de Gruyter Studies in Organization 40

Blunt / Jones: Managing Organisations in Africa

de Gruyter Studies in Organization

International Management, Organization and Policy Analysis

An international and interdisciplinary book series from de Gruyter presenting comprehensive research on aspects of international management, organization studies and comparative public policy.
It covers cross-cultural and cross-national studies of topics such as:
- management; organizations; public policy, and/or their inter-relation
- industry and regulatory policies
- business-government relations
- international organizations
- comparative institutional frameworks.

While each book in the series ideally has a comparative empirical focus, specific national studies of a general theoretical, substantive or regional interest which relate to the development of cross-cultural and comparative theory are also encouraged.
The series is designed to stimulate and encourage the exchange of ideas across linguistic, national and cultural traditions of analysis, between academic researchers, practitioners and policy makers, and between disciplinary specialisms.
The volumes present theoretical work, empirical studies, translations and 'state-of-the-art' surveys. The *international* aspects of the series is uppermost: there is a strong commitment to work which crosses and opens boundaries.

Editor:

Prof. Stewart R. Clegg, University of St. Andrews, Dept. of Management, St. Andrews, Scotland, U.K.

Advisory Board:

Prof. Nancy J. Adler, McGill University, Dept. of Management, Montreal, Quebec, Canada
Prof. Richard Hall, State University of New York at Albany, Dept. of Sociology, Albany, New York, USA
Prof. Gary Hamilton, University of California, Dept. of Sociology, Davis, California, USA
Prof. Geert Hofstede, University of Limburg, Maastricht, The Netherlands
Prof. Pradip N. Khandwalla, Indian Institute of Management, Vastrapur, Ahmedabad, India
Prof. Surendra Munshi, Sociology Group, Indian Institute of Management, Calcutta, India
Prof. Gordon Redding, University of Hong Kong, Dept. of Management Studies, Hong Kong

Peter Blunt and Merrick L. Jones

Managing Organisations in Africa

Walter de Gruyter · Berlin · New York 1992

Professor Peter Blunt
Foundation Chair in Business, Director, Graduate School of Business,
Northern Territory University, Darwin, Australia

Dr. Merrick L. Jones
Institute of Development Policy and Management,
University of Manchester, England, UK.

⊚ Printed on acid free paper which falls within the guidelines of the
ANSI to ensure permanence and durability.

Library of Congress Cataloging-in-Publication Data

Blunt, Peter, 1948-
    Managing organisations in Afrika / Peter Blunt and Merrick L.
Jones.
    (De Gruyter studies in organization)
    Includes bibliographical references and index.
    ISBN 3-11-012646-X
    1. Organizational behavior--Africa.   2. Management--Africa.
I. Jones, Merrick. II. Title. III. Series.
HD58.7.B59   1992   92-26131
658'.0096--dc20   CIP

Die Deutsche Bibliothek – Cataloging-in-Publication Data

Blunt, Peter:
Managing organisations in Africa / Peter Blunt and Merrick L.
Jones. – Berlin ; New York : de Gruyter, 1992
    (De Gruyter studies in organization ; 40)
    ISBN 3-11-012646-X
NE: Jones, Merrick L.:; GT

Typesetting: Converted by Satzpunkt Ewert, Braunschweig. –
Printing: WB-Druck, Rieden a. Forggensee. – Binding: Dieter Mikolai, Berlin.
Cover Design: Johannes Rother, Berlin.

To Professor Geoff Harcourt of the Universities of Cambridge and Adelaide for his early faith in my potential and his unwavering support throughout my career.

Peter Blunt

To Monica

Merrick L. Jones

Preface

This book expands and builds on *Organisational Theory and Behaviour: An African Perspective* which was first published in 1983. As with its predecessor, our aim has been to write a book which is helpful to anyone who is interested in organisations in Africa and their management and, in particular, in ways of making African organisations more effective and more efficient in what they do. Students of management undertaking postgraduate or undergraduate programmes of study will probably constitute the book's major audience, although we have attempted to write it in a way which will make it appealing and comprehensible to both practising managers and those with little or no work experience.

It is clear that the need for books of this type in Africa has increased with the passage of time, as we demonstrate more fully in Chapter 1. For many years, it has been widely accepted that institutional weaknesses in developing countries constitute a major obstacle to development. Resource scarcity is a major factor contributing to this state of affairs, but so also are questions of management and organisation, which are the subject of this book. Many commentators believe that such problems in Africa have worsened in recent times, particularly in public organisations, and there is persuasive evidence available to support this point of view (e.g., Adamolekun 1991a; Makharita & Brunet 1991; Phillips 1991). The consequences of such organisational ineffectiveness in Africa are clearly great: by virtue of the large numbers of people affected and, owing to their often precarious existence, their vulnerability to organisational mismanagement.

In dealing with these issues we have tried in this book to retain the distinctive qualities of the original and to augment these by, first, expanding the scope of the book to incorporate important new developments in the field of management and organisation. Second, we have included as much new empirical evidence from Africa as we could find. Third, while the focus of the book is still clearly African, in response to the increasing globalisation of commerce and trade, we have incorporated more references to the experience of Western industrialised countries and Japan, other East Asian economies such as China, and developing countries in general. Fourth, we have also made attempts explicitly to bridge the gap between theory and practice by writing in a way which is more problem oriented, rather than solely principle or theory driven, and by including at the end of every chapter a section entitled 'implications for managers and management development'. As a result of these additions and developments, this book is much longer than its predecessor. It is also, essentially, a different book.

Despite the increased length of the book, we have been unable to incorporate some material which, under ideal circumstances, we would have included. Our publishers, and we, were concerned that a longer book would have taken its price to levels which were beyond the reach of our primary target audiences, in Africa. To give a few examples, this has meant that chapters on 'researching organisations', 'selection' and 'performance management' unfortunately have had to be omitted. We had also hoped to be able to include African case examples and/or exercises at the end of each chapter, but this proved not to be possible for reasons of cost and space, too*. However, the omission of some this material is perhaps not as limiting as it might appear to be at first sight. In the case of performance management, for example, the book as a whole is concerned with the management of the performance of people and organisations in Africa. Too often in our view performance *management* is confused with performance *appraisal*, and too much time is spent by organisations on measurement – that is, appraisal – and too little on creating an organisational context which is conducive to high levels of individual and group performance. In an important sense we feel that if managers can create a positive working environment then performance appraisal almost takes care of itself. In some extreme cases it might even be seen as unnecessary. Our emphasis in this book has therefore been directed at issues such as strategy, leadership, structure, culture, motivation and job design, and roles which we feel are critical to the creation of positive working cultures. If these aspects of organisation have not been dealt with satisfactorily by managers, then imposing a system of performance appraisal, at best, will be perceived as a waste of time (because people will simply go through the motions); at worst it will be downright dysfunctional and make things worse because, say, people who do not respect their boss and do not trust him would be forced to interact formally with him in a way which might be seen to increase the opportunities for unfairness or personal reprisal rather than to reduce them. In other words, we are saying that managers and organisations who are seriously interested in performance management in Africa, as opposed to performance appraisal, will find much that is helpful to them in this book as it stands. For those who are interested in *techniques* of performance *appraisal*, many standard textbooks deal with the issues involved.

Another omission is a chapter on selection, which is clearly an important feature of managing organisations and their performance. Once again, however, it is necessary to distinguish between techniques of personnel selection, which are adequately dealt with in many texts on the subject (e.g., Blunt & Popoola 1985), and the circumstances surrounding their application. For example, a vital consideration is the motives which underlie selection. That is to say, problems of selection in Africa do not tend to arise from uncertainties about techniques, but from a wish to employ such techniques for reasons which are not so much associated with performance as with other – personal – characteristics of the individual (because, say, a manager is friendly with someone or is related to them and so on). The variables which underlie questions of this type have to do with deep-seated values and socioeconomic conditions (job scarcity, poverty etc.). Again, we think that much of what we have to say in this book is directed at the heart of the selection problem, namely, at questions of values, leadership, culture, and so on.

---

* A comparison volume, "Managing Organisations in Africa", is to be published by De Gruyter in early 1993.

Implicit, then, in the title of our book *Managing Organisations in Africa* is the management of performance as well as the creation of working environments which are pleasant to be in.

The book is divided into five sections. The first deals with the nature of African organisational environments and the nature of managerial work generally, and provides a background against which to set the material contained in the rest of the book. Subsequent sections deal in turn with managing purpose and direction, managing the work setting, managing change and conflict, and managing and developing people. Our treatment of all of these topics has been more discursive and, we would hope, more analytical than would normally be the case in a conventional management text. We have tried in this way to convey the relevance to problems of management and organisation in Africa of the material presented and, at the same time, to encourage the development of indigenous solutions which are original, or the adaptation of methods and techniques used elsewhere. This is always much easier to say than it is to do, of course, and much remains to be accomplished in the way of developing African solutions to the problems mentioned.

Lastly, we would like to express our deep-felt thanks to Hallgerd Dyrssen and Anton Johnston and others in the Public Administration and Management Division of the Swedish International Development Authority (SIDA) in Stockholm without whose financial assistance this book might not have been published. In writing this book, it was a great comfort to us to know that we had the backing of people in SIDA who understood the problems of management and organisation in Africa, and who cared about the consequences as deeply as we did. A special word of thanks also to Stewart Clegg who in his customary alert and insightful way recognised the significance of the enterprise in the wider context of international management and agreed to include the book in the Walter de Gruyter series of that name. Most of the word-processing was handled with skill, efficiency, and some critical acuity, by Hemali Seneviratne, Marla Skartvedt, and Margaret Burden to whom we extend our warm appreciation and gratitude – as we do to David Richards for his helpful comments on part of the manuscript.

Table of Contents

List of Figures

List of Tables

Part 1: Introduction

Chapter 1: African Organisational Environments

'Ex Africa semper aliqid novi' (Out of Africa always something new)
Pliny the Elder.

A recent survey of the performance of formal organisations in Africa concluded that:

"Whether or not Africa will pull out of its present doldrums may well depend on the quality of its organisation and management practices ten to fifteen years from now and beyond" (Kiggundu 1988: 239).

This book aims to contribute to the study and understanding of organisational life in Africa, particularly the management of formal organisations. In this chapter we look briefly at some of the environmental influences on African organisations and their managers. As Kiggundu (1988) points out, "in Africa, as elsewhere in developing countries, society and environment pervade organisation and management" (p. 169). As elsewhere also, there has been a tendency to focus heavily on internal organisational processes at the expense of developing a more complete understanding of the environments in which formal organisations operate. One serious effect of this, in Kiggundu's view, is that whereas African organisations may find they can apply Western management concepts and practices to their technical core with few major modifications, these imported ideas and practices are generally found to be inadequate and/or inappropriate for the organisations' relationships with their environments.

It is unrealistic to suppose that we can say anything about the contexts of African organisations which will have equal validity across the whole vast continent, even if we confine our analysis to those nations generally referred to as south of the Sahara. Nevertheless, African nations, most of which have been independent for less than forty years, do have some similar experiences and characteristics amid great diversity. It is in the nature of this book that these similarities primarily will concern us.

The elements of a national environment are of course interrelated in a complex whole. In our brief explorations of some of those elements which are significant for organisational functioning it is important to remember that we have isolated these facets artificially for analytical purposes; in reality they are not isolated in their influences on formal organisations.

1.1   The Economic Crisis

A great deal has been, and continues to be, written about Africa's seemingly endless economic crisis. Prognostications range from gloomy to ominous to catastrophic. In line with global trends, current prescriptions for the continent's economic ailments, led by the International Monetary Fund, involve rigorous austerity budgets, import restrictions, currency devaluations, reduction of government subsidies, stimulation of exports, encouragement of the private sector and foreign private investment, performance incentives, imposition of fees for public services like education and health, and drastic reductions in the size and role of the public sector.

These measures appear to be drastic, but if the descriptions of Africa's economic predicament are accurate urgent action is certainly needed. According to Kiggundu (1988), the crisis in Africa south of the Sahara is 'severe, general and worsening'; production is generally stagnant; internal and external balances are in crisis; there is a crisis in agricultural performance; there is an "institutional crisis with weak and ineffective government decision making and implementing capacity, poor investment and resource allocation decisions, weak industrial sectors, and inefficient and compromised parastatal sectors" (p. 191). Nti (1989) points to low rates of growth, falling outputs of goods and services, and food shortages. Two graphs which are showing upward trends are population, at about 3% annually overall, and inflation. Some African countries are having to spend up to 50% of their export earnings on debt servicing.

Exogenous economic factors contributing to this depressing state of affairs include drastic oil price rises, global recessions, and deteriorating terms of trade. As if this were not enough, nature has conspired in parts of Africa to produce severe deterioration in climatic conditions, through droughts, changing rainfall patterns and desertification.

Restorative measures of the type described earlier are naturally controversial. To an IMF economist they may make eminent theoretical sense, but their social repercussions may be serious. As Nti (1989) notes, for example, mass retrenchments of public sector employees – for some reason the imposed target figure always seems to be around 30% – in the context of the African extended family dependency system is likely to cause more serious problems for more people than might be the case in other socio-cultural settings. Few African nations can afford comprehensive social security systems of the type taken for granted in the wealthy industrialised countries; redundancy for one employee is likely to cause hardship to many.

At the national level the imposition of such drastic economic reforms – for instance the reduction or withdrawal of subsidies on staple foodstuffs – may lead to serious social unrest; Zambia has been a case in point. These kinds of severe economic conditions are, as Kiggundu warns, and as a number of African countries have already seen, "associated with many social, economic and political risks" (1988: 198).

Are there then any alternative or associated steps which African nations can take to escape from this economic morass? It certainly seems important that they should search for alternatives, because it is by no means clear that the current pattern of imposed recovery measures will work. Nti (1989) is unambiguous: structural adjustment pro-grammes "do not lead to the restructuring of the economy. The structure remains the same except for readjustment of the budget figures" (p. 128). Radical reductions in the size of the public sector are prescribed without any proper analysis; such across-the-board cuts are a blunt and clumsy instrument which can cause serious injuries to the patient.

Balogun (1989) finds some encouragement in what he refers to as 'recent concerted efforts' by African governments to consider other ways of overcoming these problems. Asserting that policy responses in the past to alarm signals of the dangers of economic collapse, and associated social upheaval and political instability, were largely inadequate, he points to what he calls recent 'radical policy initiatives', which actually amount to calls for:

- the formulation of effective human resource development and utilisation policies, especially in relation to the development of entrepreneurial skills;
- improved economic management through efficient allocation of resources;
- better management systems;
- reshaping of public services to be more development oriented;
- improvement of public enterprise performance; and
- the formulation of balanced population policies.

It is difficult to see anything in these generalities which would not be obvious to any secondary school student of economics. The question is: how are they to be implemented? The problem is noted by Kiggundu (1988) when he describes recommendations made by the United Nations Special Session on the African Crisis, which was held in New York in 1986. Priorities for action included "the need to improve human resources development, planning and utilisation, to strengthen local institutions ...", implying the need for "im-provements in the organisation and management of African organisations both public and private" (p. 238). As Kiggundu points out, however, there is little guidance here about how such obviously desirable improvements are to be achieved.

Balogun and Kiggundu both assert the need to develop organisations in Africa which are capable of implementing urgently needed policies. Balogun (1989) notes that the many previous attempts to resuscitate the "battered economies of Africa" (p. 227) failed mainly because the institutions for policy making and management could not anticipate and respond to changes in the environment. Likewise, Kiggundu (1988) feels that eco-nomic prescriptions of the type described have been "based on the erroneous assumption of the existence of effectively managed organisations for their implementation" (p. 200).

What seems to be obvious from this brief survey of Africa's economic crisis is that the various national and international bodies concerned can go on making recommendations and formulating new policies *ad nauseam,* but nothing much will happen in the absence of sufficient numbers of effective organisations.

1.2   Forms of Organisational Activity

As we have seen, much faith is placed, under structural adjustment programmes, in the potential of the private sector to rescue Africa from its predicament. This attitude is based more upon dissatisfaction with the performance of the public sector since independence than any clear evidence that the private sector will necessarily do much better. This section considers evidence pertaining to the effectiveness and viability of a number of different forms of organisational activity.

1.2.1   The Public Versus Private Debate

Many commentators concur in their view that the public sector in most African states has become too large, bureaucratic and change resistant. Leonard (1987) observes that, in the recent intense concern of aid donors about the quality of public sector management and ways to improve it, "emphasis is not so much upon improving the operations of the state as upon finding ways to decrease its role altogether" (p. 899). Wamwala (1989) writes of the public sector having "expanded at a feverish pace" (p. 118), and Montgomery (1987) records that it grew after independence at a faster rate than the economy.

Two points should be noted about this issue of the size of the public sector. First, there were valid reasons for African governments, immediately after independence, to expand the role and, axiomatically, the extent of their public sectors. Among these were: the commitment of many of the new nation states to socialist policies which ideologically demanded that the state should be the dominant player in development; economic nationalism; the absence generally of a strong and sufficiently large private sector – confirmed in a large scale empirical investigation in the SADCC countries of southern Africa, reported by Montgomery (1987: 922); and the desire to guarantee employment for "the new educated aspirants to elite status" (Montgomery 1987: 912).

As the previous section demonstrated, there is broad agreement among commentators concerning the poor performance of the public sector in many African countries. Balogun's (1987) views are representative: after "years of ineptitude and resistance to change" (p. 230) the generally negative image of the public sector has ensured wide acceptance of moves to reduce its size and role. Debate now focuses on the optimal relative size and roles of the public and private sectors, particularly as agents of change and development, because, as Kiggundu (1988) asserts, the pervasive role of the state is now believed to be detrimental to the development of entrepreneurship and competitive production. African governments have, in his opinion, tried to do too much in attempting to manage both government bureaucracies and business.

Current experience in Africa confirms that there are considerable difficulties involved in finding an appropriate balance between the public and private sectors. Collins (1989b) points out the methodological problems of even measuring the existing size of the public sector: there is little in the way of an empirical base for assertions of gross overstaffing. Comparisons between the size of some African public services and the United Nations secretariat would be an interesting exercise! There is also, as one might expect, little agreement about what the public sector should be left with after the radical reduction of its size and role. Balogun (1989) opts out of the argument, advocating that the appropriate balance between the public and private domains should be achieved on the basis of "what they are best placed by nature to do" (p. 231). The report of the proceedings of a conference sponsored by the (British) Overseas Development Administration (ODA 1989) is a little more specific. Some activities, the conference believed, were better left to the private sector, such as manufacturing, marketing, and some services. But certain activities should remain the direct responsibility of the state, including economic policy, law and order, regulatory and planning functions, and some social services.

Most contributors to the debate advocate a productive partnership which assumes a reduction of the role of the public sector and improvement of the institutional capacity of both sectors. This latter point is important because structural rigidity in both the public and the private sector is a barrier to growth; what is needed is "a sustained effort in the direction of institutional flexibility and reform" (Wamwala 1989: 118) in both sectors. The ODA conference (1989) made a similar point: the aim of reform should not simply be to divest the state of activities for which it is not suited, but to increase overall resource mobility.

As indicated earlier, there is little in the way of convincing empirical evidence that Africa's private sector organisations are necessarily better equipped than those in the public sector to undertake the complex business of development and change. A rare study in this area, reported by Montgomery (1987), posed the question in relation to the SADDC countries of southern Africa. The hypothesis that private sector organisations were "small, unimportant, and administratively superior" (p. 922) was supported by the data in the first two adjectives but *not* in the third. The data did not support the claim of greater rationality in the sector in terms of goal seeking. The popular expectation that managers in the private sector behave very differently from those in the public domain, similarly, was not confirmed. There were, in fact, surprisingly few differences in management styles and required skills between the public sector, the private sector, and public corporations (parastatals and public enterprises). The study noted, significantly, that 'ideological resentments' against the private sector remain. Montgomery's (1987) caution, that "current development theories that call for reliance on the private sector are not as easy to apply" (p. 922) as may have been the case elsewhere at similar stages of development, is apt.

Balogun (1989) implies similar concerns, demanding that the private sector must become more innovative and entrepreneurial, and rely less on government.

1.2.2 The Informal Sector

Associated with the public sector/private sector debate is the issue of the so-called informal sector. Now that most governments have recognised that future growth in the formal public sector is likely to be severely restricted, much interest is being shown in the employment generating potential of the informal sector. In Kiggundu's (1988) view there is "an urgent need to develop an active and fairly sizable indigenous private sector" (p. 223); this will demand a change in government policies, which at present "range from neglect to outright hostility" (p. 223).

It is perhaps worth entering a note of caution here: it would be ironic if the new faith in the promise of the informal sector were to be dashed by the very attention it is currently receiving. Whenever governments turn their attention to something which holds out some promise there is an almost obsessive tendency to fence it around with regulations and procedures – the control mechanisms which all too often concern bureaucrats far more than organisational performance. The acute danger is that the unique feature of the informal sector – its informality – will be destroyed as the state and the international aid agencies try to make use of it.

1.2.3   Public Enterprises

It is also appropriate in this section to consider very briefly current views on the role and performance of public enterprises in Africa. Following Nellis (1986), "public enterprises are defined as government owned or controlled entities which are supposed to earn the bulk of their revenues from sales, have a distinct legal identity, and are self-accounting" (p. vii). Conservative estimates indicate that there are more than 3,000 organisations in sub-Saharan Africa which satisfy the restrictions of this definition. They are important economic actors, and dominate the economies of many African countries (Nellis, 1986). In general these public sector organisations have failed to perform as was intended by their political masters. Noting the current concern about public enterprises in Africa, Kiggundu (1988) remarks on the large number of these organisations; the extent to which they dominate some economies (e.g., Zambia); their commonly politicised nature; the fact that many of them make heavy losses at the expense of the treasury; and that they tend often to be "bureaucratic, overstaffed and inefficient" (p. 202).

White (1987) comments on the heavy investments of resources in public enterprises and the disappointingly low yields which they have produced, as does Nellis (1986). White (1987) advances the following reasons for this: ambiguous and sometimes conflict-ing objectives; political interference; rotation of managers between organisations; use of unsuitable public service procedures for commercial operations; and lack of competition. In addition, the existence frequently of a weak private sector, coupled with international pricing decisions, makes African public enterprises particularly vulnerable.

Collins (1989b) has examined some of the reasons for the failures of African public enterprises. He cites problems of efficiency and overstaffing, but cautions that analysing the performance of public enterprises in Africa is difficult because of their multiple objectives, including social and non-commercial ones. Hence annual losses do not *necess-arily* prove overall poor organisational performance. A major study of public perform-ance in sub-Saharan Africa conducted by Nellis (1986) concludes that:

"African public enterprises present a depressing picture of inefficiency, losses, budgetary burdens, poor products and services, and minimal accomplishment of the non-commercial objectives so frequently used to excuse their poor economic performance" (p. ix).

Nellis (1986) has attributed these low levels of performance to poor initial investment decisions, inappropriate pricing policies, undercapitalisation and high debt/equity ratios, high inventories (which limit working capital), failures by governments to pay for services rendered resulting in tax avoidance by public enterprises, and managerial and institutional impediments including inadequate incentives and political interference in day-to-day management decisions.

Surveys of performance in the public enterprise sector have produced much debate on the steps which should be taken to improve matters. Generally, alternatives include the abolition of enterprises whose continued existence cannot be justified; privatisation of enterprises whose functions appear to be suited to private sector ownership and operation; return to the public service of the functions of some – usually minor – enterprises where there is, in the light of experience, no reason for their continued separate existence; and rehabilitation and reform of their performance, primarily through better management. Nellis (1986) has drawn up an agenda for institutional reform in Africa which we shall consider in greater detail in Chapter 3. As yet, according to White (1987), there has been little divestiture to the private sector.

The exact direction and extent of efforts to restructure the balance between the public sector, public enterprises, and private firms is not yet clear. It will obviously find different expression from country to country, and as Kiggundu (1988) believes, "for most African countries a mixed economy is the most likely scenario" (p. 203). This does not seem very dramatic, but for many African nations it will represent a radical change.

1.3 Organisation and Management

The following chapters of this book will deal in more detail with issues of African organisations and their management. In this section we briefly preview some of those issues by presenting some views about organisational performance in African countries. Consistent with the aim of this introductory chapter, this brief sample of recent views is intended to provide a contextual background to the management of African formal organisations.

Sweeping generalisations concerning the poor performance of African organisations are very common. Many of them stem from impressionistic judgments of the 'when I was in' type; and many are followed by prescriptive lectures on what African managers must do to rescue their failing organisations. For a variety of reasons, rigorous empirical research into issues of African formal organisations is sparse. Thus, judgments about their performance must necessarily be made with caution. Relevant statistics are often difficult to obtain, out of date, incomplete or unreliable. Information about organisational performance is especially scarce, particularly concerning public services and public enterprises.

Internal information systems very rarely produce data concerning job performance. Again, some of the reasons for this are discussed later.

Brown (1989) argues that such studies as there are frequently tend to have a limited systems perspective and therefore neglect environmental issues which exert crucial influences on the management of formal organisations. Much current debate, he claims, is not about organisational performance but about "assumed optimal criteria for organisational efficiency" (Brown 1989: 371). Brown rejects 'simple formula' explanations of alleged differences in management practices in Africa as compared to elsewhere – primarily of course the industrialised nations of the West – of the kind advanced for instance by Hyden (1983) and Reilly (1987). They are reductionist and they ignore obvious features of African societies "which it requires no great imaginative leap to comprehend" (Brown 1989: 375–376): political centralisation; patronage; poverty of resources; low capacities for growth; low risk political strategies; and political instability. Using data from a case study of the Liberian public service, Brown has shown that such realities provide obvious explanations for organisational performance; there is no need to resort to conspiracy theories of the kind constructed by Reilly (1987). In view of the urgent need for empirical data, Brown urges "less emphasis on assumed optimal performance criteria and more upon how organisations actually perform" (1989: 371).

Despite this dearth of reliable data about African organisational performance, it is possible to obtain some useful insights into the contemporary situation from overall trends and the small number of empirical studies which exist. Some clues emerge from the report of the Conference on Civil Service Reform (CCSR) in sub-Saharan Africa, organised by the ODA in 1989. Delegates agreed that, in general, performance of public services in the region had declined, in some cases drastically. There had been huge declines in public service incomes in some countries, which had caused serious losses of skilled manpower. Concurrently, overstaffing, caused by 'employer of last resort' policies, existed in many public services. Government budgets were overwhelmingly spent on civil service salaries. A common dilemma is how to reduce the size and cost of the civil service while increasing the rewards of those who remain, in order to produce a more efficient public service?

The symptoms of poor organisational performance identified by the CCSR included inability to make policy and routine decisions and implement them; failing services; low morale; high spending on staff; overstaffing; declining revenue; and weak financial management, budgeting, control, accounting and audit. Since independence, the Conference agreed, new demands had been placed on the civil services of African nations which emphasised their role as the motive force for development. In addition, the new and sometimes more difficult political environment made the role of the civil service more ambiguous and vulnerable. The results were often 'disappointing' and in some cases 'disastrous', but not entirely surprising considering the degree of political and economic instability.

Other factors identified during the CCSR included neglect of the civil service or "hasty and ill thought-out changes" (ODA 1989: 20), confusion concerning issues of centralisation and decentralisation of government business, and mismatches between the resources provided to public organisations and the responsibilities imposed on them. All this led the CCSR to infer the possibility that there exists in some African countries a 'crisis of governability', a real danger that "a number of governments of poorer countries might soon be unable to carry out the basic functions of law and order and service provision, let alone those summarised under the heading of 'development administration' " (ODA 1989: 19).

Balogun (1989) has provided further details of the typical pattern of public administration in African countries which contribute to the disappointing performance of public services:

- Career public servants are comfortable with bureaucratic methods of organisation and focus primarily on protocol.
- There are too many hierarchical levels, typically.
- Information systems are often chaotic.
- There frequently exist mismatches between job content and required educational attainments.
- Attachment to the principle of specialisation/ departmentalism causes jurisdictional disputes.

In short, Balogun (1989) complains of "protocol, empire building, arbitrary job creation, (and) endless form filling" (p. 230).

1.4   The Political Context

African politics are complex and sometimes baffling, as new nations experiment with different systems in attempts to find suitable patterns for governance. It is not our intention here to delve into these complexities in depth, but it is clear that political realities are a crucial element of the contexts in which African organisations function. We will refer to these issues again in various later parts of this book, so it is perhaps sufficient here to record the comments of several recent commentators.

Leonard (1987), for example, notes that the state in Africa is still a fragile institution and that political systems depend heavily on patronage: "Politics still dominates all other organisational and policy considerations" (p. 908). In his fascinating study of the careers of four eminent Kenyan managers Leonard (1988) remarks that "there is no doubt that the environment for public management is frequently inhospitable in Africa" (p. 35). One factor which emerged in the study as essential to managerial success was the building and maintenance of political connections. This consisted not in building an independent political base, but in gaining regular access to top politicians in order to influence policy decisions, supply of resources, and protection against politicisation and inappropriate policies. Such political support has to be earned through loyalty and careful network building.

Brown's (1989) Liberian case study mentioned earlier also confirms "the crucial influence of the political environment" (p. 380) on the functioning and management of African organisations, as does Nellis (1986).

1.5   The Socio-Cultural Context

The report of the recent ODA conference on civil service reform (CCSR) in sub-Saharan Africa, referred to earlier, notes that "the theme of cultural factors and their impact on civil service reform recurred repeatedly in discussions throughout the Conference" and that there was among delegates a degree of unease about "the imposition of a cultural pattern implicit in current reform approaches" (ODA 1989: 36). The delegates, despite these concerns, do not appear to have taken the issue any further.

Similarly, a report based on the proceedings of no less than four policy seminars and a 'round up workshop', involving policy makers at top political and administrative levels from 29 African countries, admits that they did not raise "the critically important issue of the impact of culture on management" (Adamolekun 1989: 17).

If the brief note in the CCSR report seems inadequate and the omission of such a 'critically important issue' from the African senior policy seminars appears astonishing, we would caution that these examples provide good evidence of the problems we all experience when trying to come to terms with cultural factors in organisational behaviour.

A recent issue of the journal of *International Studies of Management and Organisation* (Summer 1986) consists of five articles on issues in the management of African organisations. The guest editor, Augustine Ahiauzu, comments that "it is becoming increasingly widely accepted among social scientists, especially managers and organisational theorists, that patterns of management and employee behaviour in the workplace are largely culture-bound" (1986: 3). The five articles in the journal provide examples to support this view. In common with the five contributors, Ahiauzu stresses the need for empirical research in this field, particularly into 'questions of persistent interest', including:

– the nature and evolution of African management thought and work;
– the meanings of work for Africans;
– frameworks for analysis, theoretical perspectives and methodological consequences, in African organisations;
– cultural variations in African societies and their influences on organisational behaviour;
– tradition and modernity in work organisations; and
– what can be learned from the experiences of industrialised countries.

Ahiauzu's (1986) concern with the need for more research is appropriate. There is indeed a growing body of literature concerning questions of socio-cultural influences on organisational behaviour; but much of it is of poor quality, consisting of anecdotes, prescriptions based on Western experience, and fantasies. Research methodologies are often questionable, which is not altogether surprising in view of the problems of defining 'culture' and devising useful categories for investigation. As in other areas of the behavioral sciences, research has not produced conclusive evidence for or against the 'divergence' hypothesis that management is culture-bound; or the contending 'convergence' argument that the imperatives of modern complex organisations will prove so powerful and pervasive that managerial attitudes, values and behaviour will become increasingly uniform around the world.

The most influential large-scale cross-cultural studies are those of Haire, Ghiselli and Porter (1966) and Hofstede (1980, 1984). The investigation by Haire and his colleagues produced evidence indicating that in some respects managers had common views which cut across national boundaries. There was evidence also that cultural factors were significant in differences between clusters of countries with common cultural attributes. However, in the three developing countries in the study it was the shared stage of economic development which accounted for some common characteristics. Replications of the Haire *et al.* study in African countries by, among others, Blunt (1973, 1976), Howell, Strauss and Sorenson (1975), Blunt and Jones (1986), and Jones (1988a), similarly have produced evidence of 'convergent' and 'divergent' elements in the thinking and behaviour of managers.

Hofstede's (1980) massive investigation was based upon a model developed from his view that culture is essentially the collective mental programming of people in their environment. His data revealed marked differences in national cultures which would be expected to have a significant impact on organisational behaviour.

Montgomery's (1986a, 1986b, 1987) report on a large scale study of managerial behaviour in the Southern African Development Coordinating Conference (SADCC) countries provides insights into the work and attitudes of African administrators which reveal significant culturally specific influences. Montgomery's research was designed to investigate the validity of the exotic images of African management created by unsubstantiated anecdotes; this was achieved by focussing on specific contingencies in the organisational environment of these managers. We shall return to this important study and consider its findings in greater detail in the next chapter.

Balogun (1986) and De Graft-Johnson (1986) have also provided examples of specific aspects of African traditional values and practices which could be significant for an understanding of African management and systems of organisation. Murrell (1986) similarly draws attention to the realities of organisational environments in Africa which clearly do not possess the same history of modern organisational or industrial life as the West. Western management models cannot be merely adopted or copied in such environments; they have to be adapted in the 'most culturally appropriate manner'.

Leonard (1987) has provided some specific examples of cultural influences on African managers, and argues that differences in organisation behaviour between them and their counterparts in the industrialised West are due to fundamental differences in values. Leonard stresses the need to develop an understanding of the effects of such cultural realities on organisational behaviour and cautions against the unthinking transfer of alien management concepts and practices. Western social science makes certain assumptions about the functioning of formal organisations, according to Leonard (1987):

- the assumption of purposive rationality, implying commitment to organisational goals; and
- the assumption of economic rationality, which views economics as the fundamental social process which provides an understanding of all human transactions.

He asserts that such assumptions are not applicable in all societies, and that their validity in Africa is particularly limited.

As we have indicated earlier, the issues involved in the transfer of Western management concepts and practices to African environments raise many complex questions about cultural factors. There are in Africa many cultural contradictions and tensions as new nations make their painful transitions from colonial dependencies to modern nation states. The nature of this situation for individual managers is nicely captured by Balogun (1986): "As they seek to accomplish their varied tasks, they are torn between going back to the good old days of pure traditional despotism, and coming to terms with, and mastering, the alien systems of government and administration which they inherited from the colonial authorities" (p. 195).

1.6   Transportation, Communications and Technology

Africa is a gigantic continent with great river systems, mountains, deserts, lakes, forests and a huge variety of geographical and climatic conditions. Many of Africa's artificially drawn countries are landlocked. Trade links have to be maintained often across vast distances and difficult terrain. Transport links such as roads and railways are relatively undeveloped, often old and in need of updating and regular maintenance. Air transport links between different parts of the continent are often made via European cities. These and other factors make the job of the African manager additionally problematic, especially if they are combined with political instability in surrounding countries, as Jones (1989), for example, shows in the case of landlocked Malawi.

In terms of technology, as Kiggundu (1988) remarks, sub-Saharan Africa is "lagging behind in the importation and effective utilisation and management of foreign technology ... Africa is not a technology developer because almost no research and development takes place on the continent ... Africa is also a poor copier of technology ... and there is a tendency to view new technology as static, fixed ..." (pp. 216–217).

1.7   Agriculture[1]

Overall, Africans are almost as poor today as they were thirty years ago. As we indicated at the beginning of this chapter, most African states suffer from "high population growth rates, declining *per capita* food production, severe land degradation, declining export revenues, worsening trade balances and enormous debts" (Macgregor 1990: 4). The common thread running through all of these factors is agriculture. It accounts for 33 per cent of Africa's GDP, employs 66 per cent of its labour force, and produces 40 per cent of its exports. Yet today in many African countries agriculture is in crisis. It is estimated that one in four Africans (more than 100 million people) in 36 of the continent's 52 countries is threatened by famine and malnutrition. The long-term nature of the crisis is a function of deteriorating food production – which has grown by only 20 per cent in the last twenty years – and a population which has increased in size by 30 per cent over the same period.[2]

Inevitably, the people most at risk when times are hard are small scale farmers who can no longer produce enough food to feed their families. Within this group the most adversely affected are women and children; poor people in the cities who cannot afford to buy food; and refugees.

To some extent African agriculture is a victim of its colonial past and an unforgiving and uncaring world economy which is geared to serve the interests of the industrialised countries. But the agricultural crisis is also a function of internal factors, subject to internal control. The imbalance between population growth and food production, together with inept and wasteful government policies and management practices are major contributory factors – although the latter can sometimes be grossly exaggerated, and will in any case vary greatly between countries (Jamal, 1988). We have dealt already in this chapter with different forms of organisational activity and levels of performance in Africa. But the urgent need to rectify the problems mentioned is brought home by a more detailed consideration of the effects of population growth, urbanisation, and environmental depletion.

Despite the gloomy picture painted by the statistics, it is still possible to say in theory that Africa has the capacity to become self-sufficient in food. Competent management and administration has a crucial role to play in the realisation of Africa's potential in this most basic of all areas of economic and organisational activity. As the *Economist* (1990) notes: "Africa's comparative advantage may well be in farming. But efficient agriculture needs efficient towns to provide banks, marketing systems, agricultural training, and so on" (p. 20).

---

1   This section and the next two sections draw heavily on Macgregor (1990).
2   It is important to note here that aggregate figures conceal significant differences between countries – see, for example, Jamal (1988), Tabatabai (1988), and Collier (1988).

1.8   Population Growth and Urbanisation

The population of sub-Saharan Africa has doubled in size since 1965. By the year 2010 it
is expected to have risen to over 1 billion. These growth rates far exceed those of any other
continent (including Latin America and Asia). The sheer magnitude of these increases is
complicated by population distribution, density, age, and patterns of migration.

Africa as a whole cannot be said to be overpopulated. But while there are still vast
tracts of uncultivated arable land, there are larger areas of desert and semi-desert which
are virtually uninhabited, and other areas in which exhausted land is unable – because of
high population densities – to support the people who live there. Yet it is in these latter
areas (which include parts of southern West Africa, the East African lakes region, parts of
the Ethiopian highlands, and South Africa) that more than half of Africa's total population
lives. These are the areas which make the greatest demands on governments and organisations.

Urban migration and the age distribution (high proportion of young people) of Africa's
population have contributed to agriculture's reduced "percentage share of the economically active population, while the growing proportions of female and child labour have
qualitatively worsened the composition of labour resources" (Macgregor 1990: 7).

These factors clearly have major implications for public policy and the strategic
management of public sector organisations. There are signs that some African governments are beginning to take notice: for example, in Zimbabwe the government has spent
considerable sums on the development of Chitungwiza, a township some 15 miles from
the capital, Harare. Likewise, Zambia's government has attempted to develop Kafue, 30
miles from Lusaka. The idea in both cases has been to relieve congestion in the capitals;
but the costs have been hours of commuting (and waiting) for Chitungwiza's workers
and over-strained public transport systems. It is partly to escape such costs that the poor
have built their homes closer to industrial and employment centres; hence the sprawling
slums of cities like Lagos and Nairobi. The issues are pressing but far from straightforward.

Across Africa, city populations are growing at twice and three times the rate of the
general population. By the year 2020 the World Bank expects that there will be about 30
cities in the continent with populations in excess of 1 million. Some will be far bigger than
that: for example, it is predicted that Lagos will grow from 5 million to 26 million before
its population stabilises (*Economist* 1990).

1.9   Physical Environment and Resources

Deserts occupy about 40 per cent of the African land mass; dense rain forests with poor
soils account for a further 7 or 8 per cent of the continent. The remaining land is of highly
variable quality; the soils are old and easily degraded; an additional restraint (conservatio-
nists might say 'blessing') is "the widespread incidence of the tsetse fly which infests

more than two-thirds of the sub-humid zone (which) has held back the economy of entire regions" (Macgregor 1990: 8).

Rainfall is marginal and erratic, and in the semi-arid regions of the continent drought is a recurrent phenomenon.

With a diminishing supply of fertile arable land, and difficult access, a pressing concern is the rate and extent of environmental degradation in Africa, as in the rest of the world (Montgomery 1991). Macgregor (1990) is emphatic on this point:

"Africa's ecology is fragile. In the first half of the 1980's it was estimated that as many as 7,432 million hectares of land in Africa, equivalent to 26 per cent of the continent's total land area, was in the process of desertification; the Sahara Desert alone expanding at the rate of 1.5 million hectares a year" (p. 8).

Population pressures, which have resulted in overcultivation, overgrazing, and deforestation (brought about by demand for wood and construction), and increasing herd sizes, have had a major influence.

In view of the above, in Africa, as elsewhere on the planet, environmental policies should be of increasing concern to governments, corporations, associations, and even households and individuals. Unfortunately, while a few organisations and governments in Africa are trying to deal coherently with the ever increasing threats to their environments, most are ignoring, postponing, or exacerbating the problems (Montgomery 1991). Multi-national corporations have been particularly lax in this area, although public opinion worldwide has induced a more concerned and creative approach to environmental issues in recent years (Blake 1990).

1.10   Labour Market Trends

Jamal and Weeks (1988) have drawn attention to a number of labour market trends which in their view reveal "the need for a sharply revised view of African economies" (p. 273):

- Real wages of urban workers have fallen during the 1980s, in some instances dramatically. Unskilled workers have fared worst of all. With excesses of supply over demand, the minimum wage has become the actual wage for most unskilled workers.
- The security and stability of formal sector employment have diminished. Again, the limited evidence suggests that employment has declined more for unskilled workers than for the semi-skilled and skilled.
- As a result of the first two trends, the distinction between the formal and informal sectors is becoming blurred. Income differentials between the two sectors are decreasing, as are differences in lifestyles and living standards. Decreasing opportunities in the formal sector have forced many formal sector workers out into the informal sector.

- The income gap between urban workers and the rural population has decreased. According to Jamal and Weeks (1988), "in some cases the scales have even begun to tip in favour of peasant smallholders" (p. 274).
- The above four trends have contributed to a worsening distribution of income in most African countries. This contradicts the conventional wisdom which suggests that reducing the gap between urban and rural incomes automatically leads to an improved overall distribution of income. It is no longer a question of privileged urbanites versus disadvantaged farmers, but simply a question of rich versus poor, with the latter including urban wage earners, operators in the informal sector, and peasants.
- Migration from rural to urban areas seems, if anything, to have increased, despite decreasing income differentials.
- Thus, according to Jamal and Weeks (1988), we can infer that:

"Increasingly the primary dynamic distributional relationship in Africa is between rich and poor within both the urban and the rural sectors ... This tendency for the poor in both urban and rural areas to suffer most has led to interactive rural-urban survival strategies whose precise nature is not clear. However, there is evidence (particularly in the extreme case of Uganda) of nominally urban households supplementing their livelihoods from agriculture" (p. 275).

1.11   Conclusion

The aim of this first chapter has been to provide a contextual background to our examination of African formal organisations and their management, which follows. The factors briefly introduced combine to constitute crucial environmental influences on the practice of management, and organisational behaviour generally. All organisations, everywhere, function within a specific environment, and it is becoming more widely recognised in contemporary discussions of organisational performance that managers have to develop an understanding of their environments if their organisations are to survive and function effectively. We have attempted to show some of those aspects of African organisational environments which are unique or in some important ways different from those elsewhere, for a variety of reasons. In the following chapters these issues will be examined in more detail.

1.12   Implications for Managers and Management Development

For senior managers the implications of this opening chapter are of crucial importance. In Africa, where change is both rapid and in many countries turbulent, it is imperative that formal organisations develop and maintain the ability to understand their environments. Senior managers need to develop an outward-looking stance so that their organisations can monitor, anticipate, initiate and manage change. For profit-dependent enterprises this is the key to their survival; for public service organisations this is how they can make sure that their services remain relevant. Foreign managers and experts working in Africa, and foreign corporations, should pay particular attention to the issues we have raised in this chapter. Kiggundu (1991) endorses this view:

"The foreigner interested in designing, implementing and evaluating effective management development programmes must read widely in order to gain an appreciation of this diverse and complex continent, its peoples and social organisations, and the context within which organisation and management takes place" (pp. 32–33).

For management development practices the chapter suggests that managers must be alerted to the implications of change in the environment and be assisted to learn the skills of collecting, recording, analysing and synthesising information. This implies that the traditional focus of management textbooks and management teaching on the internal processes of the organisation will have to be modified. As we shall see in Chapter 13, major criticisms of the performance of management training institutes in Africa are their attachment to the textbook and their lack of contact with the world of managerial work. This chapter implies that these institutes will have to move out of the classroom and into the organisation, to identify and use learning opportunities for helping senior managers to develop their abilities in dealing with their environments. Ironically, of course, it also means that Africa's management training institutes must themselves develop similar skills. Otherwise, as has already happened in some cases, they themselves will be left behind by the changing realities of their environments.

Chapter 2: The Nature of Managerial Work

In the previous chapter we considered characteristics of the general environments of African organisations and the constraints these environments imposed on organisational functioning and effectiveness. This chapter delves within the organisation to examine the nature of managerial work and to consider the extent to which the behaviour of African managers takes on distinctive characteristics. It asks the question what do managers actually do as distinct from what are they supposed to do? This question raises another: how can an understanding of the nature of managerial work help us to improve our ability to manage organisations effectively? We shall take the view that a detailed knowledge of the nature of managerial work and its meaning, and its variations between organisations and cultures, will help us, first, to understand why organisations function in the ways that they do. And second, it will help us to devise ways for creating more effective organisations and for training and developing managers.

Our ability at present to gain such understanding in the African context is somewhat limited by the lack of direct empirical research evidence on the nature of managerial work in the continent. Nevertheless, what is known about the nature of managerial work in the West together with theory and evidence from other developing countries (e.g., China), and the small amount of African research evidence provides a basis for an informed discussion of this important topic.

2.1 The Importance of the Topic

A major reason for studying the nature of managerial work is the global expansion in the twentieth century of managerial hierarchies responsible for coordinating and controlling resources of increasing magnitude and variety (Whitley 1989), or what Chandler (1977) has referred to as the growth of the 'visible hand'. The importance of management as a distinctive activity and occupational category has developed as a function of the growth and spread of large enterprises and their increasing economic, social, political, and environmental impact. Moreover, in recent years it has been argued that the significance of management has been enhanced by the declining influence of markets, and their replacement by hierarchies, especially in newer industries (Whitley 1987).

In Africa, as we shall argue more fully below, the case for the dominance of managerial hierarchies over markets can be put with even greater force, thereby adding considerable weight to the significance of the topic in an African context. But irrespective of context, the analysis of managerial work and the development of effective managers are important simply because the growing influence and impact of managerial hierarchies has placed them among the most significant features of industrialised and industrialising societies (Whitley 1989; Willmott 1984).

2.2   What Do Managers Do?

Research findings regarding the nature of managerial work need to be distinguished, first, from the prescriptions of the 'founding fathers' of management thought, and second, from what Willmott (1984) refers to as the images and ideals of the 'pundits', that is, character-istics of management work by popular writers such as Drucker (1977) and Peters (1989). We shall take the view that the contributions of both the classical writers and the pundits suffer from a lack of empirical foundations, vagueness, and the claim that they are universally applicable.

However, as much of the received wisdom in management continues to rely heavily on such formulations, it is necessary to review briefly what they have to say.

2.2.1   Classical Theorists

The contributions of three writers stand out: Taylor (1911), Fayol (1949) and Barnard (1938). Taylor argued that the work of managers should be more scientifically based so that standardised rules and precise formulae could be used to control worker behaviour. Fayol developed a number of principles of administration, most of which were consistent with Taylor's views. These principles, which have dominated management vocabulary since they were first introduced in 1916, assert that managers plan, organise, coordinate and control (Mintzberg, 1989). Barnard's (1938) contribution, which foreshadowed the advent of so-called 'behavioral' studies of management and organisation, drew attention to management's role in developing an effective fit between the purpose of an organisa-tion and its environment and between its structure and the characteristics of its personnel. These elements of Barnard's writings continue to occupy a central position in manage-ment theory, as we shall see in subsequent chapters in this book.

2.2.2   Popular Writers on Management

Following Willmott (1984), a general idea of the characterisation of managerial work by management pundits can be gained from the writings of Dale (1965) and Drucker (1977). Dale's view is a universal one which sees the work of managers as being concerned with 'getting things done through other people' (Dale 1965: 5). Inspired by Fayol, Dale also characterises managerial work as consisting in planning, organising, staffing, directing, and controlling. He assumes, moreover, that the form of organisations and management is unproblematic and historically constant. In this view, the manager is "simply a function-ary who applies technical expertise to ensure that 'things get done' " (Willmott 1984:

354). It is assumed, further, that little if anything can be achieved without the benefits of managerial direction and control.

Unlike Dale, Drucker (1977: 25) accepts that management is "a social function embedded in a tradition of values, customs and beliefs, and in governmental and political systems". According to Drucker, competent management rests on "an understanding of the fundamentals of management" (Drucker 1977: 26). What these fundamentals entail, however, is less clear. Reference is made to the development of the skills of 'communication within organisations', 'making decisions under conditions of uncertainty', and 'strategic planning', but they are left largely undefined. One of Drucker's major recommendations is the idea that management behaviour and performance should be governed by clearly defined and achievable objectives which are directed towards the success of the whole organisation (the well known 'management by objectives').

The nature of managerial work conveyed by such popular writings is that of "the 'professional' who impartially carries out the universally and technically defined functions of management" (Willmott 1984: 355).

2.2.3   Folklore and Fact

Mintzberg (1989) asserts that none of the above helps us to understand very much about what it is that managers actually do. Neither classical nor popular writings on the subject have been very good at distinguishing 'images' (observations of managers at work) from 'ideals' (what it is thought that managers should do). From his study of various kinds of managers – foremen, factory supervisors, staff managers, sales managers, hospital administrators, presidents of companies and nations, and even street gang leaders – in the United States, Canada, Sweden, and Great Britain, Mintzberg (1989) paints a significantly different, and more valid, picture of managerial work from that presented above.

Mintzberg's (1989) account of managerial work begins with the refutation of a number of myths. The first of these is that managers are systematic planners who spend a great deal of time thinking ahead. Empirical studies have shown, however, that invariably this is not the case. Rather, managers' activities are characterised by brevity, variety, and discontinuity, and a dislike of reflection. For example, a study of 160 British middle and top managers found that their work was so discontinuous and varied that they were able to work for half an hour or more without interruption only once every two days. When planning does take place, it seems to happen implicitly and to be carried out in conjunction with or as a part of other activities. Mintzberg (1989) observes "the plans of the chief executives I studied seemed to exist only in their heads – as flexible, but often specific, intentions" (p. 11).

Another myth is that a manager spends relatively little time on operational activities, such as dealing with customers, because – like a good conductor – his job is to plan and schedule whilst others execute. However, the evidence indicates that managers devote a great deal of time to regular operational activities involving negotiations, the interpretation of 'soft' information regarding the organisation's links with its external environment, a certain amount of what Mintzberg refers to as ritual and ceremony (e.g., meeting visitors, attending official occasions, handing out long service awards etc.), and – particularly in smaller organisations – considerable contact with customers.

A third myth is that managers rely a great deal on aggregated and quantified information supplied by formal management information systems. Again, research contradicts this picture. Of the five media at their disposal – documents, telephone calls, scheduled and unscheduled meetings, and observational tours – managers appear strongly to prefer oral media, namely, telephone calls and meetings. A number of studies have shown that managers devote more than 70% of their time to oral communication (Mintzberg 1989), and place high value on 'soft' information – gossip, hearsay, and speculation – because it so often presages new developments. It is also the case that much soft information of high value never gets written down, and access to it can therefore be achieved only via informal channels.

Finally, Mintzberg discounts the proposition that management is fast becoming a science and a profession by demonstrating that much of what managers do, which involves judgment and intuition, is not amenable to scientific analysis. As Mintzberg says, many of the reasons underlying managers' work "remain locked deep inside their brains" (1989: 14) and inaccessible to observation and scientific study.

Mintzberg's own empirical investigations have led him to the conclusion that managerial work can be accurately described in terms of ten roles or coherent sets of behaviours.

2.2.4   Managerial Roles in the West[1]

Three of the ten roles stem directly from formal authority and have to do with relationships with other people (*see* Figure 2.1).

Figurehead
This aspect of managerial work is concerned with ceremonial activities associated with a manager's position as head of an organisational unit. The director or permanent secretary will receive visiting officials and dignitaries, the marketing manager will entertain valued customers by taking them to lunch, and so on. Naturally, the extent of involvement in such activities, as with the other nine roles to be discussed, will vary according to the manager's level, type of organisation, and the organisation's cultural context. In some Asian cultures, for example, ceremonial activities are central to most managers' jobs (Blunt, Richards & Wilson 1989). Their significance in Western societies is demonstrated in Mintzberg's (1973) original study where chief executive officers spent 12 percent of their contact time on ceremonial activities, and 17 percent of their incoming mail dealt with similar issues.

---

1   Much of this section is based on Mintzberg (1989).

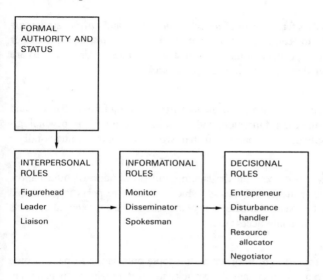

Figure 2.1 :   The Manager's Roles

Motivator

Mintzberg's (1973) original account of this role referred to it as that of 'leader'. Our own view is that his description of this role is described better by the word 'motivator'; hence our use of this term in preference to the original. In addition, however, modern debate concerning the notion of leadership – of which there has been a great deal (e.g., Bennis 1989; Kotter, 1990; Krantz 1990) – interprets the term somewhat differently, and distinguishes it quite clearly from management (Kotter 1990). We shall return to this important question later in this chapter.

The motivator role arises from the manager's responsibility for the output of others in addition to his or her own. The activities making up this role would include hiring and firing, goal setting, and performance appraisal and reward. In all of this, the manager seeks to attain some workable balance between the interests of the individual and those of the organisation.

Liaison

This role reflects the consistent research finding that managers spend as much time with peers and other people outside their own units as they do with their subordinates. Relatively little time (around 10 percent) is spent with superiors. The chief executives studied by Mintzberg had contact with a wide range of people including subordinates, clients, business associates, suppliers, managers of similar organisations, government and trade union officials, and so on. These contacts were used primarily for gathering information.

The three roles described thus far, those of *figurehead*, *motivator*, and *liaison*, are largely interpersonal in nature. As the centre of networks of interpersonal contacts, the manager becomes a key source and repository of information. The next three roles described are connected with the informational aspects of managerial work.

Monitor
This entails scanning the environment for relevant information, using formal channels and informal networks for gathering information, and creating a receptive and psychologically safe climate for unsolicited information, much of which will be transmitted orally.

Disseminator
The disseminator role is concerned with the sharing and distribution of information. Information to which the manager has access, which in many respects is privileged information, can thereby be made available to people – subordinates, external contacts etc. – who might otherwise not have access to it.

Spokesman
This role focuses on the provision of information to people outside the manager's own unit, especially those who are seen to have the capacity to exert a major influence on it. This is a particularly important aspect of the work of chief executives.

The final set of roles described by Mintzberg are *decisional* roles which make use of the manager's special access to comprehensive and up-to-date information.

Entrepreneur
This involves the manager in taking initiatives which are designed to improve the effectiveness and/or competitiveness of his unit. Such initiatives will often take the form of development projects which the manager may delegate to a subordinate. The nature and extent of these projects will frequently evolve gradually over time, as a series of small decisions or actions, rather than being the outcome of a single decision or grand plan. Mintzberg's view is that this gradual process allows managers to come to terms with the complexities of projects and to accommodate them into their busy work schedules. Some of the executives studied by Mintzberg had as many as fifty projects in a wide variety of areas (e.g., public relations, internal morale, computing systems, purchasing, and so on) in progress at the same time. These activities are subject to a continuing process of review involving the resuscitation or abandonment of existing projects and the initiation of new ones.

Disturbance Handler
As the name implies, this role is concerned with dealing with disturbances and conflicts which either occur within the manager's work unit or impinge on it in some way. Even the best run and most efficient and effective of organisations will experience disturbances because not every contingency or likely occurrence can be anticipated. As Mintzberg (1989: 20) remarks: "disturbances arise not only because poor managers ignore situations until they reach crisis proportions, but also because good managers cannot possibly anticipate all the consequences of the actions they take". It is a question of degree. On the

whole, we would expect good managers to anticipate more, and therefore to experience fewer, crises, than poor managers.

Resource Allocator
One of the manager's major activities is that of resource allocation, including financial and other resources, and time. The manager should decide how best to allocate his or her own time and the amount of time that he or she can allow to be taken up by different people. Time should also be allocated to designing the structure of the organisation and to planning; decisions taken should be integrated into the organisations strategy and should be acceptable to key individuals who are likely to be affected by them. The costs, benefits, and feasibility of proposals should be appraised, sometimes quickly, but always attempting to strike a balance between a rapid response which may be ill-considered and a delayed response which may dampen enthusiasm or depress motivation. One way around this problem which is favoured by managers is to make judgments about the person associated with a proposal rather than the proposal itself, and to approve or not approve projects on this basis.

Negotiator
This activity can occupy a considerable portion of a manager's time no matter what his or her level within the organisation might be. The scale and ramifications of negotiations conducted at different levels within the organisation will naturally vary, but the supervisor or foreman dealing with a grievance on the shop floor is likely to spend as much time negotiating as will the chief executive officer involved in a take over bid.

These ten managerial roles constitute the primary elements of an integrated whole, or gestalt. And, as indicated in Figure 2.1, to a considerable degree they are a function of the formal authority associated with a particular managerial position. However, little attention is paid by Mintzberg to 'how' and 'why' questions. His account seems mechanical and unaffected by historical and contextual factors (Willmott 1984). These questions are important to an understanding of managerial work in any context because the meaning of behaviour to individual actors themselves, and others who perceive them, matters as much or more than the behaviours themselves. Such political (not to be confused with party political) considerations are therefore vital to a full understanding of managerial work (Stewart 1989), and even more so in Africa (Jones 1990b; Leonard 1987).

It is also not certain that the so-called classical functions of management – planning, staffing, supervising etc. – are quite so insignificant a part of the manager's job as Mintzberg claims (Carroll & Gillen 1987). Indeed, empirical evidence to the contrary has been presented by Allen (1981) and Hughes & Singler (1985).

2.2.5   Comparative Evidence from China

We might reasonably expect that the nature of managerial work itself and its meaning will vary according to a wide range of factors such as size and type of organisation, managerial level, performance (Luthans, Rosenkrantz & Hennessey 1985), and so on. But perhaps one of the single most important influencing factors on organisational behaviour is culture

(Hofstede 1980; Hofstede, Neuijen, Ohayr & Sanders 1990), and a number of African writers have recently drawn attention to the importance of culture to the development of African management practice and thought (e.g., Ahiauzu 1986; Nzelibe 1986).

One of the few recent studies of managerial behaviour in a development context has been conducted in China (Boisot & Guoliang 1988). The study in question in which six Chinese state-owned enterprise directors were observed continuously for six full working days each, was a 'constructive replication' (Lykken 1968; Blunt & Jones 1986) of Mintzberg's (1973) original investigation. As one might expect there are differences and similarities between Western and Chinese managers. Contrary to the image built up in the West of idle Chinese bureaucrats sitting around drinking tea and reading newspapers, the Chinese directors on average worked longer hours each day (in large enterprises almost 12 hours per day) than their American counterparts (who worked nearly 9 hours per day). On the other hand, the activities of both groups were brief (an average of about 20 minutes duration each) and varied (between 20 and 40 activities – Chinese directors performed a greater number). However, whilst the Chinese and American samples devoted almost identical proportions of their time to their subordinates (48% and 49% respectively), Chinese managers allocated much more of their time to interactions with superiors (27% as opposed to 7% for American executives) and much less to interactions with suppliers, customers, and banks (23.5% as opposed to 44%). There were significant differences also with respect to the amount of time devoted to desk work: Chinese managers devoted 9% of their time to such activities while American managers allocated more than twice as much (20%) of their time to them. Chinese managers also spent considerably less time on the telephone (2.5% versus 6%).

But what is the meaning of these differences – that is, why do they occur? And are the observed patterns of behaviour rational and desirable given the institutional and cultural circumstances in which they occur? Possible explanations of the differences observed range from the mundane to the highly complex; the latter involving institutional and cultural considerations. At the more rudimentary level, differences in the amount of time spent on the telephone may have had to do with the inefficiencies of the telephone system in Beijing, but more likely they were due to a combination of this and a cultural preference for face-to-face contact.

More profound differences between Chinese and Western managers emerged in the nature and extent of their responsibilities for the social welfare of employees and in the variety, and level of detail, of personnel issues which found their way to high levels for resolution. Again, institutional, sociopolitical and cultural factors combined to provide the most plausible explanations. For example, Chinese state-owned enterprises assume almost total responsibility for the social and material well-being of their employees and a director is seen as the *fu mu* (father-and-mother) of his or her workers, to an extent not even seen in Japan (Dore 1987). Chinese managers are expected to display a Confucian benevolence towards their employees at all times.

"For example, he will be the one to decide on where to relocate workers who are due to retire but who remain the moral responsibility of the enterprise ... he will adjudicate on

the distribution of salaries, bonuses, and housing facilities – the latter being a key resource in the Chinese firm; and he will get intimately involved in worker welfare issues such as the construction of medical facilities or kindergartens" (Boisot & Guoliang 1988: 12).

Chinese managers are also inclined – or persuaded – to make personnel decisions which in a Western firm would be delegated to lower levels. Typical examples include (from Boisot & Guoliang 1988: 18–19):

- "A recently retired worker, who had been with the firm for a number of years, is bored sitting at home all day with nothing to do. He walks into the director's office and begs him for a part time job. The director deals with the matter himself.
- The personnel manager walks into the director's office with a list of workers and technicians who are eligible to go abroad for a training course. He asks the director to make the final selection from the list. The director obliges.
- A group of technicians and workers from one of the firm's departments comes to solicit a salary increase from the director in person.
- A worker comes to discuss a personal matter with the director: following a work accident he had to be hospitalised and his department failed to compensate him adequately. Could the director please do something about this?
- A lifelong employee comes into the office and asks the director to allocate him a flat – each enterprise builds its own but there is usually a long waiting list. His son, who is living with him, wants to get married but cannot do so until he has a home of his own.
- The wife of a trade union official has just undergone surgery. She comes to ask the director to give her a document that would make her eligible for a certain category of financial assistance".

Two complementary explanations for this type of behaviour suggest themselves. The first, which Mintzberg uses to explain similar behaviour among Western managers, is that the director is not inclined to delegate because he does not trust his subordinates, or because greater centralisation enables him to keep a closer eye on what is going on within the organisation. The second explanation is simply that everyone wants to deal directly with the manager, thereby effectively preventing delegation from taking place whether the manager would like to delegate or not.

It strikes us that while some of the underlying causes might be different, it seems likely that the demands placed upon the African manager and the way he deals with them will be similar to those observed among Chinese managers. In both cases, differences from what is observed in the West are more likely to have to do with institutional and cultural factors than, say, with a lack of managerial skill, although both may well be involved (Child & Lu 1990). It is more likely in our view that such cultural and institutional factors underlie the propensity among Chinese (Child & Lu 1990) and African (Price 1975) managers to personalise and centralise transactions to a greater extent than among Western managers.

Institutional explanatory variables emerged most clearly when it came to the power to choose which transactions would be dealt with by the application of a rule and which would be handled personally. Vengroff, Belhaj and Ndiaye (1991) observe that the major difference between the African public sector managers whom they studied and Mintzberg's managers lay in the African managers' knowledge of "and adherence to juridical rules and regulations (the so-called texts). This constitutes an extremely important aspect of the role of African managers but is not a major aspect of the roles of Western managers." (Vengroff *et al.* 1991: 107). Our view is that *lower-level* managers in developing countries are likely to behave in this way. As elsewhere in the world, senior managers have more latitude. At upper levels – in China and Africa – rules may be applied selectively according to personal or particularistic criteria. Such behaviour may permeate organisational systems, but at lower levels it is more restricted in scope, and power to behave in this way will usually be 'delegated' from above.

Many subordinates therefore become habituated to intervention from above and invite and expect it, as in the case of the subordinate who refuses to take even the most routine of decisions not governed by a rule for fear that he or she will be blamed, and punished, by a superior if something goes wrong (Blunt 1988; Richards 1991). Personal relationships between managers are of great significance everywhere, but more so we would suggest under these circumstances. From the point of view of the client as well, in Africa, as in China, it is probably true to say that "the best way to get acknowledged as such and to obtain favourable treatment is to try to personalise relationships with the manager to get him 'involved' " (Boisot & Guoliang 1988: 30).

The combination of centralisation and personalisation of relationships coupled with fear of 'failure' and responsibility for error at lower levels leads to overload at the top (Child & Lu 1990). This in turn depresses decision quality and causes inordinate delays. This is a common phenomenon throughout Africa, as noted in the report of the Zimbabwean Public Service Review Commission (ZPSRC 1989) which found that the most pervasive complaints referred to delays and lack of response.

In order to get an indication of responsiveness to the public, the ZPSRC reviewed a sample of cases 'dealt with' by two ministries over the period 1980–1987. Dates were recorded indicating when correspondence was received, whether and when acknowledgements had been made, and if and when the cases had been resolved. Out of a total of 224 cases reviewed, only 34 had been resolved by December 1988. Moreover, the average time required to deal with those cases which had been resolved was 12 months, while the average time required to send an acknowledgement was 5.5 months. Similar findings were made in a third ministry where, of 115 cases submitted between 1985 and 1988, only 20 had been resolved, with an average delay of 10 months for resolved cases.

The general implications of these and other findings mentioned up to this point are considered in the next section.

2.2.6   Current Thinking

The definitions of managerial work most favoured by practitioners and management textbooks still rely primarily on the writings of such authors as Fayol and Drucker. In these definitions, management is seen as consisting in broadly stated activities such as planning, motivating, and achieving goals through the work of others. On the whole, management researchers are less persuaded by the classical and popular schools, although some argue that classical definitions in particular should not be dismissed out of hand (e.g., Carroll & Gillen 1987; Hales 1986).

The main dissenting voices have been those of Mintzberg (1973, 1989), Stewart (1967, 1989), and Kotter (1982, 1988, 1990) who, in their observations of managerial work, have found that the manager "is not a systematic, reflective planner, deciding on the basis of 'hard' information and following through decisions; but a responsive intuitive decision-maker, with complex tasks, and decisions based on informal contacts and 'soft' information, taken at a hectic pace, (and) constrained rather than intuitive" (Harrow & Willcocks 1990: 283). We are inclined to lean in this direction ourselves, although we are far from convinced that what managers in general actually do is necessarily what they ought to do. We are also sympathetic to the view that these studies – with the possible exception of Kotter (1982) – have paid insufficient attention to the meaning of managerial work and its political make up (Willmott 1984), and to differences between the behaviour of good and bad managers (Martinko & Gardener 1990). Crucially also, studies of managerial work in general have rarely examined the "institutional contexts, market situations, internal and external social and political factors which help to explain *why* managers ... behave as they do" (Harrow & Willcocks 1990: 284). The latter being of particular significance, we would suggest, to a full understanding of managerial work in Africa.

Our own interpretation of existing theoretical and empirical evidence is summarised in the following points:

- Classical and popular definitions of management are too general to provide an accurate description of what managers actually do. However, it seems reasonable to argue that the outcomes of managerial activity can be broadly categorised in terms of planning, coordinating, motivating, and so on. It also seems reasonable to suppose that in many, if not all, circumstances these are desirable outcomes.
- Studies of managerial work such as those conducted by Mintzberg (1973) and others have greatly improved our understanding of what managers do and how they allocate their time. We see considerable added value arising from replications of this work in a development context, particularly when underlying political, cultural, and institutional factors are examined as well, as in the study of Chinese managers conducted by Boisot and Guoliang (1988).
- Stewart (1989), following Hales (1986), perceives four consistent themes emerging from empirical studies of managerial work: "(1) variation and contingency: managers' jobs differ according to their setting; (2) choice and negotiation: managers have considerable flexibility in content and style of work; (3) pressure and conflict which result in compromise and negotiation; (4) reaction and non-reflection" (p. 2). Our own experience in Africa and in other developing countries, coupled with the findings of Boisot and Guoliang (1988) and Child and Lu (1990) in China, lead us to slightly different conclusions. In particular, we would suggest that the institutional and cultural circumstances in which managers in developing countries operate restrict their ability

to choose between different courses of action. For similar reasons – particularly those associated with norms of centralised decision making and fear of failure – we would expect the actions of managers in developing countries to be more restrained and considered. That is to say, they are less likely to act without first checking with a superior and, when a superior is absent, they are more likely to suspend altogether action not governed by a rule.

– Insufficient research effort has been directed at the relationship between what managers do and what they achieve. What little evidence exists is contradictory. While one study has shown that successful managers are adept at networking activities, socialising, politicking, and conflict management, and that the need to engage in these activities lessens as the successful manager proceeds up the promotional ladder (Luthans et al. 1985), a more recent study of school principals could find no relationship between performance and managerial behaviour (Martinko & Gardner 1990). Our own view is that the behaviour of good managers, and in particular the 'how' and 'why' of such behaviour, will differ significantly from that of less effective managers. It will be necessary, however, for future studies to employ more qualitative research methodologies in order to reveal the differences of meaning, political astuteness, and values, which we feel will distinguish between good and bad managers in an African context.

– It is clear from the studies conducted in both industrialised and developing countries that managerial behaviour varies according to environmental, cultural, institutional, and demographic factors, as well as according to job type, and level within the organisation. In the latter connection, it appears that managerial work in the West becomes more fragmented and spontaneous as one moves down the organisational hierarchy (e.g., Martinko & Gardner 1990). Such spontaneity may not be much in evidence at lower levels in African organisations.

– More attention should be paid to the interpretation and meaning of managerial work and the political considerations which so often underlie it.

2.3   Managerial Work in Africa

Taken together with the general conclusions and comparative findings presented above, there is sufficient empirical (Leonard 1987; Montgomery 1987) and theoretical (Ahiauzu 1986; Jones 1988a, 1990a; Leonard 1987) research evidence on the nature of managerial work in Africa for us to make a reasonable attempt at portraying it. We shall also speculate about the underlying causes of managerial work in Africa, and its meaning.

2.3.1   Empirical Evidence

A major study conducted in 1984 by a multinational group of researchers under the direction of John Montgomery of Harvard University gathered 1,868 reports of management events – involving 'effective' and 'ineffective' behaviour – from nine countries in

Southern Africa (Angola, Botswana, Lesotho, Malawi, Mozambique, Swaziland, Tanzania, Zambia, and Zimbabwe). The events reported presented data that described the actual behaviours of managers from government, parastatal, and private organisations. In addition, 40 permanent secretaries or their deputies or equivalents completed diaries describing their activities over a period of 7–10 days which produced a total of 1,187 entries that were then coded in terms of Mintzberg's ten managerial roles (outlined above).

The study was designed to provide empirical evidence to test the validity of five common complaints about African administration: (1) that African administrative systems operate like personal fiefdoms because the notion of service to the public is much less of an incentive to perform than the economic responsibilities of managers to their immediate and extended families, and because of their inability to meet these demands from their meagre salaries; (2) that African organisations and managers are too concerned with operational issues ('fire fighting'), and questions of 'territory' and status, and too little with policy and strategy; (3) that (party) politics and ideological rhetoric interfere with the functioning and effectiveness of African organisations; (4) that high performing managers are much more likely to be found in the private sector; and (5) that African organisations and managers are conservative and change resistant, "preferring the unacceptable present to the unpredictable future" (Montgomery 1987: 913).

A later study, in part a replication, used the same categories of management actions or 'skills', but gathered data in a Francophone country, the Central African Republic (CAR), to compare with the seven Anglophone countries studied by Montgomery, "to see what commonalities exist between different bureaucracies on the continent" (Vengroff et al. 1991: 98). Data gathered on public bureaucracies in Senegal, Chad, and Zaire produced very similar findings on items common to these studies. Montgomery found that the roles of high-ranking officials included all those described by Mintzberg, and Vengroff et al. found a very similar closeness of fit with Mintzberg and even more so with the findings of those studying public sector managers (Vengroff et al. 1991: 101).

These images of managerial work in Africa are encountered so frequently in the literature, in the thinking of development management experts, and in their evaluations of development projects that they merit our close attention, for practical development reasons as well as for scientific ones.

With regard to the first proposition, Montgomery (1987: 914) concludes that "the personalistic interpretation of African bureaucracy is perhaps oversimplified, but turns out to be a recognisable explanation of observed realities". But he provides little direct evidence to support this conclusion, seeming instead to rely on inferences drawn from the fact that the behaviour of the strategic managers in his sample (permanent secretaries) was different from that described by Mintzberg (1989). In particular, he noticed that, unlike their Western counterparts, African strategic managers rarely served as organisational spokesmen, seemed unconcerned with issues involving the public, dealt with a much narrower range of issues, and in negotiations or disputes over public goods (e.g., housing, vehicles, and equipment) were concerned most about the convenience of individual users rather than the extent to which the purposes of the organisation or the interests of the public were likely to be served. While we would agree with Montgomery's conclusion, we cannot see how the evidence he presents provides very strong support for it. Also, contrary to Montgomery's findings, our own recent experience in Zimbabwe indicates that permanent secretaries regularly served as organisational spokesmen and displayed in their statements – and in some cases their actions too – a strong concern for the public (Gustafsson, Blunt, Gisle, & Sjolander 1991). This indicates the importance of considering carefully national cultural, economic, and social variables, and organisational ones, in any analysis of managerial work in Africa.

In other respects, however, the permanent secretaries studied by Montgomery engaged in all ten of the managerial roles described by Mintzberg (1989). The balance between the different roles played by the African managers emphasised for Montgomery the inward looking nature of their activities, and "displayed a kind of collective personalism" (1987: 915). The most frequently performed roles of permanent secretaries were those of resource allocator, liaison, monitor, spokesman, entrepreneur, and disseminator. Routine office chores, which were not included in the ten Mintzberg roles, came next and clearly constituted a category of some significance for permanent secretaries. Evidence of fraud, negligence, corruption, and uncooperativeness all of which are associated with personalistic, or particularistic, systems – was found, "but not necessarily in the expected order of intensity or frequency" (Montgomery 1987: 916). Moreover, many of the reported incidents were trivial:

"– My boss told me one thing and wrote another. My expectations had been raised higher and this disappointed me immensely.
– By using personal contacts, a colleague got a scholarship out of turn.
– A road examiner favoured a girl by giving her a driving licence improperly. I prepared a case for his dismissal, but my permanent secretary liked the girl and recommended no punishment.
– The draft report I prepared was circulated by my superior as his own work.
– For political reasons, a colleague of mine had me sign an apparently routine form which he was later able to use to discredit me." (Montgomery 1987: 916).

The later study, by Vengroff et al. (1991), showed that the technical expert role, added to Mintzberg's list in other studies of public sector managers, was very strong in the Central African Republic. Otherwise there was strong confirmation of Mintzberg's description of managerial activities, although there was some consolidation of the roles. For example, in the interpersonal group, the figurehead and motivator/leader roles seemed to merge, and there were strong similarities between the liaison role from the interpersonal category and the spokesman role from the informational category. "Each of his (Mintzberg's) other roles is clearly represented by a single factor in the CAR data" (Vengroff et al. 1991: 101). Comparisons were made with Montgomery's work in the SADCC countries, although it was decided that since only two of these countries, Zimbabwe and Lesotho, accounted for more than half of all the data in the 1984 study, more emphasis should be given to comparisons with these countries.

The second image of African managers – that they are more concerned with internal matters than other issues – was confirmed by Montgomery's data. His strategy for testing this proposition involved classifying the reported management events into 20 categories of activities that could be considered instrumental to national development. Examples of these development categories included: (1) "introducing a new agricultural, industrial or commercial enterprise in the country; (2) discovering a solution or a more promising approach to a significant development problem; (3) introducing a new service or programme; (4) raising standards of products or services provided; (5) securing a material advantage or resource by negotiation; (6) developing more effective working relationships with local agencies or sources of external aid" (Montgomery 1987: 917), and so on. A surprisingly high proportion (44.5%) of the management events collected by Montgomery could not be coded as having any of the 20 development purposes, and even those which were coded as having such purposes tended to be inward-looking rather than directly relevant to the development goals of the organisation. Montgomery argues that these findings might be explained partly by the African practice of "rotating personnel among jobs and sectors to advance their career prospects" (Montgomery 1987: 917). This of course limits managers' ability to come to terms with their jobs in a way which permits them to contribute significantly to organisational goals. The problem is made worse by their particularistic inclinations, as indicated above.

But as with the previous image of African managers, there is a danger of overgeneralising from the data. We can think of a number of cases in Africa where these generalisations would not be valid and where the activities of senior and middle managers accord with many of the development-related activities described by Montgomery (e.g., Gustafsson *et al.* 1991).

Where management events were coded by Montgomery as being development related, they had to do mostly with staff training and development, the improvement of management systems and discipline, and organisational design. All of these are important elements of institution building which are accorded high priority by aid organisations (e.g., Collins 1989a; SIDA 1990; Johnston & Dyrssen 1991; Palmlund 1991), and by public service review commissions (e.g., ZPSRC 1989).

In terms of the Mintzberg managerial roles, the most time consuming for African managers was that of internal resource allocator. This was true of managers in all of the disparate countries from which data were collected: socialist Tanzania, capitalist Botswana, Zimbabwe and Lesotho. The diary recordings of the permanent secretaries revealed a high degree of involvement in resource allocation activities such as the following:

"– *I met with other permanent secretaries to figure out how to reemploy young pensioners while training their replacements.*
  – *I chaired a meeting of a standing interministerial committee to consider applications from private investors in the hope of promoting productive employment.*
  – *I chaired a meeting to consider ways the government could help the cooperative movement out of its present financial difficulties.*
  – *I initiated a cabinet memorandum on the further reorganisation of the National Agriculture Marketing Board.*

- *Discussed with my deputy the issue of solving the problem of a blood transfusion team marooned in a mountain district hospital because of bad weather.*
- *Telephoned the superintendent of the national referral hospital about sending medical help to a village hit by a tornado.*
- *Dealt with the case of a subordinate who absented himself from work for the whole month and appeared on payday to collect his salary" (Montgomery 1987: 918).*

Another area of considerable activity was that of internal politicking usually involving money, jurisdiction, people, and policy in that order. As we might expect, internal politics was concerned most with funding and 'territorial' disputes as the following examples illustrate:

"– I wrote a memo to the accounts department asking them to make a payment. They refused, saying I had misinterpreted the rules, and I appealed to the Minister of Manpower Development to get the payment made.
It took a year after the approval by the donor to get the money for a project through bureaucratic channels.
- *We were charged with the task of collecting money from all the departments for damages caused by their vehicles. Those of the Defence Department frequently are at fault, but they do not bother to pay the accounts due.*
- *When I gave instructions to my subordinates, they sometimes shelved them to work first on my superior's instructions, causing delay and frustrations" (Montgomery 1987: 920).*

The suggestion that African administrative systems are adversely affected by party political interference and rhetoric, which constituted the third image of African management tested by Montgomery, was not confirmed by the data. Even at the most senior levels in the public service, he could find little evidence of such interference. Montgomery reports that permanent secretaries have managed to remain politically neutral.

Our own recent experience in Africa again points to the dangers of accepting this generalisation too easily. In Zimbabwe, for example, the newly-established Ministry of Political Affairs has recently 'poached' a whole cadre of trainees from the Ministry of Local Government Urban and Rural Development, thereby causing considerable disturbance to that Ministry's activities (Gustafsson et al. 1991). This is a clear example of the strength of influence of party politics in the functioning of public organisations. A further example, involving high levels of party political interference in an urban development project in Liberia, is supplied by Werlin (1990). In relation to public enterprise performance, Nellis (1986) is another who points to the general problem of "excessive political interference in issues and decisions that should – from an efficiency standpoint be taken by enterprise managers ... that is, specifying who should be hired, who cannot be fired, where contracts must be awarded, who should receive credit, what bills should be paid and which can safely be ignored, and where services will be provided and maintained, despite insufficient revenues" (pp. 35–36).

The fourth image of African management suggests that although the private sector in many African countries is relatively small, its effectiveness and management know-how is superior to that of government organisations. Montgomery's study produced little or no evidence to confirm this suggestion. When we think of the small-scale entrepreneur, who typically lacks management skills, and may often be semi-literate, this finding is unsurprising. What is more surprising – at least on the surface – is that Montgomery's findings indicated little or no difference between the management styles and skill requirements of large public and private organisations[2] (e.g., multinational mining companies). For example, permanent secretaries frequently carried out activities which could be classified as entrepreneurial, as revealed in the following:

" – *Chaired a meeting to formulate a strategy for sustained economic viability of a town that is wholly dependent on a mine for its economy.*
 – *Met the Director of Information and Broadcasting to consider the possibility of introducing a regular radio programme to educate the public on economic issues.*
 – *Participated in a meeting to consider what guarantees should be given to a potential investor in a hotel development project.*
 – *Chaired a meeting to consider ways of improving the housing situation in the country" (Montgomery 1987: 922).*

Managers in public, parastatal, and private organisations gave priority to the same broad areas of activity, namely, upgrading the calibre, capability, or morale of staff and imposing structures and controls on staff or vendor performance. Also, identified skill requirements for managers in the three sectors were very much the same; in particular, motivational, interpersonal relations, and personnel management skills were needed.

The final image of African organisations investigated by Montgomery – that they are very resistant to change – received some support from his findings. There were very few reports of organisational change introduced by managers on their own initiative. Even when it came to fairly low-level change managers were reluctant to take the risk without having first sought (much) higher level approval. The rigidity of the administrative systems sometimes called for the exercise of 'brute force' to get something done; on other occasions a certain amount of ingenuity was required:

" – *I consulted the under secretary about the appointment of a retired colleague. I told him that we should inform the personnel commission that he was retired; he advised me to obtain approval for the appointment first, and then inform the commission. It worked; if we had put the two together the request would have been denied.*
 – *I took a proposal to the Finance Ministry, fully justified by facts and figures, for a loan for a road service ... The officer flatly refused ... I then went straight to the Finance Minister and got the loan sanctioned.*

---

2 We shall see why the similarities between the structures of these organisations may not be so surprising after all in a later chapter.

- *When I was PS (Finance) I encountered a controversy over the implementation of a policy. I briefed the President and convinced him that my position was correct and the Ministry of Agriculture was wrong.*
- *I led a delegation abroad to negotiate a loan. The deputy minister complained that I had gone without permission. I collected information to justify the necessity of my trip and submitted it to the Cabinet Minister. Things calmed down ultimately" (Montgomery 1987: 925).*

One very significant additional factor, not previously identified in any of the other studies, "stands alone" in the opinion of Vengroff and his associates. This factor is "operating rules and procedures", which "appears to be very important in African bureaucracies, being rated extremely high in the CAR as well as in the SADCC countries" (Vengroff *et al.* 1991: 101). They say that, given the orientation and context of French colonial administration, this is not a surprising finding. However, as they note, this emphasis is found by Montgomery (1987) to be almost as great in former British colonies. Vengroff *et al* in a significant observation say:

"This may indicate something generic about administration and administrative practice in colonial and post colonial regimes in Africa or in developing nations whose policies are dominated by the bureaucracy" (1991: 101).

The greatest disparity between managerial roles in the Francophone and Anglophone African countries studied by Vengroff *et al.* was in the monitor role, which was much more important in the Francophone Central African Republic (but this may be related to differences between the samples in the two studies, as Vengroff *et al.* observe), and in leadership and supervision, which was much more important in Anglophone Zimbabwe and Lesotho, ranking right at the top. The correlations *between* the two Anglophone countries on these factors were very strong. However, the areas of greatest similarity between rankings of managerial roles in the two countries were in the spokesman (disseminator) role, in the concern for operating rules and procedures, and in the technical expertise and executive (policy analysis) roles.

The high levels of resistance to change observed in African organisations in conjunction with the preference for centralised forms of decision making mean that appeals to higher authority are still more likely to bring about change than the more fashionable forms of decentralisation favoured by some students of administration. As Montgomery (1987) rightly concludes, the changes most needed by African administrative systems – especially those involving the devolution of power – are the most difficult to bring about. We shall argue more fully in a subsequent chapter that such changes will need to be based on modified values and leadership styles, as well as the more conventional and widespread recourse to management training and development (Blunt & Jones 1991a; Collins 1989a). Making managers more risk-taking, more experimental, more outward-looking, and more client-oriented will also require the creation of institutional environments and organisational cultures which are supportive of such behaviours. There is some encouraging evidence that this is beginning to take place already in certain parts of Africa. In

Zimbabwe, for example, the government has recently approved more than 100 recommendations aimed at improving the effectiveness and efficiency of the Zimbabwean public service (ZPSRC 1989); and it has set up an implementation unit to bring about and facilitate recommended changes (Gustafsson *et al.* 1991).

This section has provided a reasonable description of managerial work in Africa which is directly comparable to accounts of managerial work in the West and in other developing countries. It has also tested the validity of a number of widely held assumptions regarding the behaviour of African managers and organisations. Tentative explanations for some of these findings have also been advanced. Drawing largely on the work of Leonard (1987), the next section extends the discussion of possible causes.

2.3.2   Influences on Public Policy

The starting point for Leonard's (1987) discussion of what he refers to as 'the political realities of African management' is that many of the differences in managerial and organisational behaviour between Africa and more industrialised parts of the world are attributable not so much to managerial or organisational failures as to "fundamental dissimilarities in the value priorities that encapsulate them" (p. 901). We share this general view (see Blunt 1990a; Blunt & Jones 1991b). It is clear also that African managers are linked to extensive networks of social obligation (Price 1975); and that values of reciprocity and social exchange that characterise African social systems still impinge directly on the working lives of African managers (Blunt 1983a; Hyden 1983). This means that:

"... African (managers) are unusual ... in the extent of their patronage obligations to poorer peoples and the strength of the moral pressures which they feel to fulfil them. For these reasons and for selfish ones that are far more universal, state organisations in Africa are extensively used to pursue informal, personal goals of their managers rather than the collective ones that are formally proclaimed" (Leonard 1987: 901).

According to Leonard (1987), this tendency finds expression at a number of different levels of organisational behaviour. At the level of public policy, he argues that the seeming economic irrationality of investment decisions and marketing strategies conceal a political rationality whose logic politicians and senior managers ignore to the detriment of development. As an example, the provision of jobs, and credit and subsidised inputs to farmers is first and foremost an act of political rationality designed to cement support and strengthen patronage networks. Any national economic benefits which might flow from such actions are of secondary consideration, and are treated as a bonus.

Under these circumstances, it is difficult to see how a recourse to market forces will have the desired effect. In this view, it is not the mechanisms of the market that are at fault, but more the rationality of the economic actors (policy makers etc.) who guide them. It is widely recognised that the survival of African states and political regimes of all political persuasions hinges on their ability to produce and distribute visible benefits to their constituencies, yet this fact does not enter explicitly – or often – enough into the calculations of development workers or governments. The prospects of achieving economic development in Africa are considerably reduced if this fact is ignored. African development is impeded all too frequently by public policies which, for political reasons, produce overvalued currencies, low prices, and monopolistic and ineffective marketing boards. The heavy burden so often imposed on agriculture is the result of deliberate policies "designed to provide the resources for the public employment and patronage which ... fragile political regimes need for their survival" (Leonard 1987: 903).

The rationality which guides such political and economic activity at the macro level not surprisingly lights the way for the activities of managers in public organisations at lower levels, as we demonstrate in the next section.

2.3.3   Leadership and Management

Leadership has reemerged as one of the key issues of effective organisation in the industrialised economies of the West (e.g., Keys & Case 1990; Kotter 1990; Zaleznik 1990). Unlike management which can be said largely to be concerned with the maintenance of consistency and order in organisations, leadership produces movement and change. There is wide agreement in Western industrialised nations that the effective leader of the new age shapes and shares a vision which provides direction, focus, meaning, and inspiration to the work of others (Conger 1989, 1991; Handy 1989; Kirkpatrick & Locke 1991; Kotter 1990). He or she must project a visible role model that embodies, and conveys in actions and words, desirable attitudes, values, and beliefs which act as catalysts for the development of an effective organisational culture. An essential ingredient of such leadership is the establishment of a set of organisational values which provide a foundation for the development and sustenance of commitment and trust. Mistrust undermines and prevents effective performance (Bartolome 1989; Blunt 1990a, 1991). Another critical element is the leader's vision which, in order to mobilise and persuade others, should possess the following qualities (after Handy 1989):

- It should be different, that is, reconstitute or reconceptualise the known and familiar.
- It should make good sense to others, or create what Handy (1989) calls the Aha Effect – "Aha – of course, now I see it". It should therefore be clearly connected to people's day-to-day working reality, but at the same time be "mind expanding", challenging, but within the bounds of reason.
- It should be succinct and easily understood; vivid and memorable; and not too long or laden with numbers and jargon.
- It should recognise that its own realisation depends upon the contributions of others, and that without them the vision will simply remain a dream.
- It should be a vision which the leader lives, one which he or she believes in and is seen to believe in. Leaders must have integrity. Their visions and values must be authentic. People must be able to believe in this authenticity.

These qualities are easy to list, but much more difficult to realise in practice. One of the most critical qualities of effective leadership, and one that is difficult to feign, is authenticity. "I believe in a kind of psychic law of management here: that workers, customers, everyone involved with a management, no matter how physically distant, can tell when it is genuine in its beliefs and when it is just mouthing the right words" (Mintzberg 1989: 275).

As we have argued elsewhere (Blunt 1991), these qualities are as important in Africa as they are anywhere else. It is clear that many of these qualities cannot be taught; and it is equally clear that values constitute the core of effective leadership. Kotter (1990) also argues that intelligence, drive and high energy, mental health, and integrity are essential ingredients of effective leadership. Kirkpatrick and Locke (1991) have added a number of important traits to this list, namely, persistence, motivation to lead (leaders must clearly want to do the job), self-confidence, knowledge of the business, charisma, creativity and flexibility. Kotter suggests that these qualities are not often found together in sufficient degrees in the same individual: "despite the ordinariness of the key attributes, remarkably few people share all (of them)" (Kotter 1990: 108). Leonard (1987) is of the same opinion: "in all parts of the world it frequently takes an exceptional person to be able to revise or set the goals and values which an organisation is going to embody" (p. 903). Nevertheless, Leonard (1987) suggests that the prospects of finding such an individual in the industrialised countries are greater because career advancement is more important to individuals in such contexts. In Africa, on the other hand, the links between a manager's career and organisational and individual effectiveness can be said to be much less reliable due to internal and external political influences. One implication of this is that "to a much greater extent than is true in the West, ... commitment must be internally generated by the manager" (Leonard 1987: 903).

Another perceived problem is that indigenous morality – and many African managers are deeply ethical, holding strong feelings of attachment and responsibility to their families and villages of origin – does not accord with bureaucratic impersonality or universalism. It may be necessary, as Leonard suggests, to work *with* this sense of morality rather than against it if the small pool of people with leadership talent are to be employed in the interests of organisational effectiveness and development. For example, "a geographically-focused project is likely to get far better leadership from an official who is from the region than from an 'objective' outsider" (Leonard 1987: 904). Leaders with the qualities outlined above are more crucial to project success, and much scarcer, than technically qualified personnel.

Neither is it necessarily the case that patron-client relationships be dysfunctional, depending on the ultimate purposes for which they are employed (Blunt 1980; Leonard 1987). Functional relationships of this kind are common in Western organisations. The difference between such relationships and other forms of patronage is that the former are used to advance, rather than retard, the attainment of organisational objectives. It is worth quoting Leonard (1987) at some length on this point:

"Managers become patrons to those of their subordinates whom they believe can best help them achieve the objectives according to which they themselves will be judged, and junior staff seek to become clients of managers who can best help them with their careers, not on the basis of some ascriptive or political tie. The resulting informal networks of obligation give flexibility and commitment to relationships that would be much less productive if they were only formal. Thus where (but only where) managers are using their patronage to reward those who are committed to the organisation's objectives, there is good reason to assist them with control over scholarships, foreign trips, and off-scale appointments. The result will be better performance from their subordinates" (p. 904).

2.4   Implications for Managers and Management Development

We can infer from the above that people who possess the potential to become good leaders are few in number – Kotter (1990) estimates less than one in fifty – and much less numerous than people who possess the potential to become good managers. As Kotter (1990) observes: "the world is full of smart people with emotional problems, mentally healthy people with only an average motivation level, people high in integrity who have average intelligence, and so on" (pp. 108–109). The good leader 'species' can therefore be said to be rare everywhere, but in Africa it is endangered by:

– the obligations of African managers to networks of kin and ethnic affiliates which may detract from their commitment to organisational objectives;
– the fact that public-policy making in Africa – perhaps to a greater degree than would be true in industrialised countries – is driven by issues of political survival involving the uneven distribution of visible resources – development projects, jobs, credit, and so on;
– the difficulties associated with developing leadership qualities themselves, which mostly cannot be taught easily because they involve values such as integrity;
– the absence of clear connections between organisational and individual behaviour and effectiveness, and career advancement;
– the apparent reluctance of donor agencies and other 'social engineers' to acknowledge the rationality of accommodating indigenous codes of ethics into development and institution building strategies so as to satisfy *both* individual and organisational objectives;
– the tendency of institution strengthening activities to focus on transference of management skills – or the 'technology' of management – and to place too little emphasis on value change, the identification and development of leadership talent, and other aspects such as organisational design and culture building, which we shall discuss in later chapters.

Good managers are also hard to find: "the scarcity of experienced managers is absolutely greater in Africa than in the Middle East, Asia or Latin America, reflecting both the poor human resource base inherited at independence, and the appointment policies followed by a number of governments, which have stressed political loyalty over operational skills" (Nellis 1986: 36).

Clearly, *both* leaders and managers are necessary for effective organisation: that is, *managers* whose activities and roles can be said largely to be concerned with the maintenance of an acceptable degree of consistency and order within organisations, and *leaders* who are concerned with establishing the direction and pace of change, aligning people, and enlisting their commitment and effort.

The material presented in this chapter also demonstrates that in many important respects the actual behaviours of African managers are quite similar to those observed among managers in other countries, although there are important differences, too. This confirms the view that there are "striking similarities between the bureaucracy of developed and developing countries" (Vengroff *et al.* 1991: 96). But does it also confirm the view that management is generic, and that Western management can be applied in different cultural settings? We would agree with Vengroff *et al.* that "while the roles may be similar, the impact of the environment on the decision processes associated with those roles is significantly different" (1991: 107). Historical factors, particularly administrative structures and practices bequeathed by colonial governments, still influence the bureaucracies of Africa, and Asia. The much stronger desire of developing country managers than of Western managers to avoid uncertainty was originally demonstrated by Hofstede (1980, 1987) and has since been confirmed with reference to Africa (e.g., Seddon 1985b), and South East Asia (e.g., Blunt 1988; Richards 1991).

Explanations for such behaviour and its meaning differ widely however. Most management training programmes in Africa would appear to operate on the assumption that the basic tenets of management – meaning planning, organising, controlling etc. – are universal and that management technology can therefore simply be transferred wholesale. We have tried to demonstrate in this chapter why this approach is wrong, and why it is that in Africa much closer attention needs to be paid – in the development of both effective leaders and managers – to values, especially those of integrity, and commitment to organisational objectives (Blunt 1990a; Nellis 1986; Washington 1988), and in public service organisations, an ethic of service to the wider public.

Part 2: Managing Purpose and Direction

Chapter 3: Strategic Management

"One of the more important things managers do is make strategy for their organisations, or at least oversee the process by which they and others make strategies. In a narrow sense, strategy-making deals with the positioning of an organisation in market niches, in other words, deciding on what products will be produced and for whom. But in a broader sense strategy-making refers to how the collective system called organisation establishes, and when necessary changes, its basic orientation. Strategy-making also takes up the complex issue of collective intention – how an organisation composed of many people makes up its mind, so to speak." (Mintzberg 1989: 25)

It is difficult to imagine how an organisation could survive if its senior managers did not attend consciously to the three elements of strategy described by Mintzberg, yet many organisations manage to do so – some even thrive – without conscious planning on the part of their senior managers. This is not to say that organisations in general would not stand to benefit from strategic management, but rather that strategic management alone cannot ensure survival and success anymore than its absence guarantees failure. As we argue repeatedly in this book, organisational effectiveness is a function of a range of internal and external factors, subject to varying levels of control, which will combine in different ways to determine how an organisation performs.

We know from our discussion in the first two chapters, however, that the external and internal environments faced by African organisations pose severe challenges to managerial skills and ingenuity. We would argue that where strategic management is not attended to consciously by senior managers the vicissitudes of African environments will impede organisational performance much more than they would do if strategic management were institutionalised. Like Collins (1989b), we take this position with the full realisation that in Africa "the development of performance – improvement strategies for public enterprise is complicated by the way in which public enterprises have at times been constrained by external or governmentally induced circumstances beyond their control (international commodity prices, staffing levels, capital and liquidity problems, etc.)" (p. 65). Our own recent experience in Africa and elsewhere leads us to the view that strategic management is crucial to improved effectiveness in organisations in both the private and public domains. Increasingly, research evidence supports this view (e.g., Whipp 1991).

In this chapter, we outline two approaches to strategic management. The first can be described as a conscious, formal, analytical approach involving managers in the organisation in systematic processes of planning, decision making, and action. The second approach is more intuitive in nature, and therefore less formalised and systematic. The latter approach draws heavily on Mintzberg's (1989) ideas on 'crafting strategy'.

3.1   Formal Strategic Management[1]

"Corporate strategy is the pattern of decisions in a company that determines and reveals its objectives, purposes, or goals, produces the principal policies and plans for achieving those goals, and defines the range of (activities the organisation) is to pursue, the kind of economic and human organisation it is or intends to be, and the nature of the economic and uneconomic contribution it intends to make to its shareholders, employees, customers, and communities ... " (Andrews 1988: 43).

An important aspect of this definition is the emphasis it places on the interdependence of purposes or goals, policies and strategies, and organised action. It is this unity and coherence which determines an organisation's ability to position itself realistically within its environment, to build a strong identity, and to make the best use of its strengths, all of which, in turn, will influence the performance of the organisation as a whole. In Greenley's (1989) view, these components of strategic management can be referred to as: analysing the environment, planning direction, planning strategy, and implementing strategy (*see* Figure 3.1).

3.1.1   Analysing the Environment

Both the internal and external environments of an organisation need to be taken into account in strategic management. By external environment we mean all those external conditions and influences that have an impact, or potential impact, on an organisation's performance and functioning. These would encompass technological, ecological, economic, industrial, social, and political factors – in short, the sorts of factors we have discussed previously in Chapters 1 and 2. Among these factors, we expect ecological and environmental concerns to become of increasing importance for public and private organisations in Africa in the future.

   On the other hand, the internal environment of the organisation reflects the total capability of the organisation including human and physical resources, the proficiency of different components of the organisation, the competence of individual managers, and the organisations culture or psychological climate.

   A thorough understanding of the organisation's internal and external environments then enables judgments to be made about opportunities and threats in relation to internal strengths and weaknesses. These judgments can then be used as a basis for decision making.

---

1   This section draws on Andrews (1988) and Greenley (1989).

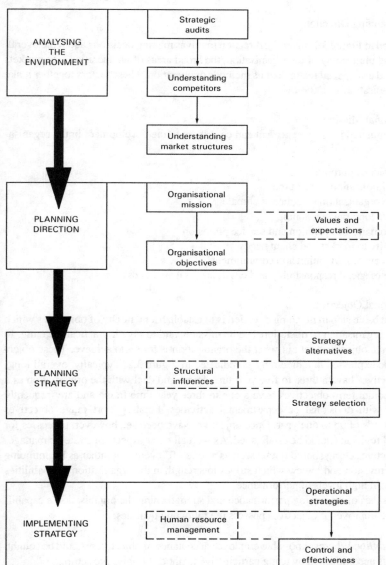

Figure 3.1: A Model of Strategic Management

3.1.2   Planning Direction

As indicated in Figure 3.1, planning direction involves making decisions about the overall purpose and philosophy of the organisation, the broad areas of its operation – or markets served – and any special features of its methods of operation. These factors together make up the organisation's *mission*.

Organisational Mission

A well formulated mission statement can contribute to the development in the organisation of:

- Unanimity of purpose
- Optimal utilisation of resources
- Positive organisational culture or climate
- Effective long range planning
- Clear domains of operation and service provision
- Sensitivity to market and client needs
- High levels of motivation and commitment
- A sense of social responsibility and environmental awareness

Organisational Objectives

The second basic step in planning direction is to establish a hierarchy of objectives which allows the organisation to operationalise its mission, and to give it practical meaning. In simple terms, objectives set out *what* the organisation is trying to achieve. These objectives can be expressed in a hierarchy as indicated in Figure 3.2. Typically, overall long-range objectives have a three to five year time frame and deal with the organisation as a whole. Medium term objectives have a one to three year time frame and are frequently associated with divisional or departmental activities. Finally, short range objectives occupy periods of up to one year. Once objectives have been set, however, processes for review and revision should be established. As with all other aspects of strategic management, objective setting should not be seen as a 'one-off' event, but rather as a continuing process of revision and review which strives to strengthen the organisation's capabilities and to sustain high levels of performance.

Our chances of improving performance and strengthening the organisation's capabilities will be improved if objectives possess the following qualities:

Acceptability: Wherever possible employee acceptance of objectives should be sought. Often this is accomplished by using participative methods of objective setting.

Flexibility: Objectives should be stated in a way which leaves them open to modification in the light of changing circumstances.

Precision: Whether stated in qualitative and/or quantitative terms, objectives should be as precise as possible in order that judgments regarding their attainment can be made.

Organisational Objectives

Figure 3.2: A Simple Hierarchy of Objectives

Challenging: Objectives should wherever possible excite interest and attention and 'stretch' the capabilities of the units or individuals to whom they are applied.

Fit: This simply means that each level of objectives needs to fit or be consistent with or contribute to higher levels in the hierarchy.

Understandability: Clearly, in order to be effective objectives must be easily understood by all affected parties. They must therefore be communicated widely and stated simply.

Attainability: Objectives should be sufficiently challenging to sustain interest and motivation, but not so challenging that they become unattainable and beyond the capabilities of the groups and/or individuals concerned.

The *process* of establishing objectives is also extremely important to the successful planning of direction. Approaches differ mostly in terms of the amount of involvement or participation of employees in the objective setting process. Participative approaches to objective setting are widely regarded as having the following advantages:

– Acceptance and commitment. Owing to their involvement in the planning process managers at all levels are more likely to be accepting of and committed to organisational objectives.
– Clear communication.

- Improved quality and range of objectives.
- More realistic objectives.

As we shall demonstrate more fully in a subsequent chapter, different organisational structures are more or less amenable to participative formal methods of objective setting and strategic management: some being better suited to top-down approaches, while others may not engage in any formal strategic management, while others still may engage in bottom-up strategic management or a combination of the two.

3.1.3   Planning Strategy

Once the direction that the organisation is to take has been established, and a hierarchy of objectives has been identified, attention shifts to the means for accomplishing objectives and aligning the organisation for movement in the desired direction.

Strategy and Structure

A major element of the planning of strategy involves the creation of suitable organisational structural mechanisms for facilitating the attainment of organisational aims. Subsequent chapters of this book consider questions of organisational structure and design in some detail. An important point which arises from our discussion of organisational structure is the idea that structure – which we shall define fully later – should be adapted to the internal and external circumstances faced by the organisation in a way which seeks to optimise the chances of effectiveness and efficiency.

This view implies that, as much as possible, structure should follow strategy. That is to say, the organisation must first decide what it wants to do, where it wants to go, and what standards it wishes to attain, and then it must structure itself (as far as this is possible) in such a way as to ensure that its aims are approached as closely as possible. While we feel that it is desirable, and rational, for structure to follow strategy, we recognise also that in many cases this will not be possible. Indeed, where old, well-established organisations exist it is likely that structure will have the effect of constraining strategy. Structure may also constrain strategy in cases where the costs (human, financial etc.) of structural change are perceived to be high: people may feel threatened or undermined by the prospect of change and this will often lead to their resisting it. This is likely to be a problem in many organisational settings, but its severity will vary according to:

The culture of the organisation: in particular, the levels of trust, openness and mutual respect that exist.

The calibre of leadership: and in particular, the extent to which leaders possess integrity, vision, and energy.

Levels of unemployment and feelings of job security: We shall see in Chapter 12 that African managers rank job security higher in importance than any other need category (e.g., Jones 1988a), and we have discussed in Chapter 2 problems associated with leadership in African organisations. Moreover, in Chapter 9, where we discuss the notion of organisational culture, we shall see that mistrust and covertness are likely features of many organisational cultures in Africa. We would argue, along with Bennis (1989) and

Kotter (1990), that where leaders have integrity, vision, intelligence, and energy; and where cultures are characterised by openness and trust the chances that structure can be made to follow strategy are greatly increased.

Influences on Strategy
There are also a number of factors which have been found to exert an influence on strategy selection.

Opportunity assessment: This simply implies that while opportunities for growth or development can often be perceived, it is not always the case that the organisation has the resources to exploit such opportunities. This calls for careful analysis of internal strengths and weaknesses in relation to perceived opportunities. Sound research will help here, but in the end the full ramifications of this type of assessment can only be addressed in an holistic, qualitative manner, that is, on the basis of managerial judgment.

Competence and resources: Distinctive competencies within the organisation should incline it to attempt to take advantage of certain opportunities, even though this may place some strain on the resources available.

Environmental threats: Important here is the capacity to predict threats rather than simply to react to them, as is more usually the case.

Managerial values and aspirations: This factor recognises that managers will have their own ideas about which strategies to pursue and will argue these strongly. Personal aspirations will play a major part in managers' assessments of preferred strategies.

Obligations to society: This influence requires the strategy selection process to take account of specific public interests that are likely to be affected by the strategies chosen. Accordingly, if the organisation's mission statement expresses a general concern for conservation of the environment, then a potential infringement of, say, water or air pollution standards should be an important consideration in strategy selection.

Strategy and organisational culture: Organisational cultures, which may be classified in a number of ways (e.g., Blunt 1991; and Chapter 9 in this book), are likely to exert an influence on a firm's strategic posture. That is, whether it adopts a posture which is aggressive, steady-state, or defensive. As we have seen already, organisational culture also affects receptiveness or willingness to change among employees, and we shall explore in greater detail in Chapter 9 elements of organisational and national culture which may serve to foster or inhibit change or to incline the organisation to adopt certain strategic postures.

It seems to us, for example, that aggressive strategic postures are less likely to be adopted in Africa, partly because by doing so organisations draw attention to themselves, or become conspicuous (which can be risky), partly because aggressive postures are more often associated with institutionalised strategic management processes and dynamic or transformational leadership, and partly because political, institutional and resource constraints restrict organisations' room to manoeuvre.

3.1.4   The Strategy Making Process

The way in which decisions are taken regarding alternative strategies is also an important ingredient of strategic management. As with most aspects of organisation and management, the extent of participation by managers at different levels in the strategic management process should vary according to the contingencies faced by the organisation (such as size, industry, competition, complexity and speed and predictability of environmental change) and in particular by the calibre and commitment of its managers. There are four basic approaches to strategy making.

Bottom-up Approach

In this approach, departments or divisions within the organisation develop long term, medium term and operational strategies which are then used as a basis for the development of the overall strategy of the organisation. The advantage of this approach is that in cases where organisations incorporate a number of disparate departments or divisions – which makes it difficult for top management to understand fully their operations, strengths and weaknesses – then it makes sense to allow the managers in those departments to devise their own strategies. The drawback of this approach is that the overall strategy of the organisation can be thrown out of balance, and the organisation may lack a clear, unified direction. As Greenley (1989) notes, "the logic and systematic planning of direction to be gained from strategic management may be lost, with the resultant compilation strategy offering little to achieve organisational mission and objectives" (p. 260).

A bottom-up approach may be less appropriate also in conditions characterised by rapid and unpredictable environmental change which require the organisation to act quickly and decisively in order to survive and prosper.

Top-down Approach

Top-down strategy making is carried out by the most senior executives in the organisation, and then transmitted down the organisation to provide a framework for the development of operational plans at lower levels in the organisation. This approach can ensure that conflicts and inconsistencies between different parts of the organisation are minimised, and it provides for greater cohesiveness and unity of purpose and direction.

The disadvantage of this approach is that it makes little formal use of the creativity and detailed insight and knowledge which could be provided by lower level managers. It may also have a dampening effect on motivation and receptiveness to change. Generally speaking, participation improves motivation and increases the likelihood of the acceptance of change (McLennan 1989).

Interactive Approach

The interactive approach involves an integration of strategies emanating from the top of the organisation and from lower levels within it. An integrated strategy results from open negotiations and exchange between managers at different levels, and allows for considerable participation by managers throughout the organisation. The major advantage of this approach is that it encourages creativity and innovation within a coherent overall strategy, which itself may be subject to change as a result of pressures from below and initiatives which are of such high value as to warrant a partial strategic reorientation within the organisation as a whole. Greenley (1989) warns, however, that the processes involved in interactive strategic management can be difficult to control and must be implemented carefully. It is also likely that as a result of the large numbers of managers involved, conflicts of interest will arise, say, over the allocation of scarce resources.

This approach is particularly well suited to complex organisations (that is, organisations whose work is diversified and difficult to understand technically) undergoing periods of change, or in their early stages of growth.

Semi-Autonomous Approach

The semi-autonomous approach allows strategic business units (or divisions or major departments within the organisation) considerable freedom in developing their own strategic initiatives and orientations which are then approved at the organisational level with little or no modification. Organisational strategy would be concerned with selecting new businesses and with setting the organisation's overall direction. Decisions at the organisational level would sometimes include the establishment, closure, or modification of strategic business units. Participation at this level would be confined to senior managers and special planners or others with specialised knowledge of matters of strategic significance.

3.1.5   Organisational Strategy Alternatives

At the organisational level, the broad strategy alternatives are *growth, stability, defence,* and *synergy.*

Growth

Growth through diversification can either involve launching new products into new markets, and therefore the establishment of a new business and new strategic business units, or the maintenance of a common thread between new and existing products. For example, a university might diversify into tourism and hospitality management where the level of qualifications and standards applied would be broadly similar to those observed in other parts of the institution, but the products and, to some degree, markets served would be different.

Two further alternatives for growth exist at the organisational level. Both entail integration: in backward integration the organisation engages in the production of items which formerly had been the inputs for an existing strategic business unit. For example, backward integration for a car manufacturer would take it into the production of component parts. Forward integration is designed to eliminate intermediaries between the organisation and the customer. For example, an oil company like BP would integrate forward if it established petrol station retail outlets.

These ends can be achieved either by the development of resources and personnel within the organisation or through takeovers or mergers. In the latter case, the acquired company forms the basis of the new strategic business unit. Another possibility is the establishment of a joint venture which itself can constitute a new strategic business unit drawing on the special skills and strengths of the parent organisations.

Stability
This entails allowing the organisation to maintain existing strategies and rates of growth. This can result from the observation that sales and growth, and performance generally, are seen to be satisfactory and expansion into new businesses may be seen as too risky.

Defence
A defensive strategy involves one of three alternatives: *turnaround*, *divestment*, and *liquidation*. A turnaround strategy entails attempts to improve the efficiency of current operations in order to enhance the organisation's competitiveness. Divestment involves the sale of a strategic business unit which is no longer performing satisfactorily or which is no longer compatible with the organisation's strategic orientation. Liquidation occurs when a strategic business unit is disbanded and its assets sold to generate cash. In the case of a single strategic business unit company, this will of course result in its closure.

Synergy
According to Ansoff (1965) a synergistic strategy is concerned with the consolidation of strengths and may consist of one or more of the following components:

- *Sales synergy* is derived from selling many products through the same distribution channels using the same sales force.
- *Operating synergy* arises from spreading operating costs across several products or services. It results in a more intensive use of resources and personnel and allows personnel to learn about operations connected with a number of products.
- *Investment synergy* is a function of shared production and research and development facilities.
- *Management synergy* is achieved where managerial skills and knowledge can be employed to benefit a number of strategic business units.

3.2 Crafting Strategy[2]

The mode of strategic management described to this point is a formal, rational, conscious procedure in which strategies and goals are *formulated*. But strategies can *emerge* as well, more or less of their own volition. In some circumstances, according to Mintzberg (1989), this evolutionary process produces better results. Largely, this is because evolutionary strategies do not make artificial distinctions between formulation – deciding what to do and how – and implementation. In the evolutionary process these two aspects of strategy form a seamless whole. They are inseparable. Mintzberg argues that this is vital for feedback: if the scene of action and implementation is cut off from the site of planning or thinking then performance will invariably suffer. Mintzberg is emphatic about this:

"The notion that strategy is something that should happen way up there, far removed from the details of running an organisation on a daily basis, is one of the great fallacies of conventional management" (1989: 31).

This point is perhaps a little over-made by Mintzberg however. Most formalised systems of strategic management, including the one we have presented in this chapter, would recognise the importance of revision, review, and feedback – that is, there would be acceptance of the necessity for contact between planning and implementation. When we referred earlier to the notion of 'live' strategic management, this is exactly what we meant. Strategic management is unlikely to be regarded by informed observers these days as a 'one-off' event.

Just as with other aspects of organisation and management, then, we endorse the view that there is no 'one best way' to make strategy. The approach adopted will vary according to the time available, that is, the urgency with which decisions and action have to be taken, and according to other variables such as the skill-levels and commitment of employees and, to some extent, the structure of the organisation. Although, in the latter regard, our inclination would be to argue that structure should follow strategy.

3.2.1 Quantum Leaps

But Mintzberg's (1989) view of effective strategic management is somewhat different. He asserts that most organisations would not be able to accept the continual turmoil and change which would accompany ongoing review and revision of strategic planning because there is a universal tendency for organisations to resist change. Instead, Mintzberg's investigations of a large number of successful organisations in the USA have revealed that organisations adopt two different modes of strategic management behaviour.

---

2   Much of this section is based on Mintzberg (1989).

"Most organisations favour ... periods of stability because they achieve success not by changing strategies but by exploiting the ones that they have. ... While this goes on, however, the world continues to change, sometimes slowly, occasionally in dramatic shifts. As a result, whether gradually or suddenly, the organisation's strategic orientation moves out of synch with its environment. Then ... a strategic revolution must take place. That long period of evolutionary change is suddenly punctuated by a brief bout of revolutionary turmoil in which the organisation quickly alters many of its established patterns. In effect, it tries to leap to a new stability quickly to reestablish an integrated posture among a new set of strategies, structure, and culture" (Mintzberg 1989: 36).

Mintzberg refers to this type of strategic management process as a 'quantum theory' approach which is particularly well suited to large, established, mass-production organisations. Organisations of this type tend to have rigid structures (what we shall refer to in Chapter 7 as 'machine bureaucracies') which are particularly resistant to change.

3.2.2   Cycles of Change

However, in more creative and flexible organisations, there are different patterns of change and stability. The periods of stability tend to be shorter because "organisations in the business of producing novel outputs apparently need to fly off in all directions from time to time to sustain their creativity" (Mintzberg 1989: 37).

The important point to bear in mind, however, is that thinking should not be separated from action. Many strategic failures are the result of either not discerning the difference between the two or misplaced emphasis on one at the expense of the other. Both are needed, but organisations seem to need to "separate in time the basic forces for change and stability, reconciling them by attending to each in turn" (Mintzberg 1989: 37–38). The lengths of periods of stability and change needed by different organisations will vary according to their circumstances or the contingencies they face – such as competition, government regulations, the availability of labour, and so on. For Mintzberg, then, "to manage strategy ... is to craft thought and action, control and learning, stability and change" (1989: 35).

3.2.3   The Craftsman's Skills

To do this well, according to Mintzberg, managers need to develop abilities which will enable them to manage stability, detect discontinuity, manage patterns, reconcile change and continuity, and they must know the business or the product well.

Managing Stability
Mintzberg's view is that managers should spend proportionately more of their time ensuring that their organisations are as effective as possible in pursuing strategies they already have, rather than devising new ones. Again, however, we feel that Mintzberg overstates his case here. Whilst we would agree that organisations need to make sure

that they perform their basic – bread and butter – functions well, we disagree that all organisations will be able to devote most of their time to such activities. This is because (for example) organisations in an early stage of development, which are attempting to carve out a niche in the market – that is, those organisations which are still in the process of determining what their range of products or services should be, and where to place emphasis – will need to spend proportionately more time on strategic management.

Nevertheless, we would agree with Mintzberg that the ability to manage stability tends these days to be relatively ignored in the literature and that it deserves more attention than it gets for the reasons Mintzberg gives. As he asserts, an obsession with change is dysfunctional: "organisations that reassess their strategies continuously are like individuals who reassess their jobs or their marriages continuously – in both cases, they can drive themselves crazy, or else reduce themselves to inaction" (Mintzberg 1989: 39). According to Mintzberg, strategic management conducted in this way is more a means for programming or scheduling strategy that has already been created rather than *creating* new strategies.

Detecting Discontinuity

Here Mintzberg argues that claims about the extraordinary rates and complexity of change in the modern world are somewhat exaggerated, and that for much of the time change is minor and temporary requiring no strategic response on the part of the organisation.

It is only occasionally, he suggests, that truly significant, and easily recognisable, change occurs in the environment. Again, while we feel that Mintzberg's views have a certain amount of general validity, we believe that African organisational environments are more vulnerable than organisations in America to profound internal (e.g., political changes) and external (e.g., changes in commodity prices) changes which do have immediate and significant effects and do require strategic responses.

Strategic management therefore poses greater challenges in Africa than in the West because not only must the African manager be able – as Mintzberg says – to "detect the subtle discontinuities that may undermine an organisation in the future" (1989: 40), but in addition he or she must be ready to make strategic responses to relatively frequent threats to organisational functioning many of which are beyond his or her control.

Knowing the Business

Effective strategic management requires managers to know their products and businesses in intimate detail. This is not just the intellectual, analytical knowledge derived from facts and figures, but more a 'feel' for the product and an intuitive understanding of the industry and competitors. "Facts are available to anyone; this kind of knowledge is not. Wisdom is the word that captures it best" (Mintzberg 1989: 41).

Managing Patterns

The good strategic manager is able both to provide vision and direction of his own and to detect or identify the emergence of patterns in other parts of the organisation which can form the basis of new strategic initiatives. However, not all of these emerging patterns will be worthwhile or desirable, and in such circumstances the manager must be prepared to 'uproot' them immediately. Yet other emerging patterns which might appear initially not to hold much promise might develop into tomorrow's winning strategy. Deciding when and how to intervene calls for fine judgment and more of the wisdom referred to in the previous section. Such wisdom involves creating a climate or culture within which strategies are encouraged to emerge, knowing when to encourage and when to discourage development and, when it is necessary to stamp out some emergent strategy quickly, and having the interpersonal skills to do it in a way which does not foster resentment or inhibit future growth.

Reconciling Change and Continuity

Lastly, strategic managers should keep in mind that their organisations' capacities to deal with periods of profound change will vary. Effective strategic management therefore calls for a balance to be struck between periods of continuity and consolidation and periods of reorientation or what Mintzberg calls 'strategic revolutions'.

"Managers who are obsessed with either change or stability are bound eventually to harm their organisations. As pattern recogniser, the manager has to be able to sense when to exploit an established crop of strategies and when to encourage new strains to displace the old" (Mintzberg 1989: 42).

3.3   Strategic Human Resource Management

Our discussion to this point has been concerned primarily with principles and processes of strategic management. But we need also to ask what forms the strategic management of people within organisations might take. How can managers ensure that their organisations' most important resource – their people – are utilised effectively and treated humanely? How can the strategic management of an organisation's human resources help it to gain and maintain a competitive advantage?

Increasingly, informed opinion indicates that a necessary first step in the strategic management of human resources is that it should become a major concern of senior line managers and not be something which is relegated to the personnel department. As Rothwell (1989) asserts, "if human resource management is to be taken seriously, personnel managers must give it away" (p. 17).

The leverage points for ensuring the effective strategic management of human resources mirror the contents of this book, namely, managing direction, managing the work setting, managing peoples' behaviour within that setting, and managing development and change. These areas must be managed in a way which reinforces the organisation's strategy and direction.

For example, when it comes to the management of the behaviour of people within the work setting, Schuler (1989) identifies six human resource management 'menus' from which different practices can be selected in order to support a particular strategic orientation. A summary of these menus is provided in Table 3.1.

The practices described in Table 3.1 are mostly self-explanatory, but a more detailed explanation of the staffing menu in that Table will indicate how the choices listed can be interpreted and applied.

Recruitment

Choices here include whether to recruit internally or externally. Internal recruitment carries with it implicit costs for training and development of personnel, but may have beneficial effects on motivation. External recruitment, on the other hand, may enable the firm to acquire new skills and values, thereby permitting it to do things which it could not do before; it could also give the organisation a means for bringing about culture change, that is, altering the psychological climate within the organisation.

Career Paths

Here the organisation needs to decide between broad career paths which allow for skill diversity or narrow career paths which make for greater specialisation and in some cases more rapid advancement.

Promotions

Several promotion ladders (or ways to proceed up the organisation) enable managers to be promoted while remaining in their own areas of specialisation. Fewer promotion ladders, or a single ladder, enhances the value of promotion and increases the competition for it. A related consideration is whether to employ explicit or implicit criteria for promotion. Implicit criteria may increase flexibility of decision making, but also increases the opportunity for malpractice. Explicit criteria, on the other hand, have the virtues of clarity and openness, making it easier for employees to determine the legitimacy and fairness of promotions.

Socialisation

This refers to the amount of emphasis placed by the organisation on inculcating in new employees the organisation's values and attitudes. Organisations with a strong, effective culture will devote considerable time and energy to ensuring that newcomers are thoroughly indoctrinated in the company's philosophy and ways of doing things. This can help to ensure unity of purpose, commitment, and involvement in the new employee.

Openness

A final choice in the staffing menu is the degree of openness. Open procedures can be seen to be fair and can engender trust and honesty. Closed or secretive selection and staffing procedures may save time, but can depress morale if decision makers cannot be trusted to act impartially.

Table 3.1: Human Resource Management Practice Menus (Schuler 1989)

Planning choices

Informal	Formal
Short term	Long term
Explicit job analysis	Implicit job analysis
Job simplification	Job enrichment
Low employee participation	High employee participation

Staffing choices

Internal sources	External sources
Narrow paths	Broad paths
Single ladder	Multiple ladders
Explicit criteria	Implicit criteria
Limited socialisation	Extensive socialisation
Closed procedures	Open procedures

Appraising Choices

Behavioural criteria	Results criteria
Purposes: development	Remedial, maintenance
Low employee participation	High employee participation
Short-term criteria	Long-term criteria
Individual criteria	Group criteria

Compensating choices

Low base salaries	High base salaries
Internal equity	External equity
Few ferks	Many perks
Standard, fixed package	Flexible package
Low participation	High participation
No incentices	Many incentives
Short-term incentices	Long-term incentives
No employment security	High employment security
Hierarchical	Egalitarian
No ownership	Extensice ownership

Training and development

Short term	Long term
Narrow applicaton	Broad application
Unplanned, unsystematic	Planned, systematic
Individual orientation	Group orientation
Low participation	High participation

Labour-management relations

Traditional	Cooperative

These, then, are just a few examples of the strategic choices which can be made among human resource management practices so that the competitiveness of the organisation, or its strategic position in the market place, can be maintained, enhanced, or reoriented.

Nicholson, Rees and Brooks-Rooney (1990) conclude from their study of a sample of British firms that:

"Human resources management techniques have an important role to play in facilitating strategic coherence and innovation from inception to diffusion ... all are potentially important for their capacity to create and sustain the organisational networks and media through which flow knowledge, ideas and influence" (p. 530).

3.4   Issues of Strategic Management in Africa

As we have seen in Chapter 1, public enterprises in Africa account for a significant proportion of organisational activity in the continent. In the words of Collins (1989b), "public enterprises in Africa dominate the economies of many countries and are active in major sectors and their infrastructure" (p. 65). We have seen also that the performance of public enterprises in Africa has not lived up to expectations (e.g., Luke 1984; Lee & Nellis 1990; Werlin 1991), although there have been success stories (e.g., TANESCO, Tanzania's Electricity Corporation, and the Ethiopian Telecommunications Authority) and, in some respects, comparisons with success rates achieved elsewhere in the world are not unfavourable (Collins 1989b).

In the socialist countries of Africa, dissatisfaction with state-owned enterprise performance has stemmed from production inefficiencies, declines in productivity and general levels of production, and low product quality. Lee and Nellis (1990) confirm that "state-owned enterprises in socialist countries have never achieved the efficiency, productivity and related performance levels expected of them ... and their performance has in the main deteriorated in recent years" (p. 30). Though the severity of the problems may be less pronounced and widespread, much the same can be said for public enterprises in Africa.

Accordingly, as elsewhere in the world, the strategic management of state-owned or public enterprises in Africa has been concerned to improve performance levels and to stem the flow of state subsidies, thereby reducing the strain imposed on the public purse. In many countries around the world, the privatisation of public enterprises has become a fashionable strategy for attempting to realise these objectives. Is this a realistic expectation? What does the evidence say?

3.4.1   Public versus Private

Proponents of privatisation posit a number of standard arguments and assertions in its support. First, that private enterprises are more efficient because competition forces them to be so. Second, that privatisation results in greater competition and the creation of an enterprise culture. Third, that it increases consumer choice. Fourth, that it reduces trade union bargaining power because private enterprises can fail and workers can lose their jobs. Fifth, that private enterprises are better for ideological reasons. The first, second and fifth of these propositions are assertions which have the character of metaphysical doctrines: either one believes them or one does not. The third is only true in some circumstances because in many instances of privatisation government monopolies simply become private monopolies. The fourth proposition makes sense intuitively and enjoys considerable empirical support.

In our view, a general case for privatisation is difficult to sustain with the available evidence, although opinions vary on this point and privatisation enjoys unequivocal support from some well known analysts (e.g., Lee & Nellis 1990). First, it is crucial to bear in mind that privatisation, or form of ownership, is only one of a number of variables which can effect enterprise efficiency and effectiveness. Others, some of which are addressed in this book, include leadership, organisational structure, organisational culture, the calibre and commitment of employees, and the quality of strategic management of enterprises. It is entirely feasible that the performance of public enterprises could be improved significantly by attending to these sorts of considerations (see also Werlin 1991). This tends not to happen, however; perhaps because it is simpler and more attractive in the short term (because of the injections of capital which result from the sale of government assets) for governments to sell a public enterprise rather than attempt to reform it. Although in some instances – as in the case of British Airways – governments will sometimes do both. That is, they will improve the performance of the state-owned enterprise, precisely because they want to sell it, and in order that they will be able to do so for a good price.

In the case of British Airways, in 1981 the Thatcher government in Britain appointed a dynamic and, some would say, ruthless new Chairman (Lord King) to resuscitate the ailing airline, which was overstaffed, plagued by union problems, and regarded by many as a less than desirable airline to fly with. Within months of his appointment, Lord King got rid of 15,000 positions (more than 20%), fired more than two thirds of the Board of Directors, appointed a new managing director, and embarked on a strenuous campaign to improve service, subdue the unions, and eliminate the competition. In the latter respect, he is widely thought to have been instrumental in bringing about the demise of Laker Airways – which was threatening to undermine British Airways' cross-Atlantic routes to the USA – and the takeover of British Caledonian. By 1987, when British Airways shares were floated on the stock market, the company had won consecutive annual awards for the best airline, and the share flotation was over-subscribed ten fold. British Airways' continued success under Lord King after 1987 can be seen to have had relatively little to do with its privatisation and much more to do with the leadership and management skills of Lord King himself, and institutional factors associated with British Airways' status as the national carrier, and so on.

This case illustrates another important general point about privatisation, namely, that whether to privatise or take some other restorative measure should be a function of the nature of a particular enterprise, its environment, the feasibility of alternative measures and, especially, possible hidden costs. Collins (1989b) is explicit about this:

"The obvious alternative (to privatisation) is to see whether the overall efficiency of the public enterprise can be improved without any shift in ownership" (p. 74).

He recommends a number of steps to be taken in the making of such an evaluation (presented here in a different order and with slightly different emphases):

Step 1 – Aims and Objectives
Any process of organisational analysis should begin by examining the mission, purpose, aims and objectives of the organisation: have these been clearly set out? Do they exist at all? If so, are they widely understood and accepted? Have they been widely discussed? Are they subject to review and revision? If so, by whom and how often, and how is this done? And so on.

Step 2 – Performance Criteria
The identification of aims and objectives should provide a basis for developing individual, group, and organisational performance criteria. This in turn creates the opportunity for establishing reasonable links between performance and reward.

Step 3 – Organisational Analysis
Here attempts are made to identify the constraints affecting enterprise performance, as well as ways of removing them. It asks the question 'how well is the organisation managing to achieve its objectives?' This diagnostic process would address many of the areas mentioned already such as the nature of leadership within the enterprise, its structure, government institutional arrangements, information systems, accounting and audit, and so on.

Step 4 – Implementation and Monitoring
If the first three steps produce a plan of action which seems to have a reasonable prospect of success, then implementation and monitoring procedures must be devised. And, as in the case of British Airways, even if the decision is to sell, it may be worthwhile to rehabilitate in any case. Collins (1989b) reinforces this point:

"As part of a strategy of ultimate privatisation it may be advantageous for government to take all measures to rehabilitate the public enterprise prior to sale in order to obtain the best price" (p. 75).

Kiggundu (1989) has also attempted to identify factors which influence success among state-owned enterprises in Africa. He refers to examples such as the Kenya Tea Development Authority, the Botswana Meat Commission, the Tanzanian Electricity Company (TANESCO), the Ethiopian Telecommunications Authority, Ethiopian Airlines, and the

Cotton Development Authority of Madagascar (HASYMA). According to Kiggundu (1989), successful public enterprises are characterised by:

1. simple structures and clear objectives;
2. technological awareness and industry knowledge;
3. effective and frequent communication with the parent ministry;
4. effective and efficient financial management;
5. systematic human resource development and utilisation;
6. and reasonable staffing levels and selective use of expatriates and outside consultants.

In Africa, decisions regarding privatisation need to be informed by a number of additional considerations. First, in many African countries public enterprises have been severely handicapped by government policies committed to price control, especially for foodstuffs and other basic essentials (e.g., cement, transport, housing etc.). Second, poor government investment decisions (e.g., siting a factory in a particular locality for political reasons – away from raw materials and markets) might undermine chances of success from the outset. Third, international commodity prices, which are beyond the control of public enterprises, may account for many performance failures. Collins (1989b) mentions the cases of Niger, where a "collapse in the price of uranium undermined heavy state investments ...; in Benin where state textiles lost a major market after Nigeria closed its borders in 1983 ... (and) Zambia in the late 1960s (where) the partial nationalisation of the copper industry was followed by a collapse of prices on the world market" (p. 69). Further, public enterprises in Africa, and elsewhere in the developing world, serve an employment function. They therefore tend to be overstaffed, and public sector employment regulations make it difficult to shed staff, especially at lower levels. Conversely, fifth, poor conditions of service in the public sector in Africa cause high levels of turnover among top public enterprise managers and technical staff. Sixth, many public enterprises in East and West Africa have suffered from the beginning from an inadequate capital structure. In other cases, promised government subsidies have not been forthcoming, leaving some public enterprises with no alternative but to borrow at much higher interest rates in commercial capital markets (Collins 1989b).

Moreover, Nellis (1986) draws our attention to the difficulties African governments face in dealing with powerful private corporations skilled at negotiating favourable terms of investment and operation. He cites the case of a near defunct Togolese steel mill which was leased to a private foreign entrepreneur on terms which included tax free importation of all raw materials, and a modest annual lease of US$ 175,000 which was a fraction of the interest charge repayments to which the Government of Togo was committed owing to the large initial investment. In this instance, the Togolese Government claimed to be concerned to create a favourable investment climate for foreign investors. But the chance that new entrants would demand equally favourable terms to those enjoyed by the steel mill seems to have been overlooked. The original decision was difficult to defend also because the mill could have been shut down and sold, and the high cost manufactured goods could have been imported more cheaply overall. The number of local people employed – 75 – was insufficient to justify the costly measures taken.

Nellis (1986) warns that "the Togolese steel mill case illustrates that more is at stake than privatisation *per se*. African governments must be strengthened in their capacity to select public enterprise candidates for divestiture, to market these enterprises and to negotiate mutually beneficial sales, lease or management contracts with private sector parties" (p. 48).

It is also clear that more innovative strategies may have to be considered. One example would be 'leveraged buy-outs', where managers and/or employees of an organisation purchase it from its owners by raising capital from a third party in exchange for equity. Nellis (1986) quotes the example of a leveraged buy-out of an agro-industry state-owned enterprise in the Ivory Coast which involved the International Finance Corporation. Also, the Government of Togo was assisted by the World Bank to prepare potentially 'salable' public enterprises by encouraging careful studies of their past performance, assets, and perceived potential (Nellis 1986).

A final set of considerations which needs to be borne in mind concerns the possible hidden-costs of privatisation arising from difficulties associated with measuring the quality of performance of private enterprises in certain spheres, and the resistance of such enterprises to external assessment. This is particularly important in Africa where government regulations and regulatory authorities are perhaps not as well established or as consistently conscientious as they are in some other parts of the world. A few examples will serve to illustrate the point.

In one study of health care provision in the USA, for-profit and not-for-profit old people's homes were compared on a number of indices. It was discovered that while private (for-profit) homes operated at lower costs per patient than publicly owned homes, they used four times the quantity of sedatives per patient – clearly, the profit motive in private homes resulted in patients being sedated in order to reduce the costs of caring for them .

One of the most celebrated examples of privatisation is that of the American domestic airline industry which was deregulated in the early 1980s. In order to increase competition among airline companies, government controls over the allocation of routes were removed so that airlines could fly to any destination within the USA. The benefits for the consumer included greater choice of airline, more flights, and reduced travel costs (on some routes fares fell in real terms by as much as 50% in the 1980s). The number of passenger miles flown by the American public per year doubled during the 1980s. It is also true to say, however, that the quality of service fell alarmingly. In order to remain competitive, airlines were forced to reduce staff numbers and make staff work longer hours, sometimes illegally. In the eyes of many consumers American airlines became like cattle trains. Most worrying of all, however, were the possible effects on safety. In some instances, pilots were required to fly more than the maximum number of hours per month with inadequate breaks between flights, and less was spent on preventative maintenance. It is perhaps not a coincidence that the worst accident in American airline history occurred during this period when a Delta Airlines' jet crashed, with more than 140 people killed and only one survivor. The Commission of Enquiry appointed to investigate the crash attributed it to pilot error.

A third example involves garbage disposal (and the disposal of toxic wastes more generally). Many government authorities in the West contract out garbage disposal to private organisations. Western consumer societies produce mountains of garbage so garbage disposal is big business. A major problem with garbage disposal is that it contains many different kinds of toxic wastes which are difficult to dispose of safely or to contain. Over time they seep into the water table and surrounding ecosystems and pollute land, drinking water and water used for irrigation. It is extremely difficult for governments to ensure that contractors who undertake this kind of work are disposing of the waste products safely. This is because it is difficult in the first place to determine whether chemicals and toxic wastes from a garbage dump are in fact leaking into the ecosystem. Many years can go by before the effects are detected in human and animal diseases and mortality rates. In the second place, the private companies concerned will resist government attempts to investigate this aspect of their performance.

African countries are particularly susceptible to the dumping of toxic wastes by private foreign companies. According to Donaldson (1989):

"During 1988, virtually every country from Morocco to the Congo ... received offers from companies seeking cheap sites for dumping wastes. In preceding years, the United States and Europe had become enormously expensive for dumping, in large part because of the costly safety measures mandated by US and European governments" (pp. 66–67).

In 1988, for example, Guinea-Bissau agreed to bury 15 million tons of toxic wastes from Europe. The government was paid US$ 120 million, only a little less than the country's GNP. Similarly in Nigeria, in 1987, toxic wastes were unloaded from European ships by port workers wearing only sandals and shorts. The workers were unaware of the toxicity of the cargo. This hazardous material had entered the country against the wishes of the Nigerian government by virtue of a loophole in existing legislation. "The example reveals the difficulty many developing countries have in formulating the sophisticated language and regulatory procedures necessary to control high-technology hazards" (Donaldson 1989: 67).

According to Ghai (1985), it is also possible to show that drives for privatisation in Africa, such as those of the World Bank, are based on false assumptions and misleading data. In particular, he argues that the World Bank's rationale overlooks the diversity of aims of public enterprises in Africa and the fact that they operate in highly uncompetitive markets. In the absence of competitive market forces it makes little sense, he argues, to advocate privatisation. His preference is to improve the management and organisation of state-owned enterprises rather than selling them off to private interests. This point of view is shared by Jorgensen, Hafsi and Kiggundu (1986) and Kiggundu (1988).

We would agree with Kiggundu's (1989) conclusion that "each developing country should develop its own reform package that combines different strategies ranging from internal management improvements to complete divestiture. Even if the ultimate objective of reform is total divestiture, in the short run it may be prudent to rehabilitate the state-owned enterprise and turn it into a productive and commercially attractive organisation" (p. 269).

It should also be kept in mind that there is always likely to be a substantial public enterprise sector in Africa. While it is conceivable that traditional public enterprise activities, such as utilities (power, water etc.), might be privatised, it is not at all likely according to Nellis (1986). African governments regard certain service monopolies as too 'strategic' to privatise. Frequently, these strategically important state-owned enterprises are also the largest employers, and the most inefficient and ineffective. It is likely therefore that there will always be a need for the rehabilitation and institution building of public enterprises in Africa.

Many African countries have begun to address the issues involved; for example, the detailed analyses of past performance and problems of 54 state-owned enterprises (out of a total of 70) conducted by the Government of Niger in 1983–84. Similar studies have been conducted with World Bank help in other parts of West Africa, and also in Burundi, Madagascar, the Sudan, and Zaire (Nellis 1986).

3.4.2   The Management of Development Projects[3]

The successful management of development projects in Africa is a major factor in the development process. A recent study of eleven development projects drawn from six different countries (Bangladesh, Botswana, India, Sri Lanka, Tanzania and Zimbabwe) has identified a number of factors which contribute to the success of such projects.

Project Goals

All of the successful projects reviewed had clearly identifiable goals which were widely endorsed and understood by those involved. But attention was also given to the maintenance within project organisations themselves of certain levels of managerial competence and organisational functioning. Kaul mentions the Kuwadzana Housing project in Harare, Zimbabwe as a project with a clearly defined goal of providing "aided self-help housing under specific conditions and for a specific income group" (1989: 16).

Project Leadership and Organisational Culture

According to Kaul (1989), committed, imaginative, and stable leadership is a key ingredient of project success.

This is a requirement not only at the top of the organisation but of leaders at different levels throughout the organisation – project leaders, change agents, local leaders, and team leaders.

---

3   Much of this section is based on Kaul (1989).

"Moreover, these qualities need to permeate throughout the organisation; in other words they should be part of the organisational 'culture'. Individual leaders play a vital role in developing that culture" (Kaul 1989: 17).

We share Kaul's (1989) view about the importance of organisational culture for effectiveness and efficiency in organisations and we explore the topic in some detail in Chapter 9.

Involvement of Beneficiaries

This factor implies that projects should be concerned first and foremost with establishing goals and methods of working which reflect the genuine needs of the beneficiaries. Second, it should entail what Kaul (1989) refers to as a 'high concern for people as human beings', meaning that interventions and objectives should be sensitive to local customs and values. Third, it implies that beneficiaries should wherever possible be involved in the planning and implementation of development projects "if assets and resources are to be maintained and development is to be sustainable" (Kaul 1989: 18).

Special efforts must also be made to ensure that target groups receive the intended benefits and that these benefits are not siphoned-off by high or middle level strata in the social structure.

People also need to have some material reward for their efforts, so long as these do not become ends in themselves, thereby subverting the ultimate aims of the development project. Consciousness raising through participation and learning-by-doing should be regarded as important elements of project management and implementation. Effective participation can only take place if it is preceded by the decentralisation of project management and the establishment of local accountability. Moreover, such participation should not necessarily be restricted to project design and implementation; in many cases it can prove to be of benefit to both beneficiaries and donors when employed in project evaluation.

Anatomy of Project Management

Significant decentralisation of policy-making and implementation to the project level should be considered. This should be viewed primarily as a means for ensuring and facilitating beneficiary participation, "rather than concentrating power in the hands of project management" (Kaul 1989: 20). Matrix and adhocracy structural configurations (*see* Chapter 7 for more detail on these structural forms) are likely to be appropriate in these circumstances. This will mean that project managers or leaders will have to adopt roles more akin to those of facilitator or change agent and use control procedures other than direct supervision and various forms of standardisation (*see* Chapter 6). At the same time, project managers will need to maintain sufficient organisational controls to ensure that a balance is struck between direction, effectiveness, efficiency and the satisfaction of beneficiary needs and interests. This takes time. Where time is at a premium, other approaches – involving reduced levels of participation – will need to be considered.

Accountability

Development projects should clearly be accountable for the effective and efficient implementation and monitoring of development plans, but in addition they should be accountable to the recipients or beneficiaries of development aid. An organisational structure which is decentralised and participative – that is, one which allows for the involvement of local (beneficiary) groups and organisations in project planning and implementation - will frequently help to ensure that projects are accountable to the intended recipients of development aid.

It can be expected, however, that the demands of project sponsors (funding agencies and/or government bodies) will be somewhat different from, and sometimes in conflict with, those of recipients. This calls for skillful management, trust, and openness in communication. It also calls for a careful assessment by all parties of performance criteria to be used in the measurement of project success.

Feedback

All of the case studies reviewed by Kaul (1989) demonstrated the importance of the monitoring of progress and the revision of aims and objectives. Flexible project structures with decentralised decision making power are capable of adjusting relatively quickly to changing circumstances so as to optimise the attainment of project objectives. Regular feedback from a 'live' and continuing process of review of progress is essential to maintaining effectiveness and efficiency in goal attainment. The institutionalisation of this process is essential also to the strengthening and development of the project organisation itself the idea of organisational learning is central to the successful development and growth of project organisations. Kaul (1989) observes:

"goals set by the (project) organisation have to be interpreted in two different ways – there is the actual measurable achievement and there is also the broader goal of consciousness raising and the developing of sustainable organisations" (p. 22).

Staff Motivation and Development

Project managers should be committed, skilled in interpersonal and inter-cultural communication, motivated and energetic, and concerned about human welfare. As far as possible, according to Kaul, training for project staff should be action-oriented, that is, learning by doing. Local level change agents – that is, community members participating as change agents in project planning and implementation – will need to be provided with material rewards or incentives to maintain long term commitment and motivation. As experience at this level provides a useful basis for movement upwards through the project organisation, career development prospects can act as effective incentives for local change agents.

The success of development projects is clearly an issue of strategic significance to all developing countries. This section has described those aspects of strategic human resource management which have been found to be critical to project success. The strategic management of people in organisations seeks to answer such questions as, how can we make the best use of our human resources in the attainment of organisational objectives?

What short term, medium term, and long term strategies will we need to employ in order to develop the work force characteristics (skills, values, attitudes etc.) and organisational culture necessary to ensure effective and efficient organisational performance in the pursuit of organisational goals and objectives?

Kiggundu (1989) summarises the position well:

"In strategic human resource management, all programmes, projects, and activities relating to the HRM function such as selection, assessment and performance appraisal, reward and control systems, and training and development must be designed, implemented and evaluated in the context of the organisation's mission, business strategy, goals, and objectives. In this regard, human resource management becomes an important consideration in the process of overall formulation and implementation of strategic plans" (p. 157).

3.5   Implications for Managers and Management Development

In a recent survey of management 'experts' (mainly university professors in well known business schools) in the USA, Lyles (1990) asked respondents to indicate the topics which will have the "most relevance to practising general managers in the next ten years" (p. 369). Of the ten most frequently mentioned items, five had to do with various aspects of strategic management. The item reckoned to be the most important was that of 'international/ global competition' which is clearly a significant component of strategic management in today's global marketplace. In public and private organisations alike, therefore, strategic management is likely in the 1990s, in Africa as elsewhere in the world, to be an area of activity which occupies – or should occupy – a significant proportion of managers' time. Whether it be the more formal, analytical processes described in the first part of this chapter or the more intuitive, qualitative approach favoured by Mintzberg, managers will increasingly need to engage in strategic management in order to ensure organisational survival, success, and employee well-being. The extent of managerial involvement will vary, according to level in the organisation and area of specialisation, and as a function of the type of organisation, its size, employee characteristics, and other features of its internal and external environments. But whatever the intensity of strategic management thought necessary for a particular organisation at a particular time, it is likely to remain true for some time to come that strategic management will be one of the most important things that managers do.

Accordingly, it is our view that management training and development of all types (classroom based, experiential, action-oriented, and so on) will need to pay greater attention in the future to the principles and processes of the strategic management of organisations and to strategic human resource management (e.g., Collins & Wallis 1990). No longer should it be the case that human resource management issues are viewed as the sole concern of personnel specialists. From the chief executive down through all areas of the organisation, strategic human resource management should increasingly be the province of all managers. This implies that general managers should receive training in areas – such as motivation, selection, performance appraisal, organisational development, leadership, team building, and so on – previously thought to be the province of specialists. In particular, as Hendry and Pettigrew (1990) have recently argued, managers should be made aware that structure, culture, and human resource management need not always *follow* strategy, and that in some cases they can precede it. This implies that human resource management "need not be simply reactive to strategy, but can contribute to it through the development of culture, as well as to the frames of reference of those managers who make strategy" (Hendry & Pettigrew 1990: 35).

The most outstandingly successful contemporary examples of strategic human resource management in practice are probably those of Japanese enterprises. For example, Oliver and Davies (1990) provide stark evidence of Japanese superiority over Western business performance in the electromechanical components industry (*see* Table 3.2). Whether or not these practices are freely transferable across cultural and national boundaries is much less certain, however. Recent research in the United Kingdom

Table 3.2: Japanese and Western Business Performance in the Electro-mechanical Components Industry (Oliver & Davies 1990)

Performance Indicator	Japan	Western
Sales per employee per annum	$ 150 K	$ 85 K
Stock turnover ratio	15	5
Ratio indirect: direct labour	1:2	3:2
Lead times (development and manufacture)	50%	100%

indicates that Japanese enterprises will frequently modify their human resource management practices to suit local circumstances (e.g., Gleave & Oliver 1990) and that, where this is not done carefully, casualties may result. The same can be said for Japanese manufacturing methods – such as total quality control (TQC) and just-in-time (JIT) production and supply of bought-out parts – as noted by Oliver and Davies (1990):

"Japanese manufacturing methods, if implemented seriously, carry significant implications for the political and cultural maps within organisations. Their introduction is liable to create both winners and losers; their successful operation requires the acceptance of a quite different set of working rules ... the successful implementation, and subsequent operation, of these techniques is as much a problem of social control as of industrial engineering" (p. 569).

But these are sophisticated human resource management strategies which may need to be based on, and therefore preceded by, more fundamental developments in Africa. For example, Kiggundu (1988, 1989) draws attention to the lack of skilled human resources in the public and private sectors and, where skills do exist, their underutilisation through misplacement, inappropriate recruitment and selection, poor job and organisational design, and so on. Kiggundu (1988) also mentions problems of motivation "caused by organisational continued poor performance, which leads to employee frustration and alienation as the organisation fails to provide the opportunity to satisfy the employee's salient needs" (p. 235). He suggests that there is insufficient appreciation and understanding of human resource management principles, strategies, and techniques in African organisations. This highlights the need for widespread basic training in strategic human resource management and strategic management to continue apace. More importantly, it reemphasises the urgency of establishing organisational systems which allow and encourage such skills and knowledge to be applied in the interests of organisational effectiveness and efficiency.

A key element in the establishment of such organisational systems is that of leadership and, in particular, what we shall refer to as transformational leadership. Leadership is the subject of the next chapter.

Chapter 4: Leadership and Management Styles

"It is ironic that despite an immense amount of research, managers and researchers still know virtually nothing about the essence of leadership, about why some people follow and others lead. Leadership remains a mysterious chemistry; catchall words such as charisma proclaim our ignorance" (Mintzberg 1989: 51).

At first sight Mintzberg's assertion might seem somewhat negative, depressing for those who seek to understand organisational behaviour. What he says is true, but his choice of words is important. We can certainly point to large bodies of research and scholarly writings on the subject of leadership, and when we examine them it is clear that to varying degrees they seem to illuminate some of its aspects. A number of well known theories of leadership are attractive to managers because they seem in many ways to correspond to their experience. And several theories are persuasive for scholars and management educators because of their elegance and logic. Nevertheless, perhaps the most common response to our existing concepts is that they go some way to enlarging our understanding of leadership yet each is somehow incomplete; in Mintzberg's language, the 'essence' remains elusive. We can claim to 'know' little about the essence, but we have some useful models which provide alternative ways of looking at the practice of leadership and studying its mysteries. Mintzberg's reference to 'chemistry' reminds us that leadership involves relationships between individuals. And he warns against the dangers of tautological argument about leadership when he selects 'charisma' as an indication of our ignorance.

At the beginning of our chapter on leadership and management styles, it is useful to acknowledge, with Mintzberg, that this is perhaps the most complex and elusive aspect of our study of the management of complex organisations. As Kotter (1988) wryly remarks, "leadership is a murky subject where opinions abound" (p. 25). As usual in organisation and management sciences, the research evidence emanates preponderantly from the industrialised nations of the West.

Leadership research in African formal organisations is rare, although issues of national leadership are of great interest. Most of Africa's nations have been sovereign independent states for less than forty years, and the imprint of the individuals who led their struggles for independence from the imperial powers is still fresh. In many African countries it is possible to identify one individual who dominated the processes of securing independence and beginning the building of a new nation, an almost unparalleled feat of leadership. Several of these nationalist leaders remain, having achieved formal authority as presidents of their countries. Their leadership is a frequent topic of discussion and debate. Yet when we look for empirical information about the practice of leadership in Africa's formal organisations we find very little.

In this chapter we briefly examine some of the approaches to the study of leadership in organisations and several influential theories. Closely connected with the topic of leadership is that of management style, and later we present the very limited available data concerning African managers.

4.1   Approaches to the Study of Leadership

One of the difficulties which Mintzberg highlights for us is the lack of precision we find in discussions and theories about leadership in organisations. Writers disagree, for example, about the differences between management and leadership, and debate the manager's role in providing leadership. Another problem is that leadership is a topic of general interest and discussion, on which many laymen will happily express their views; in common with several other issues studied in the behavioural sciences, the layman is frequently heard to observe that the findings of research on leadership are 'obvious'. Obversely, other findings, and some theories, seem unnecessarily arcane or unrelated to reality. It is useful to keep these difficulties in mind when we consider approaches to the study of the subject.

The literature of management and formal organisations has commonly included issues of power, authority, influence, and motivation among its concerns. Many studies of managerial attitudes (e.g., Haire *et al.* 1966) have revealed that for most managers it is the power and authority inherent in managerial work which makes it attractive. Most theorists see authority as the right to expect conformity with instructions which is bestowed on the manager by her position in the organisational hierarchy. In order to translate this expectation into reality, the manager has to learn how to use her authority in ways which influence the behaviour of subordinates in desired directions: she must lead. As Mintzberg (1989) succinctly observes, "the influence of the manager is most clearly seen in the leader role. Formal authority vests the manager with great potential power; leadership determines in large part how much of it he or she will in fact use" (Mintzberg 1989: 16).

The issue of the leader's power to influence the behaviour of others is also addressed by Hellriegel, Slocum and Woodman (1989). In their analysis they identify five sources of power which the skillful manager uses in appropriate combinations. They fall into two groups: organisational power and personal power. The three types of organisational power are:

- Legitimate power, which derives from the leader's formal position in the organisation and confers the right to give orders.
- Reward power, which emphasises the possibility that subordinates may comply with instructions because the leader is empowered to provide and withhold rewards (such as pay increases and interesting work).
- Coercive power, which gives the leader the right to threaten and impose punishment when her orders are not followed.

The leader's personal power is of two kinds:

- Referent power, which resides in the leader's personal characteristics which are admired by followers, such as integrity or courage (i.e., 'charisma'); followers comply willingly because they desire the leader's approval or because they want to be like him.
- Expert power, which elicits compliance from followers because they recognise the leader's particular competence or expertise which they need in order to perform their jobs (Hellriegel *et al.* 1989: 270–271).

In the 1960's and 1970's the role of the individual manager as a leader tended to receive relatively little attention, as the influence of the 'human relations movement' focussed attention more on work groups, shared responsibility for leadership, and consensus modes of decision making. More recently, however, individual leadership in formal organisations has again attracted attention, largely because of studies of apparently successful enterprises, of the kind so well publicised by Peters and Waterman (1982). New words have come into fashion under the influence of such studies: out go 'objectives', 'groups', 'interpersonal skills', 'participative management'; replaced by 'excellence', 'value-driven', 'total quality', 'entrepreneurship', and 'mission'.

The emphasis in this new paradigm is on leadership. Leadership is differentiated from management, primarily in the sense that effective organisations are said to owe their success to acts of individual leadership. An individual provides a vision of what the organisation should be. He communicates this vision, and he creates organisational conditions conducive to entrepreneurial performance. This is leadership. Managers keep the enterprise on target, in accordance with the leader's vision. Emphasising 'transformational leadership' as a key element in building organisational cultures in developing countries, Blunt (1991) observes that "there is wide agreement that the effective leader of the new age shapes and shares a vision which provides direction, focus, meaning and inspiration to the work of others" (Blunt 1991: 65).

It is true that this view contrasts with those which had held centre stage for several decades previously, but it is not altogether novel. Selznick (1957) sees the key aspects of the leadership role as defining the organisation's mission; inspiring others to pursue the mission; defending the organisation against attacks on its integrity and values; managing internal conflicts; managing the organisation's relationships with its environment; and securing the services of capable, committed employees. Kotter's (1988) more contemporary contribution emphasises Selznick's first two points, which he labels:

- Creating an agenda for change. This involves a vision which acknowledges the interests of those involved, and a strategy for its achievement that takes into account the relevant environmental and organisational factors.
- Building a strong implementation network. This includes 'supportive relationships with the key sources of power' which the leader will need to enlist, relationships which will ensure cooperation, compliance and teamwork, and a committed core group (Kotter 1988: 20).

Leonard (1987) observes that Selznick's view emphasises the central significance of values in the leader's role, particularly in defining the organisational vision and securing the commitment of others in the organisation to it, observing that 'it frequently takes an exceptional person' to do so (Leonard 1987: 903). This point is emphasised also by Mant (1983): "... the 'management' demands of most managerial jobs are not especially onerous, but leadership (which involves sticking your neck out and some moral fortitude) seems to be a more elusive quality" (p. 227).

The current focus on organisational missions and the inspirational component of leadership has led many commentators to examine the organisation's need to balance leadership and management. According to The *Economist* magazine of June 2, 1990 (p. 87), leading companies "know that being over-led and under-managed is just as dangerous as being under-led and over-managed ... Their ideal, unsurprisingly, is a combination of strong management and firm leadership." In this view the distinctions between management and leadership roles are clear. "A leader ... challenges the status quo; a manager accepts it ... To managers, systems and structure are all." Leaders bring change; managers bring consistency, control, and order to complexity. The *Economist* article notes that it is rare for an individual to combine both leadership and managerial abilities. Organisations will need to build 'leadership teams' which combine the best leaders and the best managers. But this is not a return to the old human relations 'groupism'; it is a deliberate effort to recognise the distinctions between management and leadership and to get managers and leaders to influence each other.

Having introduced some of the influences on current thinking about leadership and management, we now examine very briefly a selection of theories which exemplify the major approaches to the study of the subject. Leadership theories do not fall conveniently into clear categories, but it is clear that leadership involves a leader, some followers, the mission, objective or task to be achieved, and the situation in which the action occurs. In what follows we see that the various approaches to the study of leadership focus on one or more of these elements.

4.1.1   The 'Great Man' Approach

We do not need to spend much time on this approach. The fundamental assumption behind it is the common 'wisdom' that leaders are born, not made. Thus studies consisted of examining the origins and actions of individuals who were generally acknowledged to have been famous leaders.

It is obviously fallacious to assert that certain rare individuals emerge from their mothers' wombs endowed with the skills and knowledge which will enable them to lead others. The behavioural sciences tell us that most human behaviour, particularly our social behaviour – of which leadership is an example – is learned. For scientists, and incidentally for management educators, the 'great man' approach is a dead end. It is now discarded as a rational way to study leadership. However, it is amazing how common the belief still is among laymen that leaders are indeed born, not made. Occasionally, this old saw is used to defend an argument that, because of its mysterious nature, leadership is not an ability which can be learned. As we will see in later chapters, leadership probably cannot be learned in a classroom; but it is clear that individuals do learn how to influence the behaviour of others and that, to some extent, the skills they use in doing so can be analysed.

4.1.2   The Traits Approach

Many studies have focussed on the physical and personality traits – or characteristics – of leaders. The aim has been to establish whether there are any traits which are common among leaders. On the whole, results have been disappointing. As Hellriegel *et al.* (1989) reveal, "although more than 100 personality traits of successful leaders have been identified, no consistent patterns have been found" (p. 272).

Although the traits approach has been largely discarded, Hellriegel and his colleagues suggest that there is evidence to indicate that four characteristics do in fact appear to be common to most (not all) successful leaders. These are:

– Intelligence, which in leaders tends to be superior to that of their followers.
– Maturity and breadth of interests.
– Inner motivation and achievement drive.
– 'People-centred' behaviours – the ability to respect and work well with others.

4.1.3   Behavioural Approaches

An alternative to trying to identify common traits is to focus on the *behaviour* of leaders. Such studies have indicated that successful leaders achieve a balance between the need to be task-centred in their relationships with subordinates, and the need to be considerate and supportive towards them.

The most extensive investigations of leadership behaviour, known as the Ohio State leadership studies programme, labelled these two dimensions 'consideration' and 'initiating structure'. As the name implies, leadership behaviour which tends to emphasise consideration involves relatively close, open, trusting relationships with subordinates. The leader is approachable, supportive and flexible, and is concerned with the welfare of subordinates as individuals. As would be expected, the leader who emphasises the consideration dimension of leadership tends to produce group harmony and cohesion, and to provide a high degree of job satisfaction among subordinates who enjoy participative modes of management.

Structure, in this scheme, concerns the leader's emphasis on the achievement of organisational objectives, the group as a work unit, and the completion of specific tasks in accordance with deadlines. This emphasis would be expected, at least over the short run, to encourage high output, but where it is pursued to the exclusion of consideration high levels of employee dissatisfaction may be expected. Blake and Mouton's (1985) famous 'managerial grid' is based on the need to balance the two leadership emphases (which they label concern for people and concern for production). As might be expected, the Ohio State studies and the Blake and Mouton grid appear to indicate that leaders should stress both people and task. However, as Mullins (1989) observes, "the evidence is not conclusive and much seems to depend on situational factors", which the model neglects (p. 432).

Another approach which focuses on the behaviour of the leader considers how she uses her authority to achieve organisational goals: her leadership *style*. Perhaps the best known model of leadership styles is that developed by Tannenbaum and Schmidt (1973). They have constructed a continuum of leadership styles which illustrates that as the leader uses less of her authority the subordinates' area of freedom expands. At one extreme of the continuum, the boss-centred end, the leader makes decisions and informs the work group; in the next position the leader makes the decision and puts some effort into persuading the work group to accept it; next the leader tells the work group what he is thinking concerning a decision he is about to make and gives them an opportunity to ask questions; in the next position on the continuum the leader presents his tentative decision to the work group and makes it clear that he is open to persuasion to change it; next the leader presents the problem to the work group, obtains their suggestions, and makes the decision; at the next point a critical change occurs – the leader no longer makes the decision but defines the limits and asks the work group (which now includes himself) to make the decision; at this extreme of the continuum the leader allows subordinates to work and make decisions themselves within agreed limits.

As we move along the continuum we can identify four main styles of leadership, labelled 'tell', 'sell', 'consult', and 'join', by Tannenbaum and Schmidt. They further hypothesise that certain sets of forces will be influential in deciding which styles of leadership will be appropriate:

- Forces in the leader, which include the leader's personality, values, knowledge, experience, confidence in subordinates, and sense of security.
- Forces in the subordinates, including tolerance of ambiguity, experience, extent of dependency needs, interest in assuming responsibility and participating in decisions, and identification with organisational goals.
- Forces in the situation. These would include the nature of the problem, level of group performance, time pressure, and the type of organisation.
- Forces outside the organisation, in its environment.

In Tannenbaum and Schmidt's view, effective leaders understand these forces and are able to adjust their behaviour in response to the balance of forces at any particular time.

4.1.4   Contingency Approaches

The interaction of leadership behaviour and situation which is acknowledged in the Tannenbaum and Schmidt model is the express focus of contingency (situational) approaches to the study of leadership. Here we examine very briefly some of the more influential contingency theories, starting with perhaps the most well known.

Fiedler: Contingency Model of Leadership Effectiveness

In contrast to Tannenbaum and Schmidt's view, Fiedler (1967) argues that it is very difficult for a leader to adapt his style to the situation; leaders will tend to stick to their preferred and customary styles. Since no one style of leadership is appropriate for all situations, the alternatives are to change the leader to fit the situation or to modify the situation to fit the leader's style. In Fiedler's scheme the leader's effectiveness is determined by three factors:

- Leader-subordinate relationship, which refers to the degree to which subordinates accept the leader.
- Task structure, relating to the degree to which subordinates' jobs are structured and defined.
- Position power, which concerns the extent of the leader's powers of reward and coercion.

In order to measure leadership performance, Fiedler developed a novel – and controversial – device, the 'least preferred co-worker' (LPC) scale. Leaders are asked to think of the people they have worked with and to identify from them their least preferred colleague, whom they then rate on 18 scales; for example, 'pleasant – unpleasant', and 'friendly – unfriendly'. A low score on the scale indicates that the leader views the LPC in negative terms, and so the leader is classed as being task-oriented.

Fiedler constructed eight combinations of group-task situations from the three variables mentioned above. It appears that a task-oriented leader tends to be more effective for two of the combinations: first, when the situation is very favourable – involving a good relationship between the leader and the subordinates, a structured task, and high position power; and second, when the situation is very unfavourable – involving a poor leader-subordinate relationship, lack of task structure, and low position power. The task-oriented leader is said by Fiedler to be less effective in situations involving the other possible combinations of relationship, task structure, and position power.

The relationship-oriented leader is more likely to be effective when the situation is moderately favourable and the variables are mixed. In other words, it is the degree to which the situation is favourable which determines the appropriate leader behaviour.

For reasons which are probably obvious even from this brief description, Fiedler's model has attracted a great deal of criticism. The LPC instrument is regarded as one-dimensional, failing to acknowledge the huge complexity of leadership. Also, Fiedler's view that leaders generally find it very difficult to modify their preferred leadership styles is questioned, especially by management educators. The logic of his argument is that leaders should be selected to fit the situation – hardly a practical strategy in changing organisations – or that the situation, including the leader-subordinate relationship, the task structure, and the position power, might be changed to fit the leader's customary behaviour. Again this seems unrealistic, given the dynamic nature of organisational situations, and that leader-subordinate relationships are influenced primarily by the leader's behaviour patterns. Fiedler's work has nevertheless proved to be influential because it was one of the first theories to demonstrate clearly that there can not be one best leadership style and because it attempted to measure leadership effectiveness.

House: Path-Goal Theory

Based on expectancy theories of individual motivation, House's model (House 1971) concerns subordinates' levels of job satisfaction. The hypothesis is that the leader can enhance performance levels by deliberately seeking to increase job satisfaction. This includes helping subordinates to understand the task and removing obstacles to task performance. The path-goal model suggests that subordinates will perform to the extent that the leader carries out these enabling roles, so that good performance leads to enhanced job satisfaction.

The House theory identifies four types of leadership behaviour:

- Directive leadership, similar to the Ohio State 'initiating structure', which focuses on task clarity, work schedules, rules, performance standards, coordination, and detailed guidance of subordinates.
- Supportive leadership, in which the leader is considerate of the needs of subordinates and encourages an open, friendly climate at work; similar to Ohio State's 'consideration'.
- Participative leadership, where the leader, before making decisions, consults subordinates and genuinely considers their views.
- Achievement-oriented leadership, which emphasises the achievement of high levels of performance by setting challenging objectives and demonstrating the leader's confidence in the abilities of subordinates.

According to House's theory, it is possible for leaders to use whichever of the four styles is appropriate in different situations, the two major situational variables being:

- The personal characteristics of subordinates, which will influence their perceptions of and reactions to the leader's behaviour.
- The nature of the task, which relates to the extent to which it is structured and to the degree of goal clarity.

It can be seen, then, that path-goal theory emphasises the interaction between leader and followers: the leader uses the appropriate one of the four types of leadership behaviour to influence the perceptions and motivation of the subordinates, and to help them to achieve their goals. As Mullins (1989) remarks, in this model:

"Effective leadership behaviour is based …on both the willingness of the manager to help subordinates and the needs of subordinates for help. Leadership behaviour will be motivational to the extent that it provides necessary direction, guidance and support, helps clarify path-goal relationships and removes any obstacles which hinder attainment of goals" (Mullins 1989: 442).

We may note here that both Fiedler and House, while attempting to construct scientific theories about leadership, start from firm *assumptions* about the basic possibilities of leadership behaviour. Fiedler's is that it is very difficult for a leader to vary his accustomed behaviour to any significant degree. House, in contrast, assumes that the leader can effectively use one of (House's) four leadership behaviours where the situation demands it.

Vroom and Yetton: Contingency Model

In another contingency model, Vroom and Yetton (1973) focus on the decision making elements of leadership. Their model – later elaborated by Vroom and Jago (1988) – identifies five decision making behaviours (where A denotes autocratic, C means consultation, and G stands for group):

A.1   The leader makes the decision on the basis of the information she has.

A.11 The leader makes the decision after obtaining specifically requested information from subordinates.

C.1   The leader makes the decision after sharing the problem with appropriate subordinates individually.

C.11 The leader makes the decision after sharing the problem with his subordinates as a group and obtaining their views.

G.11 The leader shares the problem with the group. He functions primarily in a chairperson role, helping the group to achieve consensus rather than influencing subordinates to accept his views.

In advancing this continuum, from autocratic to participative, Vroom and Yetton note the following important aspects of decision making:

– Quality, which refers to the actual effects which the decision has on the performance of the work group.
– Acceptance, the degree to which the decision elicits commitment by the group.
– Timeliness, concerns the appropriateness of the time taken related to the nature of the problem addressed by the decision.

Vroom and Yetton (and later Vroom and Jago) constructed 'decision trees' which recognise that "there are tradeoffs among four criteria by which a leader's decision making behaviour can be evaluated: decision quality, subordinate commitment, time, and subordinate development" (Hellriegel *et al.* 1989: 288). These decision trees provide several rules which can guide the leader in avoiding unsuitable decision styles and selecting a style appropriate to the situation.

The Vroom and Yetton/Vroom and Jago model elaborates the interrelationship between leadership behaviour and contingencies in the workplace, and offers algorithmic guidelines for selecting appropriate decision making behaviours. In this sense it may be considered to address practical issues of leadership behaviour to a greater extent than other models.

4.1.5   The Functional Approach

So called because its starting point is that a leader, whether formally appointed or not, provides certain *functions* that the work group needs, the functional approach to leadership is associated primarily with the work of Adair (1984). Adair's model, which he calls action-centred leadership, is often neglected in American textbooks but it has achieved a degree of recognition worldwide much in excess of less accessible theories.

According to Adair's model, the effective leader must meet three interdependent sets of needs: the need to achieve the task; the need to maintain the work team (the leader's subordinates); and the needs of individual team members. In each area the leader must perform a number of functions:

– Functions related to the common *task* include defining of the group's tasks; planning the work required; allocating resources; organising duties and roles; controlling quality; monitoring performance; and reviewing progress.
– Functions related to the maintenance of the work *team* include establishing and maintaining team morale; encouraging team cohesion; setting standards; maintaining discipline; facilitating communication in the team; training the team as a unit; and appointing sub-leaders.
– Functions related to needs of *individuals* in the team include being sensitive to the differing needs of individuals in the work setting; helping with personal problems; reinforcing good individual performance with praise; dealing with conflicts between the needs of the group and needs of individuals in the group; and training individuals.

Not surprisingly, Adair's model asserts that the successful leader constantly seeks to integrate these three sets of interrelated needs. To do this, the leader must be aware of what is happening in the group and have an understanding of the dynamics of interactions in the group. She must have a keen awareness of what leadership function is required at any particular time, and the ability to perform that function.

Adair's work has achieved wide recognition because it presents an easily understandable model of the leader's functions in the work situation. In addition, unlike many theorists, he has developed from his model a training package, which claims to develop leadership skills and has been used by a large number of enterprises.

4.1.6   Summary

We have briefly explored several of the more influential approaches to the study of leadership. Our exploration perhaps illustrates the complexities of the processes of leadership about which we cautioned at the beginning of the chapter. The theories we have examined have different starting points, different emphases, and start from different assumptions about the nature of the phenomenon under discussion. Thus we find models which focus on the styles of behaviour which the leader may use, his relationship with his subordinates, the demands of the task, the situation in which leadership occurs, the needs of the subordinates as a work team and as individuals, on decision making, and on the interdependence of two or more of these variables.

It is perhaps worth reminding ourselves that our interest in theories of leadership is more than academic; we are interested in the leadership roles involved in the management of formal organisations. As we noted earlier, there is no general consensus on the question of the relationship between management and leadership. However, there has in recent years been a renewed interest in the role of individual leadership in organisations; attempts have been made to differentiate between organisational functions which demand acts of individual leadership and those which appear to be more routine in nature. In current writing on the subject – in the West – there is a degree of agreement that, as Hellriegel *et al.* (1989) assert, "leadership is a process of creating a vision for others and having the power to translate the vision into reality and sustain it" (p. 293).

How far has this current view found acceptance and expression in African organisations? This is our focus in the following section.

4.2 Leadership and Management Styles in African Organisations

As we observed at the opening of this chapter, relatively little is known about leadership and management styles in Africa. A small number of studies have included leadership in their compass, but we look in vain for substantive empirical investigations of leadership styles and practices in African organisations. Neither have any indigenous models of leadership been developed to date in Africa. Such evidence as we have seems to suggest that organisational leadership is urgently needed, but at present is in short supply. There is some sort of consensus also about the predominant management style in the continent's formal organisations: it is generally reckoned to be towards the authoritarian end of the continuum (from participative to authoritarian, i.e., more 'tell' than 'join'). Kiggundu (1988), for example, in his usual forthright style observes that "there is an acute shortage of quality leadership and management in Africa", yet this is a critical but neglected element in linking the "hopes … of the vast majority of Africans, and the harsh realities of scarcity, deprivation, despair, and powerlessness that have come to characterise the continent" (p. 226). In the face of this desperate situation, Kiggundu asserts, prevailing management styles are authoritarian, personalised, politicised, and "not conducive for management development and the emergence of new leadership. Entrepreneurial, creative, and development talents are suppressed in favour of bureaucratic risk-aversive administration based on absolute obedience" (p. 226).

Choudhry (1986) is of a similar opinion: "… the general tone of management in Africa is prescriptive … often authoritarian, inflexible, and insensitive …" (p. 93). In the view of Abudu (1986) some of the causes of this style of management can be traced to Africa's colonial past. Colonial administrators had scant faith in the ability of their African subordinates and therefore tended to keep all managerial authority in their own hands. The menial work which was assigned to subordinates was closely supervised. No real authority was delegated. And thus was created the typical African management style which tends to concentrate managerial authority and functions in a small number of positions at the apex of the organisation.

One of the very few empirical investigations which touches upon questions of leadership in African organisations is the large-scale study of managerial behaviour in the SADCC countries of southern Africa, reported by Montgomery (1987). One of its findings was that the managers in the study appeared "conservative, preferring the unacceptable present to the unpredictable future" (Montgomery 1987: 913). Data from the investigation also seem to support the assumption that African managers are concerned more with matters of internal administration than with policy issues, developmental goals, and public welfare. Montgomery remarks on the "aloofness of public managers from public responses" (1987: 916), which may be a symptom of their concerns with internal issues of resource allocation and relationships, and consequent lack of attention to the achievement of organisational goals. In Montgomery's view, "this finding may well be unique to Africa. It suggests that African managers find their greatest concerns (and triumphs) in administrative rather than substantive issues" (1986b: 24). From the orthodox viewpoint of Western notions of leadership in organisations, this finding does appear unusual. As Leonard (1987) observes, "the largest part of a leader's efforts is probably directed at factors that are external to his (or her) organisation" (p. 900). If Montgomery's finding is correct, it has serious implications for the performance of African organisations. Such emphatic concern for internal organisational issues and relative neglect of the organisation's purpose and objectives – the classic caricature which has earned the once neutral word 'bureaucrat' its now pejorative associations – is hardly likely to provide the dynamic organisational performance which Africa so urgently needs.

Associated with this inward-looking tendency, Montgomery found that the main task of managers in government was the management and allocation of resources. Data indicated that managers were heavily involved in "even trivial details of resource management" (Montgomery 1987: 919). Montgomery observes that this is not especially surprising, given that many African nations are so poor in resources. This argument is also advanced by Brown (1989) when he says that "an important and undervalued function of bureaucracies in politically unstable societies is the search for stability, and that incorporation plays as important a role as task performance in defining their rationale" (p. 376). Task performance, in such circumstances, frequently receives relatively low priority and is likely to be relegated further by more urgent concerns. Brown sees this as a distinctive feature of some Third World bureaucracies, which involves a high degree of solidarity among administrators observable in "an extraordinarily forgiving attitude towards individual misdemeanours and an apparent absence of linkage between performance and reward" (1989: 376). Brown (1989) provides an insight into such aspects of managerial behaviour, which a Western executive would probably find perplexing, when he perceptively observes that "the motivation to participate is not of the same quality analytically as the motivation to perform" (p. 376). Here Brown is touching on a distinctive and significant element in many African cultures – the strong social bonds which are so important for the individual. This element, Brown suggests, finds expression in formal organisations in what he calls 'incorporation', which means inclusion in the social group. This motivation, we may suppose, will be stronger than the motivation to perform tasks for the organisation, and will involve loyalties to individuals rather than to the organisation.

The SADDC study reported by Montgomery also provides support for the picture of the authoritarian leadership styles and hierarchical structures outlined earlier. Kiggundu (1988) remarks that this type of organisational milieu promotes fear in the system, as power is so concentrated at the top. Data from the SADCC study suggest that "the most successful strategies in interorganisational transactions involved appeals to higher authority rather than attempts to reach new agreements ..." (Montgomery 1987: 924). One serious consequence of this type of management style, reported by Montgomery, is that "top managers in Africa ... rarely display leadership by undertaking administrative reforms" (Montgomery 1986b: 25). This is hardly surprising because, in any system, initiatives for organisational change involve some form of risk taking – or at least perceived risk taking. This is the last type of managerial behaviour to be encouraged by the kind of autocratic culture which appears to be typical of many African organisations.

Yet risk taking is identified by Leonard (1988) as one of the essential attributes of managerial success, in his fascinating study of four outstanding Kenyan managers. Leonard found that these managers shared several attributes: "political connections, professional competence and integrity, access to donor resources, and skill at maintaining staff quality and commitment through the trials of Africanisation" (1988: 40). A common factor was that all four managers at some stage put their careers at risk in their determination to pursue the objectives they had set for their organisations. Their leadership style was distinctive also in that, in contrast to the customary situation discussed above, they "were careful to place the interests of the organisations they served above their own pursuit of personal gain" (Leonard 1988: 38). Leonard sees this as a manifestation of their 'professional integrity'.

It appears that Leonard's four managers were successful because they departed in several crucial respects from the norm of African leadership style. In particular, what is clear from our discussion so far is that, in contrast to the position which is claimed to prevail in Western enterprises, African managers are not driven primarily by organisational missions and objectives; neither, if the very limited available evidence is to be believed, do their loyalties lie mainly with their organisations.

A consequence of this, according to both White (1987) and Leonard (1987), is that the link – assumed in Western organisations – between organisational goals and the manager's career rarely exists in Africa; "to a much greater extent than is true in the West, then, commitment must be internally generated by the manager" (Leonard 1987: 903).

Summary
Our brief survey of the available relevant literature about leadership and management styles in Africa perhaps provides some clues concerning the reasons for current dissatis-

faction with the performance of African organisations and attempts at reform, particularly in the public sector. The picture presented is not encouraging, as the following passage by Kiggundu illustrates:

"There would be an atmosphere of management by crisis as events would seem to take everybody by surprise. Conflicts would tend to be avoided, smoothed over rather than directly confronted ... Although there would be a lot of activities in these organisations, very few people would be able to assess how well or badly they or the organisation as a whole are performing" (Kigggundu 1988: 225).

Yet, while Kiggundu might thus capture some of the problematic reality of organisational life in Africa, it is important to remain objective in our search for understanding of the complex issues involved. Nzelibe (1986), for example, illustrates how we might proceed. He believes that there is a fundamental conflict between Western and African 'management thought'. "Whereas Western management thought advocates Eurocentrism, individualism and modernity, African management thought emphasises ethnocentrism, traditionalism, communalism, and cooperative teamwork" (Nzelibe, 1986, p. 11). Nzelibe's view is that the exclusion of these modes of African management thought has caused many of the problems of organisational performance we have been examining throughout this book. How far this is so, we can establish, as he confirms, only by empirical research. Nzelibe's approach – seeking to understand current trends in the management of African organisations – offers a constructive alternative to criticising and bemoaning the situation. On this optimistic note, we conclude with a quotation by Leonard:

"To summarise, leadership is an art rather than a science, the most political of the management skills. Most of its requisites are abundant among African managers ..."
(Leonard 1987: 905).

4.3   Implications for Managers and Management Development

We have noted the resurgence in recent years of interest in the leadership role in Western formal organisations. There is a discernible consensus among many theorists and practitioners concerning the crucial role of the leader in providing and communicating an organisational mission, and getting commitment to it. However, the limited available information about African organisations suggests that managers generally do not consider organisational objectives and performance to be their main priority. If this is so, then it is unlikely at present that many African managers will fulfil this Western perception of the leadership role in formal organisations.

It seems important that African managers should examine their roles from this perspective. What are the consequences for organisational performance of their apparent inward-looking perspective? How do African organisations define their long-term purposes? Who is responsible for communicating this and ensuring the commitment of organisational members? If these roles are not performed by senior managers, how are they to be fulfilled? Such questions appear especially critical at a time when organisational reforms are under way and increasing emphasis is being placed on efficiency and effectiveness, particularly in the public sector.

For management development, leadership poses both a puzzle and a challenge. In addition to questions about the nature of leadership and its place in the job of the manager, thoughtful management educators have also to ask: how are leadership skills learned, is there a role for formal classroom training? We emphasise 'thoughtful' because so many management training courses claim to teach leadership skills – some in one day! No one would argue that theories of leadership can be taught in the classroom, but knowledge of theories does not enhance the ability to lead. Claims to the contrary are absurd and must be challenged. Management educators must search for an understanding of leadership behaviour in African organisations. We need to go beyond teaching leadership concepts, to develop strategies for helping managers to learn the leadership skills so necessary for organisational performance. We shall examine this issue more closely in our final chapter.

Part 3:   Managing the Work Setting

Chapter 5:   Organisations as Sociotechnical Systems

Kurt Lewin's assertion that 'there is nothing so practical as a good theory' is particularly appropriate for this chapter. Understanding organisations, one of man's most complex creations, is both essential and difficult. This is demonstrated particularly in relation to formal organisations in Africa: such is the dearth of reliable information that we cannot make confident statements about how African organisations function or how their managers might best be helped to develop their managerial skills. We have noted that much of the literature on African organisations and their management is unsatisfactory because it is anecdotal ('when I was in') and/or prescriptive. What we urgently need is description. However, when we are attempting to describe something as complex as organisational behaviour *and* to understand it, we need a conceptual framework within which we can analyse and compare our findings. In this chapter we look at the evolution and applications of a particularly powerful and productive tool for organisational analysis: sociotechnical systems theory.

Studying organisations from a sociotechnical systems point of view began in earnest in the early 1950s in England. The approach differs from earlier ones, such as scientific management and human relations, in that it is not biased towards either the technical or the social aspects of work and organisation, but gives emphasis to both, and their interaction with the environment. In other words, the organisation is perceived as an open system, susceptible to external influences, and interdependent with its environment. Regarding an organisation as an open system means that it is seen as possessing similar attributes to a biological organism. Organisations, like their biological analogues, take in from the environment, and modify, matter, energy and information with the aim of achieving stability and survival. More concretely, factories and other organisations take as their inputs, people, information and materials; productive work is carried out within the system to transform these inputs, and a finished product or service eventually emerges. This cycle of activity can only be maintained by a continuing intake of energy from the environment which in its turn depends on the continuing production of an output. A motor vehicle assembly plant, for example, clearly has to sell its products in order to buy raw materials and pay wage labour. Sociotechnical systems theorists have incorporated this view of an organisation as an open system into their thinking.[1]

From a methodological standpoint, sociotechnical systems theorists are idiographic – that is to say, their research tends to be conducted on one, or a small number, of

---

1   For a more detailed exposition of organisations as open systems see Katz and Kahn (1966: 14–29) and Barko and Pasmore (1986).

organisations at a time and they are not much concerned with scientific method. Rarely do we see sophisticated statistical techniques applied to the data collected by sociotechnical systems theorists. Moreover, sociotechnical systems theorists are likely to work jointly with members of an organisation on a problem or problems, a method which has been termed action research. This method allows the members of an organisation to acquire insights and solutions which are of use to them, and at the same time allows researchers to gather data of scientific value (Cherns 1972; Cummings 1986; Peters & Robinson 1984; Sommer 1987). According to Hutton's (1972) dimensions, action research includes elements of 'conceptual (scientific) interest', 'fundamental applicability' and 'short-term usefulness or topicality'.

This chapter traces the development of sociotechnical systems theory from its foundations, in the coal-mining study of Trist and Bamforth (1951), through applications in India and Norway to the present (*see* Barko & Pasmore 1986). The historical account reveals that "attempts to maximise efficiency of the technical system, if social and psychological needs are not also satisfied, lead to sub-optimal performance" and that "the converse is also true" (Miller 1975: 350). The expressed interest in the 'optimisation' of performance has been interpreted by at least one critic as a means of increasing productivity through the intensification of labour (Kelly 1978). This, together with a number of other criticisms, will be reviewed in the concluding part of this chapter, as will the value of sociotechnical systems theory for African students interested in organisations and their management (*see* Kiggundu 1986).

5.1   British Coal-Mining Studies

The pioneering study in this field was conducted by members of the Tavistock Institute in the coal mines of Durham in the north of England (Trist & Bamforth 1951). The study took the form of a natural experiment which evaluated the social, psychological and organisational consequences of a change of work methods brought about by the introduction of more advanced technology, a mechanical coal-cutter. The change entailed the effective destruction of the traditional 'hand-got' system of coal mining and its replacement with a 'long-wall' system. As we shall see in greater detail below, despite its technological superiority, the new method caused many problems which were reflected in high levels of stress and absenteeism among the miners, and in low productivity norms. The problems were overcome by introducing a system of mining which attended to both the social and the technical aspects of work underground. Nowadays this might seem to be a fairly obvious and commonsensical remedy, but at the time the state of knowledge was such that there were few precedents, and no clear guidelines as to how problems of this nature might be solved. The dominant methods of work in the early 1950s were still derived largely from the factory and were not suited to the vastly different circumstances of underground mining. Trist and Bamforth (1951) emphasise this point themselves: "a complicated, rigid and large-scale work system (was) borrowed with too little modification from an engineering culture appropriate to the radically different situation of the factory" (p. 367). The findings made by Trist and Bamforth (1951) supplied a model whose ramifications have since been felt by many organisations, and those who work in them, study them and design them. We shall now consider each of the major phases of their study.

5.1.1   The Traditional, Hand-got System of Coal Mining

The traditional, hand-got system of mining relied on small, semi-autonomous work groups underground. The groups comprised three interdependent pairs of miners with the occasional addition of one or two extra men. Each pair of miners worked on a separate shift. All of the miners had the skills necessary to perform every task required of them in preparing and getting the coal and transporting it to the surface. This meant that each shift would proceed with its work at its own pace, and succeeding shifts would simply take up where previous ones had left off.

Other characteristics of the traditional system included the fact that the groups were self-selected. That is to say, if for some reason a member of the group dropped out, his replacement was selected by the remaining members of the group. This factor, together with the hazardous working conditions underground where high levels of mutual trust and dependence were necessary, helped to produce highly cohesive groups. Such cohesiveness was reinforced further by kinship affiliations, the maintenance of social relationships in the wider community, and the fact that all members of the group were paid the same wages, based on the productivity of the group as a whole. Finally, work groups in the traditional system required no direct supervision. Trist and Bamforth (1951) described the situation like this:

"A primary work organisation of this type has the advantage of placing responsibility for the complete coal-getting task squarely on the shoulders of a single, small, face-to-face group which experiences the entire cycle of operations within the compass of its member- ship. For each participant the task has total significance and dynamic closure ... Leader- ship and 'supervision' were internal to the group, which had a quality of responsible autonomy. The capacity of these groups for self-regulation was a function of the whole- ness of their work task ... A whole has power as an independent detachment, but a part requires external control" (pp. 345–6).

Nevertheless, earning a living using the traditional hand-got method was far from easy. The dark, the cramped working conditions and the dangers of roof collapse or floor buckling, combined with the variable accessibility of coal on different faces (some coal was soft and easier to work), all told heavily on the miners: "to earn a living under hand- got conditions often entailed physical effort of a formidable order, and possession of exceptional skill was required to extract a bare existence from a hard seam with a bad roof" (Trist & Bamforth 1951: 347). In order to maintain a random distribution of good and bad faces, a lottery system, known as cavilling, was used periodically. This helped to ensure that in the long run all groups would have an equal share of good and bad faces, and that earnings would be roughly the same. And although the 'struggle was harsh', the traditional system was comprehensible to the miners, and seen as being fair. They had a clear overall picture of the scheme of things in the mine, which was largely destroyed with the advent of the new technology. The hand-got system "contained its bad in a way that did not destroy its good" (Trist & Bamforth 1951: 349), and this balance was maintained despite the unusually difficult working conditions, the often meagre rewards, and at times bitter rivalries between different groups of miners.

5.1.2 Mechanisation and the Conventional Long-wall Method

As a result of advances in mining technology, new, mechanised coal-cutters and conveyors were introduced into some of the Durham coal mines. Mechanisation made it possible to work a single, long face instead of a series of short faces as had been the case under the hand-got system. The long faces measured about 75 metres whereas the short faces had been about 5 to 10 metres in length. Along with the move to greater mechanisation came a fairly strict division of labour which entailed splitting the three phases of the coal-mining cycle between three shifts. Each shift specialised in one of the three phases of the cycle: the first shift prepared the coal by undercutting the face with the mechanical coal-cutter and drilling holes in the face for explosives, which were fired by a shot firer at the end of the shift. The second shift was the 'ripping' shift responsible for ensuring that the roof was advanced and supported safely, and that the conveyor was assembled in its new location at an appropriate distance from the face. The third shift was involved with 'filling', or breaking the coal up into manageable sizes and loading it on to the conveyor. The shifts were manned by 40 to 50 workers plus a number of supervisors and other support personnel. Problems associated with the new methods of working included:

1. Morale was adversely affected by the disbanding of the small, cohesive, multi-skilled, autonomous work groups and their replacement by large impersonal groups with specialised skills.
2. Owing to the increased length of the face, the dark and the difficult working conditions, communication and coordination among men on the shift was poor.
3. It therefore became necessary to introduce direct supervision which contravened the traditional role of the underground supervisor who formerly had acted simply as a safety monitor, and provider of other necessary services.
4. The interdependence of the shifts meant that if one shift encountered difficulties on its part of the cycle and was unable to complete its work, then the next shift could not carry out its tasks satisfactorily, and the whole mining cycle was thus disrupted.

All this led to high levels of stress among the men, the setting of low productivity norms, and a general increase in intergroup and interpersonal conflicts. Trist and Bamforth noted that the strain of controlling the cycle of activities involved in the long-wall system "tends to produce a group 'culture' of angry and suspicious bargaining" (1951: 366), and leads to high levels of tension and anxiety among all those involved.

5.1.3   The Composite Long-wall Method

The composite method drew on the advantages of the hand-got and conventional systems. It restored to the workers underground some of the autonomy they had had in the traditional system by creating forty-man self-selected groups which spanned three shifts. Once again, as in the hand-got system, an incoming shift began work where the previous shift had ended. Although individual miners no longer needed to be able to perform all the tasks likely to be encountered underground, each *shift* had to have all the necessary skills spread among its members so that any stage of the mining cycle could be tackled. There was therefore a blend of job variety and job specialisation in the composite system because all members rotated through a number of different jobs during the course of the shift, but were not required individually to have a complete range of mining skills. Partly as a result of such multi-skilling, an incentive pay system was introduced to reward *group* productivity, and this, in conjunction with self-selection and more harmonious interdependencies between shifts, significantly reduced the levels of absenteeism and the amount of time lost due to stoppages. Moreover, group cohesiveness was considerably enhanced, and because direct supervision of the shifts was no longer necessary, anxiety and frustration among the supervisors lessened significantly. A summary of some of the results is presented in Tables 5.1, 5.2 and 5.3.

Table 5.1: Absence Rates (per cent of possible shifts) (Trist *et al.* 1963)

Reason for Absence	Conventional Longwall	Composite Longwall
	%	%
No reason given	4.3	0.4
Sickness and other	8.9	4.6
Accident	6.8	3.2
Total	20.0	8.2

To sum up, the composite long-wall method was a compromise between earlier systems of mining and those thought initially to be suited to higher levels of mechanisation. It constituted a joint optimisation of the social and the technical systems. The major implication of the study was fairly clear: namely, that if one system, say the technical, were maximised at the expense of the other, then the result would lead to decreasing morale, performance, attendance, and so on. The results of this study also suggested that for a given technology a number of methods of organisation were possible which depended on several other factors – for example, social and cultural considerations and the physical characteristics of the work setting – as well as the technology itself. This observation led to the idea of *organisational choice*. That is to say, the coal-mining studies showed the limitations of earlier approaches which had implied that there was *one best way* to organise work. Instead, Trist and Bamforth (1951) concluded that different methods of work may be used according to the extent to which they satisfy the requirements of the tasks to be performed and the social and psychological needs of the workers. The form of work organisation most suited to the Durham coal mines was the *autonomous work group*. Such groups were multi-skilled so that they could perform all the tasks necessary for the completion of a whole piece of work, required little or no direct supervision, and were able to make decisions regarding the allocation of work and, in some cases, the selection of work mates. Later in this chapter, and in the next, we shall see how the autonomous work group has become an appealing, popular and in many instances effective method of organising work and overcoming worker dissatisfaction which continues to be applied in modern organisations throughout the world (e.g., Cordery, Mueller & Smith 1991). We shall also see, however, that in doing so it may have taken on some of the characteristics of the approaches it was meant to have superseded; in other words, that it too may now be regarded by some as being the *one best way* to organise work.

Table 5.2: State of Cycle Progress at End of Filling Shift (per cent of cycles) (Trist *et al.* 1963)

State of Cycle Progress	Conventional Longwall	Composite Longwall
	%	%
In advance	0	22
Normal	31	73
Lagging	69	5
All cycles	100	100

Table 5.3: Productivity as a Percentage of Estimated Face Potential (Trist *et al.* 1963)

	Conventional Longwall	Composite Longwall
	%	%
Without allowance for haulage system efficiency	67	95
With allowance	78	95

5.2   Indian Weaving Studies

Shortly after the publication of the Trist and Bamforth (1951) study, another member of the Tavistock Institute, Rice (1953, 1958), conducted an experiment based on sociotechnical systems theory at the Calico Mills in Ahmedabad, India. He made explicit the connections between sociotechnical systems theory and his investigation of work organisation at the textile mills.

"Attempts were made to take into account both the independent and interdependent properties of the social, technological and economic dimensions of existing sociotechnical systems, and to establish new systems in which all dimensions were more adequately inter-related than they had previously been" (Rice 1958: 4).

Rather like the problems encountered in the coal mining study, the major difficulty confronting management in the textile mills had to do with the introduction of a new technology consisting of automatic looms. The new looms had failed to provide the expected increases in productivity. In terms of both quality and quantity, production was no better than it had been with the old, manually-operated looms. To accommodate the new technology, management had restructured the organisation so that it looked like Figure 5.1. Twelve highly specialised roles had been created and these were distributed among a group of 29 workers whose work was highly interdependent, but whose patterns of interaction were complicated and confused. The new system did not include any form of individual or group incentive payment scheme.

Rice analysed the tasks being performed and found that they could be split into two main types: weaving and those activities connected with 'gating' (fitting new warp-yarn), and loom maintenance. This meant that it was possible to include all of the skills necessary for textile production in small, relatively autonomous groups. Rice suggested therefore that the work be reorganised to allow a group of workers to be responsible for a group of looms. The proposed structure, which was accepted by management, is set out in Figure 5.2. The proposals were also accepted with enthusiasm by the workers themselves, and before long four experimental semi-autonomous work groups had been set up. After an initial settling-down period, the new system resulted in marked improvements in quality and quantity. With respect to the latter, cloth production averaged 95 per cent of estimated potential as compared to 80 per cent before the redesign.

Similar successes were achieved in the non-automatic loom-shed experiment, conducted in 1954. Once again, the basis of Rice's redesign proposals was the creation of small semi-autonomous work groups responsible for carrying out all of the tasks of maintenance and weaving on groups of forty looms. This meant that a semi-autonomous group of 11 workers was able to perform the work of the 22 workers who had been required under the previous system. In addition to the restructuring, minimum rates of pay were increased and bonus payments for both quality and quantity were introduced. At the worker's request, the bonuses were paid according to group as opposed to individual performance.

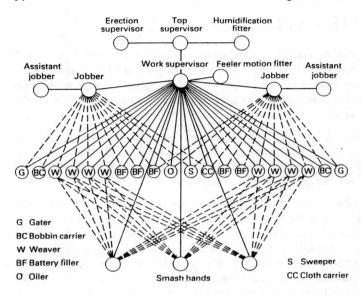

Figure 5.1: Structure of Ahmedabad Textile Weaving Shed Before Reorganisation (Emery & Trist 1981)

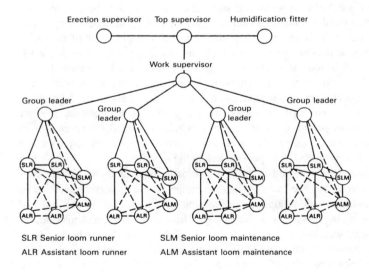

Figure 5.2: Structure of Ahmedabad Textile Weaving Shed After Reorganisation (Emery & Trist 1981)

Apart from some understandable adverse reaction in the community to the reduced manning effects of the new system,[2] it was well received and had the desired effects on cloth quality and productivity. Other results included a 59 per cent reduction in damages to machines and a 55 per cent average increase in earnings per group. All this enabled Rice to conclude that:

"The immediate practical result of the experiment has been to demonstrate that in the Calico Mills the breakdown of the 'whole' task of weaving into component operations, each performed by a different worker, and the reintegration of the workers into an internally structured work-group that performs the 'whole' task on a group of looms, can be accomplished in one process provided that permissive and collaborative relationships can be built up between all those concerned ... The conclusion was reached that the acceptance of the new system and the determination to make it work were due to its providing more opportunities for effective task performance and for the building of stable and secure small work group relationships" (Rice 1958: 166).

A follow-up study conducted by Miller in 1970 indicated that the group system of working which had been instituted by Rice more than 15 years earlier had evolved in a variety of ways. In one part of the mill the group system still operated as it had when Rice first introduced it. Workers displayed high levels of cooperation and identified strongly with their work groups. Their place of work in the mill had retained the name 'experimental shed', and more than half of the workers who had participated in the original groups were still there. The cloth woven was basically the same as it had been before, and "norms of performance seemed to have persisted for 14 years. It was as though the shed had been held within a kind of stasis – a monument to the original experiment" (Miller 1975: 377).

In other parts of the mill, however, the group system established by Rice had deteriorated badly, and in some cases had reverted back to the methods used before Rice's intervention. The breakdown of the group method of working was explained by Miller largely in terms of factors operating in the organisation's external environment. The pressures on output and quality brought about by the company's attempts to enter new markets, and its inability to obtain crucial spare parts, affected different parts of the organisation to varying degrees. Miller observed a correspondence in 1970 between a weaving shed's sensitivity to these external contingencies and the level of degeneration of the group system: the greater the experienced pressure to produce more and of better quality, the more was expected of machines and workers. As a result, the machines broke down more frequently and as the parts needed for their repair were unavailable, there were continual production problems. Managers of the sheds so affected, in their attempts to improve production, reverted to close supervision and specialised work roles, thus de-

---

2 Employees in the experimental shed were seen as supporting the reduced levels of employment, and were consequently subject to picketing from members of the local community to prevent them from working; their families were threatened, and there was one instance of a worker being stoned.

stroying the autonomous group method of working. It was also suggested that the survival of Rice's autonomous groups depended partly on the number of original experimental group members still working in the sheds. Miller supposed that: "to the extent that (surviving) group members had internalised this method of working they could be expected to be better able to maintain resistance and to resist incoming disturbances" (1975: 303).

Rice's experiments in India have, nevertheless, been regarded by most observers as a powerful corroboration of sociotechnical systems theory. To begin with, they showed that the sociotechnical approach was not limited to a particular cultural setting or type of technology: there were clear and substantial differences between the Indian and British studies in these respects. In the second place, Rice demonstrated that it was possible using sociotechnical systems theory to intervene actively and change the way an organisation functioned. The coal mining studies, remember, had been primarily a natural experiment which had simply monitored developments in mining as they had taken place. Third, the experiments were also taken as confirmation of the principle of organisational choice and the general applicability of autonomous work groups (Cummings & Srivastva 1977). Autonomous work groups also featured prominently in work experiments conducted in Norway in the early to mid 1960s, and these constitute our last examples of the application of sociotechnical principles to the analysis and design of organisations.

5.3   Norwegian Studies

The third series of experiments whose results we shall review in this chapter were conducted by Emery and Thorsrud (1964, 1975) in a number of Norwegian organisations. These studies differed from those carried out in the British coal mines and the Indian textile mills in a number of respects. First, they were instigated and sponsored by *national* employer and labour organisations in Norway, and were intended, if successful, to provide working models to facilitate the diffusion of the new methods of work to organisations throughout Norwegian society. In Norway, "a (sociotechnical) project is developed not just because management is interested in more effective organisational functioning, but also because of the strategic importance of developing a more democratic society" (Elden 1986: 246). Second, although the theoretical foundations of the studies were still provided by sociotechnical systems theory, a noticeable shift in emphasis occurred – away from a focus on autonomous work groups alone, and towards a focus on a combination of work group and individual job design considerations. The latter resulted in a set of basic job design criteria which were regarded as necessary to satisfy the general human requirements of work. Third, the researchers were more explicit in their treatment of organisations as open systems, and to that extent anticipated some of the problems encountered in India and identified by Miller (1975) in his follow-up study of Rice's work. Emery and Thorsrud (1975) emphasised the point that the task of management was continually to maintain as close a correspondence as possible between the actual and potential capacities of the organisation and the actual and potential requirements of the environment. "In other words, the primary task of management is the boundary control of the enterprise" (Emery & Thorsrud 1975: 4).

To assist with the process of dissemination, the experiments were conducted in a number of prestigious firms in various industries (e.g., metal working, paper pulp and chemical). The researchers' overall objective was to design work in such a way that it lessened the alienation of the worker from his productive activity, but did not adversely affect productivity and profitability. On the whole, the experiments managed to achieve the desired reductions in alienation, as well as improvements in productivity, via the creation of semi-autonomous, multi-skilled work groups and the design of individual jobs in accordance with certain psychological requirements of work. This led to the development of detailed principles for the redesigning of jobs at both the individual and group levels. According to Emery and Thorsrud (1975), work should be designed in such a way that it satisfies the following psychological conditions.

5.3.1   At the Level of the Individual

1. 'Adequate elbow room': the feeling that workers have control over their own activities, but not so much as to prevent them from knowing what to do next.
2. Opportunities for continuing learning on the job: this requires reasonable goal-setting and prompt feedback of results so that behaviour can be corrected quickly.
3. Recognition and appreciation of one's work, and conditions which are conducive to respect and help from work mates.
4. Optimal levels of variety and challenge: workers should be able to vary their activities so as to minimise fatigue and boredom. "The optimum level would be that which allows the operator to take a rest from a high level of attention or effort or a demanding activity by working at another related but less demanding task and, conversely, allows him to stretch himself and his capacities after a period of routine activity" (Emery & Thorsrud 1975: 13).
5. A sense that one's work makes a meaningful contribution to social welfare: meaningfulness in work includes both the quality and worth to society of a product, and having a perception of the whole product. "That is, not something that could as well be done by a trained monkey or an industrial robot machine" (Emery & Emery 1975: 2). Having a perception of the whole product is easier where tasks, which may require varying levels of attention and effort and different types of skill, are *interdependent* – so that performing one activity leads to another and makes its performance easier or improves it in some way. This enables the worker to develop methods of working which are appropriate, and to relate his own job to those of others. In addition, the tasks to be performed should wherever possible include factors – skills, knowledge, etc. – which are respected in the community.

5.3.2   At the Level of the Group

6. Allowing for interlocking tasks, job rotation or physical proximity where there is a
   necessary interdependence between the output of one group and the input of another.
   At the very least, this facilitates communication, and lessens friction, recriminations
   and scape-goating.
7. Allowing for interlocking tasks, job rotation or physical proximity where high levels of
   stress are associated with the job. Stress can arise, as we shall see in a later chapter,
   from role ambiguity and role conflict, but it may also be caused by what might appear
   at first sight to be fairly innocuous factors such as boredom, concentration, isolation or
   the physical demands of the job if these are maintained for long periods.
8. Allowing for interlocking tasks, job rotation or physical proximity where the job in
   question does not make a clear contribution to the usefulness of the end product.
9. Where jobs are connected through job rotation or interlocking tasks, workers should
   also have the freedom to set standards and maintain some control over boundary tasks
   those tasks which entail some degree of interaction or dependence on groups, resources or individuals outside of the group. Provision should also be made for performance feedback or knowledge of results. Finally, there must be "some semblance of
   an overall task which makes a contribution to the social utility of the product"
   (Emery & Thorsrud 1975: 14).

The Norwegian studies provided strong confirmation of the effectiveness of the sociotechnical systems approach to organisational analysis and design through its successful
application in yet another cultural setting. They also gave considerable impetus to worker
participation programmes in a number of countries in the 1970s. The roots of new
organisational forms in Sweden, Australia, Canada, the USA, Denmark and Germany
(Cordery et al. 1991; Elden 1986; Kolodny & Stjernberg 1986), for example, can be
traced directly to the studies conducted by Emery and Thorsrud, and others, in Norway;
and, as we shall see in Chapter 8, Thorsrud has also been involved with the development
of new forms of work organisation in Tanzania. Sociotechnical systems theory has
therefore become closely identified with new forms of work organisation which have
given to those at lower levels in the organisation greater autonomy and decision making
power. According to Emery and Thorsrud (1975):

*"The sociotechnical approach implies a radically different view of the organisation.
Indeed, it emphasises, not the sharp differentiations between jobs, but the interdependencies among tasks. With this as a point of departure, we can take care that the authority to
control an activity is placed where control can most effectively be carried out – at
whatever level in the organisation. This central idea of the sociotechnical system can be a
determining factor in shaping the structure of the organisation and the levels it may
contain. The organisation thus becomes task-oriented rather than person-oriented. The
psychological job demands we have discussed, as well as the requirements of the
technology itself, seem to indicate that the influence which has traditionally been placed
higher up in the organisation should be moved much further down and quite often right*

down to the shop floor. In principle, this is what has been called 'delegation of responsi-
bility'. What is new in the field experiments is that they seem to give more systematic
knowledge of the technological and social conditions necessary for such delegation of
authority. *A decisive element is the fact that the reallocation of responsibility provides, on*
the whole, better control of the system – its boundary conditions as well as its internal
variations – without requiring the human beings involved to be controlled by coercion"
(p. 121).

Critics of sociotechnical system theory, however, have argued that it simply provides
management with another set of tools for increasing worker productivity. Kelly (1978),
for example, has suggested that "the achievement of sociotechnical theory has been to
discover the limiting conditions – high product or process uncertainty – beyond which
certain tenets of scientific management cease to be economically effective" (p. 1083). We
shall consider this and one or two additional points of criticism later.

5.4   Organisational Choice in Africa

Few managers of enterprises in Africa seem to regard them as open sociotechnical
systems subject to the idea of organisational choice. On the contrary, it appears instead
that decision makers in many African organisations are still persuaded by the 'one best
way' view: essentially the bureaucratic model. There is therefore very little autonomy and
decision making power to be found at the lower levels of the majority of public and
private enterprises in Africa (Blunt 1978: Elkan 1960; Henley 1973; Jones 1988a). This
picture is supported by a study in Kenya by Nicholson, Ostrom, Bowles and Long (1985),
reported by Kiggundu (1988). In its description of 'a typical government agency' the
study, as is so often the case, found it to be too large overall, mismanaged, and with a poor
sense of direction. More significantly for our present discussion, it was found that it was in
the lower ranks where people had little to do while senior managers were overworked: a
typical indication that managers are not willing to delegate any autonomy of action. For
the organisation this is likely to result in "a debilitating unwillingness to take independent
action" (Kiggundu 1988: 225).

5.4.1   Zambian Copper Mines

Even in the mining industry where, as we have just seen, there are striking examples of the
appropriateness of the sociotechnical systems perspective, there has been little deviation
from strict, hierarchical controls which effectively prevent workers from developing new
skills and using their initiative. Burawoy (1972), for example, explicitly compared the
systems of work operating in the Zambian copper mines with those found to be the most
efficient by Trist, Higgin, Murray and Pollock (1963) in the British coal mines. Twenty
years after the original study by Trist and Bamforth (1951), Burawoy observed:

"Despite the development of the labour force in many areas, management has intensified rather than relaxed the division of labour, close supervision and the disciplinary code ... The contradiction between the maturation of the labour force and the fossilisation of a system of industrial organisation based on an intensive division of labour has inevitably promoted frustrations amongst those workers who are not content with a job which leaves little room for initiative and responsibility. For others the job becomes a mechanical process devoid of meaning except as a source of income. The system inevitably discourages any interest in efficiency or productivity" (1972: 270).

Burawoy suggests that the trouble with introducing a more adapted form of work organisation, based, say, on semi-autonomous, multi-skilled work groups, was that management, as well as government bodies in Zambia, subscribed to the 'myth of worker indolence'. Naturally, if it is widely believed that workers are lazy and will not expend effort voluntarily, then strict disciplinary systems and forms of control become the basis of work organisation. What was needed, therefore, Burawoy argued was for government and management to place greater faith in the abilities and willingness to work of the Zambian worker.

According to Austin (1990), perceptions about the intrinsic worth of people, whether they are regarded as mainly good or evil or neutral, are socially and culturally based. Austin notes the following implications for managers:

"A belief that humans are basically good and trustworthy will lead to looser controls; a view that they cannot be trusted will call forth tighter controls and supervision. Where trust is low, delegation of authority tends to be low and decision making more autocratic; relations tend to be more adversarial and less collegial" (1990: 64–65).

5.4.2   Sudan Railways

A more recent investigation of organisational choice in Africa has been conducted by Ketchum (1984) in his sociotechnical analysis of the Sudan Railways. The study was conducted at the request of the World Bank who were considering making a loan to the Sudanese Government in order to establish a new railway workshop, and wanted to explore the viability of designing a working environment along sociotechnical lines with the aim of improving both productivity and quality of working life.

The existing Sudan Railways workshops suffered from many of the problems encountered in developing countries generally: delays, lack of spare parts and tools, an abnormally high incidence of accidents (*see* Blunt & Popoola 1985), poor worker management relations, high absenteeism caused by shortages of basic foodstuffs and consumer goods (workers would leave their jobs in order to queue for scarce commodities), complaints of bias in promotion, selection, and reward, and low productivity. Ketchum (1984) felt that some of these problems were soluble using sociotechnical systems principles. However, his report is concerned only with the redesign of the workshop at Sennar. No data are presented on the effects of the new design on the performance criteria mentioned earlier.

Also, we cannot help but feel that at least some of the enthusiasm for sociotechnical ideas which Ketchum ascribes to Sudanese workers and managers – working, as he admits, "in an environment where pay is at or just above subsistence level" (1984: 152) – derived from the fact that the sociotechnical ideas were closely bound up with the loan package from the World Bank. There was also the not inconsiderable incentive associated with the prospect of "the entire team … (undergoing) intensive training in the United States" (Ketchum 1984: 152). As we shall see later in this book, concerns about the material incentives associated with new working arrangements are by no means confined to workers in developing countries. On the contrary, the evidence suggests that workers everywhere are all too aware of the possibility that managers may be looking for greater returns, or increased productivity, at no additional cost. It is therefore more than a little fanciful to suppose that the 'romance' of greater job variety or meaning can make up for basic need satisfaction. The lesson is surely that in conditions of hardship and poverty, in order to reap the full potential of sociotechnical or any other form of job or structural redesign, attention must also be paid to the material rewards associated with any reform.

5.5   Criticisms of Sociotechnical Systems Theory

There has been little detailed critical analysis of sociotechnical systems theory, particularly as it might be applied in Africa. Kelly's (1978, 1982) appraisals are some of the few closely argued critiques of sociotechnical systems theory in general. The points he makes are of importance because they show that it is possible to read the written accounts of studies informed by sociotechnical systems theory in a manner other than that intended by the authors, without doing violence to, or reading too much into, the evidence they present. In other words, it is not difficult to find plausible alternative explanations of the data to those put forward by the sociotechnical systems theorists themselves. The thrust of Kelly's analysis suggests, once again, that workers may be getting less – in terms of improved quality of work – than they have been led to expect.

We know that in the industrialised nations of the West worker suspicion of management and organisational designers and other experts is widespread, and in many cases quite justified. And even in Norway, in one of a number of carefully selected organisations, Emery and Thorsrud (1975) encountered considerable resistance to their activities:

"The initial agreement had been reached in an atmosphere of considerable suspicion and mistrust … Thus the collaboration of union officials and management seemed strange and aroused suspicions; the presence of research people involved the more familiar image of managerially oriented consultants; the meetings, votes and requests for volunteers smelt of manipulation in a process traditionally governed by dictates or voting with one's feet; the challenge to a working method apparently dictated by technological necessity just seemed quixotic" (p. 47).

There is no reason to suppose that similar reactions would not be likely in Africa, and it is therefore necessary that organisational designers, and others, be aware of the conflict-creating potential – no matter how slight – of the approaches they adopt. Safavi's (1981) review of management education in Africa concludes that organisational theory and behaviour courses in many of the management education programmes of 43 countries give insufficient consideration to the attitudes of workers, and that as a result African managers are insensitive to the needs and feelings of workers. In a similar vein, Msekwa (1975) has explained the occurrence of a number of Tanzanian strikes in terms of the disrespectful behaviour of managers towards workers.

More recently, Kiggundu (1986) found that applications of sociotechnical systems theory in developing countries, including Africa, had been "spotty and limited in scope" (p. 341). His view is that the theory itself is robust, but that its application in developing countries has been limited by the 'prevailing conditions' in developing countries, the operating methods of Western change agents in those countries, the potential for change-oriented action by local managers and stakeholders, and the quality of partnerships between Western change agents and local role players. Kiggundu (1986) asserts that, in contrast to the principles of sociotechnical systems theory which espouse open systems and democratic values and practices in the workplace, organisations in most developing countries are bureaucratic, mechanistic and autocratic. He lists the factors which, he claims, cause problems in attempting to apply sociotechnical systems thinking in developing countries, including:

"Organisations in developing countries exhibit dysfunctional modes of conflict management, closer social and emotional interactions, intergroup rivalry, little capacity for openness, trust, and the rational expression of feelings, and well established hierarchical and social status barriers" (Kiggundu 1986: 343).

The problem with this line of reasoning is that aspects of organisational life like those described above are surely familiar to all of us as common realities in organisations, or parts of organisations, everywhere. To designate them as true only for developing countries is to ignore the reality of organisational life the world over. In fact, what he is describing, on the basis of very little empirical evidence, are more likely to be variations on a universal theme rather than attributes of Third World organisations only. This point is reinforced by Ketchum (1984) who found the feelings and reactions of Sudan Railway workers and managers to be "similar to those of their counterparts in industrialised countries" (p. 135). Moreover, Ketchum is decidedly sanguine about the usefulness of sociotechnical systems in developing countries, based on his experience in the Sudan. In answer to the question, "Are the (sociotechnical) principles yielding superior economic and social outcomes in developed countries feasible in developing countries?" his response was "a tentative, but hearty, yes" (1984: 136).

Kiggundu's argument that sociotechnical systems theory is limited in its usefulness in developing country contexts appears to rest on his apparent assumption that the theory was developed as a strategy for organisational change rather than as an explanation of the consequences of organisational change. Hence, we should not conclude, with him, that special arrangements need to be made in order for sociotechnical systems thinking to be fruitful in Africa (and other developing regions). We would argue that sociotechnical systems theory is singularly equipped to acknowledge variations in organisational behaviour and environmental change. What needs to be done before we can make such confident assertions about 'most' developing countries is to identify reliably what these variations actually are.

Some major general criticisms of sociotechnical systems theory have been made by Kelly (1978, 1982) and these are set out below.

5.5.1   Economic Considerations are Given Precedence over Worker Autonomy

Despite the expressed commitment to autonomous work groups, much of the work redesign in India, Britain and Norway actually entailed significant curtailments of worker autonomy, with precedence being given instead to economic considerations. Kelly points out that in one of the Norwegian experiments, conducted in a wire-drawing mill, the creation of autonomous work groups led to fewer men being employed. The researchers felt obliged to insist on this because it was "difficult to see how (the workers) would make effective use of the time saved" (Emery & Thorsrud 1975: 30). In other words, autonomous work groups were only regarded as viable so long as they were able to improve efficiency. Kelly provides similar instances from the weaving and mining studies, and concluded that the "three studies indicate the necessity (in sociotechnical terms) for the prefixing of 'responsible' before the word autonomy, for where autonomy clashed with the employer's economic demands ..., or was giving them no advantage ... it was curtailed. In all cases economic imperatives were uppermost" (1978: 1080).

5.5.2   Sociotechnical Design Results in the Intensification of Labour

Rather than affording equal emphasis to the social and technical systems, Kelly argues that the technical systems in Britain, India and Norway were taken as given, and the studies were actually concerned with adapting the social systems to them. In practice, this turned out in every case to involve the intensification of labour, that is, an increase in workload per man and/or a faster pace of working. As we have seen, in one of the Indian weaving sheds manning was reduced by 50 per cent, and Rice (1958) himself reports that "there were many complaints of tiredness caused by so much extra walking ... At all conferences they said that they worked much harder than in the other sheds" (pp. 146–7). Similar evidence was produced by Kelly in relation to the Durham coal mining study and the Norwegian studies.

5.5.3   The Positive Effects of Sociotechnical Design Could be Due in Part to Pay Incentives

There is some evidence to suggest that sociotechnical systems theorists have underestimated the significance of pay as an explanatory variable in their studies. For example, one of the major complaints about the conventional long-wall method was the fact that owing to the complex system of payments certain tasks which were carried out underground went unrewarded. This had effects such as the following: "Minor maintenance, for example, if not the responsibility of Group A, would not be carried out by them since it would only consume time without simultaneously yielding a financial reward" (Kelly 1978: 1088). The composite system overcame this problem by ensuring that all tasks necessary for the extraction of coal were rewarded. Moreover, there had been a long tradition of pay bargaining in the Durham coal mines, both in the hand-got and conventional systems, and this too indicated the significance of pay to the miners.

Rice may also have been guilty of underemphasising the significance of pay. Members of the autonomous weaving groups which were set up received increases in their basic monthly pay ranging from nil, for a small number, up to as much as 44 per cent. An incentive payment system was also introduced, so that each worker received a small rise in pay on attaining a predetermined production target of 85 per cent of full potential. The observed increases in loom efficiency – from 80 to almost 90 per cent – were hardly surprising, therefore, and could well have been as much due to the payment schemes as they were to changed methods of work. Miller (1975) acknowledges this possibility by allowing for the "possible relevance" of the "diminishing 'bite' of the bonus system" (p. 381) in explaining the situation which prevailed in the textile mills some fifteen years later. Arguments like the above can also be advanced in relation to the Norwegian studies, and to other experiments, conducted in the USA, by Trist, Susman and Brown (1977).

How did this evidence affect the status of sociotechnical systems theory and the claims of its proponents? More than anything else, perhaps, it provided a healthy correction to the tendency to regard the autonomous work group as the new panacea. Like job enrichment, and other management fads before it, there was a danger of claiming too much too soon. The idea of *organisational choice* which had been the cornerstone of early sociotechnical work was becoming lost in a series of studies which seemed to be saying that autonomous group working was the best way to achieve organisational and employee goals. But although Kelly's points introduced a note of caution and promoted a more balanced appreciation of sociotechnical systems theory, they did not on their own falsify its major claims, since:

"The evidence in these cases is not unequivocal, ... many other changes took place in pay levels and incentives. It is theoretically possible then that the payment changes did not cause the performance changes, but resulted from them, and that performance improvements stemmed from other factors, such as increased job challenge" (Kelly 1978: 1072).

5.6   Conclusion

Treating organisations as open sociotechnical systems is still a dominant perspective in organisational theory. It is to be found, for example, in the 'quality of working life' movement which is preoccupied with the humanisation of work through sociotechnical design. Cherns and Davis (1975: 6) propose that "far from imposing economic costs", humanising work through sociotechnical design "yields societal, personal, and economic gains".

As we have seen, systems thinking, in the form of sociotechnical systems theory, has been applied to formal organisations for several decades. A recent development in systems thinking concerns the notion of 'hard' and 'soft' systems theory. According to Checkland (1981), who is perhaps the preeminent soft systems thinker, methodologies like systems engineering and systems analysis "assume that problems can be formulated as the making of a choice between alternative means of achieving a known end. The belief that real-world problems can be formulated in this way is the distinguishing feature of all 'hard' systems thinking" (p. 15). Checkland suggests that the concept of *'human activity system'* is profoundly different from the concepts of 'natural' and 'designed' systems because the perceptions of the human actors infuse human activity systems with many alternative meanings. In Checkland's (1981) view, this makes it impossible to construct testable objective accounts of organisational life.

Checkland remarks on some similarities between the soft systems approach and that of the sociotechnical systems movement. He notes that Warmington, Lupton and Gribbin (1977), using sociotechnical systems thinking, deliberately neglected the concept of organisational goal because it was seen as contributing little of value to attempts to assess organisational performance. Thus, Checkland notes, "their core paradigm is ... one of *learning* rather than *optimisation* and that is where lies the resemblance to soft systems methodology" (1981: 258).

Using this paradigm in relation to the African situation, it can be asserted that only those organisations which become *learning communities* have a chance of surviving and performing in an era of accelerating and complex change. We shall return to this notion – of the learning community – in later chapters.

The meeting between new technological systems and old social systems is probably nowhere more evident than it is in Africa, yet there appear to have been relatively few serious attempts made to address the issues involved. Where attempts have been made, with one or two exceptions they have been hampered by the absence of a clear theoretical framework which serves to make the data intelligible and comparable with studies conducted elsewhere (e.g., Okediji 1965), and they have failed to give equal prominence to the social and technical aspects of organisational life. As Brown (1989) observes, "the systems perspective in studies of Third World management tends ... to be a rather qualified phenomenon" (p. 371). Sociotechnical systems theory provides a framework for the development of an understanding of such issues in Africa, and for urgently needed empirical research.

Jones (1990b), for instance, claims that the application of the basic systems model, described at the beginning of this chapter, can demonstrate the importance of two major factors in considering questions of organisational performance in the context of African public administration. First, the serious effects of the common tendency in African public organisations to focus almost exclusively on inputs – 'the vast increases in spending on health, education, housing and so on' – whilst neglecting to consider 'outputs/outcomes achieved in terms of quantity, quality, service, and client satisfaction'. As Jones (1990b) points out, "no useful judgment of performance is possible unless inputs and outputs are considered together" (p. 59). The second factor is the rapid, and frequently turbulent, nature of change in African environments. Sociotechnical systems concepts are invaluable in understanding such developments and for initiating, monitoring and managing complex change in the organisation's environment.

Moreover, the utility of systems theory has been evaluated in a number of cultural settings with favourable, though not unequivocal, results. Trist (1975), and Cherns and Davis (1975), all leading 'elders' of the sociotechnical systems school of thought, have advocated it as a valuable approach to organisational analysis and design in developing countries. They argue that the chance is there for developing countries to profit and learn from the mistakes made in the industrialised nations of the West. Rather than taking the Western pattern as an inevitable consequence of industrialisation and progress, developing nations should aim from the beginning to attend to the social repercussions of rapid industrialisation and change. This is consistent with the sociotechnical systems point of view, as expressed by Cummings (1986):

"Sociotechnical systems theory has come a long way from the British coal mines, spreading across diverse nations and industries ..., developed numerous concepts and practices, and ... produced a rich set of applications. What will continue to hold the field together and make sociotechnical systems powerful are a shared set of values as to how persons should be treated in the work place and a deep-seated belief in the importance of organisational choice" (p. 360).

This reinforces the need in Africa to question the (Western) norms and values which are imported together with advanced technologies: "Without this sociotechnical assessment the developing countries are importing the quality of working life of their people along with the imported technology" (Cherns & Davis 1975: 24). Many parts of Africa today stand on the brink of rapid industrialisation, and there will be no better opportunity than now exists to direct development in a manner which benefits the social and technological needs of its people. Tragically, the signs are that the Western agenda of industrialisation along with widespread alienation, the destruction of family structures and values, and ugly urban growth, is being repeated in Africa. Much is said about social considerations in development planning, but all too little gets done.

One of the problems is that quality of working life considerations are seen as being less urgent, politically, than other social issues. When compared with the desperate need in African countries to create employment, quality of working life is regarded as a barely affordable luxury. Cherns and Davis (1975) reveal the fallacy in this line of reasoning nicely:

"This generally held notion is, however, a misreading based on false historicism. Because industrialisation was accompanied in the past by a widespread decline in the quality of working life, it has become accepted that the price of industrialisation is alienation as well as dense urbanisation. Yet neither of these consequences is an inevitable concomitant of industrialisation. Furthermore, the currently present symptoms of dissatisfaction in advanced countries appear to be largely associated with, and more than partially the outcome of, steps taken to advance the efficiency of work organisations. Again the ills are seen as part of the cost of efficient operation. Costs they are, but paradoxically uncosted: necessary costs they are not. Newly industrialising countries need no more follow the road of 'scientific management' than they need begin their industrialisation with the James Watt steam engine" (p. 22).

5.7   Implications for Managers and Management Development

It is not only the academics who are interested in finding some answers to puzzling questions about African organisations and how they work. African managers are themselves daily confronted by such questions; trained primarily in Western management theories and practices and frequently having Western managers as their only role models, how are they to answer such questions? More importantly, how are they to develop management practices which are appropriate to African, rather than Western, contexts?

Systems thinking is not difficult. By this we mean that it is not difficult to incorporate the fundamental notions of systems thinking into one's framework for thinking about organisational and managerial issues. Perhaps the most urgent task for African senior managers is to breathe life into the failing bureaucracies which they inherited at independence. To do this they will need an understanding of organisational alternatives and of the changes occurring in their organisations' environments. Sociotechnical systems theory offers a practical tool for understanding; the critical – and all too frequently missing – prerequisite for initiating and managing change.

The implications of this for management development are not that African managers must be necessarily educated in the details of systems theory, but that management education strategies and methods could usefully encourage managers to think in systems terms, within a systems framework. However many times it has been said, many managers still do not act in a way which acknowledges the critical starting point of systems thinking: that all parts of the organisation, internally and in their interaction with the environment, are interdependent. All too frequently we observe changes being made in African organisations for example, some of the reforms being recommended and imposed under the structural adjustment programmes mentioned in Chapter 1 which fail because they ignore this fundamental reality.

Chapter 6:   Organisational Structure and Design

In the decade up to 1986, Rondinelli (1986) reports that international donors had spent more than US$ 13 billion on development aid to sub-Saharan Africa, but that few signs of economic progress were evident in the region. The General Accounting Office of USAID acknowledged the contribution to this situation of a range of economic, political, and physical problems common to the area, but noted that a major weakness was the "capabilities of the Sahelian governments to plan and manage economic development and to coordinate donor activities" (*quoted* in Rondinelli 1986: 422).

In an effort to deepen its understanding of the reasons for organisational failure, USAID reviewed more than 1,000 of its projects undertaken in Africa over a period of ten years. This was followed by a content analysis of 277 project reports which sought to identify common factors explaining project performance. In addition, detailed case analyses of six large-scale agricultural and rural development projects were carried out, one in each of six African countries (Zaire, Kenya, Senegal, Niger, Liberia, and Lesotho).

High on the list of problems identified by these investigations were those associated with organisational structure and design. Organisational problems, involving inadequate support systems and ineffective organisational relationships, occurred in more than 91% of the 277 African project reports subjected to content analysis. The investigators deduced from their analysis that:

"An appropriate organisational structure for a project is a crucial variable in its success, but that there are no universally applicable arrangements. In some cases strengthening existing organisations was most effective; in other cases, new organisations had to be created to overcome constraints and obstacles to change" (Rondinelli 1986: 430).

This quotation conveys the essence of a contingency approach to organisational structure and design – that there is 'no one best way' – which is the cornerstone of this chapter and an underlying theme of this book. Below we define and analyse the concepts of organisational structure and contingency theory, and trace the evolution of these ideas from empirical research and theorising conducted in the West from the 1950s through to the present.

6.1   Organisational Structure

James Kamau made simple wooden bed frames in his small shed in one of the poorer areas of Nairobi, Mathari Valley. His work involved a number of different tasks: buying timber, transporting it, cutting the timber into suitable lengths, sanding and smoothing the edges, joining the pieces of wood together, and taking the finished products to the market to be sold. As it was a small business, the management and completion of these tasks presented few difficulties: Kamau did everything himself.[1]

Kamau was a skilled carpenter.[1] His beds were sturdy and fairly priced, and he had a good reputation as an honest and hard working man among the traders at the market. But like many Kenyans, Kamau had great responsibilities. He needed to finance his small farm in Thika, pay for his children's school uniforms and fees, feed himself and his family (including three wives and many children), support a number of unemployed relatives, and perhaps save a little for emergencies. In short, he needed more money. Fortunately, the demand for his beds was so strong that he sold them as fast as he could make them. He therefore decided to increase the number of beds he made by taking on a young nephew, Ben Kimani, as an apprentice. This meant that Kamau now had to divide up the work to be done. Since Kimani was still learning the trade, it was decided that he would transport the timber and the finished beds to the market in a hand cart, keep the tools clean and oiled, and look after the shed during Kamau's absences. He would also, of course, be taught carpentry skills. Now that two people were involved, some coordination of the work was necessary, but this was easily achieved through informal communication between the two men.

Business continued to boom, so that before long Kamau was again selling every bed he could make as fast as he could make it. Kamau could see that he needed to expand further, but this time instead of employing another apprentice he decided to take on carpenters who had been trained at one of the local technical colleges. He therefore employed four additional young carpenters who were able to start making beds, and other basic items of furniture (e.g., tables and chairs), almost immediately. Even with six people working in the (by now) cramped shed, and with a wider range of products, coordination of the various activities still did not present much of a problem.

However, a few months later when two more carpenters were hired, problems began to emerge. One day Kamau came into the shed to find three of the carpenters sitting about talking with no work to do. Apparently, the hand cart was no longer large enough to supply them with a sufficient quantity of timber to keep them all working. In addition, as all of the men were now fully trained carpenters, nobody was keen to do the less prestigious, menial task of fetching the timber. At this point, it became clear to Kamau that informal methods of coordination were no longer satisfactory. Kamau himself was spending less and less time in the workshop and more time visiting customers. His furniture was now

---

1 This is a hypothetical but far from trivial example. The furniture industry in Kenya, and in other African countries, employs large numbers of people, both in the rural and urban areas. House (1981) has noted that in the rural areas of Kenya "the small-scale, self-employed ... carpenter is ubiquitous, constructing basic items of furniture for home use and the market" (p. 338). In 1977 at least 27,000 rural families in Kenya were "involved in some way in the furniture industry ..., (and) slightly more than 4,000 persons were employed in the formal modern or enumerated sector, while urban informal sector employment exceeded 2,000 in 1975" (House 1981: 339).

being sold in a few shops in River Road as well as in the market. Kimani was therefore made workshop supervisor responsible for coordinating the work of the six carpenters in the shed.

The business kept on growing. The workshop was moved to a more spacious building, closer to the major customers in River Road, and it became obvious to Kamau that the work would have to be organised formally. Luckily, he was able to call on the advice of a friend who owned a similar business and had run it successfully for many years. This friend recommended that Kamau's small work-force be split up into groups so that each group was responsible for making a certain type of furniture: one would make only beds, another tables, another chairs, and so on. Thus, the work to be done was divided up and allocated to four specialised groups. Two men were also employed to transport the timber and finished products in a small second-hand lorry that Kamau had bought for the purpose.

Kamau's ambition and success were limitless. Before long, the chance came to diversify into other areas: first, built-in cupboards and cabinets in offices and private homes, and finally special custom-made pieces of furniture for wealthier clients. The business was subsequently split into three divisions. One produced fairly standard lines of furniture (the original items plus one or two others, e.g., beds, chairs, tables, and book-shelves), another dealt with special orders, and the third was responsible for built-in cabinets, etc., in clients' premises. From his office overlooking the factory floor, Kamau coordinated the activities of the divisions by reviewing their performance regularly and by taking appropriate action when sales figures or profits were below budget. The firm became known as Kamau Enterprises.

6.1.1   Defining Organisational Structure

This simplified example illustrates two basic principles of work organisation, whether it be the manufacture of tractors or the operation of a school: first, the *division of labour* into logical work groups to carry out the tasks which need to be performed; and second, the coordination of those tasks to accomplish the work. *The structure of an organisation can therefore be defined as the ways in which it chooses to divide its labour into separate work groups, and how it coordinates their activities.* These two basic activities are also widely referred to in the literature as *differentiation* and *integration*. As we shall see, factors in organisations' external environments and factors within organisations themselves affect the ways in which organisations differentiate and integrate their activities. The purpose of this chapter is to consider the various coordinating mechanisms which an organisation might use, the different shapes that organisational structures can take, and finally the range of variables which have been found to influence an organisation's structure.

6.1.2   Methods of Coordination

The division of labour in Kamau's business was a relatively straightforward affair. It was possible to combine tasks into logical groupings without too much difficulty. Kamau divided his workers into groups according to what they produced.[2] However, as it grew, the coordination of Kamau's firm proved to be more complicated. Following Mintzberg (1979, 1983), there are five conventional ways in which organisations coordinate their activities.

Mutual Adjustment

This method relies on informal communication to achieve the desired coordination of work. In its early period of growth, remember, Kamau's firm was able to employ this method successfully. Control of work under mutual adjustment resides with the workers themselves. As we might expect, this method works best in relatively small and simple organisations. But it is also a method which is suited to coordination in some of the most complicated organisations. Organisations with thousands of highly trained specialists, such as those involved in the USA's space programme, use mutual adjustment as a method of coordination. The reason for this is that at the beginning of such highly complex projects nobody can be sure how, exactly, they are going to develop. Accordingly, the organisation needs to remain extremely flexible, able to learn as it goes along, and to adapt quickly. Mutual adjustment permits such flexibility.

Direct Supervision

In this method, coordination is achieved by having one individual take responsibility for seeing that the work of others is performed satisfactorily. It is used in organisations which have passed through the early stages of their development. In our example, as business expanded, Kimani was made supervisor in charge of the six carpenters in the workshop.

Standardisation of the Work Processes

It is also possible to coordinate work through standardisation. This is achieved by deciding in advance how tasks are to be carried out and coordinated so as to ensure the predictability of behaviour. Workers on an assembly line have their tasks standardised in such a manner that they are rarely faced with any new or unexpected occurrence. They know exactly what to expect of their workmates and can proceed with their own work accordingly. Standardisation is usually applied to work which can be broken down into fairly simple operations which then become routine. In Kamau's factory, for example, the division dealing with fairly basic lines of furniture could probably standardise its work in this way, whereas the division dealing with special orders would be less suited to standardisation.

Standardisation of work processes is perhaps seen in its most extreme form on the assembly line where the worker is required to perform the same simple operation over and over again. Coordination of the work in such a setting is therefore determined primarily by whoever designed the assembly line. The assembly line worker consequently requires

---

2   Other bases for the division of work include: (1) time (e.g., shift or no-shift workers); (2) location (e.g., Accra, Kumasi); (3) process (e.g., packaging, stacking); (4) customer (e.g., the public or other firms).

little direct supervision. To take a less extreme example, a parcel clerk in a busy post office in, say, Ibadan or Blantyre must also perform basically the same standard operations, but is less confined by technology (as in the assembly line example). He has more opportunity to interact with colleagues and customers, but still, because of the fairly routine nature of his work, requires relatively little direct supervision. Like the assembly line worker, the essential elements of the parcel clerk's job have been determined in advanced.

Standardisation of the Product

Here the worker is told that certain outputs or performance standards are required of him, but he is allowed some freedom to determine how these ends are achieved. For instance, night watchmen whose work is governed by a punch clock are required to do so many beats of their patrol during the course of their shift, and not to rest for longer than a certain period. A watchman can therefore choose within these performance limits when he is going to do a beat, where he will rest and for how long, and so on. Similarly, a taxi driver in Nairobi or Lagos knows where his passengers must be delivered, but will take different routes according to the time of day and other occurrences which may threaten to impede his progress (e.g., presidential motorcade, or heavy traffic, or road repairs, etc.).

At Kamau Enterprises the three divisions were required to meet profit and sales targets which may also be regarded as coordination through standardisation of performance or product.

Standardisation of Skills

Under certain circumstances it is not possible to standardise either the work processes or the product. In such instances it may, however, be possible to standardise the workers employed in terms of their skills and abilities and perhaps also in terms of their orientations to work and motivation, although the latter are difficult to measure accurately. Colonial powers in Africa routinely adopted this method. Owing to the huge distances involved and, in the early days at least, difficulties with communication and travel, it was virtually impossible for the colonial authorities in London to coordinate the activities of their far flung officers. The solution they adopted was that of standardising the worker so that his output became predictable and reliable. To achieve this end, the men selected for colonial service were trained in special training establishments, and most had very similar class and educational backgrounds. The English public school, for example, was regarded as the ideal breeding ground for future members of the colonial service. On a much smaller scale, Kamau employed a similar tactic when he hired trained carpenters who shared his system of values, whose skill levels were similar, and who could therefore be relied upon to carry out the work required of them.

Even the most complex of tasks can be coordinated in this way. Members of a surgical operating team need not have worked together before in order for them to be able to remove an appendix because they have each been thoroughly trained in their respective areas and know what to expect of one another. Coordination is achieved through the standardisation of their skills.

Kiggundu (1989) asserts that while standardisation of knowledge, skills, beliefs and attitudes in organisations in industrialised countries is highly developed, this is much less the case in developing countries: "nonstandardisation of knowledge, skills and organisational norms is one of their most serious problems" (p. 109). Moreover, the need for such standardisation in African organisations is acute because of the large numbers of jobs which are carried out in remote areas far away from supervising authorities.

The five methods of coordination described are suited to work of varying complexity. Mutual adjustment is suited to relatively simple work, involving small numbers of people. Larger groups and more complicated work require supervision. Further increases in size and complexity then necessitate the use of standardisation of either the product, the work processes or the worker himself, or some combination of these. And where it becomes impossible to standardise, coordination reverts to the simplest yet most flexible and adaptable method, mutual adjustment.

It should not be assumed, however, that an organisation will only use one method of coordination at a time. Most organisations employ, at the same time, a number of the coordination methods mentioned above. To return to Kamau Enterprises, a mixture of direct supervision, standardisation, and mutual adjustment was to be found. In fact, in nearly all organisations a certain amount of mutual adjustment and direct supervision is necessary, no matter how much it is possible to standardise. Supervisors are required to provide direction and information, or to coordinate interactions with other parts of the organisation, and workers must be able to deal with minor interruptions or unexpected problems as they occur if their work is not to be seriously disrupted.

Another way of looking at the organisation as it grows and becomes more complex is to focus on the different types of personnel that are needed, and the, in some senses, separate parts of the organisation they come to occupy. This is the subject of the next section.

6.1.3 Basic Components of Organisational Structure[3]

At the beginning, Kamau Enterprises was a simple organisation where the workers were able to coordinate their activities satisfactorily through mutual adjustment. They, the *operators* of the enterprise, were essentially self-sufficient. With growth and increasing complexity, however, we saw the need for direct supervision emerge. A manager or supervisor was needed to coordinate the activities of the operators. Whereas previously the operators had coordinated themselves and divided up the work as they saw fit, the appearance of the manager introduced an *administrative* layer into the organisation's structure: a group of people responsible for coordinating the work of others. When an organisation keeps on growing in this fashion, the initial administrative layer has superimposed upon it another administrative layer to coordinate its work, and so on until a *hierarchy* or *line* of authority is built up.

---

3   Much of this section is adapted from Mintzberg (1979).

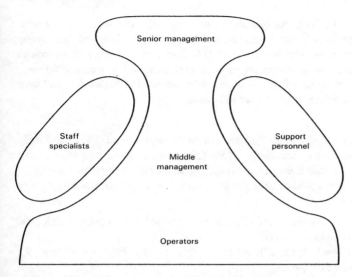

Figure 6.1: The Five Basic Components of Organisations (Mintzberg 1979)

Later still, as size and complexity continue to increase, the organisation adopts methods of standardisation. Much of this standardisation is the responsibility of *staff specialists*. For instance, responsibility for the standardisation of outputs falls under the jurisdiction of accountants, production engineers, and quality control managers; and the standardisation of work processes usually falls to industrial engineers and work study specialists. This introduces a third element into the organisation, a cadre of staff specialists who take over from the managers (who in turn, remember, had taken over coordination from the operators themselves) certain responsibilities for coordination, by instituting various methods of standardisation to either complement or supersede direct supervision.

The result of all this is an organisation composed of a basic core of *operators* who carry out the fundamental work tasks, of actually making the products or performing the services, and an *administrative* element of line and staff managers who take the major responsibility for coordinating the work. This administrative element can be subdivided further into three basic units:

1. Higher-level line managers and their personal staff, the 'big men' at the top whom we shall call simply *senior management*.
2. Middle-ranking line managers who form a link and communication channel between the operators and senior management, whom we shall refer to as *middle management*.
3. Specialist staff managers who are concerned with the standardisation of work, and such areas as personnel and maintenance. We shall refer to this group as *staff specialists*.

So far, then, we have identified four distinct components within the organisation: operators, senior managers, middle managers, and staff specialists. A fifth and final group comprises *support personnel* who provide services to other parts of the organisation such as legal advice, research and development, canteen services, cleaning, message delivery, etc. These five basic elements of the organisation are depicted in Figure 6.1, and their functions will now be defined in greater detail below.

Operators

These are the people who work in the 'boiler room' of the organisation. They are directly concerned in their day to day activities with the production of goods and services: the carpenters and transporters in Kamau Enterprises, or postal clerks in the Lagos G.P.O., or assembly line workers in a vehicle manufacturing plant. Operators carry out four major activities:

1. They obtain the raw materials and other inputs required for production (e.g., the transporters at Kamau Enterprises).
2. They carry out the work on these inputs to turn them into the final product (e.g., the carpenters at Kamau Enterprises).
3. They sell and distribute the finished product (e.g., the postal clerk who sells stamps in the Lagos post office, and, again, the transporters at Kamau Enterprises).
4. They offer direct support to the other three functions by, for example, maintaining equipment and keeping stock records.

But as we have noted, most organisations – apart, that is, from the very smallest and simplest of work organisations – also develop administrative components: staff specialists, middle management, support personnel, and senior management.

Senior Management

Senior managers are obviously located at the top of the organisation. In most work organisations in the Western world, and Africa, they have overall responsibility for the organisation. For the purposes of this discussion, we shall include in this group senior managers' personal assistants, although we shall focus our attention on the senior managers themselves. Senior managers are responsible for ensuring that the organisation does what it was intended to do by those who have power over it: government agencies, shareholders, owners, and so on. The duties of senior management can be divided up into discrete areas of activity and responsibility.

1. Senior managers are involved in the supervision of work, either directly, or indirectly through middle managers. What does supervision entail? It usually covers the making of major decisions affecting other groups within the organisation or ratifying decisions made by employees; the assignment of resources and people to different areas or activities; the resolution of conflict within the organisation; the dissemination of information; and the staffing, rewarding, and motivating of employees. In short, in most organisations senior managers are there to try to ensure that the organisation survives and runs smoothly.

2. Senior managers are also charged with governing the relationship between the organisation and the outside world, its environment. This role is frequently called 'boundary control'. It involves the maintenance of harmonious relationships with other organisations (e.g., trade unions); the development of high-level contacts in other organisations (e.g., government, suppliers, retailers); the provision of information concerning the organisation to other bodies, the entertainment of valued customers or clients; and so on.

3. Boundary control also means that senior management must take responsibility for determining the direction and pace of change in the organisation, so that it can stay ahead of competition, or improve its services to the public. Senior managers must therefore be perpetually alert to changes in the wider environment which could affect the smooth-running of their organisation.

These tasks require senior management to be flexible and adaptable. Coordination at this level – that is, among the senior managers themselves – is therefore nearly always achieved through mutual adjustment.

Middle Management

Large organisations need more than a few senior managers to coordinate and control their activities. At the lowest level of middle management, small work groups are supervised by a foreman or supervisor. A number of such units may then be supervised by a middle manager, and so on up the organisation's hierarchy. The supervisory work of the middle manager comprises the following major activities.

1. He gathers information on the performance of his subordinates, and passes this in summarised form to higher levels. For example, Kimani, who eventually became manager of the furniture division of Kamau Enterprises with two supervisors beneath him, reported regularly to Kamau on the performance of the work groups under his control.

2. He interrupts the flow of information or work which has risen from lower levels in the organisation, sifts through it, deals with that material which falls within his jurisdiction, and allows the rest to progress through to senior levels. Thus, Kimani might deal himself with minor squabbles or disagreements which arose between his supervisors or workers, but a case involving, say, suspected theft by one of the supervisors would probably need to be brought to the attention of Kamau.

3. He sifts pieces of information and resources flowing *down* the organisation's hierarchy and allocates and deals with them accordingly.

4. He also has a limited boundary control function – limited because it is confined to other units which directly impinge on the operation of the middle manager's own unit. Such units could be other departments within the same organisation – e.g., production, marketing, and research – or customers in the organisation's environment. Kimani, for example, in his new role as division manager, would need to maintain good contacts with his major customers.

In essence, a middle manager operates in a localised area within the organisation in much the same way as a senior manager does for the organisation as a whole.

Staff Specialists

Staff specialists are not directly engaged in the firm's primary production or service activities. They are mainly concerned with facilitating the work of those who are directly engaged in the firm's major activities. They would include in their ranks personnel specialists (responsible for advising on the recruitment, selection, placement, and development of personnel, or the standardisation of skills); work study experts who standardise work processes; and planning and control specialists, such as accountants and long-range planners, who standardise outputs. The relationships which this group has with other components of the organisation need to be fairly flexible. Consequently, the work of its members is usually coordinated through mutual adjustment.

Smaller firms, like Kamau's, might only have one or two such specialists; say, an accountant, and a production engineer responsible for scheduling. Kamau's firm is still probably not large enough to require the services of a personnel specialist, although the day is not too far off when it might. In the meantime, Kamau himself deals with hiring and firing. Large government departments, however, such as a ministry of education, or a ministry of works, would have a number of staff specialists.

Support Personnel

The type of service or support provided to the rest of the organisation by members of this component is quite different from that provided by staff specialists. They do not generally give advice to senior and middle management, and neither do they have much to do with standardisation. The services they offer include canteen facilities, mail sorting, research and development, and public relations. People in this category can be found at all levels of the organisation: for instance, some support personnel, who do give advice, such as legal experts, may have quite senior positions. But, by definition, support personnel are not directly involved in the major production or service activities of the organisation. Finally, the methods of coordination appropriate for support personnel vary tremendously, from mutual adjustment in research and development through standardisation of work methods in the canteen to standardisation of skills in the legal area.

Why is it necessary for organisations to have support personnel? How, for example, might Kamau's firm benefit? Robbins (1990) has proposed that organisations attempt wherever possible to reduce uncertainty. One way of doing this is to include within the confines of the organisation services or skills upon which it has some degree of dependence. For instance, instead of workers at Kamau Enterprises having to go outside the firm to buy and eat their lunch, the day might come when Kamau's firm was large enough to maintain its own canteen facilities. This way the organisation would be more certain about the quality, or nutritional value, of the food eaten by its employees, and there would also be less likelihood of absences from work owing to delays in travel, and so on. Receptionists would be another group included in the support personnel category. And this too is a support service which might be of benefit to Kamau Enterprises; to greet customers or suppliers who came to the firm's premises, to arrange meetings and appointments, and to convey visitors to the relevant person or part of the organisation.

Organisations in Africa have always had senior managers and operators, and, where they were large enough, middle managers. More recently, as levels of technological and managerial sophistication have advanced, numbers of staff specialists have increased, but there would probably still be fewer of them in African firms than in firms of comparable size and type in the industrialised nations. Part of the reason for this difference, particularly in private enterprises, is the availability of cheap labour and the consequent lack of incentive to standardise work processes through mechanisation. Consequently, the need for the type of staff specialist we have discussed has not arisen as much in Africa as it has in the industrialised nations. However, the growth of the manufacturing sectors of most African countries makes it likely that the need for staff specialists will be more widely felt in the next decade and beyond.

A similar argument can be applied to *certain parts* of the support personnel component. African organisations are likely to have fewer of certain types of support personnel too. This is due in part to the fact that labour has much less power, generally speaking, in Africa than it does in the West. Trade unions have relatively little influence on employers. When this is coupled with the fact that there are many more people looking for work than there are jobs, it can be seen that organisations experience only minor pressure, or none at all, from their lower-level employees. As a result, there is little or no call for industrial relations experts or lawyers to be kept permanently in an organisation's employ, and canteen facilities, especially in private organisations, are not the norm. Most of the members of, say, a typical medium-size manufacturing organisation in Africa would therefore be integral parts of the three central components, that is, senior managers, middle managers and operators. There would be a reasonable number of support personnel – cleaners, receptionists, messengers, and perhaps canteen workers – but relatively few staff specialists. The five structural components in an African manufacturing organ-isation might take the form depicted in Figure 6.2. It can be seen that the ratio of operators and managers to support personnel in our 'typical' manufacturing firm is high.

Civil service organisations in Africa would probably have a much lower ratio than this, that is, proportionately more support personnel and specialist staff than a manufacturing concern. In fact, typically, government organisations throughout Africa would have grossly inflated staff numbers, and particularly in the support personnel component. A vivid example of this is provided by Ayeni's (1987) investigation of Nigeria's Public Complaints Commission. Ayeni contrasts the size of the Nigerian Public Complaints Commission of 1,780 employees (1,425 of whom were junior support staff, namely, typists, messengers, drivers and janitors) and its productivity (1.7 complaints per year per staff member) with those of ombudsman's offices in other parts of the world. In Finland, for example, the ombudsman's office had six staff who dealt with an average of 167 complaints each per year. Sweden's ombudsman's office contained 15 staff with an average annual case load per staff member of 200.

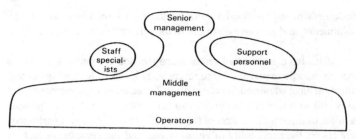

Figure 6.2: A Typical Manufacturing Organisation in Africa

The latter part of our discussion has implied that an organisation's structure, in terms of the methods of coordination it employs and the relative sizes of its major components, is influenced – perhaps even determined – by forces exerted upon it from within (recall the example of the relative lack of standardisation through mechanisation in many Third World organisations) and without (recall the effects of weak trade unions). The structure of Kamau Enterprises in its various stages of growth can be analysed in terms of the variety of influences exerted upon it: from the environment (strong demands for furniture), from senior management (Kamau's ambition, drive, and foresight), and from the operators (reluctance of skilled carpenters to do unskilled work such as fetching the timber). These influences are known as *contingencies*. Their effects have been widely studied and are the subject of the next section. This stream of research has culminated in what might be termed a situational or contingency approach to organisational studies. Lorsch and Lawrence (1970) provided some of the initial direction for this approach:

"During the past few years there has been evident a new trend in the study of organisational phenomena. Underlying this new approach is the idea that the internal functioning of organisations must be consistent with the demands of the organisation's tasks, technology, or external environment, and the needs of its members if the organisation is to be effective. Rather than searching for the panacea or the one best way to organise under all conditions, investigators have more and more tended to examine the functioning of organisations in relation to the needs of their particular members and the external pressures facing them. Basically, this approach seems to be leading to the development of a contingency theory of organisation with the appropriate internal states and processes of the organisation contingent upon external requirements and member needs" (p. 1).

Accordingly, the next section examines variables in the organisation's internal and external *contexts* or environments which appear to influence its structure.

6.2.   Major Influences on Organisational Structure

Most of the research on this topic has been conducted in the industrialised nations of the West, mainly the USA and Britain. Virtually no research on the determinants of organisational structure has been carried out in Africa, although there are a few exceptions, including a comparative study of US and Nigerian organisations by Scott, Dornbusch and Utande (1979), and a study of two Kenyan organisations (Blunt 1980). For the moment at any rate, this means that some reliance must be placed on American and British findings. This naturally raises the question of relevance. Hickson, McMillan, Azumi, and Horvath (1979) have posed the question: "How far is organisation theory an American edifice fabricated on a foundation of West European Weberian thought? How far is it relevant to Asia, Africa, or wherever?" (p. 25). To answer this question, there are at least two positive contributions which existing research has to offer. First, the research which has been carried out to date has highlighted a number of crucial variables in an organisation's context which appear to influence its structure. African researchers who seek to address similar issues therefore have a store of comparative data to which they can refer in the early, exploratory phases of their work. Second, measures have been developed for collecting information on organisational structure and context which seems to be readily obtainable in most, if not all, countries. Third, it is probable that the direction of the relationships between structural and contextual variables observed in the West is likely to hold good in other parts of the world, including Africa. The small amount of cross-national research which has appeared in the literature reveals a reasonably high degree of consistency in this regard. Hickson, Hinings, McMillan, and Schwitter (1974) are particularly sanguine on this point:

"The consistency of the relationships between variables of organisation context and of organisation structure found in data from seventy manufacturing units in the United States, Britain, and Canada supports the 'bold' hypothesis that these relationships ... will hold for work organisations in all societies" (p. 74).

To take a more specific example, it has been found that the amount of formalisation (the degree to which rules, procedures, instructions, and information in general appear in a *written* form) in an organisation increases with its size, as measured by the number of employees. Accordingly, if Hickson *et al.* (1974) are correct, we would expect to find that although, say, Nigerian organisations of a certain type tended in general to be less formalised than Canadian ones, bigger Nigerian organisations would still be more formalised than smaller ones. Writers who hold this point of view therefore regard certain relationships between structure and context as being *culture-free*. A case has also been made, however, for the "uniqueness" of *cultural-effect*. That is to say, certain observed differences cannot, it is argued, be satisfactorily explained in terms of the global contextual factors described by those who accept the culture-free argument. A cultural explanation of differences between organisations is to be found in the work of Maurice (1979). He was able to explain observed differences between a German firm and a French firm more fully in terms of cultural factors operating in the two countries than by reference to more "usual" contextual or contingency factors such as management style. Partly as a result of the fact that the economic dominance of Japan and the emergence of the newly industrialising economies of East Asia (Hong Kong, South Korea, Singapore, and Taiwan) has been attributed to some degree to cultural factors (e.g., Hofstede & Bond 1988; Whitley 1990), cultural explanations have gained in strength in recent years (Adler 1991).

The position adopted here will be that both points of view have something to offer. We argue the importance of culture consistently in this book. We cannot therefore ignore the wider implications of its possible effects on organisational structure and functioning. By the same token, there are certain relationships, such as that between organisational size and formalisation, which have yet to be directly and consistently refuted by empirical research. These reasonably well established connections should also be described.

Some of the earliest and most robust work in this field analysed the relationship between technology and organisational structure, and this is where we shall begin. Other major influences we shall discuss are: the organisation's external environment, organisational size, and strategic choice. We shall deal with the important question of culture in some detail in Chapter 9.

6.2.1   Technology

The idea that technology influences organisational structure has its foundations in the work of Woodward (1958, 1965, 1970). She and a number of colleagues working in the south of England in the mid-1950s studied 91 percent of the firms in the area employing more than 100 people. The majority of the 100 or so organisations studied employed between 250 and 1,000 people. The sample was drawn from a wide variety of industries with electronic, chemical, and engineering firms predominating.

The original aim of the survey was to analyse the methods of organisation and management employed by local firms, and to develop hypotheses for future research. Data collection was based on structured interviews, observation, and analysis of company records. Information was collected on the following:

1. The history and goals of each firm.
2. The type of manufacturing process used by each firm, or its *technology*.
3. The effectiveness or success of the firm, as measured by market share, share prices, and the opinions of senior executives in each industry.
4. The firm's style of management, as indicated by the degree of formalisation (*written* rules, procedures, and communication) and the division of labour.
5. The organisational structure of each firm in terms of such factors as the span of control (e.g., number of operators under one supervisor), and number of levels of authority in the organisation.

Early analyses of the data showed that there were obvious differences in the structures of the firms studied. For instance, the spans of control of managing directors varied between two and eighteen, the number of authority levels in middle and senior management ran between two and twelve, and the ratio of production workers to staff specialists went from less than 1:1 to more than 10:1. The researchers were naturally eager to explain the observed differences. However, their initial attempts to do so, using such factors as organisational size and organisational effectiveness, failed: for example, Woodward noted that "the 20 firms assessed as 'above average' in success had little in common organisationally" (1965: 33). Eventually the researchers turned to technology for a possible explanation of their findings. Using technology as their criterion, Woodward and her colleagues classified the firms into three main groups:

1. Unit or small batch production – in Kamau Enterprises this would take place in the division responsible for making special pieces of furniture according to customer requirements. That is to say, production consists of small numbers of specially made items.
2. Large batch and mass production – in Kamau Enterprises this would take place in the division responsible for making standard pieces of furniture in large numbers. An assembly line in a car factory would be another example.
3. Process production of gasses or chemicals requiring long or continuous runs using the same procedures over and over again. An example of an organisation using this technology would be an oil refinery.

Woodward felt that as one moved along the scale of technical complexity, so it became easier to control the operations involved. In her own words:

"Moving along the scale ... it becomes increasingly possible to exercise control over manufacturing operations the physical limitations of production becoming better known and understood. Targets can be set and reached more effectively in continuous flow production plants than they can in the most up-to-date and efficient batch production firms and the factors likely to limit performance can be allowed for. However well developed production procedures may be in batch production firms, there will be a degree of uncertainty in the prediction of results" (Woodward 1965: 40).

In terms of our earlier discussion, Woodward is saying that as the complexity of technology increases, so it becomes more and more amenable to coordination through the standardisation of work processes. Simple technologies which are often found in small batch and craft production are more difficult to coordinate and control because only small numbers of each product are made, and the products themselves differ widely. The special orders division of Kamau's organisation, for example, might be contracted to make three large round tables of certain dimensions for a conference room in a large hotel one week, and a specially designed display cabinet for a museum the next week. In each case, the work processes would differ, as would the amount of time required to complete the jobs, yet the technology required would be simple, and the same in both instances. However, because of the need for great flexibility in such work, it would be a mistake to attempt to coordinate it through the standardisation of the work processes; and, by definition, standardisation of the product is ruled out. The most suitable method of coordination is therefore mutual adjustment, which increases the degree of uncertainty involved, but permits the maintenance of flexibility. In addition, as with Kamau's carpenters, it is frequently possible to improve coordination in small batch production through the standardisation of skills.

On the other hand, process production technologies, such as those employed in, say, a Nigerian oil refinery, have long production runs (that is, the same basic production process is repeated time and again), and use highly complex technologies to produce the finished goods – in this case refined oil. Such work processes are obviously highly standardised and therefore much easier to coordinate and control. Mintzberg (1979) remarks, "the giant oil refinery ... (can be) operated by six people, and even they only serve as monitors; the technical system runs itself" (p. 258).

Returning to Woodward's study, it soon became apparent to the researchers that each production category or technology seemed to be suited to a particular type of organisational structure. There also appeared to be a link between organisational structure and success within each of the three major production categories. These results are summarised in Table 6.1.

A number of studies have attempted to replicate Woodward's original findings, and some were moderately successful in doing so (e.g., Harvey 1967; Zwerman 1970). Indeed, so influential has Woodward's work been that a number of organisational theorists, notably Perrow (1967) and Thompson (1967), have developed models which give technology a prime place in determining an organisation's structure. These writers interpret the term technology in a much broader sense than Woodward, thereby enabling them to apply the concept to all types of organisations. Perrow (1970), for instance, defines technology as "the actions that an individual performs upon an object, with or without the aid of tools or mechanical devices, in order to make some change in that object" (p. 80). The 'object' mentioned can be anything at all, from a form being processed by a clerk in a government agency to a piece of leather in a shoe factory.

Robbins (1990) has concluded that "the technological imperative, if it exists, ... is most likely to apply only to small organisations and to those structural arrangements at or near the operating core" (p. 201). It seems also that other factors may exert a greater influence. A British group of researchers, at the University of Aston in Birmingham, England, were among the first to cast some doubt on the prominence of technology as a determinant of organisational structure. The Aston studies, as they are now called, found that a number of other factors, a major one of which was organisational size, seemed to have more influence on an organisation's structure than did technology.

Table 6.1 : Major Relationships Between Organisational Structure and Technology Among Successful Firms in Woodward's Research

Technology	Structural 'Effects'		General characteristics of structure
	Lower levels of organisation (operators)	Higher levels of organisation (senior management)	
Unit and small batch production	Informal coordination though mutual adjustment with narrow spans of control. Some direct supervision with good relationships between operators and supervisors. Skilled, craft work.	Informal coordination through mutual adjustment; no distinction between line and staff managers.	Simple structure; few senior managers, and no technical specialists.
Large batch and mass production	Standardisation of work processes with wide spans of control. Work is routine and unskilled.	Coordination through standardisation of management and administrative processes; highly formalised.	Clearly defined positions; clear chain of command; large numbers of technical specialists. Much hostility between different components of the organisation.
Process production	Coordination through standardisation of work, and mechanisation which approaches automation. Few unskilled operators – instead, skilled workers to maintain machinery. Skilled supervisors with narrow spans of control, but good relations between the two.	Few line managers and technical specialists – mainly support staff or professional engineers who design new systems, and control their own work through mutual adjustment.	Much more flexible structure. Large numbers of support staff and relatively few operators. Line/staff distinction blurred.

6.2.2   Organisational Size

In some quarters, so strong is the belief that size (as measured by number of employees)[4] determines certain features of organisational structure that it has led to statements such as the following:

"In all countries, big organisations will be the most formalised and specialised in structure. This is because everywhere growth means reaping economies of scale and of expertise by dividing labour still further, and as the knowledge possessed by any one person of what is happening in the organisation becomes a smaller part of the whole, so more formalised documentation of action and intended action is required for control. Non-formalised custom is inadequate to control large numbers in organisations with a turnover of personnel" (Hickson et al. 1979: 37).

Put simply, as the size of the organisation increases it requires a larger number of coordinative devices to run it. So, large organisations rely more on written rules and regulations, and written communication. In other words, they are more formalised. This generally means that large numbers of administrative personnel (middle managers), and technical specialists are required. Consequently, we find that in large organisations there are clear and strong lines of demarcation drawn between different parts of the organisation: between operators and middle management, between middle management and senior management, and so on.

Unlike the results obtained by Woodward, where technology was found to have the greatest influence on structure, the Aston studies found *organisational size* to be the most powerful predictor. This apparent contradiction may be due in part to the fact that the organisations studied by Woodward were, in general, much smaller than those studied by the Aston group; the latter included firms employing between 300 and 25,000 people, whereas Woodward's sample included only 17 firms with more than 1,000 employees. The stronger relationship between technology and structure found in smaller firms may be due to the fact that more parts of the organisation are directly affected by the technology employed. This probably explains why, in the Aston studies, technology was found to be related to those aspects of structure upon which it impinged directly, like the supervisor's span of control. Pugh and Hinings (1976) have therefore suggested that: "Structural variables will be associated with operations technology only where they are centred on the work flow. This effect appears in such characteristics as the proportion of employees in functions like maintenance and production control" (p. 172).

---

4   But even this apparently straightforward criterion is problematic for the simple reason that what constitutes a large organisation in one industry may not in another. Robbins (1990) rightly observes that "a small beauty parlour may have three employees; while one with 50 employees would be quite large. On the other hand, a steel plant with 200 employees is small in an industry where average plants employ several thousand workers" (p. 151). For most intents and purposes, however an organisation employing in excess of 2,000 employees can be said to be large.

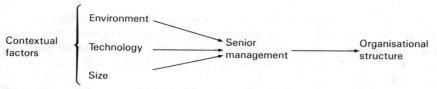

Figure 6.3 : The Relationship Between Context and Structure According to Child (1972)

One criticism levelled at the original Aston studies was that they had given insufficient attention to the role of senior managers or decision-makers in the whole process of an organisation's structural development. Child (1972, 1984), who was responsible for this criticism, felt that executives interpret the same environmental or contextual factors differently, and to some degree organisations' structures reflect these differences. According to this line of thinking, senior management acts as a mediating variable between contextual factors and organisational structure, as depicted in Figure 6.3. They make *strategic choices* about what they consider to be appropriate structures for the contingencies they perceive (see Donaldson 1985). By way of example, Kamau might have opted to react to the same contextual factors in an entirely different manner to the one that he chose, and the structure of his organisation would have differed accordingly.

Parkinson's Law
Parkinson's now well known credo that 'work expands to fill the time available for its completion' arose from his research into the relationship between organisation size and the size of the administrative component in the British Royal Navy between 1914 and 1928. His conclusion that in government at least "there need be little or no relationship between the work to be done and the size of the staff to which it may be assigned" (Parkinson 1957: 33) seems particularly relevant to Africa as our earlier example of the Public Complaints Commission in Nigeria has already demonstrated (Ayeni 1987). Briefly, Parkinson found that between 1914 and 1928, the number of warships in the British Royal Navy declined by nearly 68 percent, total personnel numbers declined by 32 percent, but certain categories of administrative personnel (on-shore administrators and clerks) rose by 40 percent, and the number of officers increased by an astonishing 78 percent. Considerable research has subsequently been conducted into the relationship between organisational size and the size of the administrative component (support staff component). Ideally, we would hope that economies of scale would accompany increasing size, meaning that the relative size of the support staff component would reduce as the overall size of the organisation increased. Research results confirm this expectation under certain circumstances (where there are managerial incentives for this to happen). But research findings also indicate that economies of scale tail off after a certain size threshold is reached and support staff numbers begin to increase because coordination becomes more complicated after a certain point and this requires additional manpower.

Other factors relevant to the generality of Parkinson's claims are organisation type, environmental change and complexity, technology, and whether the organisation is in a state of growth or decline.

The absence of incentives in many government organisations for managers to resist Parkinson's law, and the fact that in Africa there would be incentives (derived from social approval of behaviour which conforms to customary practice) for it to operate, suggest that it would have fairly widespread validity in Africa. Nevertheless, it should not be accepted as a general law.

To this point, we have considered two major influences on organisational structure: technology, and size, and we have mentioned a third, strategic choice. A fourth set of factors which has been found to have a bearing on organisational structure is the external environment of the organisation. We shall include under the heading external environment wider economic, technological, and social considerations. Culture, which is an important element of the organisation's external environment, warrants special attention in the African setting and will be treated separately later.

6.2.3   External Environment

In Chapter 1 we mentioned the dynamism and complexity which characterise the environments of organisations in Africa. One of the best known studies of the relationship between an organisation's external environment and its structure was conducted by Emery and Trist (1965). These authors categorised the environment into four types, or 'causal textures' as they called them. Each type of environment is conducive to the development of certain organisational structures. The environments and corresponding structures proposed by Emery and Trist, which were based in part on a case study of a British food canning firm, are outlined below.

Placid, Randomised Environment
This is the simplest environment and one which is not likely to be encountered by present day organisations either in Africa or the West. It corresponds to the economists' pure competition market. The environment is stable and unchanging, but resources are dispersed almost randomly within it, and are therefore not logically connected. This makes it difficult for the organisation to predict what will happen in its environment. Such an environment is conducive to small, independent organisations with simple structures. Little forward planning is possible and the organisation proceeds through trial and error.

Placid, Clustered Environment
Here the environment is still not subject to rapid change, but is more predictable owing to the existence of logical, causal connections between resources and other elements within it. An organisation's survival and success depends on its being able to predict the environment, and therefore planning becomes important. Organisations tend to be larger and more hierarchically structured.

Disturbed, Reactive Environment
The major difference between this environment and the preceding one is the existence of a number of similar organisations competing for the same resources. This is a dominant feature of this type of environment. The ability to predict the environment and to plan

accurately is complicated by the existence of competitors; relative power becomes a vital consideration. As Aldrich (1979) states, "larger size might give organisations such power, and over time the larger organisations might drive out the smaller ones" (p. 72). Such an environment also promotes structural flexibility, and encourages decentralisation.

Turbulent Environment

This is a highly complex, rapidly changing environment, characterised by multiple connections between resources and other elements within it. Three factors contribute to this state of change and complexity. First, adaptation to the third type of environment mentioned above increases the links between competing organisations (that is, what happens to one often affects the other and they are all – because of their competition over the same resources, customers, etc. – subject to similar pressures), and this in turn creates a backwash effect, from the organisations to the environment itself. For example, demand for particular goods and services can be created through advertising. Second, there is an increasing interdependence between organisations and society in general. Organisations come to depend heavily on customers and client groups within certain parts of society, and society in turn depends on formal organisations for certain goods and services. Third, competition and rapidly changing environments make it necessary for organisations to rely increasingly on research and development activities, which themselves help to speed up the general rate of change. Organisations operating in this type of environment need to be extremely flexible, with heavy reliance being placed on mutual adjustment as a method of coordination among middle and senior management personnel.

Very similar results to those of Emery and Trist had been obtained in an earlier study by Burns and Stalker (1961). The latter examined 20 firms in Britain, drawn mainly from the electronics industry, but including a large engineering firm and a manufacturer of artificial fibres (rayon). These researchers were also interested in studying the relationship between organisational structure and environment. They were able to distinguish two types of organisational structure, each of which was suited to a particular external environment. The first type of structure, which they labelled mechanistic, seemed appropriate for organisations operating in stable environmental conditions; the second, which they called organic, was more suited to dynamic or changing environmental conditions. This led them to the conclusion that an organisation's structure and management system depended to a large degree on extrinsic factors or on the organisation's external environment. In their own words:

"These extrinsic factors are all, in our view, identifiable as different rates of technical or market change. By change we mean the appearance of novelties; i.e., new scientific discoveries or technical inventions, and requirements for products of a kind not previously available or demanded" (Burns & Stalker 1961: 96).

The terms mechanistic and organic are now widely used in the literature to refer to two distinctive forms of organisational structure. They are perhaps best described by the authors themselves.

Mechanistic Structures

"In mechanistic systems the problems and tasks facing the concern as a whole are broken down into specialisms. Each individual pursues his task as something distinct from the real tasks of the concern as a whole; as if it were the subject of a subcontract. 'Somebody at the top' is responsible for seeing to its relevance. The technical methods, duties, and powers attached to each functional role are precisely defined. Interaction within management tends to be vertical, i.e., between superior and subordinate. Operations and working behaviour are governed by instructions and decisions issued by superiors. This command hierarchy is maintained by the implicit assumption that all knowledge about the situation of the firm and its tasks is, or should be, available only to the head of the firm. Management, often visualised as the complex hierarchy familiar in organisation charts, operates a simple control system, with information flowing up through a succession of filters, and decisions and instructions flowing downwards through a succession of amplifiers" (Burns & Stalker 1961; 5–6).

Organic Structures

"Organic systems are adapted to unstable conditions, when problems and requirements for action arise which cannot be broken down and distributed among specialist roles within a clearly defined hierarchy. Individuals have to perform their special tasks in the light of their knowledge of the tasks of the firm as a whole. Jobs lose much of their formal definition in terms of methods, duties, and powers, which have to be redefined continually by interaction with others participating in a task. Interaction runs laterally as much as vertically. Communication between people of different ranks tends to resemble lateral consultation rather than vertical command. Omniscience can no longer be imparted to the head of the concern" (Burns & Stalker 1961: 5–6).

These studies, in conjunction with others such as those of Lawrence and Lorsch (1967) in the U.S.A., have helped to improve our understanding of the ways in which organisations are affected by their external environments. Organisations facing relatively stable and predictable environments tend to have structures which rely on direct supervision, formalisation, and standardisation – in short, they tend to be mechanistic. Conversely, those organisations which have to cope with dynamic, changing environments must exhibit similar characteristics themselves in order to survive. They therefore tend to have organic, flexible structures. It is also important to remember, however, that departments or groups within organisations often have to deal with quite different sub-environments, and their structures are likely to vary accordingly. In other words, a single organisation may contain both mechanistic and organic subsystems.

But are the implications of all these studies restricted to organisations in Britain and the U.S.A., where the studies themselves were carried out? Do the findings apply to different cultures? Or, more precisely, how might organisational structure be affected by culture? How does its influence compare to that of technology or size or the wider external environment? These are questions which will be taken up in Chapter 9.

6.3.   Organisational Structures in Africa

On the basis of studies conducted by Nicholson, Ostrom and Bowles (1985) in Kenya, research evidence analysed by Blunt (1983a), and his own experiences of organisations in Uganda, Kenya and Ghana, Kiggundu (1989) has drawn up a structural profile of a 'typical' organisation in a developing country (*see* Figure 6.4). Kiggundu suggests that top managers in a typical organisation in a developing country are authoritarian and paternalistic, autocratic, overworked, highly educated, articulate and widely travelled. However, they tend also not to provide much in the way of visionary leadership or example. Organisations typically do not have clearly stated and widely understood missions or objectives; they are heavily politicised, and have weak executive support systems. In Kiggundu's view, senior managers also devote too much of their time to extra-organisational activities which have little to do with the organisation's interests, such as political, tribal, religious, or personal family and business activities. Middle managers, on the other hand, are seen by Kiggundu as possessing inadequate management and administrative skills, insufficient industry specific knowledge and experience, low levels of motivation, and to be risk averse, unwilling to take independent action or initiative, to favour close direct supervision over other methods of coordination and, like senior management, to be unwilling to delegate. As a whole, middle lines in developing country organisations are understaffed and are characterised by weak and/or inappropriate management and organisation systems and controls. At the operating levels, developing country organisations are judged by Kiggundu (1989) to be inefficient and costly, and overstaffed. Operators tend to be underutilised, underpaid, and not to be rewarded according to performance. This results in low morale, lack of commitment, high turnover and absenteeism. Moreover, he sees the boundaries of the organisation as being "rather porous, leaving the vital technical core of the organisation unprotected and susceptible to abuse by outside societal interests" (Kiggundu, 1989: 10). In Figure 6.4, the extended connecting lines between different levels represent inadequate coordination and communication between the different parts of the organisation, while the broken line surrounding the operating core indicates the permeability of organisational boundaries at that level.

Like Kiggundu (1989), we acknowledge that there will be many exceptions to this model in Africa and elsewhere in the developing world. But we can see some value in describing an undesirable end state in order that it may serve as a stark reminder of a common African organisational scenario.

It is also worth noting that other commentators have recently arrived at very similar conclusions to those of Kiggundu. For example, Jreisat (1988) has described a number of structural and administrative deficiencies common to seven Arab countries, including Sudan and Morocco, which broadly corroborate Kiggundu's conclusions.

TOP MANAGEMENT

- Overworked
- Authoritarian paternalistic
- Centralised control and decision making
- No clear mission or sense of direction
- Extensive extra-organisation activities
- Politicised
- Weak executive support systems
- Learned, articulate, travelled

MIDDLE MANAGEMENT

- Weak management systems and controls
- Inadequate management and administrative skills
- Lack of specific industry knowledge and experience
- Understaffed
- Risk averse, unwilling to take independent action or initiative
- Exercise close supervision, little delegation
- Low levels of motivation

OPERATING LEVELS

- Inefficient, high cost operations
- Low productivity
- Overstaffed, underutilised
- Low pay
- Poor morale
- Weak boundaries and unprotected vital technical core

Figure 6.4: A General Profile of a Developing Country Organisation

6.4. Implications for Managers and Management Development

In this chapter we have defined and analysed some basic components of organisational structure and methods of coordination and control, and examined the range and nature of the variables which have been found to influence them. We have seen that there are a multitude of factors to which managers and organisational designers need to attend when considering how to structure their organisation's activities, among them: size, technology, culture, environment, and growth. The bulk of the Western literature points to size as a variable of great significance, but more studies are beginning to appear which indicate that culture and environment may, under certain circumstances, supersede other variables, including size, as influences on particular aspects of organisational structure.

The whole question of organisational design in Africa is complicated greatly by the, generally speaking, more turbulent and changing political, economic, and social environments encountered on the continent, and by severe resource and infrastructural constraints. The effects of size on organisational structure, for example, are most evident in stable environments: unstable or variable environments disturb this relationship. Child (1978) has commented on this quite clearly:

"When there is not much variability in the environment, the need to develop organisation to suit size becomes relatively more dominant. In this environment, the better-performing companies tend to develop formalised structures at a faster rate as they grow than do poor performers. When the environment is a variable one, however, these differences in structural development are reduced, because the contingency of coping with uncertainty tends to offset the contingency of coping with large scale ... The picture is complex indeed" (pp. 400–401).

However, perhaps the single most important conclusion to be drawn from this chapter is that organisational structure as we have defined it should be seen as an organisational design *variable*, something which managers should not take as given but should view as a feature of organisation which can and, when circumstances demand it, should be changed in order to improve organisational performance and employee well-being. The recognition of this fact is, of course, a necessary step; more difficult will be the creation of political conditions within African organisations which are sufficient to bring about management-designed structural change in the interests of the attainment of organisational goals. The implications for management training and development are clear. These ideas should constitute a central part of any management training and development programme.

The next chapter in this book considers a broad range of configurations of organisational structure which can be used as frameworks for assessing the fit between existing organisational structures and their internal and external environments, and as targets for setting the direction, and gauging the pace, of structural change.

Chapter 7:   Configurations of Organisational Structure

Elsewhere in this book we consider questions associated with organisational change and development in Africa (*see* Chapter 10). There we make the point that a great deal of what passes for organisational change and development in Africa, as elsewhere in the world, is overly mechanistic: that it gives insufficient attention to the human consequences of change and justifiable anticipatory fears which change arouses in people. A common feature of such mechanistic change is a general interest in the structure of organisations, which is usually taken to mean the domains of activity with which organisations or units within them are concerned. As we saw in the last chapter, organisational structure is a more complicated and inclusive concept than that because it refers also to methods of coordination and questions of managerial style. But applications in Africa of even the more restricted notion of organisational structure have suffered from a limited knowledge among those responsible for undertaking organisational redesign of the variety of organisational forms available, and the circumstances in which each of these forms has been found to work best. This chapter attempts to fill such knowledge gaps with a series of rationally constructed models of organisational structure along with accounts of the internal and external environments to which they appear to be best suited.

In addition to providing a detailed description of organisational structure the previous chapter reviewed the major empirical studies of the variables associated with it. This massive and complicated body of research has been synthesised by Mintzberg (1979, 1983, 1988, 1989) into six basic configurations depicting the relationships between distinctive structural forms and associated sets of environmental contingencies. These configurations are the subject of this chapter.

7.1   Mintzberg's Six Structural Configurations

This section describes and discusses the major characteristics of Mintzberg's six structural forms: the simple structure, the machine bureaucracy, the professional bureaucracy, the divisionalised form, the adhocracy, and the missionary organisation; and the environmental factors associated with them. Each of the structural forms outlined below can be differentiated according to the method of coordination used, the type of decentralisation employed (vertical or horizontal), and the part of the organisation that plays the most important role. Vertical decentralisation is concerned with the delegation of decision making power down the organisational hierarchy from the strategic apex. Three design considerations arise: which decision making powers should be delegated, how far down should the devolution of power go, and how should the power delegated to lower levels be coordinated? Horizontal decentralisation occurs when power is shifted from managers to non-managers (for example, technical specialists and support staff).

The six structural forms which are summarised in Table 7.1 can be explained by regarding the organisation as being pulled in a particular direction by one of its component parts. Most organisations will, of course, be subjected to simultaneous, though varying, pulls in a number of directions, but one will usually dominate, thereby inclining the structure towards one of the configurations mentioned.

So, for example, *under suitable conditions* (more about these later), a pull for centralisation from the strategic apex coupled with coordination through direct supervision is likely to result in a *simple structure*.

Similarly, we have seen that the major function of staff specialists is to standardise work processes. When conditions favour this method of coordination, the organisation structures itself as a *machine bureaucracy*.

On the other hand, members of the operating core who seek to minimise the influence of administrators – managers as well as staff specialists – by promoting coordination through the standardisation of skills and horizontal and vertical decentralisation, exert a pull for professionalism. When conditions are conducive to this pull, the organisation structures itself as a *professional bureaucracy*.

When managers of the middle line are intent on achieving greater autonomy, they do so by drawing power down from the strategic apex and, where necessary, up from the operating core. This results in a form of limited vertical decentralisation, and the splitting of the organisation into market-based units with high levels of autonomy. Coordination is achieved primarily through the standardisation of outputs. Where circumstances favour this pull, the *divisionalised form* results.

The influence of support personnel is maximised not when they are autonomous, but when, owing to their expertise, their participation or collaboration in decision making is sought. This occurs when the organisation is structured into work constellations to which power is decentralised selectively, and which achieve coordination through mutual adjustment. Where conditions are conducive to this pull to collaborate, the *adhocracy* results.

A key element in the formation of the sixth configuration, the *missionary organisation*, is the existence at the top of the organisation of strong, transformational leadership which is able to construct and transmit a clear organisational mission and purpose, along with committed employees at all levels.

7.1.1   Dimensions of Organisational Environments

Before we discuss each of the configurations in more detail, it is necessary to define some of the key terms we shall use in our discussion of organisational environments.

Environment

An organisation's environment consists of virtually everything outside the organisation: the store of knowledge upon which it must draw; the nature of its products, customers, and competitors; its geographical location; and the economic, political, and social conditions

Table 7.1: Major Characteristics of Mintzberg's Structural Configurations (Mintzberg, 1983, 1989)

Structural Form	Prime Coordinating Mechanism	Key Part of Organisation	Type of Decentralisation
Simple structure	Direct supervision	Strategic apex (senior Management)	Vertical and horizontal
Machine bureaucracy	Standardisation of work processes	Staff specialists (technostructure)	Limited horizontal decentralisation
Professional bureaucracy	Standardisation of skills	Operating core	Vertical and horizontal decentralisation
Divisionalised form	Standardisation of outputs	Middle line	Limited vertical decentralisation
Adhocracy	Mutual adjustment	Support staff	Selective decentralisation
Missionary organisation	Standardisation of norms and values	Strategic apex and whole organisation	Vertical and horizontal decentralisation

in which it must operate. But the organisation's internal environment is also important, particularly in so far as the skills and commitment of its members are concerned. However, our analysis in this chapter focuses on the organisation's external environment.

Stability

An organisation's environment can range from *stable* to *dynamic*, from that of a craftsman who turns out the same pieces of furniture year after year to that of the management consultant who is continually faced with novel challenges. Many factors can make an environment dynamic: for example, unstable economic or political conditions, unexpected changes in customer demand, or rapidly changing technologies as in electronics manufacturing. Note that we use the term dynamic here to mean *unpredictable* rather than *variable*. Variability may be predictable.

Complexity

An organisation's environment can vary from simple to complex (here, in terms of the store of knowledge upon which it draws). The major dimension of complexity has to do with the *comprehensibility* of the work to be done. We assume here, however, that where (as, say, in the automobile industry) industries have been employing a standardised, though complicated, technology for long periods their environments will be simple. There are two reasons for this. First, there has been sufficient time to assimilate the accumulated store of knowledge. Second, the technologies involved have not been the subject of radical change, and are capable of being broken down into comprehensible parts.

Market Diversity

Market diversity may be a function of a wide variety of clients, products, services, or of geographical areas in which outputs are sold.

Hostility

Hostility in an organisation's environment may be a function of competition, the availability of resources, or interactions with government, unions, and other outside bodies.

Naturally, organisations are faced with multiple environments. Political conditions may be relatively stable, but economic ones dynamic; products may be complex, but marketing channels simple, and so on. Having said this, however, we should add that frequently one aspect in particular of an organisation's environment may dominate to such an extent that it affects the entire organisation.

7.1.2   The Simple Structure (SS)

Key part of the organisation:	Strategic apex (senior management)
Main method of coordination:	Direct supervision
Major structural characteristics:	Centralisation; organic structure
Environmental factors:	Young; small; uncomplicated technical system; simple, dynamic environment; either extreme hostility in environment or strong power needs of chief executive.

As Figure 7.1 shows, and the term simple structure[1] implies, this structure typically has few support staff, little or no technostructure, a loose division of labour, little differentiation between units, and a small managerial hierarchy. Its behaviour is not formalised and it makes little or no use of planning, training, and formal liaison devices. More than anything else, perhaps, it is organic. An organic structure is characterised by the absence of standardisation; remember, a bureaucratic structure lies at the opposite end of the (standardisation) continuum.

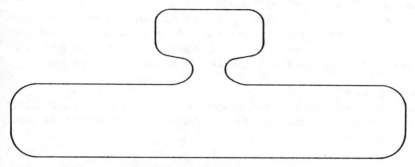

Figure 7.1: The Simple Structure (Mintzberg 1983)

The strategic apex is the key part of the structure, and very often this consists of a single individual. This individual typically has a wide span of control, and coordinates activities between units which, if they exist at all, are grouped on a loose functional basis. Communication is informal, work flows are flexible, and there is relatively little job specialisation.

New organisations tend to have SSs no matter what their environments or technical systems are like. The SS is therefore a *stage of development* through which most organisations pass in their formative years. Five other factors are conducive to the development of SSs:

Simple and Dynamic Environments
The single individual is more likely to be able to comprehend such an environment (that is, an uncomplicated technical knowledge base or system), and at the same time maintain sufficient flexibility to deal with its dynamism.

Small Size
Work tends to be less repetitive in small organisations, and therefore less standardisation is called for. Communication is most convenient and effective when it is informal. And in very small organisations there is little or no need even for direct supervision: coordination can be achieved through mutual adjustment.

---

1   In his later work, Mintzberg (1989) refers to this configuration as an *entrepreneurial* one.

Extreme Hostility
With some exceptions (e.g., organisations like the Red Cross – whose main mission it is to deal with crises – may be organised according to bureaucratic principles and employ standardised procedures), crisis, and the consequent need for rapid, coordinated responses, also compels the organisation to place power exclusively in the hands of the chief executive.

Personal Characteristics of the Chief Executive
There are at least two possibilities here. In the first place, a chief executive who hoards power and strongly resists what he perceives to be threats to his personal control will incline the organisation towards a SS. Second, charismatic individuals, or those upon whom power is lavished, exert much the same kind of influence on the organisation.

Owner Management
SSs are probably associated more with owner management than with any other single factor: such organisations exhibit most of the characteristics of the SS in some of its most uncontaminated forms.

7.1.3   The Machine Bureaucracy (MB)

Key part of the organisation:	Technostructure (staff specialists)
Main method of coordination:	Standardisation of work processes
Major structural characteristics:	Behaviour formalisation[2]; vertical and horizontal job specialisation; usually functional grouping; large operating-unit size; vertical centralisation and limited horizontal decentralisation; action planning
Environmental factors:	Old; large; regulating, non-automated technical system; simple, stable environment; external control; not in vogue.

This structural configuration is the one which comes closest to the Weberian bureaucracy. It incorporates standardised responsibilities and qualifications for its members, standardised communication channels and work rules, and a clearly defined hierarchy of authority. It is a structural type which has its foundations in the Industrial Revolution, and which Woodward observed in the mass production firms she studied.

The outstanding features of the machine bureaucracy are discussed in greater detail below.

---

2   The formalisation of behaviour in organisations represents the organisation's method of defining or limiting the activities and discretion of its members. Formalisation can be achieved in three ways. First, specifications, such as those contained in a job description, can be attached to individual jobs. Second, specifications can be made in relation to the flow of work. Third general rules governing everything from dress to timeliness and the use of forms can be laid down.

The Operating Core

The tasks carried out in the operating core are generally simple and repetitive in nature, require relatively low levels of skill, and consequently little training. This goes hand-in-hand with sharp divisions of labour and high degrees of vertical and horizontal specialisation. Coordination is achieved primarily through the standardisation of work processes, and behaviour is formalised (i.e., highly regulated). First-line managers do not engage in much direct supervision because standardisation and formalisation achieve most coordination objectives. This state of affairs is conducive to the formation of extremely large units in the operating core.

The Administrative Component

The insulation of the operating core from external disturbances is facilitated by a highly developed administrative structure. This elaborate structure can be described in terms of the following major components:

The Middle Line

Middle line managers perform three major activities. First, they deal with any problems which may arise among the highly specialised members of the operating core. Despite the already mentioned high levels of standardisation in the operating core, problems and conflicts inevitably occur. As operators are prevented – by extensive standardisation of the work processes which inhibits informal communication – from dealing with such problems themselves through mutual adjustment, some direct intervention (supervision) by management is called for. To facilitate such supervision, operators are grouped into functional units dealing with distinct parts of the work flow. For similar reasons, functional groupings are found throughout the organisation's hierarchy: from production and maintenance, who look to the plant manager for problem resolution, to marketing and manufacturing who might appeal to the chief executive.

A second function of middle-line managers is to liaise with staff specialists in the technostructure and to implement their standards in the operating core. Third, as indicated in an earlier chapter, the middle-manager also sifts information flowing up the organisation from lower levels and amplifies decisions flowing down the organisation from senior management. In addition, the middle manager explains and directs the implementation of decisions and action plans (responses to information received) emanating from above. Many of these tasks demand frequent personal interaction with subordinates, specialists, and supervisors which limits the middle manager's capacity to supervise large numbers of people. Accordingly, administrative units above the operating core tend to be small in size and to be part of a tall hierarchy (that is, one containing a large number of administrative levels).

The Technostructure (staff specialists)

Owing to the importance in the MB of standardisation of the work processes, the staff specialists who design the systems assume a strategic position, and their part of the organisation, the technostructure, becomes the most vital structural component. This takes place in spite of the sharp distinctions made in the MB between line and staff personnel: officially, staff specialists only have advisory powers, while line managers retain formal control over operating units. But, because of the critical nature of their activities, staff specialists such as work study experts, quality control engineers, planners, budgeters, accountants, MIS people, and so on, acquire considerable *informal* power.

The staff specialists' influence is extended further by the fact that standardisation in the MB is not confined to the operating core. Rules and regulations govern behaviour throughout the organisation. Formal communication is favoured at all levels, and clear lines of responsibility and zones of decision making power are drawn. We do not mean to say here that the work of senior managers is tightly constrained, but to suggest that relative to other configurations behaviour at every level in the MB is more formalised.

Moreover, the MB emphasises division of labour and unit differentiation more than any other of the structural configurations to be dealt with here. Unlike the SS, for example, neither managers nor staff specialists are likely to be seen working alongside operators. The administrative structure is clearly separated from the operating core.

The Obsession with Control

The structure and functioning of the MB – rigid divisions of labour, elaborate rules and regulations, the routine, repetitive nature of work in the operating core – give rise to alienation[3] and conflict. The MB's obsession with control is partly designed to ameliorate the effects of such conflict. It attempts to do this by smothering the *symptoms* of conflict with a blanket of tight control procedures rather than creating an atmosphere where conflicts can be brought out into the open and their possible causes analysed and resolved.

Another preoccupation of the MB is uncertainty. Of course, most organisations are concerned with uncertainty, but the MB carries it to the extreme.

The Strategic Apex

While staff specialists in the technostructure retain most of the informal power in the MB, formal power rests in the hands of senior managers in the strategic apex. This formal power is exercised in three major spheres of influence. First, the strategic apex exercises its formal power at middle levels of the organisation – where there exist highly differentiated units such as engineering, marketing, and manufacturing (in mass production firms) – because the need at that level for the formalisation of behaviour to be augmented by some other coordinative device is rarely satisfied. This is because, on the face of it, a flexible method of coordination such as mutual adjustment would seem

---

3 Following Seeman (1959), alienating work is work which leads to feelings of powerlessness, meaninglessness, normlessness, self estrangement, and social isolation.

to be best suited to the organisation's requirements. But informal communication is not encouraged in the MB. Status differences between line and staff, and between managers at different levels, and the general emphasis on vertical reporting relationships and formal communication all act as effective barriers to the type of informal communication upon which mutual adjustment depends. As a result, much of the interaction between units at the middle level is coordinated in a top-down fashion by senior managers through direct supervision. In an important sense, managers at the strategic apex are the only ones with a perspective broad enough to encompass the activities of differentiated units and to channel them towards organisational (as opposed to departmental or individual) objectives. As Mintzberg (1983) says, "everyone else in the structure is a specialist, concerned with a single link in the chain of activities that produces the outputs" (p. 169).

Not surprisingly, strategy making is the second major domain of managers in the strategic apex. Relevant information is transmitted up the organisation where it is moulded into an integrated strategy. Its aim is to tie all the decisional threads of the organisation together. Exceptions or anomalies which are encountered in implementing strategy are referred back up the hierarchy. Where a number of differentiated units are affected (by the anomaly), the matter finds its way back to the strategic apex for resolution. Resulting decisions and action plans are then, once again, transmitted down the organisation. We can contrast this process with that which obtains where *work constellations* are the primary structural feature: that is, where formal power is allocated to various constellations in the organisation and where decision making and implementation take place in localised areas. In the MB, on the other hand, the stra-

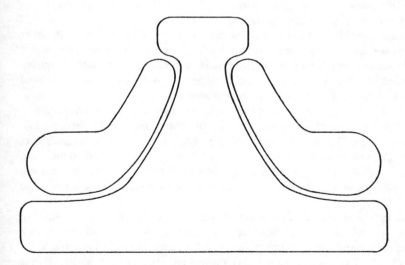

Figure 7.2: The Machine Bureaucracy (Mintzberg 1983)

tegic apex decides and instructs and the middle line and operating core implement – at least in theory (we shall have something to say about practical considerations in a moment).

Our discussion thus far suggests a structure something like that depicted in Figure 7.2; that is, a fully developed administrative and support structure (focused on the operating core), substantial operating units at lower levels, but narrower administrative ones in the middle line, which shape the tall hierarchy of authority.

Finally, the third major function of senior management is to deal with the major conflicts – the 'tummy rumbles' – of the organisation. Bearing in mind what we said earlier in this regard (that, in the MB, conflict tends to be smothered rather than exposed to analysis), the effect of the strategic apex is very much that of a cork in a bottle. Accordingly, to stretch the analogy further, if the cork pops (or conflict is not contained), it is usually senior managers who go with it.

The Environment

Above all, the ideal environment for the MB is one that is simple and stable. In addition, MBs tend to be old and large, and to have regulating technical systems which make work routine and therefore allow it to be easily formalised. Technical systems tend not to be complicated, otherwise considerable formal power would be lost to staff specialists. This in turn would create a form of decentralisation quite out of keeping with the MB.

Neither are highly automated technical systems suited to the MB as these do away, by definition, with routine operating work. Accordingly, while the organisation might make considerable use of mechanisation and computers because its work is standardised, it only retains the distinctive qualities of the MB so long as such technical systems do not displace large numbers of unskilled operators.

Mass production firms provide the clearest examples of the MB: after raw materials or components are taken in from the environment, the mass-production firm operates very much as a closed system that transforms these inputs into marketable products through a series of standardised operations. These horizontal operations are divided into functional departments which report up the vertical chain of authority.

But MBs are obviously to be found elsewhere. For instance, many service organisations are MBs. In these organisations, the assembly line workers of the mass production firm are replaced by banks of switchboard operators in the telephone organisation, clusters of office clerks in the insurance company, and by rows of tellers in the bank. The operating work carried out in these organisations is routine and non-professional and consequently just as amenable to formalisation as the work of the assembly line worker.

External control is another factor which impels organisations towards the MB. For example, government bodies are often subject to high degrees of external control. Post offices and tax departments are bureaucratic not just because they are accountable to the public. Their behaviour towards clients and employees must be seen to be fair so rules and regulations abound.

Two other factors appear to incline an organisation's structure towards the MB. The first is *control*. Since control is such a dominant feature of the MB, organisations with a 'control mission' – such as police forces, prisons, and security companies are attracted to this type of structure. The second factor is safety. In order to minimise risks, organisations in which safety is a major goal – e.g., airlines and fire services – formalise their procedures extensively. Airline maintenance staff, for example, must clearly carry out standardised, precise safety and maintenance checks. Similarly, firemen must know exactly what to do when they arrive at the scene of a fire.

While the environments of these organisations appear to be dynamic, they in fact present quite predictable contingencies. The organisations concerned will have faced similar situations on countless occasions in the past. Clearly, though, this is not to say that in unexpected or unusual circumstances all organisations would maintain the rigid structure of a MB: some would no doubt convert temporarily to an organic structure until the (novel) crisis had passed.

We conclude our discussion of the MB with three general observations: one positive, two negative. First, we would agree with Mintzberg (1983) that "when an integrated set of simple, repetitive tasks must be performed precisely and consistently by human beings, the MB is the most efficient structure – indeed, the only conceivable one" (p. 176). But second, hand-in-hand with these efficiencies go severe human problems in the operating core. Frequently, the type of work required of operators results in widespread alienation (e.g., Blauner 1964; Blunt 1982; Schrank 1978). Joan Woodward recognised this many years ago when she spoke of irreconcilable conflicts between the social and technical systems. What is good for production in the MB is simply not good for people. And while responses will vary according to individual orientations to work, a common sentiment is expressed in the following reaction of an American factory worker:

"My attitude is that I don't get excited about my job. I do my job but I don't say whoopee-doo. The day I get excited about my job is the day I go to a head shrinker. How are you gonna get excited about pullin' steel? How are you gonna get excited when you're tired and want to sit down? ... Unless a guy's a nut, he never thinks about work or talks about it. Maybe about baseball or about getting drunk the other night or he got laid or he didn't get laid. I'd say one out of a hundred will actually get excited about work" (Shostak 1980: 57).

Our third concluding observation on the MB has to do with problems of adaptation at the strategic apex. Environments these days – as we have repeatedly observed – are subject to more rapid change than ever before. These changes generate non-routine problems which the MB is not well equipped to handle. This is because non-routine problems in the MB are passed up the strategic apex for resolution. A rapidly changing environment naturally generates many unusual problems, and consequently information channels leading to the strategic apex become clogged, overload may occur among senior managers, delays ensue, or decisions are made too hastily by people (senior managers) divorced from the 'problem scene'.

You might think, given the existence of modern management information systems, that MBs should be capable of dealing with these types of (rapidly occurring, non-routine) problems. The trouble is, however, that because of the tall administrative structure of the MB, the upward flow of information is subject to distortion. Such distortions are frequently intentional. For a variety of reasons, different individuals and levels within the organisation want to present their own views of the problems (e.g., views which minimise their own culpability). As a result, 'bad' news usually gets selected out, so that the information which eventually finds its way to the strategic apex is often a curious mishmash of leftovers – what different people at different levels feel they can safely leave in.

Another drawback of management information systems is that they are primarily sources of 'hard' – that is, quantitative – data. As we saw in Chapter 3, there is considerable evidence to suggest that managers need to base their strategic decisions as much – or more – on 'soft', specific, and timely information as they do on quantitative information which in any case frequently arrives too late to allow a rapid response. Mintzberg adds:

"Gossip, hearsay, speculation – the softest kind of information – warn the manager of impending problems; the management information system (MIS) all too often records for posterity that these problems have long since arrived. Moreover, a good deal of important information never even gets into the MIS. The mood in the factory, the conflict between two managers, the reasons for a lost sale – this kind of rich information never becomes the kind of fact that the traditional MIS can handle. So the information of the MIS, by the time it reaches the strategic apex – after being filtered and aggregated through the levels of the administrative hierarchy – is often so bland that the top manager cannot rely on it. In a changing environment, that manager finds himself out of touch" (1983: 184–185).

To conclude, it should be clear by now that MBs work best in stable environments. All personnel are expected to conform to rules and regulations and not to innovate. Managers are rewarded for improving operating efficiency, reducing costs, and tightening controls and standards, rather than taking risks, trying out new methods or encouraging creative problem solving. In short, the MB is an inflexible configuration; efficient in a closely defined realm of activity and clumsy and virtually unmanageable in an environment that is either dynamic or complex. However, so long as there is a demand for standardised, cheap goods and services, and so long as there are people able and willing to do what is required more efficiently than automated machines, the MB, with all its deficiencies, will remain.

7.1.4   The Professional Bureaucracy (PB)

Key part of the organisation:	Operating core
Main method of coordination:	Standardisation of skills
Major structural characteristics:	Horizontal job specialisation; vertical and horizontal decentralisation; emphasis on training
Environmental factors:	Complex; stable; non-regulating non-sophisticated technical systems; fashionable.

The professional bureaucracy is the term we shall use to describe organisations which are bureaucratic[4] but not centralised. PBs are decentralised because their work is stable and complex and must therefore be controlled directly by the operators who do the work. The method of coordination which accommodates both decentralisation and standardisation at the same time is the *standardisation of skills*. Universities, hospitals, schools, and accounting firms are frequently structured in this way. All of them produce standard products or services by relying on the knowledge and skills of their operating professionals.

We can achieve a deeper understanding of the PB by considering the following structural characteristics.

The Work of the Operating Core

The work of the PB is carried out by highly trained and suitably indoctrinated professionals who have considerable autonomy. Horizontally, their work is highly specialised, but vertically it is enlarged. The professional in the operating core works relatively independently of her colleagues, but maintains close links with the clients she serves. Coordination is achieved through the standardisation of skills and knowledge so that, in most instances, the professional knows what to expect of her colleagues. But while knowledge and skills – such as those involved, say, in a surgical operation which can be reduced to a list of essential steps – are standardised in the PB, they are sufficiently complex to demand considerable discretion on the part of those professionals who apply them. There are therefore likely to be differences between professionals (for example, lecturers, surgeons, teachers, etc.) with respect to the ways in which standardised knowledge and skills are employed.

The Bureaucratic Aspects of the Structure

The lengthy and intensive periods of training undergone by professionals in the operating core ensure that they bring with them into the organisation a set of standards which, to a substantial degree, makes their work self-regulating. Unlike the MB, therefore, which

---

4   We can define a structure (or organisation) as bureaucratic to the extent that its behaviour is predetermined or predictable, that is, the degree to which it is standardised (be it in terms of work processes, outputs, or skills, and *irrespective* of the degree to which it is centralised).

generates its own standards, professionals in the PB derive their standards from extensive training and the professional associations to which they belong.

Other forms of standardisation are simply not suited to the PB. Work processes in the PB are not amenable to standardisation because they are too complex; and work outputs are not amenable to accurate measurement, which clearly makes their standardisation difficult. Let us consider the example of a clinical psychologist. His or her work may include therapy sessions with patients, case conferences (where diagnoses, treatments, progress, and prognoses are discussed), ward visits, reading of technical journals, and research. None of these activities is easily programmed (standardised). The 'outputs' of the clinical psychologist are equally difficult to standardise. Take, for instance, the problem of trying to define accurately what constitutes a cure in the treatment of psychological disorders.

The Importance of the Operating Core

Everything we have said so far about the PB – for example its emphasis on highly skilled, professional operators who are subject to few formal controls apart from those implicit in their training – suggests that the operating core is its most important structural component. The only other part of the organisation which is highly developed in the PB is the support staff component. In universities, for example, libraries, sporting facilities, computer and printing departments, publishing houses, and staff clubs are all engaged in routine service or support work which can be formalised. This means that the high cost members of the operating core can focus their attention on the primary tasks of the organisation. Where support staff components do not function as they should, and professional operators must devote time to these activities, the primary tasks of the organisation suffer accordingly (some of the most vivid illustrations of this point are to be found in PBs in developing countries – e.g., Blunt 1988).

Figure 7.3 shows that the technostructure and middle line of management are not highly developed in the PB. As there is little or no scope for planning or formalising the work of the operating core, there is not much need for an elaborate technostructure (except in-so-far as non-professional support staff are concerned). Likewise, the middle line in the PB is sparsely populated.

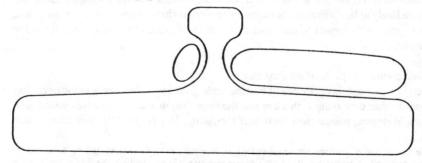

Figure 7.3 : The Professional Bureaucracy (Mintzberg, 1983)

Decentralisation in the PB

Most of the points we have made about the PB suggest that considerable power and autonomy are vested in professional operators. The complex nature of the operator's work and its importance to the organisation are the major sources of professional power in the PB.

The Administrative Structure

The administrative structure of the PB is composed of two parallel yet opposite systems: a democratic, bottom-up administrative hierarchy for professionals, and a top-down MB-like system for support staff (*see* Figure 7.4).

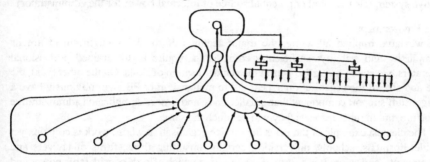

Figure 7.4: Parallel Administrative Hierarchies in the Professional Bureaucracy (Mintzberg 1983)

The Role of the Professional Administrator

While the professional administrator has little direct control over operators in the PB, she exerts considerable informal influence by virtue of certain of her responsibilities. Perhaps the most important aspect of the administrator's role in this connection is her deep daily involvement, and therefore her keen understanding, of the administrative process. She knows the ins and outs of the complicated democratic decision making process and – very often – has cultivated dependable informal contacts at pressure points. In the case of a university, for example, the professor or lecturer who is oriented to research and writing, and resents being distracted from this aspect of her work, surrenders – by default – some of her power in the broader organisational context to the professional (academic) administrator. Such administrators can be instrumental in obtaining the best possible 'deals' for their departments or faculties. And, to the extent that they are seen to be successful in this, they are accorded considerable informal power.

A second source of informal power for the professional administrator is her boundary control function, between the operating professionals in the organisation and external bodies such as government, the media, and clients. In this role, the professional administrator acts both as a buffer between the organisation and the outside world, and as a procurer of resources, new clients, and so on.

It is worth reiterating, however, that these informal powers are only retained by the professional administrator in the PB so long as, in the eyes of professional operators, she is effective in the spheres of activity mentioned.

Strategy Formulation
Strategy in the PB is largely a function of strategic initiatives on the part of professionals within the organisation: to purchase a new piece of equipment in a hospital, to set up a new degree programme in a university, or to develop a specialised department in an accounting firm. To effect these initiatives the professional operator relies heavily on the professional administrator, for it is she who is able to negotiate the complicated administrative system (clearly another potential source of informal power for the administrator).

The Environment
As we have implied all along, the major features of the PB's environment are its complexity and stability: sufficiently complex to require highly trained professional operators, yet stable enough to permit the standardisation of skills. On the other hand, the age and size of the organisation appear not to matter. Larger PBs will obviously have a bigger staff support component than smaller ones, and a more complicated administrative structure, but in other respects they will be much the same.

The clearest example of the PB is the service organisation whose work is complex yet stable: hospitals, schools, universities, certain consulting firms, firms of lawyers and accountants, and so on. It is a form of organisation which affords considerable power and autonomy to members of its operating core, and provides them with stable and challenging working environments. Yet it is not without its problems, some of them stemming directly from the very freedom, autonomy, and complexity which make the PB such an attractive organisation in which to work.

Problems Associated with the PB
We have stressed that the professional operator in the PB has considerable autonomy. He or she is virtually self-controlling. This means that the organisation has little opportunity to overcome deficiencies in performance which the professional does not perceive in the first place or, if she does, chooses to ignore.

Where professionals are either incompetent or unconscientious, because of the organisation's lack of influence over them, severe problems can arise and these frequently become institutionalised. From the point of view of the client, differing levels of competence are a problem because, in most instances, he either has no choice in the matter or is unable to make informed, valid judgments about the relative merits of different professionals. This hit-or-miss approach on the part of the client often has dire consequences, yet the PB is not in a position to alter things quickly. Profound remedies will necessitate improved selection procedures, leadership and management styles and, as we shall argue more fully in Chapter 9, the creation of positive working cultures. These are all relatively long term measures.

The second general problem, that of the unconscientious professional, raises slightly different issues. This person might not keep abreast of developments in his discipline, or choose to pursue his own interests irrespective of his client's needs: as in the case of the therapist who feels that all patients should receive behaviour therapy, or the consulting firm which applies the same packaged system or formula to all problems of a particular type (one package for selection problems, another for design problems and so on), or the teacher who uses the lecture method irrespective of the size and nature of his audience or other considerations. Yet again, however, we find that in all except the most severe cases – for example, the lecturer who repeatedly fails to show up for classes – the PB is powerless to do anything. Its position is made worse by the fact that it is difficult to appraise professional outputs in any case: to show unequivocally that one form of therapy or treatment is superior to another, or that one form of teaching is better than another, or that one legal adviser does a better job than another. Under these circumstances, the PB is understandably reluctant to stick its neck out. It is unlikely to attempt the difficult task of censuring its own professionals (who fiercely resist any kind of interference) when neither professional associations (in all but the most exceptional circumstances) nor – until recently – the public seem inclined to do so.

Another problem with the PB – like all bureaucracies – is its lack of flexibility. Members of PBs are usually reluctant to meddle with well-established procedures which have been designed for stable environments. And even when it is agreed that change is necessary, it takes a long time to effect. The bottom-up nature of the organisation has a lot to do with this as a majority of organisational members, not just a few managers or professional representatives, must agree on the nature of change and the way that it is introduced.

When such problems are perceived by clients, nonprofessional administrators, members of society at large, or government a frequent response is to try to control the professional's work by using one or other of the methods of coordination: direct supervision, standardisation of the work processes, or standardisation of outputs. For reasons which should be clear by now, these attempts to control the work of the professional rarely succeed. Supervisors divorced from the professional activities which they are meant to be supervising, and frequently ignorant of them, are therefore likely to resort to nuisance behaviour (like the school supervisor who sits-in on a class for ten minutes in order to get the 'feel' of teacher behaviour, or the departmental head who routinely 'pops in' to see subordinates at 4.55 on Friday afternoons). Similarly, attempts to standardise work processes and work outputs usually fail because the work is complex and results are difficult to measure. As Mintzberg says, "complex work processes cannot be formalised by rules and regulations, and vague outputs cannot be standardised by planning and control systems" (1983: 211). Where such measures are applied, the outcome is usually a drop in morale and motivation among the professionals affected. It means that many professionals will simply work to satisfy the rules and regulations instead of serving their clients.

The upshot of all this is that complex work of the type performed in the PB simply cannot be carried out effectively unless it is controlled by the operators who do it. And while there are costs to be borne in such a system, they are usually less severe than those associated with the introduction of rigid, centralised controls which drive the PB to become like a MB. The effect of bureaucratisation, as Mintzberg points out, is to throw the baby out with the bathwater. Controls of the type found in the MB do not usually improve the performance of professional work. They merely constrain everything: responsible and irresponsible behaviour alike, and innovation. And where – as would presumably be the case in most PBs – responsible behaviour is the norm, such controls only serve to reduce organisational effectiveness.

This is not to say that PBs should be immune from any form of control because clearly they are not, and nor should they be. External financial controls are imposed on PBs, and legislation against excessively irresponsible professional behaviour exists. Internal control, however, is a different matter. Effective changes in this arena will take considerable ingenuity to devise, and many years to implement. Our own view is that effective performance management resides in the wider issues discussed in this book, such as strategic management, leadership, organisational culture and structure. If managers can get these things right, performance control largely takes care of itself.

7.1.5   The Divisionalised Form (DF)

Key part of the organisation:	Middle line
Main method of coordination:	Standardisation of outputs
Major structural characteristics:	Market grouping; performance appraisal system; limited vertical decentralisation
Environmental factors:	Diversified markets; old; large; power needs of middle managers.

The divisionalised form is seen most widely in the private sector. The majority of large industrial enterprises use this type of structure. As the term suggests, the DF is characterised by *divisions* at the middle line which have considerable autonomy. Interactions between divisions and overall coordination are dealt with by a central administration or headquarters. This means that unlike the PB, which is a bottom-up structure, the flow of power in the DF is top-down. For this reason, and others we shall consider shortly, the structures of individual divisions tend toward the MB.

More than any other of the structural configurations mentioned, the DF incorporates within an overarching structural framework clearly distinguishable structural entities which correspond to divisions. The major focus of this discussion is on the relationship between these divisions and the central (headquarters) administration, or between the *top of the middle line* of the organisation and its *strategic apex*.

Major Structural Characteristics (of the organisation as a whole)
Divisions are usually formed on the basis of markets served, and are given decision making power over issues affecting their own operations. Interdependence between divisions is limited by the fact that operating functions – such as purchasing, manu-

facturing, and marketing – are duplicated. This operational autonomy naturally reduces the coordinative load imposed by individual divisions on the strategic apex. It therefore is conducive to wide spans of control at the strategic apex which permit a single organisation to incorporate a relatively large number of semi-autonomous divisions.

But how are the divisions coordinated or controlled by the strategic apex? Control is exercised mostly in a *post hoc*, or after the fact, fashion. Typically, quantitative measures of profit, market share, sales growth, and return on investment are used to appraise divisional performance. That is to say, coordination is achieved primarily through the standardisation of outputs.

Other methods of coordination employed by the strategic apex include standardisation of skills and a certain amount of direct supervision. As managers in charge of individual divisions play such a great part in determining overall organisational effectiveness, the selection and training of these people assume great importance (hence the standardisation of skills). Direct supervision (by the strategic apex of divisional managers – the middle line) is put into effect only when performance at the middle line is not up to standard.

Major Structural Characteristics of the Divisions
One of the major effects in the DF of coordination through the standardisation of outputs is the creation of MB structures in the divisions. This happens because the MB can be treated as a single highly integrated entity (in contrast, say, to the PB) with unified goals. These goals lend themselves well to relatively precise quantitative assessment, and hence, of course, to coordination through the standardisation of outputs.

The Distribution of Power in the DF
As we have said, individual divisions in the DF are given considerable operational autonomy to achieve output goals. The power of the strategic apex is most visible in five areas.

1. Determination of Overall Product-Market Strategy

The strategic apex determines which products are made, which markets are served, the allocation of products or markets to divisions, and the creation or closure of divisions themselves.

2. Allocation of Overall Financial Resources

This entails, for example, the transfer of funds from more successful to less successful divisions, the procurement of additional funds in capital markets, and the authorisation of major capital expenditure within divisions.

3. Design of Divisional Performance Appraisal Systems

With the aid of staff specialists, managers in the strategic apex decide on performance measures, frequency of assessment, and a suitable MIS system for the transmission of data. They are also responsible for the operation of the system.

4. Appointment and Replacement of Divisional Managers

5. Provision of Shared Support Services

These would clearly preclude support services which need to be physically contiguous to the divisions they serve (e.g., canteen facilities, market research, and so on). On the other hand, services and specialist advice which cut across divisional boundaries can be provided by headquarters (e.g., financial services, and legal advice).

Major Contingencies

Three types of market diversity – product and service, client, and location – constitute the major environmental influence on the DF. All three are frequently associated with divisionalisation.

A second contingency – technology – encourages divisionalisation *only* in circumstances where it is economically feasible to separate the organisation's technical system into divisional units. For example, in the case of a geographically dispersed cement company, it is economical because of the nature of the technical systems employed to duplicate these in various locations. An aluminium company, on the other hand, might only be able to afford one smelter. However, where divisionalisation has occurred as a consequence of product diversity, separation of the technical system is a *sine qua non* of effectiveness. Different products clearly require different technical systems.

A third consideration is that, because of the favoured method of coordination in the DF (standardisation of outputs), this form of organisation works best in relatively simple and stable environments, as does the MB. In environments which are dynamic and complex, it is extremely difficult to standardise outputs. Accordingly, when an organisation divisionalises in an environment other than one which is simple and stable, it assumes a hybrid structure. As coordination through the standardisation of outputs is no longer feasible, some other form of coordination must be used. For instance, reliance on direct supervision produces a hybrid simple structure, and so on.

Older, larger organisations are more likely to diversify and then to divisionalise. There are several possible explanations for this association. Mintzberg suggests risk aversion (diversification spreads risk), market dominance or saturation (which leads to a search for new opportunities), and the type of manager found in the middle line (divisionalisation nurtures aggressive, high-performing managers who press for further diversification and growth) as probable reasons for the connections between large size and divisionalisation. Diversification is seen by Mintzberg as being the mediating variable. That is to say, large size leads to diversification which in turn leads to divisionalisation.

Another contingency which plays an important role in the development of the DF (which is alluded to above, but warrants separate treatment) is the power needs of top managers. The DF is easily the most effective medium for personal aggrandizement. This feature of the DF is not always conducive to organisational effectiveness. Other problems associated with the DF are the subject of the next section.

Problems Associated with the DF

One of the major problems associated with the DF concerns the relative autonomy afforded divisions by the strategic apex. There will be instances when senior managers in the strategic apex are reluctant to delegate sufficient power to enable divisional managers to carry out their responsibilities effectively.. In effect, this defeats a major purpose of divisionalisation and can lead to severe interpersonal conflicts and ill-feeling. These, in turn, are likely to have damaging consequences for organisational performance.

Problems of this type sometimes arise in response to the introduction of sophisticated management information systems. We mentioned earlier that such systems are not always conducive to good decision making, especially when those making the decisions are far removed from the problem sources and the settings in which decisions are implemented. Speed of transmission of information, and quantity, are rarely sufficient to ensure high quality decision making. The softer, richer detail of informal communication is also needed.

On the other hand, it sometimes happens that divisional managers, who have the most detailed and up-to-date knowledge, are not willing to make it available to senior managers so as to enable them to make well-informed decisions in their formal spheres of influence (say, with respect to the standardisation of outputs or major capital expenditure). This has been found to be a major problem in joint-venture and state-owned enterprises in China (Child 1991), and elsewhere in the developing world (Kiggundu 1989). Why does information withholding occur? One reason is that divisional managers resent the close control over outputs exercised by senior managers because it stifles innovation and creativity. Another reason concerns the virtual obsession with quantitative measures among those members of the strategic apex who favour coordination through the standardisation of outputs. Such measures are frequently used to the almost total exclusion of more qualitative – less easily measured – goals such as pride in one's work, product quality, customer service, and environmental considerations. As it is often difficult to separate neatly economic considerations from social ones in organisational action, the control system of the DF compels it to behave, "at best socially unresponsively, at worst socially irresponsibly" (Mintzberg 1983: 247).

A third problem arises from the strong direct relationship between the DF and large size. We have suggested before that the DF is most often associated with big organisations, and that it is conducive to further growth. Large organisations tend to be more bureaucratic, and this may be regarded as a social cost in societies which already have large numbers of bureaucracies.

The DF does not work well in the public sector. There are several reasons for this. First, public organisations generally are less able to divest themselves of ineffective divisions. Second, public service regulations governing appointment, tenure, and performance appraisal are frequently such that it is difficult to do anything about ineffective individuals, too. But the most important reason is that of measurement: public institutions are more likely to have social goals which are difficult to measure quantitatively. Without such measurement, the DF in its pure form tends not to function as well as it would under other circumstances.

As a result, government institutions which need to have market-based divisions resort to other methods of coordination which are not ideally suited to the DF. A common reaction is to coordinate via direct supervision and formalisation (from the strategic apex). Hence the frequently heard complaints from government departments which are constrained by numerous rules and regulations and therefore lack the autonomy they need to function effectively.

Perhaps the best method to employ in these circumstances (i.e., in public organisations where the DF is necessary) is to appoint divisional managers who are committed to the social goals of the organisation. Unfortunately, this method is much easier to recommend than it is to implement, as the selection problems posed by such a method are immense.

7.1.6   The Adhocracy

Key parts of the organisation:	Support staff and operating core
Main method of coordination:	Mutual adjustment
Major structural characteristics:	Organic; selective decentralisation; horizontal job specialisation; liaison devices; training; functional and market grouping concurrently
Environmental factors:	Complex; dynamic; young; sophisticated and often automated technical systems.

The adhocracy is the structural configuration most suited to sophisticated innovation. Innovation implies a search for new ways of doing things, or a breaking away from established patterns. By definition, therefore, the adhocracy cannot employ any form of standardisation as its major coordinative device. It has none of the characteristics of the MB. There is little or no formalisation of behaviour, no sharp divisions of labour, and no importance is attached to tight planning and control systems. More than anything else, the adhocracy must remain flexible.

The major structural features of the adhocracy are described in greater detail below.

Expert Power
Owing to the complex and dynamic environment in which it operates, the adhocracy must employ and give considerable autonomy and power to experts. However, unlike the PB which relies on the standardisation of skills for coordinating the work of its professional operators, the adhocracy very often needs to build on existing individual skills in a variety of ways thereby ruling out their standardisation.

Interaction Between Experts
Moreover, innovation in complex fields not only requires continuing learning, but also constant interaction between people with different specialist backgrounds. Again, unlike the PB whose professionals rarely cross disciplinary boundaries, professionals in the adhocracy must coordinate their efforts.

Matrix Sub-Structure
Project team work provides a vehicle for such cooperation. For housekeeping purposes, professionals are grouped in functional units, but are assigned to project teams for innovative work. This, of course, is basically a matrix structure (Knight 1977).

Mutual Adjustment
We have already ruled out any form of standardisation in the adhocracy because of the complexity and dynamism of its environment. We can rule out direct supervision for the same reasons. Coordination must rest with the people who have the knowledge and expertise, the professionals themselves. Mutual adjustment between professionals in the operating core is therefore the major coordinative method used in conjunction with liaison devices.

Liaison Positions
Liaison between functional units and project teams is facilitated by 'boundary riders' or integrating managers.

Selective Decentralisation
Reliance on highly trained experts in the adhocracy naturally inclines it to decentralise selectively. Decentralisation in the adhocracy is selective because it takes place according to the nature of the decisions to be made. It occurs in both the horizontal and vertical dimensions because experts are located throughout the structure.

Mintzberg goes on to distinguish in structural terms between what he calls the *operating adhocracy* and the *administrative adhocracy*. We shall include these in our overall discussion of the adhocracy's structural features.

The Operating Adhocracy
The operating adhocracy carries out its innovative work on the behalf of its clients. Advertising agencies and certain types of consulting firms are examples of this kind of organisation. An important structural characteristic of the operating adhocracy is that no distinction is made between administrative and operating work. This is because it is often difficult in project work to differentiate clearly between the planning and design of the work and its execution. Consequently,

"managers of the middle line and members of what in other organisations would be called the support staff – typically a highly trained and important group in the operating adhocracy – may take their place right alongside the operating specialists on the project teams" (Mintzberg 1983: 258).

The Administrative Adhocracy

Unlike the operating adhocracy, the administrative adhocracy undertakes projects for its own ends, and distinguishes between its administrative component and its operating core. This distinction becomes necessary when the organisation needs to be innovative in an area which is managed best as a MB. There are three paths open to the organisation under such circumstances. First, it can do away with its operating core altogether by contracting out the work to other organisations; or, second, it can separate-off its operating core from its administrative component. Both options allow the organisation to focus on development work. The first by containing its innovative work in what Mintzberg calls an administrative component consisting of experts and support staff, and the second by simply getting rid of non-innovative work altogether. A third possibility is that the operating core is automated and it therefore virtually runs itself.

Few Staff Specialists

The fact that the adhocracy makes little use of standardisation to coordinate its activities means that it has little need for staff specialists.

Strategy Formation

Strategy formation in the adhocracy is more a function of decisions made about particular projects than it is a conscious activity on the part of senior management. When innovation is the primary activity of an organisation, the results of its work can rarely be predetermined. Under these circumstances, attempts to formulate strategy are pointless or, even worse, counter-productive (because they limit the organisation's flexibility). At most, therefore, we might encounter a general form of action planning which sets out broad, flexible guidelines within which projects are carried out, with specific decisions flowing from these to form the basis of strategy. To reiterate, it is only through the making of specific (project) decisions – which projects to undertake and whether these succeed or not – that strategies evolve in the adhocracy.

Functions of Senior Management

Both because of the nature of its activities and the creative experts it employs, the adhocracy throws up difficult human resource problems. These usually entail interpersonal rivalry and conflict, and their resolution requires considerable human relations skill on the part of senior managers in the strategic apex. Top managers must also have close personal contact with individual projects in order to maintain some form of performance control. However, perhaps the most important function of senior management in the adhocracy is to liaise with the external environment. This is particularly so, of course, in the case of the operating adhocracy which relies on external clients for its project work. For instance, a consulting firm which engages primarily in innovative work would not survive very long if it was not constantly on the look out for new clients.

Environmental Factors

The dominating environmental influences which incline organisations toward adhocracy are complexity and dynamism. The environment is dynamic because innovative work is unpredictable; it is also clearly complex because innovative work involves sophisticated knowledge and skills.

Yet these broad terms – dynamism and complexity – encompass many different contingencies which exert pressure in different ways and at varying intensities. As a result, variants of the adhocracy configuration emerge. To give just two examples, Mintzberg (1983) describes the entrepreneurial adhocracy and the competitive adhocracy.

The Entrepreneurial Adhocracy

This structural configuration is a hybrid of the adhocracy and the simple structure. Typically, they are small firms controlled by a single individual. 'Unit producers' which custom-make all their products to order might be structured in this way. The major factors in this type of organisation's environment are obviously frequent and unpredictable product change, and hence dynamism; and specialised skill and knowledge requirements, and hence complexity.

Another example is provided by the small newspaper or magazine which might involve elements of the administrative adhocracy and the simple structure. Again, the environment of this type of organisation is clearly dynamic and complex. The work of photographers, reporters, and editors must be synthesised, and this calls for adhocracy. On the other hand, the distribution and printing functions of such an enterprise are relatively stable activities which can be structurally separated from other parts of the organisation and lend themselves to being organised as a MB. But because the organisation is small, a single individual, the editor, retains overall control of the enterprise as in the SS.

The Competitive Adhocracy

This organisational type is most often found in environments where *product competition* is the major determinant of dynamism and complexity. Product competition is more difficult to deal with than, say, competition based on pricing or marketing, and so adhocracy is called for.

Although strictly speaking they are not environmental factors, two other variables exert an important influence on the operating adhocracy: *success* and *aging*. Both of these factors incline the organisation toward the PB. This happens because success makes the organisation concentrate its activities in one or two areas, making for more stability, greater security of tenure, and so on, which are all features of the PB. Age also has this effect.

The administrative adhocracy, on the other hand, cannot respond in this way to success and aging without threatening its own survival. A newspaper would collapse very quickly if it ceased to be innovative and flexible.

Problems Associated with the Adhocracy

The adhocracy is the least researched configuration of the six discussed in this chapter. It is a relatively new form of organisation and there has therefore not been sufficient time for practical experience and research to generate much evidence. The little that there is suggests three major problems.

Ambiguity and Individual Differences: The adhocracy is both organic and decentralised. It is characterised by fluidity, uncertainty, and ambiguity. Some people simply do not like working in such conditions. They prefer more structure, more stability, and well-defined relationships. Even committed members of adhocracies periodically experience frustration and dissatisfaction with its dominant features. Many years ago, Burns and Stalker (1961) reported that "in these situations, all managers some of the time, and many managers all of the time, yearn for more definition and structure" (pp. 122–123). As a consequence, adhocracies are frequently riddled with political intrigue of a particularly virulent kind. The organic nature of the structure (and therefore the absence of clear rules and regulations, and so on) means that political infighting takes place with no holds barred. As we indicated earlier, a major task of senior management is to see that the widespread conflict and aggression which results is allowed to work itself out in a way which threatens neither organisational performance nor individual autonomy and creativity.

Organisational Effectiveness and Time Consumption: In the adhocracy, because of its organic, decentralised structure and the nature of its work, ideas take a long time to develop, and decisions take a long time to make. Unlike the MB where, when a decision needs to be taken, a senior manager does so quickly, in the Adhocracy everyone must have a say. But widespread involvement of this type can have decided benefits, too. For one thing it can foster general support for decisions and hence facilitate successful implementation. In the MB, remember, the opposite is likely to occur because operators have not been involved in the decision making process and are therefore more likely to resist implementation. The problem of time consumption in the adhocracy therefore lies in determining when the cost/benefit ratio of the democratic process has reached unacceptable limits.

Pressures to Bureaucratise: The first two problems mentioned generate pressure to bureaucratise. Bureaucracy is clearly anathema to creative, innovative work, and must therefore be resisted. This is problematic.

7.1.7   The Missionary Organisation (MO)[5]

Key parts of the organisation:	Strategic apex and organisation as a whole
Main method of coordination:	Standardisation of norms and values
Major structural characteristics:	Small units, loosely organised and highly decentralised, but with strong normative controls
Environmental factors:	Can be workable in most external environmental settings; internal environment must possess committed employees; more difficult in environments where work is primarily professional or innovative.

---

5   This section is based on Mintzberg (1989).

The emergence in the 1980s of organisational culture as a widely acknowledged major influence on organisational performance led Mintzberg (1988, 1989) to develop his sixth configuration of organisational structure. It is based partly on Japanese methods of organisation which place such heavy reliance on the creation of cohesive, positive working cultures for bringing about and sustaining high levels of quality and productivity. The psychological climate, or culture, which results gives an organisation its own distinctive 'personality' and 'feel'. We can sense very quickly differences between organisations' cultures. Mintzberg (1989) prefers to use the term *ideology* to describe these intangible yet very real organisational characteristics. He defines ideology thus:

"specifically, an ideology is taken here to mean a rich system of values and beliefs about an organisation, shared by its members, that distinguishes it from other organisations ... the key feature of such an ideology is its unifying power. It ties the individual to the organisation, generating an 'esprit de corps', a 'sense of mission', in effect, an integration of individual and organisational goals that can produce synergy" (Mintzberg 1989: 224).

In Chapter 9, we shall examine the concepts of organisational culture and national culture more fully. Here, for the sake of completeness, we provide an account of Mintzberg's general interpretation of the notion of ideology in organisations.

There are two broad sets of circumstances in which we can perceive the missionary configuration most clearly. The first, which we can call the missionary organisation *per se*, occurs in organisations which are clearly committed to some unifying and inspiring purpose which members of the organisation can easily identify with; this makes the organisation distinctive, and places it in a market niche where the ideology can grow and strengthen. Mintzberg (1989) mentions the traditional Israeli kibbutz as a classic example of the MO.

The second set of circumstances is where a strong ideology is *overlaid* on some other structural configuration. This, according to Mintzberg, is what Japanese enterprises – such as Toyota and Honda – manage to do so successfully; and it is what many American and other Western firms are trying to emulate with varying degrees of success.

The Formation of Organisational Ideology

The following conditions are necessary for the establishment of a strong organisational ideology:

Mission and Leadership: Charismatic, transformational leaders who are able to inspire a group of like-minded organisational members to pursue shared goals, and who can establish trust and loyalty among followers, lay the foundations of organisational ideology. This is much easier to accomplish in a new or developing organisation than it is in an established one.

Myths and Traditions: Once established, an organisational ideology is reinforced and sustained through myths, stories, and legends which recount significant events in the organisation's history. This provides members with a common store of experiences expressed in language which only they – the initiated – can understand and appreciate.

Identification: This can be developed in a number of ways: first, it can occur *naturally*, simply because a new member is attracted to the organisation's ideology. Second, new members can be *selected* because they are seen to possess appropriate values, attitudes, and beliefs. Third, identification can be *evoked* through induction programmes in which new members are *indoctrinated* and *socialised* so as to reinforce natural or selected commitment. Fourth, the weakest form of identification is based on *calculation*, in which individuals conform to the demands of organisational ideology in order to acquire material rewards such as pay and promotion, and other benefits.

The Missionary Organisation

Two aspects of the MO stand out. First, it has a clear and inspirational purpose, and dynamic leadership, which bind its members together. Second, it relies on the standardisation of norms and values to achieve control and coordination. This latter characteristic means that it is also fundamentally a bureaucracy, and in this sense, therefore, quite rigid (that is, inflexible about its mission and ideology). But it also means that there tend to be few formal rules and regulations, and little in the way of formal planning and control, so hardly any technostructure or hierarchy of authority is necessary. All of these things are in a sense already built-in to member behaviour by virtue of their shared values and beliefs and strong commitment to the mission of the organisation. In this situation, leadership and management is concerned much less with the imposition of direction than with "the protection and enhancement of the common ideology; the leader is expected to inspire others to pursue the mission, perhaps also to interpret the mission, but never to change the mission" (Mintzberg 1989: 229). It is also important in the MO that organisational units remain small in size so that strong ideology can be maintained through personal contact. Mintzberg also suggests that the egalitarianism of the MO is better suited to agriculture than to industry because technology, expertise, and job specialisation (associated with industry) increase the needs for an administrative hierarchy.

Types of Pure Missionary Organisation

Mintzberg identifies three types of pure MO.

Reformers: These MOs attempt to change the world directly. The most obvious examples are religious organisations, but others would include environmental and conservation organisations such as Greenpeace and Friends of the Earth.

Converters: These organisations attempt to change the world indirectly "by attracting members and changing them" (Mintzberg 1989: 231). For example, Alcoholics Anonymous attempts to reduce alcoholism by discouraging its members from drinking. A reformer MO, on the other hand, would attempt to reduce alcoholism by lobbying for government legislation to prevent the sale of liquor.

Cloisters: 'Total institutions' (Goffman 1961) are those which exert a complete control over their members' lives by housing them physically, and restricting their behaviour organisationally (e.g., mental hospitals, prisons, etc.). The cloister MO is similar, in that it is a 'closed system', but rather than having a 'control' mission, as in the case of a prison or a mental hospital, it is designed to "allow its members to pursue a unique lifestyle" (Mintzberg 1989: 232). Monasteries provide a clear example of this type of organisation. However, such organisations, because they are closed-off from the outside world, face problems of isolation and of renewal (of finding new members).

Ideology as an Overlay on Other Structural Configurations

Most MOs would fall into this category. The pure form of MO would simply not be applicable to most organisations. Accordingly, where other structural configurations can benefit from stronger ideology or culture, or where such ideology already exists, it tends to be an overlay on a more conventional structural form. For example, Toyota and McDonald's both have strong organisational cultures or ideologies which have been superimposed on machine bureaucracy configurations. In the case of Toyota, loyalty and commitment to the firm are key elements which are reinforced by human resource management practices such as lifetime employment, consensus decision making, collective responsibility, seniority-based promotion, implicit, informal control, little specialisation, single-status facilities (dress, canteen, parking etc.), and a concern for the general welfare of employees (Oliver & Wilkinson 1988; Gleave & Oliver 1990; Whitley 1990).

But it is easier to superimpose an MO on some configurations than on others. Simple structures (or entrepreneurial configurations) and machine bureaucracies would seem to be the most amenable.

Simple structures and entrepreneurial configurations are the most likely to have a strong charismatic leader who can create and share an inspirational vision and inspire others to work hard to realise it. The process will be less straightforward in the machine bureaucracy because of alienation and high levels of calculative involvement or instrumental orientations to work (we shall discuss these ideas more fully in Chapter 9) at lower levels within the operating core. The divisionalised form will pose similar problems, complicated by the fact that different divisions will have different missions.

However, perhaps the most serious obstacles to the superimposition of the MO are to be found in the professional bureaucracy and the adhocracy. This is because expertise in organisations – a major feature of the professional bureaucracy – fosters status differentials which cut across the egalitarian ideals of the MO. In the adhocracy, on the other hand, higher levels of role ambiguity and uncertainty are frequently associated with political intrigue and interpersonal conflicts which are anathema to the MO. Nevertheless, because, as Mintzberg says, "these organisations often have missions that are either intrinsically noble or exciting (such as curing the ill or developing high-technology products) ... ideological overlays may in fact occur with some frequency" (1989: 235).

It seems likely to us that the MO configuration will become more common in different countries around the world, either as a function of direct 'Japanisation' (Oliver & Wilkinson 1988), such as that taking place in Britain and elsewhere, or as a result of attempts by Western organisations to emulate the Japanese. We feel that many African cultures may be particularly suited to this form of organisation (Blunt 1978). But we are equally persuaded that these configurations will not take root in Africa until appropriate institutional frameworks and imperatives of effective organisation – such as strategic management, effective transformational leadership, and clear links between performance and reward – have been established (Blunt 1990a, 1991).

7.2   Implications for Managers and Management Development

This chapter has extended our case for what is known as the contingency approach to organisational analysis. Contingency theory disclaims the view that there is one best way to organise in all situations. It suggests instead that organisational structure will vary according to a range of internal and external contingencies. The six structural types described are merely illustrative of adaptive response to frequently encountered clusters of contingencies. At most, they represent rough benchmarks for the analysis of the structure and functioning of individual organisations.

Mintzberg (1989) argues that his configurations of organisational structure extend earlier versions of contingency theory by introducing notions of power and culture into the equation. This is consistent with our own position, which might better be described now as *neo* contingency theory. Our position incorporates also what we might call Mintzberg's 'creativity' hypothesis, which states:

"The most interesting organisations ... invent novel approaches that solve festering problems and so provide all of us with new ways to deal with our world of organisations. Their effectiveness depends on ... two things: a rich understanding of the world of organisations and a propensity to (use) that knowledge in creative ways" (1989: 281).

The strategic management of organisations and the people within them is clearly of critical importance to the effectiveness of organisations everywhere. For example, Dowling and Schuler (1991) suggest that "the fundamental strategic management problem is to keep the strategy, structure and human resource dimensions of the organisation in direct alignment" (p. 19). So far in this book we have discussed the first of these fundamentals (strategy), and mentioned certain aspects of the third (human resource management). This chapter offers a framework for dealing with the second fundamental, that of organisational structure.

However, our presentation and discussion of the six configurations should not be taken to imply that these are all that is needed to describe accurately the structure of any organisation, or that any particular organisational structure will fit neatly into one of the configurations. This is clearly not the case. Indeed, it is probably safe to say that most organisations will display characteristics of more than one configuration, thereby constituting what Mintzberg (1989) calls a 'hybrid' structure. Mintzberg's (1989) investigations of this question in Canada reveal that about 50% of organisations would have hybrid structures, about 20% simple structures, about 10% would be divisionalised forms, and adhocracies and professional bureaucracies would account for about 5% each. In our experience, managers invariably derive considerable insight from being able to use these configurations to analyse the structures of their own organisations.

It also seem reasonable to suppose – given the markedly different features of each configuration and our increasing understanding of national cultural differences (*see* Chapter 9) – that the frequency with which we observe structural types will vary as a function of national culture. It seems clear, for example, that the overseas Chinese have a preference for family businesses which resemble the simple structure, while the South Korean business groups (*chaebol*) are most similar to the divisionalised form, and Japanese firms conform more closely to the missionary form (e.g., Redding 1989; Whitley 1990). American industry, on the other hand, appears to have a greater proportion of machine bureaucracies than we might see in other countries (Mintzberg 1989). This may be dysfunctional in today's world markets. American industry is still striving for a fit between strategy, structure, culture, human resources, and environment which many organisations, particularly in East Asian countries such as Japan, Singapore, Taiwan, and Korea, manage to have achieved sufficiently to maintain their competitiveness. In Africa, our view is that machine bureaucratic-like structures dominate in public and private organisations. This imposes severe limits on organisational effectiveness, and poses considerable challenges for organisational design: that is, improving the fit between organisations and their internal and external environments.

Accordingly, the job for managers everywhere is to strive to achieve a fit between the various dimensions (strategy, structure, culture, etc.) of organisation. The configurations we have discussed can be enormously helpful in this respect. As Mintzberg (1989) asserts, "configuration helps not only to understand organisations but also to manage them. It facilitates diagnosis ... and that in turn facilitates prescription" (p. 261).

Our *neo* contingency approach to organisation and management therefore incorporates the idea of fit between organisations and their internal and external environments – defined in the broadest terms. A detailed understanding of the various components, and the creative use of this knowledge, will clearly help to ensure that such fit is attained. It is clear also that managers can acquire a great deal of this knowledge through training, and that management training programmes should take greater account of such strategic issues as structure and culture. Once again, however, in Africa we feel that the critical step of implementation and knowledge *use* can only be taken in institutional and organis-ational environments which differ radically from many of those extant in the continent.

Chapter 8:   Participation and Decentralisation

For some twenty years or more, a key feature of the debate surrounding new forms of work organisation has been the distribution of power within them. Decentralisation and participation are both concerned with this question although the term 'decentralisation' tends to be used more in connection with public organisations, while 'participation' tends to be the expression employed to describe similar organisational arrangements in private enterprises. Partly for these reasons two separate literatures have developed in parallel. The gap between them is particularly evident in the development context, where decentralisation has been a central topic for many years (e.g., Conyers 1984), but where the notions of contingency theory until recently were regarded as new ideas (e.g., Conyers 1986).

But despite some conceptual difficulties, the ideas of decentralisation have had a major impact on public organisations in Africa (Adamolekun 1991b; Adamolekun, Robert & Laleye 1990). Notions of worker participation have also been applied and debated in development settings, including Africa, but with less frequency; their impact in private and public enterprises has been less marked (e.g., Kanawaty & Thorsrud 1981).

This chapter analyses the notions of participation and decentralisation, and provides examples of them from a number of African countries. These notions are at the centre of major industrial reform programmes, both current (e.g., China) and planned (e.g., Vietnam), in many parts of the world, and the literature on the issues involved is growing steadily; of particular interest for socialist countries in transition is the increasingly well-documented experience of the Peoples' Republic of China (e.g., Child & Lu 1990; White 1991a, 1991b). Evidence from this country and from other sources continues to suggest that the redistribution of power in organisations can lead to higher levels of effectiveness and improved quality of working life, but only in certain circumstances. Neither decentralisation nor participation should be regarded as a panacea for problems of organisation, or development more generally. We advocate this view knowingly, at a time when the sweeping economic reforms taking place – and in prospect – in the centrally controlled command economies of Eastern Europe, the former Soviet Union, China, and Vietnam are creating a tidal wave of pressure in favour of open markets, economic liberalisation, and decentralisation. In the minds of an increasing number of economists and other social engineers, market liberalisation and the decentralisation of control are seen as necessary and inseparable conditions for economic development (e.g., Sommariva, *in press*). Although we do not have the space to argue it here, we are not persuaded that a new 'one best way' has been discovered. It seems to us that there is more than enough evidence to suggest that sustained high levels of economic performance are associated with a variety of organisational forms, and that decisions regarding which organisational form to use should be based on the circumstances in which it is to be employed and, in particular, the goals of the organisation, the nature of the work force, and the institutional frameworks in which it is embedded (Clegg 1990).

8.1   Participation

There is a persistent doubt among workers as to whether participation is simply another management device designed to elicit greater productivity or whether it is a genuine attempt both to humanise work and to improve organisational effectiveness. Pateman's (1970) classic definition of the term acknowledged this uncertainty by describing situations in which workers are offered full explanations of decisions already make by management as *pseudo participation*. Here, measures to increase productivity are introduced by stealth, under the cover of what is frequently a facade of concern for the opinions and needs of workers. Pateman sees *full participation* existing only in circumstances where each member of an organisation, or decision making body within it, has equal power to determine the outcome of deliberations associated with the decisions in question. *Partial participation* occurs where there is mutual exchange of information and influence between two parties before a decision is taken, but the right to decide finally resides in one group alone (usually management). However, for convenience, in the present discussion, the term participation will be used to refer to both partial and full participation.

8.1.1   Levels of Participation

Three levels of participation have been identified by Wall and Lischeron (1977): local, medium and distant.

Local Participation

This is broadly analogous to what transpires in the previously mentioned semi-autonomous work group (see Chapter 5). Workers exert an influence on decisions which affect their own jobs: how the work is to be carried out, and how tasks are to be scheduled and allocated among individuals. Such decision making is confined to certain localised areas of the organisation, and therefore has limited relevance for the organisation as a whole.

Medium Participation

This encompasses the broad range of decision making activities which normally are associated with middle management jobs. These decisions affect more people in the organisation, say a whole department or division, and include such matters as personnel selection and placement, performance appraisal, training, and the purchase of equipment and materials. In the case of personnel selection, for example, a participative approach might entail the involvement in parts of the selection process of those who work in the same department as, or interact with, the position to be filled. Where training is concerned, decisions as to who should be trained, and how, might be arrived at collectively by those involved.

Distant Participation

This takes place at the highest levels of an organisation. Decisions taken, which affect everyone in the organisation and the organisation's relationship with its environment, are no longer the sole responsibility of senior management. Distant participation usually means that representatives from other parts of the organisation take part in the decision making process. Decisions thus made help to determine the growth and diversification of the organisation, and overall questions of policy.

The *form* of participation (or the methods and systems through which participation takes place) which is most appropriate depends partly on the level at which it occurs.

8.1.2 Forms of Participation

The major distinction here is drawn between *direct* and *indirect* forms of participation, or what Walker (1974) calls *descending* and *ascending* participation. The former, direct participation, refers to situations in which individual workers participate personally in decision making. They actively contribute to decision making procedures by speaking for themselves or presenting their own views in a context which grants them equal power to other participants. Indirect participation, on the other hand, involves participation through representation. Typically, elected worker representatives from lower levels of the organisation serve on decision making or advisory committees at higher levels in the organisation, and thus represent the views of their constituents.

8.2 Decentralisation

Following Conyers (1984), our definition of decentralisation includes the notions of devolution and deconcentration. It "is confined to decentralisation of government and, in the main, to decentralisation to sub-national levels (territorial decentralisation) rather than decentralisation to parastatal or non-government organisations (functional decentralisation); (and) defined relatively broadly as any transfer of power from the centre to such sub-national level" (Conyers 1984: 187).

Now that we have a clearer picture of what is implied by the terms decentralisation and participation, we are in a position to examine some African examples.

8.3 African Examples of Participation

So far, most worker participation schemes in Africa have been of the indirect or representative kind, but attempts are also being made to introduce direct forms of participation. Algeria has probably had more experience than any other African country with worker participation, or workers' self-management as it is called there, and accordingly that is where our discussion begins.

8.3.1   Algeria[1]

One of the major products of the Algerian revolution, which began with independence in the summer of 1962, was the workers' committees which were set up to manage agricultural estates and factories. These committees became formally known as *autogestion* (self-management). Their aim was to break down the rigid forms of organisation inherited from the colonial period, and to provide instead decentralised and democratic organisations which ensured humane working conditions and protected the dignity of all employees. These were laudable objectives, but they were to meet with mixed success in the years after independence up to the present (Clegg 1971; Nellis 1983; Lee & Nellis 1990). The history of these developments is instructive because it highlights a number of problems common to many countries in Africa, and the Third World in general. This section describes the Algerian form of self-management and analyses the reasons for its uneven progress.

Algerian Self-Management

The Algerian system of self-management (*autogestion*) was instituted by the government of Algeria's first Chief of State, Ahmed Ben Bella, with the publication, on 22 March 1963, of the *decrets de mars*.

Initial Developments: Autogestion

The *decrets de mars* provided for the organisation and management of manufacturing, mining and 'artisanal' concerns as well as agricultural enterprises. The proposed system of self-management consisted of four basic parts: the workers' general assembly; the workers' council; the management committee; and the director. These parts provided a framework for a combination of ascending and descending participation (*see* Blunt 1983).

The Fate of Self-Management Before 1970

The way in which Algerian workers reacted to self-management can be explained partly in terms of cultural norms and values. Clegg (1971) advances this argument when he states: "In order to assess the ability or desire of workers to participate in management, the role played by work in their lives must be gauged" (p. 170). Clegg suggests, and we would agree, that in societies like Algeria where there are high levels of unemployment or underemployment, severe constraints are placed on the worker, and work takes on a special meaning, which we describe later in this book as an instrumental orientation. Like workers all over Africa, the majority of Algerian workers "were, and still are, deeply immersed in an everyday struggle for material survival where the next job or the next wage packet becomes the limit of their horizon. Their attitude to self-management is radically circumscribed by this context. They tend to visualise their job in an instrumental fashion, according to the equation work equals money and security" (Clegg 1971: 172–3). Clegg argues, in fact, that the initial successes of self-management were due to material necessity: the collapse of colonial rule had left a vacuum in the organisational infrastruc-

---

1   This section draws heavily on Clegg (1971) and Nellis (1977, 1980, 1983).

ture of the country. In Clegg's view, the workers were faced with the choice of taking over the means of production themselves, or of economic ruin. There was little or no class consciousness in this movement, but simply a desire to ensure material survival. To quote Clegg again,

"The workers did not form comites de gestion in 1962 and thus implicitly seize control of the means of production for purely political reasons. They did so because not to work meant to starve and because elimination of the capitalist owner would mean higher wages" (1971: 173).

This instrumental orientation on the part of the workers was anticipated by the *decrets de mars* in the recommendations it contained for the distribution of profits. Workers were provided with a clear financial incentive to participate in the management of their organisations. But, with only a few exceptions, these incentives were never paid, and thus the workers' major hopes and needs were left unfulfilled. Widespread disillusionment followed quickly, and by 1964 the system of self-management was beginning to break down.

Their preoccupation with the satisfaction of material needs did not in itself indicate that the workers were hostile to self-management *per se* or incapable of making it work. It did show, however, that where basic needs are largely unfulfilled the success or failure of a system like self-management rests not so much on its ideological appeal or its recognition of higher-level needs like self-actualisation or autonomy, but rather on its ability to provide for the material well-being of participants. In other words, the early Algerian experience demonstrates that in order to be accepted, an alternative form of organisation operating in a climate of basic need deficiency first needs to demonstrate it capacity for satisfying such needs. Once this is accomplished, the implications that the system has for quality of working life and humanist ideals become increasingly important. This is not to say that workers who are concerned about basic need satisfaction are incapable of appreciating the workings of self-management. On the contrary, the Algerian evidence indicates that they understood the system and were able to assume control, but quickly lost interest when it failed to help them attain their major objective: the satisfaction of basic needs.

The 1971 Charter for la Gestion Socialiste des Enterprises
In certain respects the 1971 charter was similar to the *decrets de mars*. But, importantly, it sought also to ensure fair remuneration, a guarantee of social rights, protection against unemployment, equal pay for equal work, and opportunities for training (Nellis 1977).

While there were some similarities between the 1971 and 1963 charters, the tenor and detail of *la gestion socialiste* reflected a greater concern for productivity, and provided a dominant role for the representatives of management. Nevertheless, workers in public enterprises were given the opportunity to influence, if not determine, decisions associated with their own working lives, and the representatives of management, at the very least, had to modify their operational styles in order to accommodate themselves to this novel and challenging climate.

Self-Management After 1971: Implementation
The new charter, and an accompanying legal code, appeared in November 1971, but the
first practical application did not occur until January 1974. The pattern established in this
initial phase – of selecting small groups of enterprises, dividing them into units, conducting 'campaigns of explanation', selecting candidates, and then holding elections – was
repeated throughout 1975 and 1976. Nellis (1977) reports that by mid-1976 about 40
organisations, employing some 140,000 workers, were operating according to the principles of *la gestion socialiste*. Other industrial enterprises were being prepared for the new
system of management, and planning had begun for social service organisations and the
public administration sector. But the new system also encountered a number of problems.

Self-Management After 1971: Difficulties and Prospects
A noteworthy feature of the evaluation process of self-management in Algeria has been
the steady stream of information which has emerged. This material indicates that the
major difficulty emanates from the traditional clash of interests between workers and
managers. Managers have been accused of sabotaging the spirit and the letter of the
charter by ignoring the advice of the assemblies, and by withholding data necessary for
the making of decisions. Another reason for the limited implementation of *la gestion socialiste* "has been the leadership's view of the Algerian work force as a sort of pre-
proletariat, recently and violently torn from its peasant origins and culture, and in need of
a lengthy and closely supervised apprenticeship before it can be entrusted with the full
range of powers envisaged by the new system" (Nellis 1977: 549).

In 1980 Nellis concluded that "the Algerians have more trouble than most fitting the
ordinariness of their present practice to the grandeur of their ideology, and in spite of a
few areas of participatory progress, the ideology is more likely to be adjusted than the
practice" (1980: 420). He noted also an increasing tendency in Algeria to deal with
bureaucratic inefficiency and organisational malfunctioning by adopting "production
oriented, basically Western-devised procedures" (Nellis 1980: 420). This seems to have
been borne out by more recent developments (*see* Lee & Nellis 1990). Participatory institutions, it seems, have not helped to silence the complaints of the public who are served
by the Algerian administrative system. Rudeness, slowness, inefficiency, indifference and
corruption abound.

8.3.2   Tanzania

The foundations of indirect forms of worker participation in Tanzania were laid by the
country's first president, Julius K. Nyerere, in a circular issued in January 1970. The
circular decreed a significant increase in the representation and involvement of workers in
the management of enterprises. Formerly, worker representation had been confined to
workers' committees which had been set up in 1964 to act on behalf of workers in relation
to conditions of service, warnings, unfair dismissals and the like. But while the workers'
committees performed a valuable service, because of their restricted advisory powers they
did little to improve the workers' level of motivation or their understanding of the

functioning and purpose of the organisation as a whole. President Nyerere implied this himself in a much-quoted address at the opening of the Friendship Textile Mill in July 1968:

"We ask the people to work hard, yet in modern factories each man and woman is doing only a very small part of the whole process of production. How can he really go on year in year out taking a pride in that one job? The imaginative people can do it, but for the majority it is very hard to relate one simple task to the total output of the factory. Often the worker does not even know where his task fits into the whole scheme of things; he does not know what the factory as a whole is aiming at, and he does not know what progress they are making towards their combined aims. It is not sensible to expect people to be enthusiastic about their jobs under these circumstances" (Presidential Circular No. 1 of 1970: 1).

From the beginning, therefore, the proposals for worker participation in Tanzania were intended to improve both productivity and the quality of working life.

Indirect Participation in Tanzania

In February 1970 all parastatal organisations were directed to establish *workers' councils* as soon as possible, "to further industrial democracy in relation to the economic functions of the enterprise, and give the workers a greater and more direct responsibility in production" (Presidential Circular No. 1 of 1970: 3). Membership of the workers' councils was to be constituted as follows:

(a) the Chairman of the Party (TANU) branch established at the organisation;
(b) the manager or general manager;
(c) all heads of departments or sections;
(d) all members of the workers' committee;
(e) representatives elected in proportion to the number of employees in different departments or sections, provided that their number when added to category (d) was not greater than three-quarters of the total permanent membership (a), (b), (c) and (d).

Provision was also made for co-opting members from outside the enterprise, as and when required. These were to be selected jointly by management and the National Union of Tanzania Workers (NUTA), which was also entitled to have a representative. Fifty per cent of the membership was required for a quorum, and meetings were to be held at least once every six months, with emergency meetings being held whenever the need arose.

The functions of the workers' councils, as described in the Presidential Circular of 1970, are set out below:

1. to advise on the requirements of the existing wages and incomes policy as announced by the government from time to time;
2. to advise on the marketing of the commodity produced;
3. to advise on matters relating to the quality and quantity of the commodity produced;
4. to advise on planning;

5. to advise on other aspects of productivity, such as works and enterprise organisation, technical knowledge and workers' education;
6. to receive and discuss the balance sheet.

Parastatal organisations were also directed to set up *executive committees*, consisting of the general manager as chairman, heads of departments or sections, and workers' representatives elected by the workers' council from among the worker members of the council, to a maximum of not more than one-third of the total membership of the executive committee. Executive committees were empowered to scrutinise financial and production estimates, labour productivity programmes, export and marketing programmes and so on; and to advise generally on the efficient running of the organisation.

The formal role of the workers' councils is clearly an advisory one, but according to Jackson (1979), they have played an active part in furthering workers' interests, and the expectation has developed among workers "that whatever is decided by the workers' council should be automatically implemented by the board of directors" (p. 239). Jackson's general evaluation of the usefulness of the workers' councils and executive committees is a positive one, and he refers to instances where the technical know-how of workers has proved valuable in investment planning and other areas of management.

Detailed published case studies of the effectiveness of worker participation in Tanzania are scarce, however. One of the few is that of Maseko (1976) whose assessment of worker participation in the Friendship Textile Mill and the Tanganyika Electricity Supply Company for the most part supports the favourable impression gained by Jackson (1979). A problem which did emerge, however, was that of reluctance on the part of managers to allow workers to participate in decision making. Specifically, Maseko (1976) refers to secrecy and the withholding of information, and a generally autocratic manner on the part of managers: the latter behaviour has been officially censured, and is widely disapproved of in Tanzania. A set of guidelines issued by TANU deals with this issue in paragraph 15:

"There must be a deliberate effort to build equality between leaders and those whom they lead. For a Tanzanian leader it must be forbidden to be arrogant, extravagant, contemptuous and oppressive. The Tanzanian leader has to be a person who respects people, scorns ostentation and who is not a tyrant" (quoted in Jackson 1979: 240).

Shortly after the publication of these guidelines, there was considerable industrial unrest designed to expose and get rid of 'arrogant' and 'contemptuous' managers, and to achieve better working conditions and higher pay (Mihyo 1975). Some managers were literally locked out of plants, and workers simultaneously raised their productivity in order to demonstrate that the managers in question were superfluous. With a few exceptions – one being the Mount Carmel Rubber Factory documented by Mihyo (1975) – government was sympathetic to worker demands and willing to take note of their needs.

Later developments in indirect forms of participation in Tanzania were displayed in the replacement, in parastatal organisations, of boards of directors by management committees. This step was taken in order to limit the number of directorships which civil servants could hold and to increase the representation of citizens who were not civil servants. The directive was issued, in the form of circular from the president's office, in December 1974. The relevant excerpt reads:

"What we want in the Tanzanian situation are boards or management committees in which most of the directors are the workers themselves ... . In these committees 40 per cent will be people from outside the industry. The general manager of the industry or company will be the chairman of the committee and he is included in the 60 per cent of the members who are not workers of the industry" (quoted in *Jackson 1979: 241*).

The circular stipulated further that the workers nominated to be members of the management committees should be strong leaders in the workers' councils. In 1976 legislation was passed – the Parastatal Organisations Act – which specified that for all parastatal organisations nominated by the Minister responsible for that particular industry management committees would take the place of boards of directors.

Experiments with direct forms of participation have also been conducted in Tanzania, as we shall now see.

Direct Participation in Tanzania

A number of examples of direct participation in Tanzania have been provided by Kanawaty and Thorsrud (1981). The approach adopted by these researchers drew heavily on the Tavistock model described in Chapter 5, and applications of this framework in Norway and Sweden (e.g., Clarke 1989). Positive results were observed in two enterprises, a fishnet manufacturing firm and a forwarding and transport firm; marginal results were noted in one enterprise; and three enterprises were described as 'non-starters'. From these and a number of other case studies involving Indian organisations, Kanawaty and Thorsrud (1981) were able to draw general conclusions with respect to factors which facilitated, or hindered, the introduction, acceptance and effectiveness of direct forms of worker participation.

All of the firms which took part in the study were invited to attend a two-day induction workshop before changes were implemented. The workshop served to introduce participants to the idea of alternative forms of work organisation; to provide some basic guidelines for job and organisational design; to set out minimum conditions for group working; and to discuss implications for supervision and training and strategies for the introduction of change. Participants were then encouraged to work in company groups in order to define more closely problems in their own organisations and methods of dealing with them.

Positive Results

The pre-change work situation in the fish net plant was organised on an individual basis. Each worker operated one or more machines and was rewarded through incentive payments based on his own performance. This was the cause of considerable hostility and rivalry between workers. Absenteeism was also a major problem. The change to direct participation entailed the modification of individual work to group work in three sections of the plant, and the basis of the incentive scheme was adapted to group, as opposed to individual, performance. Several positive results were achieved, including higher levels of output, which generated extra income for the workers involved, improved cooperation between workers, and reduced levels of absenteeism. Similar successes were achieved in other parts of the plant. Two years after the initial changes were introduced, production for the firm as a whole was 17 per cent above target as compared with the corresponding month two years earlier when it had been 9 per cent below target. During the same period, overall absenteeism dropped from 8.9 to 1.9 per cent. Finally, job rotation improved to an extent which permitted the company to grant annual leave without closing down the plant.

At the forwarding and transport firm, work reorganisation began in the maintenance workshop and then spread to other departments. Four major task and skill groupings were identified in the workshop; mechanical repairs, auto-electric wiring, panel beating and tyre repairs. Only four of the twelve permanent employees were skilled mechanics; the remainder being assistants. The relatively unskilled assistants reported high levels of job dissatisfaction owing to the absence of promotional opportunities and the inadequate training facilities provided by the firm. There were also difficulties caused by the great pressure of work, which meant that many repair jobs had to be sent out to other firms.

The change to greater direct participation was achieved through each of the skilled mechanics agreeing to train three unskilled workers for a period of three months in his own speciality. Workers were then rotated for successive periods of three months to skilled mechanics in other areas. After a year, each of the operators had become reasonably skilled at the four major trades. Now that a pool of multiskilled workers existed, it was possible for rotation between tasks to occur, which helped to reduce the monotony of the work and to prevent boredom. As a result of these changes, expensive outside repair work became unnecessary, cooperation improved, opportunities for learning increased, and wages rose to match the workers' newly acquired skills. Positive results of much the same nature were subsequently achieved in other sections of the firm. Two years later there was a much higher rate of utilisation of vehicles and equipment, the firm's safety record had improved, training on the job had increased, leading to substantial wage rises, and absenteeism had fallen from 16.6 to 8 per cent.

Marginal Results

Work organisation in the cement company studied was confined to a small section with a staff of four electrical maintenance workers, each of whom had specialised skills. Again, the major feature of the altered working arrangements entailed job rotation, with the aims of producing multiskilled workers as opposed to specialists, and reducing monotony. The initial results were promising: maintenance took less time and job satisfaction rose. However, efforts to diffuse these methods to other parts of the organisation were opposed by the predominantly (80 per cent) foreign management, who contended that the risks involved in a major work reorganisation programme were too great.

The Non-Starters

Three firms were included in this group: a farm implements company, a bank and a cigarette company. In the farm implements firm, failure was put down to complete lack of interest and support on the part of management. At the bank, bureaucratic methods were too deeply entrenched; in the cigarette company, management felt that "participation of shop floor workers ... was unnecessary" (Kanawaty & Thorsrud 1981: 272).

Implications of the Results Achieved

There is nothing in these results to suggest that direct forms of worker participation are not as applicable in developing countries as they are in more advanced countries. But in accordance with conclusions reached elsewhere in this book, Kanawaty and Thorsrud (1981) acknowledge the importance of cultural factors: "social and cultural differences, however, dictate locally developed approaches rather than uniformly applied imported solutions" (p. 273). An unexpected finding was that the educational level of workers did not appear to be a critical factor in determining the success or failure of work reorganis-ation. Good results were obtained with illiterate workers as well as highly educated technical personnel. The major requirements seemed to be that all participants be willing and capable of learning on the job. Other factors which were conducive to success were:

1. *Careful selection of the enterprise and the point of entry:*
   First it was essential that management and unions were agreeable to the introduction of direct worker participation, and second, that there were good chances of success in the initial sites of work reorganisation.
2. *Thorough preparation of selected enterprises:*
   This entailed careful and detailed explanation of what was likely to be involved in work redesign, and participative problem identification and site selection involving as many people who were likely to be affected as possible.
3. *Internalisation of problems:*
   This was achieved by involving the work groups themselves in the redesign process. Workers were thus able to see that the problems being tackled were of direct relevance to their own work, and they became committed to the success of the new working arrangements.
4. *Maintenance of momentum:*
   In the organisations where positive results were achieved, work reorganisation was a continuing process and not an isolated event. Changes spread throughout the organis-ation.
5. *Wage incentives:*
   Kanawaty and Thorsrud (1981) regarded this as a crucial issue in Tanzania and other developing countries: "This is something one has be to very clear about right from the outset. Group work implies a revision of wages and incentives. In the two successful Tanzanian cases, wages were revised to compensate upgraded skills or the acquisition of new skills, and individual incentives were changed to group incentives ... Workers were motivated by the expectation that their wages would improve once they learnt more skills on the production line" (Kanawaty & Thorsrud 1981: 275).
6. *Mutual support between projects:*
   This applied to different projects mounted in the same organisation and to projects in a number of organisations.

Factors associated with failed work redesign attempts included the obverse of all of those mentioned above, plus the following:

1. *Changes in personnel:*
   The replacement of key managers or workers contributed to poor performance.
2. *Worker mistrust of change agents and/or management:*
   This was critical to the success or failure of the work redesign efforts. Capturing the workers' interest and commitment proved to be impossible under conditions of mistrust or suspicion.
3. *Rigid bureaucracy and autocratic management:*
   These were, and are, among the greatest impediments to the introduction of alternative forms of work organisation.

To sum up, the Tanzanian experience illustrates that new forms of work organisation are as applicable in developing countries as they are elsewhere, with the important proviso that they will probably work best where basic material needs are relatively well satisfied, and where thorough preparatory work has been done in advance. It is essential that the support of the managers, unions and workers involved be secured beforehand; that change agents receive proper instruction; and that supporting and advisory bodies exist to assist the work teams and to help maintain momentum. Perhaps most important of all in the African context, however, are the questions of basic need satisfaction and the modification of wages and incentive schemes. These last two factors in particular played a major role in Algeria, and although they were less explicitly and less frequently articulated in the Tanzanian programmes, they were no less important.

8.3.3   Zambia

Legal provision for indirect forms of worker participation in Zambia came into force in May 1976. By July 1978 there were 113 *works councils* in existence. The initiative for these developments had been provided by President Kenneth D. Kaunda in 1969. Originally, the intention had been to adopt the Yugoslavian system of workers' councils, which have fairly wide powers in the organisation. In the end, however, it was decided that workers' councils were probably too radical a departure from former systems and instead the West German model was followed. The *works councils* of the West German system tend to be dominated, to a greater degree than the original Yugoslavian workers' councils, by management, and they have relatively little real decision making power (Quemby 1975).

Works Councils in Zambia

The powers of the Zambian works councils have been restricted further by resistance from private enterprise (Fincham & Zulu 1979). The commercial farmers' lobby, for example, was strongly opposed to the idea of worker participation. Its efforts succeeded in raising the lower limit, where worker participation in the form of works councils became compulsory, from firms employing 25 workers to those employing 100 workers or more.

Moreover, a new category of worker, known as the 'eligible employee', was introduced which excluded part-time, seasonal and casual workers. As a high proportion of farm labour is hired on these terms, the vast majority of commercial farms did not have to form works councils.

Under the Act, the following powers are granted to works councils:

1. They are able to veto decisions in the fields of personnel management and industrial relations. Questions relating to recruitment and selection, remuneration of hourly-paid employees, discipline and redundancy must be agreed upon by a majority of the council before decisions can be implemented.
2. They may offer advice on matters pertaining to employee health and welfare. In practice, this means that management is required to obtain the opinion of the works council but not necessarily to heed it.
3. They are entitled to be informed of decisions already taken by management with respect to investment policy, financial control and economic planning. That is to say, management still retains the right to make the majority of decisions relating to the firm as a whole.

A point worth noting here is that the Act requires that the deliberations of works councils be kept secret from anyone outside the council. No information on matters discussed by works councils can therefore be passed to operators or shop floor workers. The size of works councils varies between three and fifteen members. They are composed of one-third management and two-thirds elected worker representatives. Worker members are elected by the eligible members of the work force by secret ballot, while management members are appointed by the chief executive. Council meetings are meant to take place regularly but not more than once a month.

An indication of how seriously the government regards worker participation is to be seen in the existence of an Industrial Participatory Democracy Department in the Office of the Prime Minister. How seriously workers and managers treat the matter is a different question, of course; one that has been researched by Fincham and Zulu (1979).

Attitudes Towards Worker Participation in Zambia

In December 1977, Fincham and Zulu (1979) conducted a questionnaire survey among members of works councils on the usefulness of this method of participation. Their survey included employees of public and private organisations. About 70 per cent of both management and workers felt that the councils were working quite well. Managers in private enterprise were the least enthusiastic about the concept, while workers in private firms were the most enthusiastic about its potential. More than half the respondents indicated that council meetings were marked by conflict, and that agreements were reached rarely and with difficulty. With respect to the implementation of decisions taken by the works councils, 70 per cent of management thought that 'agreed actions' were 'always implemented'; on the other hand, 73 per cent of workers thought that they were only implemented 'sometimes' or 'seldom'. In private firms the disagreement between management and workers on this issue was even more marked: 100 per cent of managers in private enterprise maintained that decisions taken by works councils were always implemented, while only 18 per cent of worker members in private firms shared this view. A disturbing feature of the responses concerned the number of worker representatives (46 per cent) who felt that their security of tenure was threatened when they spoke in council debates.

Fincham and Zulu (1979) also surveyed the attitudes of workers who were not members of works councils. While the majority of workers interviewed saw the potential of works councils for facilitating communication between management and workers, they complained that worker council members rarely discussed the agenda with them:

"Many workers were emphatic about wanting to know the agenda before meetings – aware that discussion with their representatives before decisions were taken was important. It seems that the great emphasis on secrecy in the industrial relations Act is having the effect of isolating councils from workers" (Fincham & Zulu 1979: 221).

But this is not the whole picture. There are a few documented case examples of the effectiveness of worker participation in Zambia. Martin (1980), for instance, describes the successful application, to squatter resettlement and upgrading, of a form of worker participation in management. Other research into forms of worker participation in Zambia (Blunt 1984) reveals a number of notable exceptions. To take just one example, a leading hotel in Lusaka operated a works council system of worker participation which was described – by one of its expatriate managers with extensive international experience – as the 'most successful I have come across anywhere'. The works council had *decision making* (veto) powers in relation to hiring and firing, discipline, promotion and employee welfare. Council authority extended also to the ratification of evidence in disciplinary matters: that is to say, a worker member of the council was needed to witness and verify instances of drunkenness, negligence or theft in order for the evidence to be admissible. The serving chairman of the council was a storeman (not a particularly senior position in the hotel) who had been elected by a majority vote among members of the council.

This is clearly an example of full participation, at the medium level, in the sense described by Pateman (1970), and referred to at the beginning of this chapter. The hotel management felt that the success of the works council played a great part in what was described as the 'extremely high levels of morale among all employees, and the low levels of turnover and absenteeism'. Many instances were recounted which indicated the extent of employee commitment over and above the call of duty. More research on successful organisations like this needs to be done before firm generalisations can be made, but this case, like some of those in Tanzania, does demonstrate the potential benefits that alternative forms of organisations hold for enterprises, their employees and their clients.

8.4   Some Examples of Decentralisation in Africa[2]

In this section we examine briefly some examples of local government organisation in the Ivory Coast, Senegal, Nigeria, Zambia and Kenya, and discuss the possible effects of the different policies employed.

8.4.1   Ivory Coast

Municipal government institutions in the Ivory Coast consist of two principal bodies: the municipal council and the municipal executive. The municipal council is elected by secret ballot on the basis of universal suffrage for a five year period. Communes of 10,000 members or less are served by a 25 member council; council size increases to a maximum of 50 elected members for communes with populations in excess of 100,000. The council has advisory powers only in relation to the formulation of regional economic and social development plans, which must be forwarded to the sponsoring central government department for assessment and approval. Such matters as the commune's budget, staff establishment, and the management and continuance/discontinuance of council services would be considered, and recommendations made.

The municipal executive consists of the mayor and his deputies; all of whom are elected by the municipal councillors. The executive is charged with determining the business to be dealt with at council meetings: supervising the collection of municipal income taxes and other levies, and overseeing municipal works. Executive meetings are not open to the public.

The mayor is responsible for the general administration of the commune, and has powers over local authority employees, the transfer of land, gifts, legacies and other assets, and so on. He is also responsible to the relevant government agency for the maintenance of law and order, public safety, peace, security, health, and the implementation of social, economic and cultural development policies determined by the central government.

Financial and human resources are provided to municipal governments by the central authority. Aloki (1989) concludes that: "broadly speaking, the territorial administrative breakdown is guided, in the main, by principles based on considerations of a technical order" (p. 408).

8.4.2   Senegal

According to Vengroff and Johnston (1987), "decentralisation efforts in Francophone African countries are both rarer and far less ambitious than those in Anglophone states. The decentralisation programme launched by Senegal over a decade ago is an important exception" (p. 273).

---

2   This section is based largely on Aloki (1989), Conyers (1986) and Cohen & Hook (1987).

Rural communities in Senegal comprise villages within a geographical area of a radius of 5–10 km and have populations of between 5,000 and 8,000. Rural councils govern community affairs. Two thirds of council members are elected by universal suffrage from candidates nominated by political parties. The remaining members are representatives drawn from cooperatives in the community. "The chairman of the rural council is elected by the council from among those of its members elected by universal suffrage" (Aloki 1989: 409).

Authority is devolved to rural councils which gives them powers to determine land usage, settlement of land tenure disputes, and the erection of temporary and permanent dwellings within their boundaries. Budgetary matters are determined centrally, but many community activities are financed from revenue generated by rural land taxes, although communities have no control over the rate of taxation (Vengroff & Johnston 1987).

The council chairman has similar powers and responsibilities to those of a mayor in a municipal setting: he or she is responsible for the promulgation and enforcement of statutes and regulations, and the maintenance of law and order, public security and hygiene. He or she is the person to whom the village chiefs in the community report.

As opposed to the Ivory Coast, where development policy is designed to encourage export oriented agricultural production driven by large commercial farming operations, policy in Senegal is intended more to encourage and facilitate local agricultural production for internal consumption. Local government in Senegal probably has more power for this reason, and there are greater attempts made there to distribute technical know-how, and equipment, to peasant farmers. According to Aloki (1989), in 1985, such policy "was strengthened ... by widening (rural competency) to include ore-working (phosphates), crop diversification, the 'Senegalisation' of jobs and ... less externally reliant development. This helped increase peasant farmer responsibility, while relaxing the framework of (central) government ... supervision and laying the emphasis on food self-sufficiency" (p. 412).

However, if we accept that financial autonomy is one of the critical features of successful decentralisation, we are forced to modify slightly our assessment of the Senegalese case. As with many other instances of decentralisation in Africa, in Senegal "authority is ... delegated to local organisations but they are not given the resources to perform their new functions" (Rondinelli, Nellis & Cheema 1984: 31). Moreover, those units charged with providing technical support to rural communities, the CERs (*Centres d' Expansion Rural*), are themselves underfinanced and under-staffed. Vengroff and Johnston (1987) conclude:

"The fact that the budgets of the rural communities were extremely small, and that even services such as water and health are still lacking in most rural areas, suggest that it will be many years before the orientation of the councils can be expected to change. Demands for very basic services such as health and water continue to dominate the thinking of rural councils. Council resources are so limited that even these fundamental needs are, at best, only partially dealt with. The involvement of the councils in 'productive' projects only

seems possible through external financing. However, the council itself generally has little or no influence over externally funded projects" (pp. 286–287).

8.4.3   Nigeria

There are three main areas of local government in Nigeria: councils consisting of directly elected and government appointed members; local offices of the various ministries; and central government branches responsible for providing a variety of services.

Councils are headed by a chairman elected by the councillors. Councils have two committees, one dealing with general and financial affairs, the other with education. Committee members are elected from the Council by the Council. "Political leaders also sit on the Council in order to supervise the use of federal technical and financial assistance provided to local government" (Aloki 1989: 412).

The chief executive of local government in Nigeria is the local government chairman who is appointed by central government and selected from traditional leaders in the area. This person has overall authority over all arms of local government, with the exception of the armed forces and the police. Primary responsibilities of this office include education, health, hygiene, road construction and maintenance, garbage collection and disposal, agricultural extension services, and so on.

Funding for all local government operations is determined centrally. Human resources are also allocated centrally – by the Ministry of Local Government and Chieftaincy Affairs – and costs are recovered from state budgets.

Aloki's view is that the Nigerian government is successfully pursuing a decentralist policy aimed at stimulating agricultural self-sufficiency by improving distribution channels for seed and fertilizer, increasing levels of mechanisation of cereal farms, providing credit facilities, management and training services, building of grain storage facilities, and establishing efficient and effective marketing mechanisms. General economic policies which set guaranteed minimum producer prices for certain foodstuffs, ban the importation of certain foods, and provide for dam construction and irrigation projects are also supportive of the government's decentralist strategy.

8.4.4   Zambia

According to Conyers (1986), Zambia's 1980 decentralisation reforms are similar to those introduced in a number of African countries. Aimed at increasing public participation through participatory democracy, the Zambian reforms had two main features. In the first place, local government councils were replaced by district councils made up of locally elected officials of the national party (UNIP), members of parliament from the area, and officials appointed by UNIP headquarters. The district governor, "an appointed official who is head of the party and the government at district level" (Conyers 1986: 596), acts as chairman of the district council. In the second place, district councils have (theoretically) assumed responsibility for all central and local government functions in their areas of jurisdiction including some control over staff and finance.

These reforms have advanced the cause of decentralisation in that the new district councils have considerably more delegated power and authority than their predecessors, the local government councils, but can be said to have retarded it in that there is less local representation on district councils than was the case with the local government councils. It is also clear, according to Conyers (1986), that "one of the main objectives (of the reforms) was to strengthen the role of the national party and improve central government administration. This does not necessarily mean that the majority of local people will not benefit from the reforms, but it does not guarantee that they will" (p. 596).

8.4.5   Kenya[3]

The rationale for decentralised planning in Kenya has a number of strands. First, it was recognised that agriculture is one of the mainstays of economic development and that agricultural productivity is sensitive to the degree of centralisation/ decentralisation in planning. Second, information on local areas, on which to base centralised planning, was either not available or unreliable. Third, special expertise and knowledge existed in local areas and this needed to be tapped effectively. Fourth, as with all change, involvement in the design process and problem solving by local people was thought likely to increase commitment to change and facilitate its introduction. Fifth, owing to "significant ecological, demographic and historical differences between and within regions and districts (it was) ... difficult to formulate a coherent national approach to national development" (Cohen & Hook 1987: 79). Lastly, it was thought that decentralised planning would have the benefits of: highlighting government budgetary allocations, thereby increasing the possibilities for greater equity and rationality in budgetary decision making by central authorities; increasing the likelihood of identifying groups or areas of special local need such as pastoralists, women, the landless, and so on; and improving the coordination and control of operating ministries, development programmes and projects in a particular area.

Standing in the way of such decentralised planning were a number of obstacles, including a lack of know-how at the centre for creating and managing a decentralised planning system; relatively low levels of enthusiasm for the idea among local government officials and field ministry officers who saw themselves as owing allegiance first and foremost to their own authority or ministry rather than to the planning ministry; concern among field professionals that increased decentralisation would create more opportunities for politically motivated behaviour, at the expense of technical and other considerations; concern that regional imbalances brought to light through the new planning process might foment political unrest; a reluctance by officials at the centre to relinquish power; and the view held by "some national political leaders that centralisation of decision making was essential to nation-building" (Cohen & Hook 1987: 79).

---

3   Much of this section is adapted from Cohen & Hook (1987).

The arguments presented above in favour of decentralised planning in Kenya, and the constraints which needed to be overcome in institutionalising the system, are likely to be among those which would need to be taken into account in assessing the viability of decentralisation in many African contexts. A number of important inferences from the Kenyan experience have been drawn by Cohen and Hook (1987), and these might well constitute useful guideposts to decentralisation elsewhere in the African continent.

Discretionary Funds and Local Authority over Them
Unless discretionary funds of a sufficient magnitude to satisfy at least some local needs are made available for local authority allocation, decentralised planning is unlikely to be taken seriously by local leaders. Cohen and Hook (1987) suggest two possibilities: first, the establishment of donor and government-financed local development funds (of sufficient size) from which districts would be able to draw agreed shares to be spent as they saw fit; and second, allowing districts the authority to generate their own revenue to "support the recurrent costs which the district focus will generate but which government cannot afford and donors will not support" (p. 86).

Management Capacity at the Local Level
In Kenya, District Development Committees were too large (70–90 members), met too infrequently, and probably lacked the management skills – particularly in such areas as financial management – needed to manage operating ministry programmes and projects effectively and efficiently.

Training and Staff Development
The Kenyan experience highlights the need for training at all levels in such areas as: district-based government development strategies, procedures and regulations; longer term technical training in, for example, various aspects of management; training of trainers; and so on.

Local Infrastructure
Decentralisation can complicate the completion and maintenance of local infrastructure projects (e.g., roads, bridges etc.) because projects planned locally are dependent on operating ministry officials for their implementation, and on "vulnerable recurrent budget lines in those ministries responsible for the maintenance of projects financed" (Cohen & Hook 1987: 87). Donors are unlikely to fund the recurrent costs of development projects. Likewise, local self-help movements (such as *harambee* in Kenya) cannot be expected either to foot the bill for recurrent expenditure, as it is likely to be viewed as a form of taxation by local residents.

District-Level Staffing
For effective performance in the districts, service in outlying rural areas must be made attractive to experienced and capable officers by providing them with career paths and enhanced promotion prospects. Greater training of district staff in such areas as planning

techniques, budget management, and project implementation and control is also called for. Other necessary conditions, according to Cohen and Hook (1987), include the provision of adequate staff housing and logistical support.

District Data Needs
The ability and willingness must exist at the centre to provide timely information necessary for the planning and implementation of development activities; a corollary of this is the existence in the districts of officers who can interpret and make use of such information.

Local Project Preparation
The success of decentralisation depends to a considerable extent on the ability of district authorities to formulate and argue viable project proposals. In Kenya, project handbooks and 'standard design manuals' have been developed and distributed to assist in this.

Rural-Urban Links
Increasingly, districts will have to devise investment plans that are designed to create infrastructures capable of attracting and sustaining manufacturing enterprise, distributor-ships of agricultural products, and an active informal sector. This will require policies at the national level which encourage the growth of small towns; actively expand the provision to the districts of goods and services necessary to improve agricultural produc-tivity; stimulate private investment in outlying areas; and enhance the revenue generating capacity of local authorities so they can promote their own development.

National Political Factors
There must clearly be support for decentralisation from the highest authority in the land. In the case of Kenya, decentralisation programmes receive direct support from President Moi and the Office of the President. Cohen and Hook (1987) attribute the "rapid gains of recent years" in Kenya "to changes in national leadership, economic vision, and political imperatives" (p. 89).

Popular Participation
To make the best use of local knowledge, to ensure continuity of thinking, and to encourage the commitment of the local population, it is necessary for there to be a degree of popular participation in planning. To safeguard against the possibility of centrally funded recurrent expenditure, such participation should take place within centrally de-vised guidelines.

Scope of District Development Plans
District development plans should encompass both the activities of local authorities and non-governmental organisations (NGOs) and, in particular, the relationship between the two.

Sectoral Ministry Responses
The operating ministries have a crucial role to play in supporting effective decentralisa-tion: "if they fail to establish guidelines for district activities in their sector, neglect to

incorporate district priorities into their budgets, or do not redeploy competent staff to the field, decentralisation is unlikely to succeed" (Cohen & Hook 1987: 90). Recent studies in Kenya have indicated that ministries:

1. are uncertain about which activities should be transferred to the districts;
2. have difficulties recruiting competent staff to send to the districts;
3. pay insufficient attention to training;
4. do not know how to develop budget management systems appropriate for decentralised functioning and;
5. are unable to monitor and control district development projects effectively.

Interministerial Cooperation and Coordination
Interministerial cooperation and coordination is also essential for effective decentralisation. Resources must be made available to support this, and political support from the top must again be clearly in evidence.

Consolidation of Planning Strategies, and Review
Effective strategic management should be a live process of review and revision. The same is true of planning for decentralisation. Periods of consolidation must be followed by careful evaluation and, if necessary, the revision and modification of development strategies.

8.5   Implications for Managers and Management Development

In this chapter we have analysed and described some of the most advanced forms of organisation in Africa. We have chosen to concentrate on the examples provided partly because they are relatively well documented but also because their experiences are instructive. But these are by no means the only examples of innovative organisational design in Africa. Other examples, particularly in the agricultural sphere, where participative methods of organisation are most obviously, and appropriately, connected with traditional practice have existed for some time, for example, in Dahomey, Guinea, Mali, Niger and Uganda (e.g., Nash, Dandler & Hopkins 1976).

Something which is borne out by most of the evidence reviewed here on decentralisation and participation is that basic needs must be catered for in conjunction with higher-order needs (quality of working life). Many researchers in Africa recognise this point (e.g., Blunt 1983; Clegg 1971; Kanawaty & Thorsrud 1981; Mihyo 1975), but it is also essential that policy makers keep it in mind, lest worker participation and decentralisation become simply additional empty phrases in the government or party official's kit-bag. The incomes and social responsibilities of African workers, and their need for job security, are such that one cannot ignore hygiene factors (material rewards, working conditions, etc.) and expect decentralisation and worker participation schemes to succeed. Kanawaty and Thorsrud (1981) stress the importance of this aspect of organisational design in developing countries: "One of the most important issues, probably even more crucial in developing countries, is wages" (p. 275). This view is implicit, as we saw in Chapter 5, in work redesign in the Western world too, and on occasions it is explicitly stated:

"Humanistic work and productivity are inevitably intertwined and we cannot ignore the productivity side without risking retrogression back down some Maslowian-type hierarchy to lower order concerns. Workers are unlikely to be concerned about humanistic work design if there is an insufficient amount of work, if there is insufficient income etc. At these points, security concerns overpower interests in self-actualisation" (Bowers 1977: 151).

Finally, when the clients of public and private enterprises complain of corruption and inefficiency and that 'nothing works', they are, at the same time, sounding a warning to organisational designers. They are saying, in effect, that alternative forms of organisation involving participation and decentralisation must do something to improve the performance of organisations which serve the public. Unless this happens, disillusionment will quickly set in, and alternative forms of organisation will be regarded simply as another passing fad to be relegated with the rest to the dustbins of history. Organisational researchers, managers, decision-makers in government, and others concerned with organisational life in Africa, have a joint responsibility to ensure that this does not happen.

Our discussion of decentralisation has demonstrated the importance to development of that topic, and its complexity. As we would expect, the success of decentralisation programmes in Africa varies enormously, with the factors outlined by Cohen and Hook (1987) explaining much of this variation: management training and development for decentralisation is clearly a central issue. But even more important, as the case of Kenya illustrates, is the question of political support from the country's leadership. This point is reinforced by Adamolekun (1991b) when he says, "ministers, party officials, and local political leaders need to have a better understanding of decentralisation requirements" (p. 290).

Another important conclusion to be drawn from our discussion of decentralisation is that, like other forms of organisation, there is no "one best way". This point is now increasingly recognised by writers on development. Conyers (1986), for example, asserts that the different forms of decentralisation "have advantages and disadvantages and the choice must depend on the objectives of decentralisation and the environment in which it will operate" (p. 599).

Chapter 9: Culture and Organisation

Organisational culture, or the "collective programming of the mind which distinguishes the members of one category of people from those of another" (Hofstede & Bond 1988), is a concept which has dominated thinking about organisations in recent times. There is now widespread acceptance of the idea that national and organisational cultures have a major impact on the structure and functioning of organisations, as well as on their performance and problems. According to Hofstede, Neuijen, Ohayu and Sanders (1990), the analytical status of the concept in organisation studies is similar to that of such established notions as strategy, structure and control. Certainly, there is no doubt that cross-national research into questions of organisational and national culture has come to be a dominant feature of the academic and professional literatures (e.g. Blunt 1988, 1991; Earley 1989; Hofstede 1984; Hofstede & Bond 1988; Lockett 1988; Singh 1990). Indeed, Bate (1990) suggests that "the 1980s are likely to go down in history as the 'decade of culture' " (p. 83). But so far it is an idea which has been applied predominantly in the industrialised West and hardly at all in developing countries, including those in Africa.

In this chapter we define the concept and review a number of seminal studies conducted in different parts of the world which shed light on possible links between national and organisational cultures and organisational performance. At the same time, we make inferences from existing knowledge and opinion, as well as our own experience, about dominant features of culture in Africa[1]. Lastly, we present a progressive series of models which link organisational culture with other aspects of organisation, with national culture, and with different stages of economic development. On this issue, a recent world-wide investigation of leadership and culture carried out by Kanter (1991) concluded that "managers' views tend to correspond more to their country's cultural heritage and less to its geographical location or its regional economic affiliations" (p. 152).

9.1 Culture Defined

According to Adler (1991), "the cultural orientation of a society reflects the complex interaction of the values, attitudes, and behaviours displayed by its members" (p. 15). On a smaller scale, organisational culture can be defined in the same way. Shared values, what people genuinely believe to be good or bad, desirable or undesirable, acceptable or unacceptable, are the essence of organisational culture. The more clearly articulated and

---

1 In attempting this ambitions task we acknowledge, with Kiggundu (1988), that we cannot do justice in the space available to the rich cultural diversity and distinctiveness of the African continent.

more widely shared these values, the more robust, effective and lasting the culture (Peters & Waterman 1982; Schein 1989). When organisational culture is strong a distinctive psychological atmosphere pervades the whole organisation. Employees display in their words and actions the characteristics that define the mission and ethos of the organisation: for example, dedication to outstanding service, openness and trust, perseverance in the face of adversity, commitment to innovation, or, in less desirable circumstances, lethargy or a sense of helplessness or futility or antipathy (Bate 1984; Morgan 1986).

The following passage, describing an African organisation, illustrates how values can affect behaviour in the workplace, and how they can help to create a certain type of psychological atmosphere or culture within organisations:

"I did not like the foreman because he did not treat me well. All the time I was working there he was always looking at me and trying to find fault with me. He was telling me how I should do the work but he did not speak to me well and told me that unless I improved my work he would fire me. I told him that I was trying to do my work well and that I wanted to learn and that it was his duty to teach me. Then one day he was very rude to me and told me that people of my tribe should go back to the country and grow food because that is all that we are good for. He was always comparing me to other people in the factory who were better workers. He said that this was due to the fact that they were of a different tribe. I spoke to the manager about my complaints and he told me that I was a good worker and not to pay any attention to those comments. Then one day the foreman complained that I had not washed my hands properly and I became angry with him. We had a quarrel and he told me that he despised people of my tribe. So I left." (Gutkind 1968: 157).

9.2   Dimensions of Culture

Recently, attempts have been made to describe organisational and national cultures in terms of a small number of key dimensions. A book published by Hofstede (1980) has provided much of the theoretical and empirical foundations for this work. He identified four cultural dimensions, the major features of which, along with their organisational manifestations, are discussed below.

9.2.1   Power Distance

Following Hofstede (1980, 1984), high power distance can be defined as a high willingness on the part of less powerful individuals in a society to accept an unequal distribution of power without question and to regard it as normal. This tendency is reflected in the following facets of organisational behaviour: close supervision is positively evaluated by operators and managers alike; employees are afraid to disagree with their supervisors; there is a low level of trust; there is strong centralisation; organisational structures are taller; and the proportion of supervisory to non-supervisory personnel is high. Other behaviours indicative of high power distance include:

- A marked unwillingness to make any decision without reference to the most senior executive in the organisation.
- In general, centralisation may be carried to quite extraordinary lengths and may appear to be regarded in itself as conferring special value on anything that is subjected to it.
- Criticism, even of a constructive kind, may be frowned upon, whatever the source.

We would agree with Kiggundu (1988) that many African cultural groups would score high on power distance. This view is consistent with the preference of senior managers in Africa not to delegate and not to engage in participative forms of management and decentralisation.

9.2.2   Uncertainty Avoidance

Uncertainty avoidance refers to the extent to which people within a culture are made nervous by situations that they consider to be unstructured, unclear, or unpredictable, and the extent to which they try to avoid such situations by adopting strict codes of behaviour and a belief in absolute truths (Hofstede 1980). Organisational manifestations of uncertainty avoidance include:

- More emotional resistance to change;
- Less risk taking;
- A preference for clear organisational structure that must be respected at all costs;
- A preference for clearly laid out rules and regulations that should not be broken;
- A strong feeling that conflict in organisations is undesirable and to be avoided whenever possible;
- A tendency to want to restrain the initiative of employees;
- A reluctance to compromise with opponents;
- A suspicion and distrust of foreigners as managers;
- More ritual behaviour; and
- Managers who are more involved in detail.

All these are characteristics of high uncertainty avoidance.

Again, we would agree with Kiggundu's (1988) observation that many African cultural groups would score high on this dimension also. This is compatible with Hofstede's analysis of the origins of the national uncertainty avoidance index where he argues that high uncertainty avoidance is associated with beginning modernisation and a high rate of change in society, and young democracies.

9.2.3   Individualism

Low individualism is characteristic of collectivist cultures and implies that individuals, because of close-knit kinship relationships, belong to tightly woven 'in groups'. The in-group whether extended family, clan, or organisation – protects the interests of its members and, in turn, expects their permanent loyalty. Organisational consequences of low individualism, which are evident in a number of African settings, include policies and practices based on loyalty and a sense of duty, promotion based on seniority, less concern with modern management ideas, and policies and practices that vary according to personal relationships between particular individuals.

With regard to the latter, certain rules and regulations – such as those pertaining to leave, housing, travel, equipment purchases, and so on – may be routinely circumvented according to mutual, but unstated, reciprocity. Where less than harmonious personal relationships are formed, however, such apparent flexibility with regard to rule conformity can quickly give way to the rigid application of precisely those rules that, under more 'favourable' circumstances, are happily circumvented.

We would expect most African cultural groups and organisations to score low on individualism, although high levels of rural-urban migration and the emergence in many African cities of an urban proletariat might be beginning to erode collectivist values (Kiggundu 1988).

9.2.4   Masculinity/ Femininity

Masculinity/ femininity is concerned with the extent to which roles for the two sexes in a culture are defined differently. Masculine cultures expect men to be assertive, ambitious, and competitive, to strive for material success, and to respect what is big, strong, and fast. They expect women to serve and to care for the nonmaterial quality of life, for children, and for the weak (Hofstede 1980). Medium masculinity in organisations implies that there are fewer women in more qualified and better paying jobs, that women in more qualified jobs tend to be assertive, and that the appeal of organisation redesign rests in its capacity to facilitate the realisation of personal ambitions.

We would anticipate that many African cultural groups and organisations would exhibit what we have termed medium masculinity.

On the basis, then, of Hofstede's four dimensions, we would hypothesise that many African countries, and organisations within them, would be characterised by high power distance, high uncertainty avoidance, low individualism, and medium masculinity. We can contrast this speculative profile with that of the USA which has relatively low power distance, high individualism, medium uncertainty avoidance, and medium masculinity; and Sweden, which has medium individualism, medium to low power distance, weak uncertainty avoidance, and high femininity.

But what is it possible to infer from the speculative profile we have constructed about the effects of culture on the effectiveness of organisations in Africa, and their susceptibility to change, and hence their adaptability? One way to find out would be to examine features of culture which have been shown to be impediments to effectiveness and the introduction of change in organisations, and to search for possible parallels between them and the African profile we have developed.

9.3   Cultural Impediments to Organisation Change

A series of studies conducted in Britain between 1975 and 1989 by Paul Bate and his colleagues at the University of Bath identified six specific aspects of organisation culture that appeared to be linked consistently with a range of problematic organisational predispositions (Bate 1984, 1990). Prominent among these dysfunctional predispositions were (1) a low commitment to and involvement in the change process, (2) erection of barriers to change, (3) a disowning of problems and an abdication of responsibility for the search for solutions, (4) over caution and a lack of decisiveness in the search for solutions, and (5) the adoption of an adversarial position on all issues regardless of whether any potential measure of agreement between the parties existed.

The six cultural orientations identified by Bate as being most closely associated with the above symptoms of organisational malaise were:

9.3.1   Unemotionality

The expression of one's real feelings about organisational issues is avoided (Bate 1984). Problems therefore tend to be internalised and to smoulder for long periods. If problems are brought into the open, they are dealt with at arm's length. Wherever possible, face-to-face confrontation is avoided. People tend to be over-cautious and inflexible. Collaborative problem solving and decision making rarely occur, and people's concerns focus on coping with the *status quo* rather than attempting to change it.

9.3.2   Depersonalisation of Problems

Never formally point an accusing finger at anyone in particular. Gossip and backbiting (that is, informal 'finger pointing') are acceptable, but formal criticism of individuals is regarded as unprofessional and destructive. Therefore, meetings rarely confront human resource problems. Avoidance behaviour of this type is widely practised and accepted, and there is a conspiracy of silence when it comes to attributing problems to particular individuals. Instead, technical or impersonal explanations are sought.

9.3.3   Subordination

Always do what's expected of you and when in doubt wait for direction from above. People suffer in silence or grumble politely when problems occur rather than attempting to do anything about them. This reinforces autocratic styles of management and decision making, with decisions being made with little consultation or explanation and with little input from lower-level employees. Managers are therefore often blissfully unaware of the existence of problems.

9.3.4   Conservatism

Change is more likely to make things worse than better. Problem solving is engaged in only halfheartedly. There is a feeling of resignation that things will never change. The mood is captured by the retort of a worker interviewed by Bate (1984): "What's the use? Participation is a load of rubbish. If we were to put anything forward, it would be squashed – a case of you can't have it, goodbye. There's no point is there?"

9.3.5   Isolationism

Do your own thing and do not trespass on other people's territory. Horizontal and vertical two-way interaction and communication tend to be limited. Highly individualistic approaches to problem solving predominate; there is little teamwork. Other people are regarded as potential threats or sources of problems rather than sources of help. Rumours abound. Expertise is underutilised. Decisions are unilateral. Chronic interpersonal conflicts are unlikely to be resolved.

9.3.6   Antipathy

Assume that most other people will oppose you. Don't trust anyone. Competing interest groups and alliances are commonplace. Relations among such groups are belligerent and untrusting. All issues involving managers and workers are seen as win-lose. Even relatively trivial matters evoke strong feelings and are bitterly contested. Such conflict is taken for granted.

There are striking parallels between the cultural orientations identified by Bate as being linked consistently with strong resistance to the introduction of organisational change, and the cultural profile that we have identified as being characteristic of African nations. The conceptual links, and their consequences for organisations, are summarised in Table 9.1.

The suggested correspondence between Bate's cultural orientations and Hofstede's cultural dimensions, as outlined in Table 9.1, was determined simply by inspection of the respective definitions. Bate's impression, which we share, was that subordination, depersonalisation, and unemotionality posed the most serious obstacles to problem solving.

While much more carefully controlled research is clearly required before firm conclusions can be reached regarding the validity of the propositions made, there is sufficient plausible evidence to warrant a note of caution. Intractable problems of organisational development encountered in Africa may well be a result of more than merely the peculiarities of a particular organisation's culture. It seems possible that work-related values operating at the macro, or national, level may be creating a general cultural atmosphere not conducive to organisational change.

This general line of reasoning has been extended by Blunt (1991) who has devised a progressive series of models of organisational culture which he argues may be observed at different stages of economic development.

Table 9.1: Organisational Outcomes of Work-Related Values in Africa

Present Study's Profile of Africa	Bate's Corresponding Cultural Orientations	Associated Organisational Outcomes
High power distance	Subordination Antipathy	Low commitment to, and involvement in, change
		Disowning of problems and an abdication of responsibility for the search for solutions
Strong uncertainty avoidance	Conservatism Depersonalisation Isolationism Subordination	Lack of openness in confronting and dealing jointly with issues
		Avoidance of data gathering on the causes of problems
Low individualism	Unemotionality Subordination	Overcaution and lack of decisiveness and creativity in problem solving
		Erection of barriers to change
Medium masculinity	Elements of subordination	Taking of adversary positions on all issues regardless of whether any potential measure of agreement between the parties exists

9.4   Organisational Culture and Economic Development: A Progressive Series of Models[2]

In the discussion which follows, culture or organisational culture refers to positive elements, where individuals or groups subscribe to organisational goals of product and service quality, and are committed and energetic in their pursuit. The psychological settings in which these elements exist or with which they coexist (either negative, confrontational, inert or latently positive), which are also cultural phenomena, are referred to below, variously, as psychological climate or atmosphere. Also, the allocation of cultural forms to different stages of development is not meant to exclude in those contexts the possibility of the existence of the other cultural forms mentioned, but simply to suggest the economic circumstances in which the cultural form in question seems to be most commonly observed or most likely to occur.

9.4.1   Fragmented (Negative) Cultures

It is proposed that fragmented (negative) cultures are descriptive of many organisations in developing countries. In general, the fragmented culture is characterised by small isolated pockets of positive values and beliefs, which are not widely shared or interconnected and are not part of an overall organisational value system. Moreover, fragmented cultures lack strong, committed, transformational leadership (Kotter 1988; Conger 1991). This may be due to the fact that in many enterprises in developing countries the scope for personal gain is greater at the top, and such positions are therefore competed for largely for this and, possibly, status-related reasons. The pockets of positive culture which do exist may have been imported by individuals or small groups, such as professional employees, who derive their positive values from the professional associations of which they are members; or by returnees from external training and development programmes.

In the fragmented (negative) culture, the prospects for maintaining such values in isolation are not good as the general psychological climate is negative, countervailing and extrinsically oriented; meaning that systemic corruption (e.g., Aina 1982; Blunt & Popoola 1985; Caiden & Caiden 1977; Gould 1980) and particularism (Price 1975) are widespread and that precedence is given to personal goals and the demands of external role-set members (kin and ethnic affiliates) at the expense of organisational goals (Blunt 1983; Blunt, Richards & Wilson 1989). The pervasiveness of such behaviour, the existence of social systems which in some ways are supportive of it, and the laxity and capriciousness of societal and organisational control procedures constitute a fertile wider social environment for the emergence of fragmented cultures of this type.

Moreover, at lower levels in the organisation there may be considerable alienation (Blunt 1982), and instrumental orientations to work (Goldthorpe *et al.* 1968) are likely to be the norm (Blunt 1983). Organisational systems are likely to be inappropriate, underde-

---

2   This section draws heavily on Blunt (1991).

Table 9.2: Fragmented (Negative) Cultures

Climate	–	systemic corruption, alienation
Culture	–	isolated, disconnected pockets
Leadership	–	ineffectice, low integrity, variable power
Organisational systems	–	inappropriate, underdeveloped, stagnant
Organisational effectiveness	–	low
Prognosis	–	degeneration culture and effectiveness, sometimes rapid
Organisation type	–	public service
Economic setting	–	developing countries
National culture	–	supportive to unsupportive

veloped and stagnant. This culture is characteristic of many public service organisations in developing countries (Blunt 1988; Price 1975).

The effectiveness of organisations possessing this cultural form tends to be very low, and culture and effectiveness may degenerate further, sometimes rapidly.

9.4.2   Fragmented (Inert) Cultures

It is suggested that the remaining command economies of Eastern Europe, and the former Soviet Union, are conducive to the development of this type of organisational culture. The fragmented (inert) culture possesses many of the same general characteristics as the first, including the likelihood of weak leadership and isolated pockets of positive culture of similar origins. However, rather than existing in a strongly negative and countervailing psychological climate, the setting is more inert or uninterested, made up of employees who are neither very alienated nor committed, and who have relatively few demands placed upon them by external role-set members. Moreover, the scope for personal aggrandizement is reduced owing to the presence and enforcement of strict legal codes and heavy punishments, and the more limited scope of particularistic ties. The scarcity of consumer goods also has a limiting effect, as do restrictions on overseas travel.

Systemic corruption is therefore less widespread. Organisational systems tend to be inappropriate and/or underdeveloped and stagnant.

The presence or absence of effective leadership in the strategic apex is a result not so much of the scope for personal excess as the presence of restrictive controls exercised by external government authorities. In these conditions, there is little incentive for strong transformational leaders to emerge and to take the risks, or assume the responsibilities, associated with positions having little real power. Accordingly, organisations with this

Table 9.3:   Fragmented (Inert) Cultures

Climate	–	uninterested, inert, low commitment, some alienation, individual corruption
Culture	–	isolated, disconnected pockets
Leadership	–	ineffectice, low power
Organisational systems	–	inappropriate, underdeveloped, stagnant
Organisational effectiveness	–	low
Prognosis	–	stagnant or slowly degenerating culture and effectiveness
Organisation type	–	state controlled
Economic setting	–	command economies (Eastern Europe, former Soviet Union)
National culture	–	supportive to unsupportive

type of culture go through the motions, but are neither efficient nor effective. They are characterised by low and slowly degenerating, or stagnant, cultures and effectiveness.

9.4.3   Fragmented (Latently Positive) Cultures

The third type of fragmented culture is differentiated by the greater likelihood of effective leadership in the strategic apex and a more benign psychological climate. It is suggested that this type of culture is representative of state-owned enterprises in the People's Republic of China (Child & Wu 1989; Henley & Nyaw 1986; Lockett 1988).

Several factors combine to produce a setting conducive to the emergence of this type of culture. First, responsibility for the general welfare of employees is assumed by the organisation and security of tenure is guaranteed. The organisation provides a comprehensive system of services of reasonable quality; housing, canteen, schooling, kindergarten, entertainment and so on. Under these circumstances, organisations are less likely to be perceived by employees as exploitative. Employees' basic needs are fulfilled. Their expectations for higher-level fulfilment at work are possibly held by conditioning at relatively low levels, and their consequent levels of šatisfaction, while not high, may be sufficient to ensure reasonable commitment and drive (Lockett 1988).

Second, the socio-cultural environment of the nation is supportive of unified, disciplined, cohesive organisational systems and cultures (Hofstede & Bond 1988). There are severe penalties for malfeasance in society and organisations and these, combined with strong respect for and acceptance of authority (high-power distance), restrict the likelihood of excessive and widespread corruption. Individual corruption is likely, systemic corruption less so. Indeed, particularism, extended family links or other personal rela-

Table 9.4: Fragmented (Latently Positive) Cultures

Climate	–	benign, latently positive, reasonable satisfaction and commitment, individual corruption
Culture	–	isolated, disconnected pockets, including apex
Leadership	–	variable effectiveness; medium to high integrity; low power
Organisational systems	–	inappropriate, underdeveloped, incremental positive change possible
Organisational effectiveness	–	medium to low
Prognosis	–	steady state, incremental +VE or – VE change
Organisation type	–	state controlled
Economic setting	–	command economies (PRC)
National culture	–	potentially supportive to supportive

tionship networks *(guanxi)* may be used in the interests of the organisations as well as of the individual (Lockett 1988). Respect for age (Nevis 1983; Lockett 1988) encourages older individuals of ability to seek positions of responsibility and leadership and to some extent ensures commitment and integrity among them. In enterprises, this possibility is increased by the strong ideological criteria employed for selection to such positions. Specialised management skills and knowledge and well-developed leadership abilities may be lacking (Lockett 1988), but there is likely to be a reasonable degree of commitment and integrity at the top. This helps also to contain the negative effects (for the individual – less so for the organisation) of the lack of authority associated with senior management positions.

As in other fragmented cultures, pockets of positive culture exist – for similar reasons – but may persist for longer in isolation because of the more benign psychological atmosphere in which they are embedded. Effectiveness, while medium to low (Lockett 1988), and culture are therefore likely to remain steady state with only small incremental positive or negative changes for localised reasons. The prospects for improvement are good, especially if structural improvements are also made; in particular, if closer relationships between authority and responsibility, and performance and reward can be introduced at all levels (individual, group and organisational) without threatening the broader – social welfare – objectives of the enterprise or its essentially egalitarian ideals.

9.4.4   Embryonic Cultures

These cultures are characterised by a series of interconnected or interlocked pockets of positive culture located in key parts of the organisation. Frequently, this is brought about by 'cultural implants' – managers with desirable values and transformational leadership qualities, and high power, placed in key positions – as a result of mergers or takeovers or some joint venture operations (e.g., Harrigan 1986; CEMI 1990); or may be a form of culture associated with new and developing organisations. A necessary feature of this form of culture, which is essential for regeneration or growth, is the existence of strong transformational leadership at the top of the organisation, supported by a network of capable and like-minded managers. This network provides the skeletal framework for culture building.

The psychological climate in which the embryonic culture is embedded is variable, from negative to latently positive, but often tends initially towards negative or hostile, as existing employees are uncertain, and fearful, of the effects of the merger or takeover and the actions, values and expectations of new managers. This may change rapidly as fears are allayed, people leave or change, and new values and attitudes are assimilated, or latently positive values are activated. Organisational systems may vary from appropriate and reasonably developed to marginal, but are likely to be improved quickly.

Levels of effectiveness associated with this culture are variable, but prospects for cultural regeneration and improving effectiveness are good. Positive change may occur rapidly.

Table 9.5: Embryonic Cultures

Climate	–	negative to latently positive; some fear, defensiveness initially
Culture	–	interconnected pockets in key locations
Leadership	–	effective, transformational, high integrity and power
Organisational systems	–	appropriate to marginal; rapid improvement likely
Organisational effectiveness	–	medium to low
Prognosis	–	rapid regeneration of culture and effectiveness likely
Organisation type	–	mergers; takeovers; joint ventures
Economic setting	–	developed (Western) and developing countries
National culture	–	unsupportive to potentially supportive

9.4.5   Apex Cultures

Apex cultures are most commonly found in enterprises in Western industrialised societies and in the branches or subsidiaries of Western multinational corporations in developing countries, including Africa. They are characterised by a solid wedge of positive values and attitudes at the top of the organisation, tapering down to a sharp point at lower levels. This culture is typical of organisations which have entrenched traditional divisions between management and workers, and where confrontation and bargaining are institutionalised. In Mintzberg's (1979) terms, such cultures would be especially likely in machine bureaucratic and divisionalised organisations, but less so in professional bureaucracies and adhocracies.

Such cultures therefore exist in organisations with established formal systems and structures and heavily politicised and confrontational informal systems. Class divisions in the wider society can reinforce these features of the apex culture (Clegg 1990). The negative elements of the psychological climate identified by Bate (1984) in his study of English enterprises would be likely to occur frequently in apex cultures, along with instrumental orientations to work at lower levels (Goldthorpe et al. 1968).

Nevertheless, reasonable, and sometimes strong, leadership, combined with a positive unified cultural core and well established systems of performance and reward, and authority and responsibility, ensure medium to high levels of effectiveness which, together with the cultural core itself, may be subject to slow regeneration.

Table 9.6: Apex Cultures

Climate	–	instrumental orientations, confrontational
Culture	–	diamond shaped; solid at top
Leadership	–	variable effectiveness
Organisation type	–	public or private; multinational
Economic setting	–	developed (Western) and developing countries
National culture	–	unsupportive to potentially supportive

9.4.6   Synergistic Cultures

Synergistic cultures exist in organisations which have achieved organisation-wide consensus about values and attitudes. There is more or less complete harmony, unity of purpose and widespread commitment to, and belief in, the organisation's mission and way of doing things. Leadership is empowered, effective and transformational. Organisational systems are likely to be appropriate and highly developed. Such cultures are associated with very high effectiveness and steady regeneration of culture and performance. They are most likely to be found in Japan and some of the East Asian economies where societal value systems infuse and reinforce organisational ones (Blunt 1990a; Hofstede & Bond 1988). In the Western industrialised economies such cultures are most likely to be found in what Mintzberg (1989) calls 'missionary organisations', which we have defined earlier in Chapter 7.

The major potential weakness of the synergistic culture is a consequence of its cultural strength and unity of purpose – a tendency to become too inward looking or to 'implode' (Mintzberg 1989). That is, the culture may breed complacency which in turn may stifle innovation. Some organisations attempt to counteract this effect by building into their cultures values which encourage risk raking, innovation and the latitude to make mistakes (Evans, Doz & Laurent 1989).

Table 9.7: Synergistic Cultures

Climate	–	positive, unified
Culture	–	unified, organisation wide
Leadership	–	effective, high integrity, transformational
Organisational systems	–	appropriate and developed
Organisational effectiveness	–	very high
Prognosis	–	steady regeneration of culture and effectiveness
Organisation type	–	private, some public
Economic setting	–	Japan; some East Asian countries (e.g., Singapore)
National culture	–	supportive

9.4.7   Cultural Progression

The forms of organisational culture outlined above constitute a progressive series, with the synergistic culture clearly being the most desirable and effective and the fragmented (negative) culture the least so. While not impossible, it is unlikely that progression through the series would involve leapfrogging one or more stages (cultural forms). Key elements of the process of cultural progression – or regeneration – include the establishment of appropriate institutional frameworks in the wider society (Clegg, Dunphy & Redding 1986), the installation of committed transformational leaders at the top of the organisation and the linking up of cultural fragments into mutually reinforcing cultural embryos. Progression from this point to the apex culture is likely to be unproblematic in many cases. However, the transition to the synergistic culture is likely to be more difficult, especially in national cultural, and institutional, settings which do not reinforce desirable behaviour, values and beliefs. The major features of each model are summarised in Table 9.8 (p. 204).

9.5   Implications for Managers and Management Development

Several practical issues for African managers and management development in Africa arise from our discussion of culture. Two stand out. First, given the importance of culture to organisational effectiveness, how can organisations in Africa set about changing their cultures? Second, given the crucial role of leadership in the process of culture change, what leadership *skills*, as distinct from the leadership qualities mentioned earlier (e.g., vision, integrity, energy etc.), are needed to bring about culture change? Third, we need to examine also the role of broader issues in culture building – particularly among lower level workers – such as job involvement, commitment and alienation in African organisations. We can refer to this category of considerations under the heading orientations to work: that is, why is it that one individual might be highly involved with his work, spend long hours working and thinking about work-related problems, and derive considerable satisfaction from his job, while another resents more or less every minute he has to spend cooped up in the office or factory and would not be there at all were it not for the fact that he needs the money.

9.5.1   Orientations to Work

Consider the following excerpts.
Ghanaian labourer:

"In fact I don't like (my job), but because I can't get any other I'm bound to it. It's the money that keeps me here" (Peil 1972: 85).

Kenyan night watchman:

"I have no choice but to come to town because I need money. Why should a man undergo such hardship for any other reason? I must help my family. If that means working every day ... I will do it. I cannot let my family suffer" (Blunt 1982: 11).

Table 9.8: Summary of Features Associated With Each Model of Organisational Culture

Model of Organisational Culture	Climate	Culture	Leadership	Organisational Systems	Organisational Effectiveness	Prognosis	Organisation Type	Economic Setting	National Culture
Fragmented (negative)	systemic corruption; alienation; instrumental orientations	isolated, disconnected pockets	ineffective; low integrity; variable power	inappropriate; under-developed; stagnant	very low	degenerating culture and effectiveness, sometimes rapid	public service	developing countries	unsupportive to potentially supportive (variable)
Fragmented (inert)	inert or uninterested; low commitment; some alienation; individual corruption	isolated, disconnected pockets	weak; ineffective; low power	inappropriate; under-developed; stagnant	low	stagnant or slowly degenerating culture and effectiveness	state controlled	command economies (Eastern Europe, former Soviet Union)	potentially supportive to unsupportive (variable)
Fragmented (latently positive)	benign; latently positive; reasonable satisfaction and commitment; individual corruption	isolated, disconnected pockets, including apex	variable effectiveness; medium to high integrity; low power	inappropriate; under-developed; incremental positve change possible	medium to low	steady state with incremental positive or negative change	state controlled	command economies (PRC)	potentially supportive to supportive (variable)
Embryonic	negative to latently positive	interconnected or interlocked pockets in key locations including apex	effective transformational; high integrity; high power	appropriate to marginal; rapidly improving	medium to low	rapid regeneration of culture and effectiveness likely	mergers; takeovers; joint ventures	developed (Western) and developing countries	unsupportive to supportive (variable)
Apex	hierarchical divisions, confrontational; instrumental orientations	diamond shaped; solid at top	variable effectiveness; high power; high integrity	appropriate; developed to well developed (variable)	medium to high	slow regeneration of culture and effectiveness	public or private; multi-national	developed (Western) and developing countries	unsupportive to supportive (variable)
Synergistic	positvie; unified	unified	effective; high integrity; transformational	appropriate and developed	very high	steady regeneration of culture and effectiveness	private; some public	Japan, some East Asian countries (e.g. Singapore)	supportive

Work as an Instrumental Activity

The quotations listed above indicate quite clearly that workers from different parts of Africa regard their jobs, and work *per se*, purely as an instrumental activity; that is, something to be tolerated in order to obtain money. To them, the meaning of work is simply that of providing enough money to satisfy their needs. A classic study conducted by Goldthorpe *et al.* (1968) in Britain suggests that workers who display an instrumental orientation towards work are much more likely to put up with unpleasant working conditions in order to maximise their monetary incomes. More precisely, according to Goldthorpe *et al.*, the values which comprise the instrumental orientation are as follows:

1. Work is regarded solely as a means to an end, as a way of obtaining the income necessary to support a valued way of life which excludes work itself.
2. Accordingly the workers' self-involvement with the organisation is 'calculative' (Etzioni 1975): that is to say, it is characterised by weak or negative sentiments and maintained only so long as it satisfies economic needs.
3. Since work is regarded as a purely instrumental activity, the involvement of the workers in their jobs is low: work neither constitutes a central life interest nor a source of psychologically significant experiences in terms of self-actualisation.
4. As a result, workers' lives are divided sharply into work and non-work activities. Work relationships are not likely to be extended outside the plant.

Understandably, instrumental orientations to work are commonplace in Africa (Blunt 1983; Kiggundu 1989). Such orientations are partly fuelled by the nature of the web of kinship obligations and demands experienced by many African workers which is well depicted in the following case of a Yoruba carpenter who had worked for a Lagos-based company for 11 years:

"Three weeks after I moved to this house with my wife one of my brother's children came to me to ask me for a job. As he was related to me I told him that he could sleep here and that I would ask the foreman whether he would take him on. The foreman refused to do so, and the result was that this young man lived with us for several weeks. He finally found a job as a messenger. About two months later a distant cousin came to me also to ask for work. He too stayed but because he was lazy he did not look for work. He stayed with us for 16 months. All this time I was working hard and doing some overtime, but it seemed that I gained nothing from this. I also had to pay some of the school fees for my two brothers and one sister. All this I had to do while at the same time my wife had three children over a period of six years. We lost the fourth child and my wife had to go into hospital for a long time.

I am working as hard as I can. I know that I am very lucky to have work because there are many thousands of people who are looking for work and some of them are nearly starving. But I wonder what to do in the future because almost every month I have somebody come to me for help. I do not earn enough to help all my relatives and friends and what I do earn does not help me a great deal. The harder I work the more my friends demand money from me. I have told the foreman that I need more money and he said that he would talk to the master about it but I know that he will not do this unless I pay him *some money. That is the way my life is at the moment. I can tell you about many people who are lucky to get work but they do not benefit themselves" (Gutkind 1968: 151–2).*

But there are also growing numbers of African workers, especially younger and more educated ones, whose commitment to urban living and modern ways is much greater, and likely to become increasingly so as time goes by. Already, in African towns and cities, there is a small but growing urban proletariat made up of those who intend not only to work in town, but also to reside there with their wives and families, to buy a home and in general to live out their time permanently in town. For this group, work is likely to be of greater personal significance. It may even assume the proportions of a dominant or central life interest as it has done for so many workers in the industrialised West.

Work as a Central Life Interest

Work as a central life interest will be regarded here simply as indicating that work is a very important part of life for the individual, and that the individual is personally affected by her whole job environment, including the work itself, her co-workers and the organisation. This inclines the individual to identify closely with her work so that what she does in her job forms a significant part of her self-image: how she sees herself, and how she would like to be seen by others. This definition of work as a central life interest makes it analogous to the concept of job involvement. Rabinowitz and Hall (1977) have presented a profile of the job-involved person based on a large number of research studies. The job-involved person:

1. believes in the Protestant work ethic (that work has moral value, that it is intrinsically good);
2. is older;
3. has strong needs for personal growth and development (to develop her potential to the full);
4. has an interesting and stimulating job;
5. participates in decisions which affect her own work;
6. has a history of good job performance; and
7. is less likely to leave the organisation.

Based on the limited amount of available data, what conclusions is it possible to draw about orientations to work in Africa? The following conclusions, stated in the form of plausible hypotheses in need of further testing, can be made:

1. Ethnic and cultural factors and other variables, such as education, which influence receptivity to change account for much of the diversity with regard to orientations to work.
2. Unlike workers in the West, more rather than fewer Africans are beginning to regard work as a central life interest.
3. Nevertheless, the vast majority of African workers can probably still best be described as having a primarily instrumental orientation to work.

4. This is especially true of unskilled lower-level workers (as is the case in the USA) and the vast numbers of unemployed, but it is also true of significant numbers of white collar and blue collar workers.
5. There is evidence of widespread worker alienation in Africa (e.g., Blunt 1982, 1983; Burawoy 1972; Mayer & Mayer 1971).

Clearly, culture building in African organisations will be inhibited by widespread alienation and instrumental orientations to work. And, as we have argued repeatedly in this book, attention to basic need satisfaction will in many organisational circumstances have to precede, or at least go hand-in-hand with, different forms of organisational development, including culture building.

9.5.2   Leadership Skills

Elsewhere in this book, we have remarked on the importance of transformational leadership to modern organisations. We have also discussed the types of individual qualities which are associated with successful leaders. But there is clearly also a range of leadership skills which contributes to leadership effectiveness. Kirkpatrick and Locke (1991) describe these as being connected with structuring the organisation, selecting and training, motivating, the constructive use of formal authority, building subordinate self-confidence, delegating, managing information, team building, and promoting change and innovation. Unlike the leadership *traits* (drive, honesty, intelligence etc.) referred to, these are all areas which are amenable to management training and development.

We would reiterate, however, that such skills are only likely to be employed in the interests of building a more effective culture and organisation if they rest on a solid foundation of key values, especially those of trust and integrity. Kirkpatrick and Locke (1991) share our view on this:

"Honesty does not require skill building; it is a virtue one achieves or rejects by choice. Organisations should look with extreme skepticism at any employee who behaves dishonestly or lacks integrity, and should certainly not reward dishonesty in any form, especially not with a promotion. The role models for honest behaviour are those at the top. On this issue, organisations get what they model, not what they preach" (p. 58).

Instrumental orientations to work combined with a scarcity of appropriate leadership in Africa clearly do not provide ideal conditions which are conducive to culture change. The ethnically heterogeneous nature of many African organisations is another complicating factor (*see* Cox 1991 for a model for analysing such organisations). But what about in circumstances where levels of commitment are reasonably high and effective leadership is present?

9.5.3   Culture Change Propositions

Arising from his extensive investigations of British Rail, Bate (1990) has developed a number of theoretical propositions concerning the process of changing organisational culture.

Initial Orientation: Breaking Out of Vicious Circles of Thinking
This involves creating in managers an awareness of new possibilities, an awareness of the importance and nature of such concepts as organisational culture and organisational development, and an awareness of how dysfunctional aspects of culture might be reflected in existing practice. Much that is negative in organisational cultures Bate (1990) attributes to 'closed loop' thinking: "namely, endless permutations of the old, and the tendency of such loops to turn into inward spirals in which thinking and action become increasingly narrow and restricted" (p. 97).

Devising Cultural Labels: Diagnosis of Present State
It is important to get managers to think in cultural terms. Naming and describing organisation cultural components and models, as we have done in this chapter, is as Bate (1990) suggests, "an indispensable part of perception and interpretation" (p. 97). Before people change something it is clearly helpful if they understand it and can think and talk about it in ways that make sense to them and to others.

Reversing Cultural Images: Visions of the Desired State
This entails creating in the minds of managers a clear idea of how they would like the culture of the organisation to be, and helping them to be able to convey this idea persuasively to others. This can result in very detailed "sets of cultural images of the 'present' and 'desired future' senior management culture" (Bate 1990: 98).

Developing New Networks of Communication and Influence
Networks of communication and influence between managers and others in the organisation are important channels for changing and maintaining culture in organisations. According to Bate (1990), they provide:

"channels of meaning ... into which ideas are introduced and subsequently defined, developed, patterned, validated, and corrected, or suppressed and invalidated. The network, not the formal authority structure, is the basic unit of cultural production and adaptation" (p. 102).

This suggests that a main focus of cultural change efforts should be networks of relationships, that is, the human mechanisms which create culture rather than the culture itself. A focus on networks of relationships rather than, say, abstract values alone has the virtue of providing more tangible targets of change. In practice this would involve "various combinations of individuals and groups of managers to negotiate and establish the terms of their interdependence in the network" (Bate 1990: 102). Cultural parameters for these discussions might be established in terms of agreement about the undesirability of the cultural impediments discussed above (*see* also Bate 1990: 90–94). Within these parameters the aim would be "to design a process that would continually recall, incorporate, and reinforce the features of the 'desired' culture" (Bate 1990: 102).

We can see from this discussion that processes of culture change are far from straightforward, and that the processes themselves demand skilled and careful management. These skills will be scarce in Africa and may need to be imported for some time to come. Great care will therefore need to be exercised in the selection of management development professionals and agents of cultural change, as indicated recently by Kiggundu (1991). Whilst the magnitude of the challenges and obstacles to cultural change facing managers and leaders in Africa is considerable, we feel that in many organisational settings the benefits to be derived from such change will repay high investments of time and energy.

Part 4: Managing Change and Conflict

Chapter 10: Organisational Development and Change

"The most striking of all impressions I have formed since I left London a month ago is of the strength of this African national consciousness ... . The wind of change is blowing through this continent."
(U.K. Prime Minister Harold Macmillan, Cape Town, 1960)

During the three decades since Macmillan made his famous speech immense changes have indeed taken place on the African continent, even in the turbulent country where he uttered his much quoted words. The former European colonies have become nation states, many after protracted struggles for independence. New roads, railways and airports have been built. New industries have been implanted. Mines have been opened. Huge cities teem with people where not so long ago there was forest or savanna. Many of the first generation of national leaders, those who led the struggles for independence, have gone. The continent has been convulsed by civil wars, coups, border disputes, insurrection, creating huge refugee problems. In some regions climatic changes and trends have caused terrible droughts while others have suffered from devastating floods. An increasing number of states have been forced to appeal to the international community for food aid, as populations increase and food production decreases. As we noted in Chapter 1, much of the news from Africa is bad news. Yet there have been notable successes, which have not received the attention – particularly in the Western media – which they merit. Nevertheless, the great excitement and promise of the early years of independence has in many African nations been replaced by a sense of disappointment, failure, disillusionment, even despair.

Yet 'development' remains the most common word in the rubric of Africa. Many governments still claim to be 'revolutionary', despite the reality that change since independence has generally not been of the revolutionary kind promised. 'Change' in education has meant more schools, more teachers, more colleges, more universities: more and more of the Western assumption that education and learning inevitably *means* schooling. 'Change' in health provision has meant more hospitals, more imported drugs, more complex procedures, more university-trained medical practitioners: more and more of the health arrangements which the rich countries of the West can afford less and less. 'Change' in organisational arrangements, where it has occurred, has meant more – and bigger – bureaucracies, more ministries, more departments, more parastatal corporations, more bureaucrats, more clerks, more office blocks, more procedures, more forms, more control mechanisms: more and more of the organisational structures and practices which are now seen to retard change and development. (It has been remarked, with irony and some justification, that in many ways the public services of some ex-British colonies in Africa bear a striking resemblance to the British civil service circa 1950, so little real change has taken place.)

It is against this background that in this chapter we examine organisational change and development, particularly in the African context.

10.1   The Nature of Organisational Change

"There is nothing more difficult to execute, nor more dubious of success, nor more dangerous to administer than to introduce a new order of things; for he who introduces it has all those who profit from the old order as his enemies, and he has only lukewarm allies in all those who might profit from the new."
(Machiavelli. *The Prince*)

The overwhelmingly distinctive characteristic of the twentieth century is change. Human civilisation has in all eras been marked by changes, but it is in this century that change has become disturbingly rapid, continuous and turbulent. Popular attention was focussed on this aspect of our world, particularly in the 1970's, by such writers as Toffler (1970), who attempted to catalogue the acceleration of changes in all aspects of human society and to predict their consequences. It is natural that those involved in the functioning and performance of formal organisations should be concerned to understand the implications of such 'future shock.' A number of writers have sought to explore and clarify the nature of organisational change. Unfortunately, much of this theorising has been of little practical value to those who have to try to monitor, cope with, initiate, and manage change. Many attempts to change organisations fail because of our incomplete understanding of the nature of change and the dearth of tools to undertake change. Yet many writers on the subject, in attempting to provide a kitbag of techniques for 'managing change', 'overcoming resistance to change', and 'dealing with conflict', fail to consider the *nature* of organisational change; thus frequently rendering their suggested techniques ineffective or even damaging.

Our understanding of the nature of organisational change has been greatly enhanced by Edgar Schein, one of the pioneers – with Bennis and Beckhard – of the approach to changing organisations which came to be known as Organisation Development (OD). In an important recent article Schein (1990) observes that in the face of the accelerating rate of change in technological, socio-cultural, political, and economic environments, managers and academics alike are increasingly concerned about the adaptive and learning capacities of organisations. Schein recognises that the nature of continuous environmental change demands more than making adjustments to current organisational practices; frequently, it requires 'genuinely *innovative* thrusts' (Schein 1990: 9), the development of capacities for institutional learning and self-design, and an understanding of change as a permanent feature of organisational life.

According to Schein (1990: 12), "the overarching determinant of how organisations work is the culture that is evolved in the organisation as its members cope with the external problems of survival in the environment and their internal problems of integration." For Schein, organisational culture consists of 'learned basic assumptions' which are considered to have been validated and which new organisational members learn as 'the correct way to perceive, think, and feel ...' This learning encompasses shared values and accepted norms, finding overt expression in the 'normal' behaviour of organisational members. Schein's crucial point about organisational culture is that it provides meaning and stability to organisational life, without which members could not function. This "underlying, often implicit and unconscious pattern of *taken for granted assumptions*" brings to organisational life a degree of essential predictability. Hence – and this is the nub of Schein's argument – "culture, once in place, is ... an inherently conservative force" (Schein 1990: 14).

As we saw in the previous chapter, the notion of organisational culture has engaged the attention of a number of writers. But few have articulated as clearly as Schein its critical importance for understanding change in organisations, particularly as a conservative force. Schein's sociotechnical systems approach to organisational change makes it clear that one cannot consider organisational processes and structures separately from culture. Both formal and informal aspects of organisational structure are reflections of the under-lying cultural reality, which serve to strengthen the organisation's stability and predict-ability. Attempts to change organisational structure – probably the most common re-sponse to a perceived need for change, especially in Africa – which are not informed by an understanding of the organisation's culture, are inevitably flawed. The question, then, is:

"is it possible to conceive of a type of culture that would be innovative, that would have as its learning dynamic the invention of environmentally responsive new solutions rather than conservative self-preservation ... a type of culture that would favour sociotechnical design innovations instead of the traditional technology driven ones?" (Schein 1990: 15).

This question, as posed by Schein, might be expressly addressed to the problems of African managers in their "overwhelmingly urgent task ... to force life into the ailing bureaucratic systems which they inherited and which have largely failed to meet the demands placed upon them since independence" (Jones 1990a: 50). Schein advances a set of hypotheses concerning the dimensions of organisational culture which influence inno-vativeness. In view of the apparent relevance of Schein's model to the African situation, we will return to his hypotheses later in this chapter and consider the extent to which African formal organisations might meet his conditions for innovation.

Another writer who has contributed importantly to our understanding of organisational change is Revans (1987, 1991), the originator, some fifty years ago, of the notion of Action Learning. Although Revans' concepts have been trivialised by many of those he labels 'charlatans' (Action Learning is, he says, so simple that it takes professors ten years to thoroughly misunderstand it!), he continues to articulate the fundamentals of Action Learning. We consider the applications of Revans' ideas to management development in Chapter 13; in this chapter we will look briefly at their implications for organisational change and development.

We noted earlier that Schein considers that the process of learning must be institution-alised in the organisation if it is to manage change successfully. For Revans, 'learning how to learn' continuously and consciously from lived experience is the key if we are to avoid being overtaken and overwhelmed by environmental change. Revans sees that the challenges of organisational life are of two kinds. Managers are regularly faced with *puzzles*. A puzzle is a challenge to which a solution or several solutions already exist: the challenge is to find the existing solution(s). The solution(s) are based on precedent cases and are stored in files, records, books, and the brains of educators – in this context, management teachers. Puzzles, then, are the routine business of administrators. The other type of organisational challenge identified by Revans is the *problem*. A problem is a challenge to which there is no known solution or answer; it is new, without precedent, and therefore cannot be tackled by reference only to the past, like a puzzle. For Revans, this is the arena of leadership where the manager must call, not on books and teachers – in this context usually operating in their 'consultant' guise – but on her 'questioning insight', on the lessons learned from her lived experience and that of her colleagues. "True learning consists mainly in the reorganisation, or reinterpretation, of what is already known" (Revans 1980: 289).

For the manager the two types of challenge are very different. The puzzle presents few real difficulties because it is not new. The problem, in contrast, is occasioned by change, and demands new solutions. Revans eloquently illustrates the frightening predicament of the manager faced with a problem:

"... when ordinary men, like hardworking managers, are confused and uneasy, but nevertheless obliged by circumstances to get something done, it is not some intellectual explanation of their emergency that they seek, followed by a logical plan of action that will get them off the hook; one cannot build intellectual edifices upon the foundation of disorder. At such times, borne down by responsibility, fear, confusion and helplessness, it is not argument one needs but support, not analysis but example, not lucidity but warmth ..." (Revans 1980: 289–290).

Revans' choice of language – 'confused, uneasy, emergency, disorder, fear, confusion, helplessness' – eloquently conveys the nature of change and its consequences for the managers of formal organisations. For Revans, such challenges can be met only if the rate of learning matches or exceeds the rate of change in the environment.

Morgan (1986) has also been concerned to articulate the nature of organisational change and development. Calling for a 'reframing of the study of change', Morgan asserts that "few organisation theorists have devoted attention to understanding the *nature* of change" (Morgan 1986: 376). Two lines of reasoning emerged from the early Greek philosophers, one emphasising the stable nature of earthly phenomena, the other, in contrast, asserting that change is omnipresent. Morgan quotes the philosopher Heraclitus to stress "the idea that the universe is in a constant state of flux embodying characteristics of both permanence *and* change" (Morgan 1986: 233):

"... you cannot step twice into the same river, for other waters are continually flowing on. Everything flows and nothing abides; everything gives way and nothing stays fixed ... It is in changing that things find repose" (Heraclitus, circa 500 B.C.).

Morgan therefore sees "that the world is itself but a moment in a more fundamental process of change." If we are to comprehend the 'logic of change', "we have to understand the movement, flux, and change that *produce* the world we experience and study" (Morgan 1986: 234).

According to Morgan, the sociotechnical analysis of the 'causal texture of environments' (Morgan 1986: 376) is one of the few contributions to the understanding of the nature of change and its impacts on organisations so far offered by organisation theory. In common with Schein, therefore, Morgan appreciates the relevance of sociotechnical systems thinking for analysing environmental change. Like Schein, also, he notes the conservative, change-resistant characteristics of culture. The artifacts which give expression to a culture serve to provide an illusion of continuity, development and immortality which is psychologically essential to us when we contemplate our own mortality. Our formal work organisations are particularly powerful artifacts in this respect; they usually survive longer than individual members (some, for centuries). In them we "find meaning and permanence ... our roles become our realities." No wonder, then, that organisations frequently perceive change as threatening to their survival, "for there is more than the survival of the organisation at stake" (Morgan 1986: 213). Such insights into the *meanings* of organisational culture and its artifacts provide an explanation for the persistence of organisational structures and processes long after they have ceased to perform any formally significant purpose. They have become ritualised and hence excluded from rational questioning. Such elements "may come to assume special significance and be preserved and retained even in the face of great pressure to change" (Morgan 1986: 221).

As with Schein's work, Morgan's analysis offers us clues to understanding the generally recognised ability of African bureaucracies, particularly in the public sector, to resist change. Many aspects of culture and organisational artifacts identified by the two writers can be seen to be powerful conservative forces in African countries, particularly in view of the need, so insistently expressed by African managers, for security (*see* Chapter 12).

The stabilising quality of organisational culture is also emphasised by Mintzberg (1989), who prefers to use the word 'ideology'. He sees it as a force for co-operation, for 'pulling together' (Mintzberg 1989: 257), which is reinforced by organisational myths about key events in the organisation's biography. It 'forms a common base for tradition', providing the organisation with 'a life of its own ... a self, a distinctive identity' (Mintzberg 1989: 226). It is not difficult to see, as Mintzberg asserts, that organisational ideology can 'hinder fundamental change', as can associated forces, "especially those for efficiency, for proficiency, and for concentration" (Mintzberg 1989: 277).

As with our previously mentioned writers, the relevance of Mintzberg's analysis for African organisations is intriguing, especially when he observes, "in my own work with organisations, the single most commonly asked question – the virtual obsession of today's managers – is how can we help bureaucracies to change" (Mintzberg 1989: 277). In earlier chapters, particularly Chapter 1, we have emphasised the overwhelming urgency of this same question for the developing countries of Africa.

10.2   Managing Change

"The philosophers have only interpreted the world in various ways, the point is to change it" (Karl Marx).

A useful recent exploration of the management of organisational change has been provided by Mullins (1989). He points out that in an era of turbulent change, organisations can perform effectively only by successfully managing their interactions with their increasingly volatile environments; this demands that they be responsive to change. Organisations have to make regular arrangements for managing continuous internal change, brought about by the need to maintain and renew resources, including people. Careful planning of manpower, maintenance, materials and equipment can facilitate this essential organisational process. "But the main pressure of change is from external forces. The organisation must be properly prepared to face the demands of a changing environment. It must give attention to its future development and success" (Mullins 1989: 499–500). An understanding of the systems nature of organisations enables us to comprehend their interdependent variables – or sub-systems – including task, technology, structure, people, and management. Such a systems perspective can be a powerful tool for understanding the organisational implications of change and for managing change.

10.2.1   Environmental Forces for Change

Mullins notes that pervasive change produces a range of forces which act on organisations. These he identifies as: the accelerating rate of technological change; the explosion of knowledge and methods of dissemination; the shortened life-cycle of many products and services (product obsolescence); changes in the composition of workforces, brought about by enhanced educational opportunities, changing lifestyles, and changes in patterns of employment; increasing emphasis on the quality of working life and the employer's responsibility for the wellbeing – physical and psychological – of the worker. It would not be too fanciful to infer that many of the trends identified by Mullins could be expected to have an even more dramatic effect in the African situation. We are thinking here, to give just one example, of the fact that many African workers are of the first generation which has made the traumatic transition from the traditional village life to wage employment, with all the cultural and psychological contradictions that process has involved (e.g., Jenkins 1982).

10.2.2   Resistance to Change

The management of change is complicated by the fact that change inevitably rarely benefits everyone; it is usually in someone's interest and thus contrary to someone else's. Or it appears to be; Checkland (1981) shows that 'human activity systems' (for instance, organisations) differ from 'hard' systems in a critical way: what happens in a human activity system is not an objective reality. It is perceived in different ways by the various groups and individuals who have a vested interest in the organisation. Checkland (1981) uses the German word '*Weltanschauung*' to convey the sense of the 'image or model of the world' which provides meaning for the individual or group: the way in which people make sense of events. The implications of Checkland's work are clear. Organisational change is not an objective reality; its meaning and significance for individuals and groups who are involved in different ways will be formed by their distinctive *Weltanschauungen*; and there may be several quite different ways in which change is perceived.

Resistance to change and acceptance of change are crucial elements in managing organisational change and development. We have noted above that fundamental aspects of organisational life can be conservative forces, resisting change. There is a danger, evident in the work of some writers, managers, and consultants, of perceiving such conservative forces as abnormalities to be condemned. This is unrealistic and illusory. The work of writers like Revans, Morgan, Mintzberg and Schein shows that much of what happens in formal work organisations is designed or intended to provide the essential elements of stability, continuity and predictability in organisational life. For example, the word 'structure', which we use to describe the designed pattern of formal internal relationships in an organisation, when applied in its original sense to a building or a bridge or an aeroplane clearly means a strong, rigid framework which can be relied upon to retain its shape and form. Even in the most flexible, freewheeling organisations, life would be intolerable without a degree of such reliability. We must be careful, therefore, to understand manifestations of resistance to desired change as normal – and from some viewpoints, valuable – mechanisms to protect the existing system.

Torrington, Weightman and Johns (1989) provide a useful distinction between four basic categories of change. The first is imposed change. For an organisation as a whole, this refers to change which is initiated or necessitated by an external force, to which the organisation has to react. Examples would be a change in the law, in the economic situation, in the national labour force, in supplies of essential resources, or in the market for particular products or services. For individuals in an organisation, change imposed by management may take a variety of forms, such as new employment conditions, new work patterns, new supervisory practices, or altered reporting relationships.

The second form is adaptation, where individuals have to change their behaviour, and perhaps values and attitudes, at the behest of others. Torrington and his colleagues point out that this can lead to real problems for the individual, who may feel uncertain about his ability to 'become the new type of person'. They suggest that perhaps the main reason for individuals taking early retirement is that "they lack the confidence to change the values and behaviours in which they have come to trust" (Torrington *et al.* 1989: 106). This example of the consequences of required adaptation to new values reinforces the point made earlier in this chapter about the conservative power of organisational culture.

The third category of change identified by Torrington and his colleagues is growth. Here, the individual is not reacting to external demands, but to "the opportunities for becoming a person of greater competence, poise and achievement" (p. 106).

Creativity is the final type of change, where the individual initiates the process of realising her ideas and bringing them to fruition. According to Torrington *et al.* (1989:

106), "most of us are probably resistant to the first, uncertain about the second, delighted with the third and excited by the fourth".

From Checkland's (1981: 180) 'soft' systems viewpoint, three types of changes are possible in organisations (his 'human activity systems'): changes in structure, changes in procedure, and changes in attitude. Structural change involves changes to the organisational framework and includes changes in functional responsibilities, changes to reporting structures and changes to groupings within the organisation. Procedural change involves changes to "the dynamic elements: the processes of reporting and informing, verbally and on paper, all the activities which go on within the (relatively) static structures." Changes of these two types are not especially difficult for management to specify or to implement. Even though such changes may possibly bring about unanticipated effects also, the act of implementation can be designed with some degree of deliberation. However, according to Checkland, this is not true (and we may think this is a good thing if we are to remain human) where changes of the third kind are involved, that is, changes in 'attitude'. These, for Checkland, include not only those changes which 'attitude surveys' claim to measure, but also "many other crucial, but intangible characteristics which reside in the individual and collective consciousness of human beings in groups" (1981: 180–181).

It seems to us that Checkland, using different, specialised systems language, is exploring the organisational cultural realities which have engaged the attention of Schein and the other scholars whose work we considered earlier in this chapter. His notion of *Weltanschauung* provides a powerful tool for understanding how individuals and groups in organisations might perceive potential changes in ways which might be simplistically put down to 'resistance to change as basic to human nature' and therefore something to be overcome by some form of force.

Mullins (1989) provides some more detailed guidance on the common reasons for resistance to organisational change. He points out that "although organisations have to adapt to their environment, they tend to feel comfortable operating within the structure, policies and procedures which have been formulated to deal with a range of present situations" (Mullins 1989: 503). Hence, organisations may tend to resist change for a number of reasons.

First, the perceived importance of stability and predictability, especially by large organisations, tends to lead to the maintenance of rigid structures, job specialisation, tight definitions of authority and responsibility, established work methods, and laid-down rules and procedures. Examples of resistance to change reinforced by such bureaucratic mechanisms are common in Africa, as we have noted in other chapters.

Second, it is often expensive to change organisations. Even changes which appear clearly desirable may be excluded or delayed because resources are needed for other essential investments. Change may appear from the accountant's point of view to represent an open-ended investment of scarce resources, perhaps with an uncertain payoff. Since public sector bureaucracies, particularly in Africa, place such heavy emphasis on inputs, it is not surprising that the accountant's cost-conscious view often carries the day there against the advocates of organisational change.

The third factor identified by Mullins concerns the fact that many organisations are bound by long-term agreements and contracts – with trades unions, suppliers, customers/ clients and government agencies – which restrict their scope for changes in direction or modes of operation.

Finally, various groups within the organisation may perceive proposed change as a threat to their influence and power, particularly in relation to decision making and control over resources and information. This protection of organisational territory may be especially trenchant where managers suspect some potential diminution of their power; for example, when some form of power-sharing scheme is proposed.

At the level of individuals in the organisation, Mullins notes some common reasons for reluctance to accept change. One is selective perception (Checkland's *Weltanschauung*), which means that individuals construct their version of organisational reality in accordance with how they see it. It is not difficult to appreciate how individuals operating within differing *Weltanschauungen* can fail to see each other's perspective. As Checkland perceptively remarks,

"(even if we are) merely talking about taking action in a human activity system then that action must seem to be 'obvious' to the people in the system, *it must fit in with the state of their perceptions of their situation and their valuations of what constitutes 'good' or 'bad' activity relative to on-going purposes"* (1981: 189).

Mullins' second point about individual resistance to organisational change concerns habitual behaviours. Habits provide security and comfort and guide actions in well established routines – routines which have presumably at some time proved to be useful. Proposed changes to well established habitual behaviour often meet with individual resistance. Even where the necessity for such changes is accepted, individuals may still find it difficult to change habitual behaviours. For instance, the introduction of 'No Smoking' rules in university classrooms has been known to cause real hardships for some students and lecturers.

Third, individuals may react against a proposed change if it is likely to increase control over them or reduce their freedom of action, or if it looks as if it will make their working life more difficult. It is often the case that, in retrospect, individuals will agree that the initial hard work, inconvenience and disruption involved in making a change was worth it, although they vehemently opposed the change when it was proposed.

Mullins notes that individuals will generally resist proposed organisational changes which appear likely – directly or indirectly – to reduce their financial rewards from work, lessen their job security, or increase the level of work required for the same pay. This, of course, is an area where trades unions are especially vigilant when scrutinising, on behalf of their members, changes proposed by employers. Many industrial disputes are caused when unions in these situations are accused of being rigid and resisting changes which are perceived by employers as imperative for organisational survival.

Another factor noted by Mullins is that many individuals find security in the past, whereas a future which looks as if it will be rather different from the past may be regarded with suspicion. Mullins points to the habit, common in bureaucracies, of retaining comfortable ways of doing things by referring to 'tried and tested' procedures; the implication being that new procedures run the risk of being less effective and therefore not worth trying.

The final reason for individual reluctance to accept organisational change suggested by Mullins is widely acknowledged yet at the same time perhaps the factor which receives least managerial attention when change is being proposed. Many aspects of organisational change can produce uncertainty, and consequently anxiety for those individuals who will be affected. As we note in the next chapter, many people in organisations suffer from damaging, and in some cases dangerous, stress. Anxiety about impending changes is an important causal factor in many instances of stress.

10.2.3   Managing Organisational Change

Advice on how managers should manage change in their organisations is available in abundance. As we noted earlier, much is in the form of neat prescriptions and kitbags of techniques. It is not surprising that such simplistic nostrums frequently fail to match the complexity of the processes of change. Some writers, however, have attempted to propose guiding principles for managers which acknowledge the complexity of their task in managing change. Morgan (1986), for example, builds on his view that "the organisation consists of interrelated subsystems of a strategic, human, technological, structural, and managerial nature, which need to be internally consistent and adapted to environmental conditions" (Morgan 1986: 63), by posing a set of questions which can clearly be seen to be of potential value to managers:

- 'What is the nature of the organisation's environment?' This involves consideration of the environment's degree of stability, the interconnections between its various elements, and changes which are occurring.
- 'What kind of strategy is being employed?' How is the organisation approaching change – reactively or proactively?
- 'What kind of technology (mechanical and non-mechanical) is being used?'
- 'What kind of people are employed, and what is the dominant "culture" or ethos within the organisation?'
- 'How is the organisation structured, and what are the dominant managerial philosophies?' (Morgan 1986: 62–63).

By asking these systemic questions, managers can obtain a rich description of the organisation in relation to its environment, which will provide a framework for initiating and managing change.

Torrington, Weightman and Johns (1989) describe an influential study by Pettigrew, following his argument that "change is not just a rational choice of events but has to be seen in its cultural historical context" (Torrington et al., 1989: 111). Pettigrew studied processes of organisational change in ICI and traced a series of events which exemplified the cultural history of the organisation. These included the existence of rational arguments for change, supported by political influence; there were powerful advocates of an emphasis on efficiency; exceptional individuals were able to foresee needed changes and to persuade others; technological obsolescence existed in some parts of the enterprise; a number of chance events occurred; and powerful environmental forces for change were evident. Generalising from his ICI study, Pettigrew recognises the problem of obtaining legitimacy for organisational change and proposes a model for managing organisational change which involves the following steps:

1. The development of concern by a subset of the organisation.
2. Acknowledgement and understanding of the problems with possible causes and alternatives by others.
3. Planning and acting to create specific change.
4. Stabilising the change, including rewards, information and power to appropriate individuals to sustain the change.

Although this model is not phrased in specifically systems terms, it is clear that the various subsystems – human, technological, cultural (particularly political influence) – identified in Morgan's questions (above) are central to the successful management of change in Pettigrew's study and conclusions.

An important implication of the work of Morgan (1986) and that of Torrington *et al.* (1989) is the critical need to give due attention to the human subsystem in initiating and managing change. Change, even potential change, can be very unsettling for those organisational members who will be – or think they will be – affected. Many organisational change efforts fail because their effects on the human subsystem are not properly managed. The proposals in many African countries to reduce the size of workforces in the public sector, often drastically, can be expected to cause vehement opposition and conflict unless those in charge of the change have the competence and commitment to manage the process sensitively.

Torrington and his colleagues propose that those in charge of organisational change should be guided, in relation to the human subsystem, by several questions:

– 'What is in it for them?' Will it be possible to demonstrate to those who will be affected by the proposed change that they will benefit in some meaningful way from it?
– 'Have they a say in the change?' It is important to encourage the commitment of those involved in organisational change by providing opportunities for *genuine* involvement in some or all stages – 'introduction, design, execution, feedback and evaluation' – of the change process.
– 'Is it clear what change is envisaged?' As we have noted earlier, change is associated with uncertainty, and frequently involves complexity, confusion, disturbance and turbulence. This is often made worse by the failure of management to articulate a clear vision of the proposed change and its intended outcomes. The vision communicated has to be practical, explaining what is proposed, who is involved, why change is being proposed, and how it is to be achieved (Torrington *et al.* 1989: 112–113).

Similar points are emphasised by Mullins (1989). Stressing the importance of human and social factors in the management of change, he asserts that "activities managed on the basis of technical efficiency alone are unlikely to lead to optimum improvement in organisational performance" (Mullins 1989: 504). It is important for successful management of organisational change to encourage an environment of trust and commitment by involving those affected in the change process, at an early stage. This inevitably demands a free and open exchange of information: facts, estimates, anticipated benefits and difficulties, opinions, feelings, concerns, doubts. As we have noted elsewhere, the limited number of reliable investigations of organisational behaviour in African countries have consistently shown that this openness is not generally a feature of organisations there. Thus there is a contradiction: the very organisations which are charged with the management of national change and development are frequently managed in ways which effectively prevent them from changing themselves, despite the urgent need for such change (e.g., Jones 1990b). It is important to stress here that involvement in change has to be *genuine* if it is to make a contribution to its successful management; as Mullins suggests, joint consultation mechanisms such as working parties and steering committees are potentially very valuable, but it is not uncommon for such bodies to be established by management to manipulate employees by giving the *appearance* of consultation and participation. Naturally, such schemes tend to make the management of change even more problematic when – inevitably – the employees, who are rarely as gullible as managers like to believe, see through the deception. This is especially likely to happen where the management regime has not previously been based on openness and participation.

Mullins takes a sociotechnical systems view of organisational change (*see* Chapter 5) when he points out the importance of considering the potential and actual impact of technological change on all aspects of the human subsystem. This will include job design; work methods and organisation; intra-group and inter-group relationships; reward systems, including incentive schemes; learning needs, including importantly new skills and values. The introduction of new technologies is not only a potential source of uncertainty and stress for employees; it frequently does actually involve changes in the relationship between workers and their work. A common consequence of automation, for instance, is to make jobs boring, repetitive and less responsible. It is important that such potential consequences of change, for the human subsystem, should be considered seriously and openly at the early stages of change and then continuously.

It is apparent from our brief discussion of some contemporary views on the management of organisational change that it is a supremely complex process. Because the rate of environmental change is accelerating and in many ways becoming increasingly turbulent, the managerial responsibility for anticipating, initiating, monitoring, interpreting and managing organisational change is becoming more and more critical. A sociotechnical systems perspective, which is implicit in the views we have discussed, emphasises the interdependence of the organisation's various subsystems. For those charged with the management of organisational change, the implications of this interdependence are particularly crucial in relation to the effects of change on the human subsystem – the employees whose working lives will be affected. It appears that many attempts to change and improve formal organisations go wrong because managers are unable and/or unwilling to consider rigorously and openly the probable and possible consequences of change for the people involved. In the African context, as Jones (1990b) observes, reform of the organisations inherited at independence, which have failed to measure up to the tasks of development, is perhaps the most urgent need. Yet the "generally ... mechanistic view of organisations, involving an unquestioned assumption that organisations function in accordance with formal policies and objectives and operate at the command of rationality ..." tends to limit organisational reform efforts to changes in *structure*, "the classic mechanistic remedy" (Jones 1990b: 61). As we saw in Chapter 1, the various reform packages being adopted currently by many African governments tend also to focus heavily on changes in the structure of public sector organisations. Little consideration seems to have been given to their chances of success, given the apparent failure to consider the implications of such changes for those affected, directly and indirectly.

Ironically, concepts and tools for the more effective management of organisational change and development have been available for some years, but appear not to have made much of an impact on the managers of African organisations or those international agencies concerned to impose organisational reforms in Africa. In the next section we look at some of the ideas of those concerned with Organisation Development (OD).

10.3   Organisation Development

"We will, within another ten years, become less concerned with 'management development' as a means of adapting the individuals to the demands of the organisation, and far more with 'organisation development' to adapt the organisation to the needs, aspirations and potential of the individual" (Drucker 1972: 41).

When Peter Drucker, the philosopher and prophet of management, made his prediction two decades ago he was in good company. Schein (1970) had come to a similar conclusion: "Good management training may ... be inseparable from broader problems of organisational change and development" (p. 48). Schein was one of the pioneers of the Organisation Development movement, which was at that time gathering force as an approach and technology for organisational change and renewal. During the following years, Organisation Development – OD as it came to be known by its practitioners and adherents – attracted the attention of managers and scholars in the industrialised nations of the West, particularly in the United States. As with all such movements, OD waned in prominence as new ideas came to the fore. Yet its influence persists as an important strand in the literature and practice of organisational change. In this section we examine briefly the conceptual basis of OD and its possible applications in African organisations.

Over the years an enormous OD literature has accumulated. Debate has persisted about its definition, its boundaries, and its limits. It is frequently frustrating for students of management and organisational behaviour to find that accounts of OD 'interventions' tend to be rather vague: "Yes I've read the books, but I still don't know what OD *is*." This lack of precision in terms of the applications of OD in real organisations is not unique in the behavioral and social sciences, of course. What gives OD its distinctive character is its base in explicit humanistic values concerning how organisations should be managed.

One of the most quoted descriptions of OD, by another pioneer, Beckhard (1969), conveys some of its fundamental character: "... an effort, planned organisation-wide and managed from the top, to increase organisation effectiveness and health through planned intervention in the organisation's 'processes', using behavioral science knowledge" (1969: 9). From this very brief definition the systems focus of OD is clear, in the notion of organisational health, an unfamiliar idea at the time, and the stress on the 'organisation-wide' nature of OD's focus.

The concepts and assumptions underlying OD are nicely articulated by Hage and Finsterbusch (1987) in their examination of organisational change as a development strategy. Rooted in the human relations approach to organisations, OD proceeds from a critical view of formal organisations: most of them have powerful dehumanising characteristics. Hence, it is asserted that organisations should be changed so that they encourage the personal growth and development of employees; they should promote openness and cooperation; they should recognise the validity and importance of open expressions of feelings. It is claimed that organisations which encourage human development and growth tend to perform well. This focus on the human subsystem of the organisation, while recognising the interdependence of all subsystems, guides OD interventions towards change efforts in the areas of organisation culture, group processes, job design, employee attitudes and motivation, and role expectations. Processes in the human subsystem which concern OD practitioners include the uses of power and influence, problem solving, decision making, communication, creativity and innovation, and the management of change and conflict. An important distinctive aspect of OD is that, unlike other strategies, it "does not assume that there is a rational order to the world or that people should be seen simply as calculators" (Hage & Finsterbusch 1987: 26). (Note the echo here of Checkland's *Weltanschauung*.) These authors remark on the clear biases, in OD assumptions, of social psychology and North American culture. Significantly for our discussion of the appropriateness of OD strategies for African organisations, their view is that these assumptions, "about openness, collaboration, and expression of feelings may not fit many non-Western cultures, while that of the need for growth and development may" (Hage & Finsterbusch 1987: 26).

It is clear that the basic thrust of OD is influenced primarily by humanistic psychology. Its major concerns are with the development of effective organisations which encourage the growth and learning of organisation members and which are thus capable of thriving in a changing environment: the notion of self-renewal. Congruent with the values which tend to guide OD strategies, its practitioners favour an approach which Schein presented as 'process consultation'. The model of the management consultant who is called into the organisation, diagnoses the problem, presents her prescription (and bill), and departs, leaving the client to implement the change, is regarded as failing to respect the abilities and learning needs of the client. Instead, the OD practitioner, as a process consultant, tends to prefer a client-centred, action research methodology which involves the follow-ing steps: contract building between the practitioner and the client to ensure that they share similar values and aims; data collection as a basis for diagnosis of organisational health; comparison of the client's needs with the data collected; generation, by the client in consultation with the practitioner, of potential action plans; evaluation of the alternative action plans in terms of their likely effects and implications, particularly possible sources of resistance; choice *by the client* of the action plan thought to be the most appropriate; implementation and monitoring of the action plan by the client, *with the active participation of the practitioner*. As mentioned earlier, OD practitioners generally have some background in the behavioral sciences, acting as agents of awareness, concerned with process issues, helping the client to manage the change, and monitoring the systemic affects of the change process. Where, as is often the case, other subsystems are involved in the change process, for example some aspect of the organisation's technology, the OD practitioner will, if necessary, advise the client to bring in specialists in the appropriate areas. The intention behind the insistence on the active role of the client is to ensure that the organisation members develop the skills to solve future problems without the help of a consultant. A crucial test of the effectiveness of an OD intervention is the extent to which the organisation has developed into a 'learning community'.

Commonly, OD process interventions tend to take the form of team building activities, goal setting and planning, intergroup problem solving, confrontation meetings (confront-ing issues), agenda setting, and management of meetings. These interventions into the processes in the human subsystem can be seen as a basically educational strategy: the intended outcomes are to make the organisation more effective *and* to ensure that the organisation 'learns how to learn' from its experience.

It is difficult to dispute that the values underlying OD are attractive: their purpose is to change organisations so that they become not only more effective agencies for providing the goods and services we want and need, but also more interesting and democratic places to work in. Perhaps the main thrust of criticism which is of most direct relevance for us has been directed at these very explicit values. As we noted earlier, Hage and Finsterbusch (1987) questioned the applicability of OD for organisations in developing countries, suggesting that the North American values to which it is committed may not be appropri-ate in other settings. We have been unable to locate any descriptions of OD interventions in African organisations which have explicitly raised these issues. We can, however, usefully pursue Hage and Finsterbusch's concerns in more general terms.

It is commonly assumed that the cultures of the United Kingdom and the United States are, for many reasons, rather similar. Indeed, a number of studies mentioned in previous chapters (e.g., Haire *et al.* 1966; Hofstede 1980) have provided evidence to support the popular wisdom. It is interesting therefore to read a thought provoking article by Steele (1976) which contradicts this view in the light of the author's experience of trying to undertake OD work in the U.K. Steele has tested several OD value assumptions against British cultural factors which he found to impede change processes. These values include: "doing better is a good thing; the facts are friendly; people should have personal owner-ship of their own lifespace; a changing environment requires the system to be adaptive in terms of its structure and processes; change does not have to be haphazard; the results of change actions are not always wholly predictable and controllable; behavioral science knowledge can contribute to organisational health" (Steele 1976: 21). Steele's findings indicate how aspects of British culture have the effect of contradicting each of these value positions, which caused him to have misgivings about whether OD could be made to work there.

In considering the potential usefulness of OD in African organisations, Steele's insights are illuminating:

"Doing OD work is always influenced by a number of factors. Prime among these factors is a hazy yet pervasive one: the cultural context of the country in which the organisation is located. The culture includes basic norms which carry over to the organisation, societal pressures and formal regulations, technology and artifacts, traditions, and basic assumptions about life which are held by the members of the organisation. The OD process grew mainly (but by no means exclusively) out of consultant experience in the US. As such, it is rooted in a particular cultural context, and one cannot assume that its chances of success are high in another country ... " (Steele 1976: 21.)

If an experienced and thoughtful OD practitioner feels moved to offer such a caution as a result of his experience of contrasts between US and British cultural realities, it is worth considering how much greater these contrasts are likely to be when OD's central values guide attempts to change African organisations. We might anticipate that the conflicts would be so pronounced as to render many OD approaches dysfunctional. A simplistic conclusion to be drawn might be that when OD is used in Africa it must be modified in order to harmonise with local cultural realities (a not uncommon device in books on management 'in developing countries'). However, as we noted earlier, the overt value base of OD change strategies is what makes the approach so distinctive. Meddling with its value base will not modify OD; it will take away the elements which make it what it is. The task is to find out which (if any) of OD's value assumptions might be congruent with African cultural factors, and whether it is possible to use OD as some sort of model or guide for the construction of approaches to organisational change and development which might be suitable for African enterprises. In this connection it is worth noting that Golembiewski (1991) enters an objection to the commonly held view that OD change efforts must achieve a 'close fit' between the values of the change agent – the OD practitioner – and the client organisation. He suggests that such a comfortable situation may not produce the confrontation of problems which an open debate about values might initiate. Such issues can be debated in an informed way only when we have relevant empirical data at our disposal.

10.4. Organisational Change in Africa

In our exploration of the nature of change and approaches to organisational change and development so far, we have where appropriate attempted to relate contemporary concepts and themes to the African arena. In this section we focus more particularly on the small amount of recent literature concerning organisational change in Africa. As a preface to this it is useful to mention a couple of points. First, as we have emphasised on several occasions in this book, there are severe limits on our ability to make confident statements about African formal organisations and their management, owing to the acute scarcity of empirical data in this area. This is particularly problematic in relation to an issue of such complexity as organisational change. Secondly, such attention as has been directed at organisational change in African countries has been overwhelmingly on reforming the public sector, impelled primarily by international agencies such as the IMF (*see* Chapter 1). Very little seems to be known about the private sector, although this may begin to receive more attention as the various attempts to reduce the size and role of the public sector gather momentum. Generally, most attention has been directed at civil service reform, which is proving to be immensely difficult to achieve. Changes in the public enterprise (or parastatal) sector appear, at least in prospect, to be less problematic, mainly because of factors such as smaller size and narrower objectives compared to national civil services. Collins (1989b), for instance, has proposed, as a 'policy alternative' to privatisation, a systematic four-step rehabilitation plan which appears feasible in relation to African public enterprises.

Although documented evidence is scarce, there seems to be a general consensus among managers and scholars that African formal organisations, particularly in the public sector, are powerfully change resistant. Montgomery (1987), for example, is probably not exaggerating when he describes Africa as "one of the most difficult administrative settings to be found anywhere in the world" (p. 913). Describing one of the few large-scale investigations to have been undertaken into organisational behaviour in Africa – its focus was the SADCC countries of southern Africa – Montgomery details a number of assumptions about African organisations which were tested by the study. One assumption was that African institutions are very resistant to change. The evidence available from the investigation tended to support this assumption. As Montgomery observes, "the system cries out for administrative reforms, (yet) the changes the administrative system needs are the hardest to bring about. Political realities tend to undermine the appearance of grand scope for administrative modernisation" (1987: 924–926).

Kiggundu (1988) also remarks on the capacity for resistance to change which appears to characterise African formal organisations, particularly in the public sector, where he says they "have demonstrated tremendous resistance to different forms of bureaucratic reorientation and reform" (p. 226).

Jones (1990b) observes that the "newly independent African nations ... inherited from their colonial former masters the bureaucratic forms which were designed primarily for the maintenance of law and order", and which have "proved extraordinarily resistant to change" (p. 59). This is particularly serious because, given the weakness of the private sector in many African countries, public institutions have been required to be the engine of national development. Jones points to problems faced by African states which are 'outside the experience of the wealthy industrialised nations'. Among these is the inescapable – but, strangely, often overlooked – fact that many African nations are poor in resources and lacking in developed infrastructure, especially in transport and communications. This poverty of resources frequently includes critical shortages of skilled manpower, including managers. In addition, few African states have the tradition of formal organisations and technological/industrial evolution which is taken for granted in the industrialised nations. This has been a factor in the failure of frequent experiments with institutional systems in a number of countries. Some of these factors, and others, lie outside the control of African governments.

"The immense complexity of maintaining a public sector charged with initiating and managing change would test the abilities of the most supremely competent managers ... such abilities were scarce at independence among Africans ... the colonial administrators had themselves never performed these tasks, and were therefore not able to pass on a tradition of dynamic management" (Jones 1990b: 60).

It could be said, then, that while the role of the state in African countries has changed drastically since independence, the machinery generally has not. Jones cites several studies – Jenkins (1982), Jones (1986a), Rutherford, (1981) – which tend to support the view of the change resistant bureaucracy as the dominant organisational form in Africa. The following inferences can be drawn from the available evidence. First, there is often a mechanistic view of organisational functioning, involving an assumption that organisations operate at the command of rationality in accordance with formal policies and goals. Such a view ignores the political, social, psychological, and irrational characteristics of organisational life, and frequently leads decision makers to see possibilities for organisational change only in terms of structural alterations. This mechanistic type of remedy often fails because it ignores the complex reality of organisations. The issue of decentralisation of authority, for instance, has been debated by academics *ad nauseam*, especially in terms of its generally disappointing track record. Yet these discussions often ignore the realities of political power and political concerns. The need to build a cohesive nation state is for many African leaders more crucial than the need to pursue democratic ideals by decentralising the very authority which they perceive as indispensable to success in the first task.

   Second, it seems that there is generally in African public organisations an emphasis on control rather than performance, emphasising inputs and internal procedures, and neglecting measures of output. Much effort is devoted to creating and staffing ever more complicated checking mechanisms while questions of individual and organisational performance receive little attention. The Report of the Zimbabwe Public Service Review Commission (ZPSRC 1989) contains rich detail of just such a state of affairs, which prompted the Commission to call for measures to move the civil service towards a more performance oriented culture.

Third, associated with the common mechanistic view of organisational functioning and the emphasis – sometimes almost obsessional – on control, is the overstaffing of the public sectors of many African countries. As we observed in Chapter 1, many current reform programmes have focussed, rather crudely, on achieving reductions in public sector staffing levels, primarily as a way of cutting costs. Jones (1990b) points out that while inflated wage bills are a serious issue for many African governments, perhaps more damaging in the long run is the effect which overstaffing almost inevitably has on morale. Many bureaucrats, whose morale is already in decline because of low pay levels as compared to the private sector, become additionally depressed by the realisation that they are actually performing no useful function.

Another factor noted by Jones (1990b) is that the civil services of many of the ex-British colonies in Africa seem to have inherited and even strengthened the 'cult of the generalist'. This ethos, long under question in the British civil service, reflects the customary British mistrust of the professional and admiration of what Steele (1976) calls the "tradition of the gifted amateur ... notions of well-roundedness and the stigma attached to those who apply themselves in an ungraceful manner to one narrow field" (p. 25). An immediate and damaging consequence of this ethos is the frequent transfers of senior generalist civil servants, often into posts which demand specialist skills, with predictable consequences.

Leonard (1987) stresses African political realities *and* our lack of real knowledge about African administrative systems and practices:

"We certainly have no knowledge of what reforms might be used to improve the perform-ance of Africa's public organisations. We can be reasonably certain that techniques imported from the West will fail unless they are revised quite fundamentally. Yet we also know that some African organisations are performing much better that others. What we do not know is why" (Leonard 1987: 906).

It is probable also that we do not know *how* to initiate and achieve appropriate organis-ational change in Africa's public administrations. A number of commentators have highlighted perceived symptoms of organisational malfunctioning and incompetence. Adamolekun (1989) describes the deliberations of policy makers at top political and administrative levels from 29 African countries, who met in no less than four 'policy seminars' and a 'round up workshop' in a variety of locations. The following were among the points which emerged. The performance of the civil services of many African states has declined so seriously that they are now *obstacles* to development, neglected by politicians, lacking commitment and dynamism, and subject to politicisation and cycles of indiscriminate expansion and periodic purges. There is an urgent need for professionalism and specialisation in the service, to arrest institutional decay and to revitalise services, to increase effectiveness and efficiency, to reform training, to undertake more research, to develop suitable salary policies, and to achieve reductions in size and effective control of growth. Attention needs to be focussed on such issues as the misallocation of skills, computerised personnel systems, inter-sectoral mobility, wage differentials between the civil service, corporate and private sectors, personnel and recruitment policies, restructuring and the simplification of rules and procedures. All this would demand political commitment to reform and to sharing information.

Such an array of problems and urgent needs is daunting indeed. It would be difficult to argue against the need for action in these and associated areas. The problem is to *implement* the recommended changes. It is, for example, easy to agree with Balogun's (1989) prescriptions: "Africa needs to completely streamline the policy-making and implementation institutions and imbue every role player with a sense of purpose and energy"; "Africa needs a new administrative/ managerial order that is adequate to the challenge"; and "emphasis should be placed on the institutionalisation of ethics of public service: accountability, loyalty (to the nation) ... integrity, and constant search for excellence" (Balogun 1989: 228–231). These gentle homilies have an undoubted inspirational appeal, but provide no guidance as to *how* they might be implemented. What, for example, is involved in 'streamlining' when applied to complex organisations? How does one 'imbue' a sense of purpose and energy in people? By what process are the ethics of public service institutionalised, and by whom? What is a bureaucrat actually expected to *do* when he is told he must constantly 'search for excellence'?

Given the difficulties in deciding *what* kind of organisational changes are likely to be successful and of knowing *how* to implement such reforms, we need to be able to identify the causes of the resistance to change which is widely acknowledged. Here, we find that very little seems to be known beyond speculation, anecdotes, and uninformed prescription. If we are to search for such causes, one starting point might be in the cultural factors which might have an impact on organisational behaviour. Choudhury (1986), for example, raises the question whether 'the African culture' "discourages innovativeness, individualism, or impersonalism and anything that prevents or challenges the valued social order and stability" (Choudury 1986: 89). At present there is no way to answer such a question with any degree of confidence, let alone identify the forms which such cultural factors might take. The Report of the Conference on Civil Service Reform in Sub-Saharan Africa, organised by Britain's Overseas Development Administration (ODA) in 1989, touches on this issue. Delegates noted that the Western legal rational bureaucratic model tended to be the basis for attempted organisational change and that diagnosis of organisational problems failed to take account of what they called 'indigenous management practices'. It was felt that the urgency of the need to 'do something' about African public service organisations tended to preclude any attempt to identify and understand such indigenous management practices, and to prescribe mechanistic reforms based on the Weberian model (*see*, also, Marsden 1991). There was a need to develop an alternative, appropriate model, which might acknowledge the "different patterns of organisation, different value systems and decision making patterns that had grown up in developing countries in response to the unique environment and traditions" (ODA 1989: 19). In this context it was recognised that for some stakeholders in any change effort the desirability of improving organisational performance, which is a central value in the West, may be secondary to social and political objectives. There have been instances where reform attempts have failed because they lacked political commitment to changes which, to the international agencies involved, seemed unquestioningly desirable, in their ignorance of the real interests of powerful stakeholders.

Another important issue identified at the ODA Conference concerns the question of *who* makes the changes: "the difficulty of asking the civil service to transform itself fundamentally at a time when the civil service was the main instrument in implementing wider structural adjustment and economic recovery programmes" (ODA 1989: 21). This issue has received little attention, yet it is central to such change efforts. Quite apart from the huge additional burdens imposed on bureaucrats by structural adjustment programmes, there must be very serious questions about their commitment and ability to manage the immensely complex processes of organisational change. Are many of them not, by training, inclination and experience, predisposed more to stability and predictability: maintenance rather than change, administering rather than managing?

10.5 Conclusion

The tribulations of President Gorbachev, daily catalogued by the world's media, provided a stark example of the pitfalls which litter the paths of those who attempt change. So common are examples of failed change efforts that one is tempted to conclude that we have really have no idea how to manage change. We noted earlier in this chapter that Reg Revans, one of the few scholars of management who have enriched our understanding of the *nature* of change, teaches us that if we are to cope with change our only weapon is our great capacity for learning. Thus we must ensure that we learn how to learn from our experiences of change efforts, whether successful or otherwise. In Africa the need for organisational change and development is, as we have seen, urgent. It is imperative that lessons be drawn from the large-scale reform programmes currently under way in many African countries. In this closing section we examine the possibilities for change in African organisations. We conclude by suggesting how workable strategies for organisational development in Africa might evolve.

Earlier in this chapter we introduced a model developed by Schein (1990) for analysing the capacity of organisations to innovate. The difficulty is that organisations are by their nature and often by design oriented toward stabilising and routinising work. "How then can one conceptualise an organisation that can function effectively yet be capable of learning so that it can adapt and innovate in response to changing environmental circumstances? How can one conceive of an organisation that can surmount its own central dynamic, that can manage the paradox of institutionalising and stabilising the process of change and innovation ... what kind of organisational culture would consistently favour innovation?" (Schein 1990: 9–10).

By posing his questions in these terms, Schein captures the fundamental contradiction in organisational change which has to be confronted by managers and change agents: that formal organisations are by nature and design better equipped to resist change than to initiate it. According to his model, innovative organisations – those best able to initiate and manage change – share the following cultural values or beliefs, explicit or implicit:

"– That the world is changeable and can be changed.
– That humans are by nature proactive problem solvers.
– That truth is pragmatically arrived at.
– That the appropriate time horizon (for change) is the near future.
– That time units should be geared to the kind of innovation being considered.
– That human nature is neutral or good and is, in any case, 'perfectible'.
– That human relationships are based on individualism and the valuing of diversity.
– That decision making is collegial/participative.
– That diverse sub-cultures are an asset to be encouraged, but that sub-cultures have to
be connected to the parent (organisational) culture" (Schein 1990: 28). (Our parentheses).

Schein's hypothesis is yet to be tested in the context of African organisational cultures. Most of the values he posits as being necessary for organisational innovation are, of course, reflections of shared values which might characterise the national culture in which the organisation functions. It is wise to note that Schein is writing from the viewpoint of an OD practitioner and organisational theorist in the USA, and thus that the values which, he claims, facilitate change are those which he has encountered in that cultural milieu. We do not have the necessary empirical evidence to support or refute the applicability of Schein's hypothesis to African organisations, but even a cursory examination of the values he cites would suggest that there might be considerable doubts about the presence of many of them in institutions there. It seems particularly questionable whether the cultures of African organisations would place value on individualism or on the notion that diverse sub-cultures should be encouraged. Other of the values might have greater or lesser degrees of applicability in African organisations. If Schein's hypothesis, based on his observations and experiences with innovative organisations, is accurate, then there must be considerable doubt concerning the ability of African organisations, particularly in the public sector, to initiate and manage change. Indeed, his insights may provide some clues as to why organisational change has generally proved to be so problematic in many African countries.

It has to be said that many of the public sector reform programmes currently underway in Africa, often under the impetus of external agencies, are either crude or simplistic. We have noted, for example, the curious coincidence that manpower cuts in the civil service – seemingly imposed with little convincing justification in many instances – are regularly in the region of 25% to 30%. We have a definite impression that those involved in these reforms are either unfamiliar with, or uninterested in, the literature of experiences with organisational change and development which might provide valuable guidance for these major and frequently controversial change efforts. We look in vain for any principles of 'good organisation' which guide these reforms. They appear to be based on mechanistic assumptions about organisational functioning and thus tend to focus on structural modification – primarily in the form of reducing total size and range of functions performed.

Hage and Finsterbusch (1987) observe perceptively in relation to developing countries that:

"We think an elaborate framework is necessary since many change efforts in the past have failed due to underestimating the complexity of the task. Often change agents worked with only one model of a good organisation or proposed only one kind of intervention, and were not sensitive to a different model or a different type of intervention being more appropriate ...they often changed too few elements for lasting effect ... " (Hage & Finsterbusch 1987: 20).

From the African point of view this is an important observation. As we have shown earlier, the dominant model for administrative reform has been the Weberian bureau-cracy, whereas "the problem of development from an organisational perspective is to stimulate the growth of a *variety* of organisations, each of which is needed to achieve certain performances" (Hage & Finsterbusch 1987: 87) (our emphasis). These authors call for an approach to organisational change which is concerned with multiple organi-sational levels and would therefore draw upon several relevant organisational disciplines. Change efforts frequently must be targeted at both organisational *and* sub-system levels. Hage and Finsterbusch assert, for instance, that many decentralisation efforts have failed because they have ignored the need for changes at the sub-system level. Changing structure but not the behaviour of people in the system – and vice versa – generally fails to produce permanent organisational improvement.

Hage and Finsterbusch (1987) propose a set of 'basic questions for development change agents':

"– Why change? What are the performance and output gaps?
– What change? Which component of the system needs to be changed?
– How to change? At what level should the intervention be instituted? Which tactics of change or ways to introduce change in an organisation are appropriate? What resources are needed for achieving change and what resources are available? What methods of data collection are useful?" (22–23).

These questions appear straightforward, but in fact if applied rigorously they offer a prospect of respecting the existing organisational culture, which, as we have argued throughout this chapter, is crucial if change efforts are to have any chance of success.

10.6   Implications for Managers and Management Development

Change is difficult. It is probably the hardest part of the manager's job. Yet for African organisations, as we have seen, change is urgently needed. Because of the factors we have discussed, particularly cultural realities, African organisations may be especially resistant to change. Organisations, as we have argued, are designed for stability, and it is unrealistic to suppose that the average manager has either the inclination or the time to go around looking for opportunities to make changes as part of his daily routine. Usually the impetus for change is provided when someone – the manager or some other concerned person or body – perceives some form of performance deficiency. When this occurs it is rarely as a result of a formal process for measuring performance: the limited evidence from Africa suggests that few organisations make any serious attempts to measure performance at the individual or organisational levels. There is a 'felt need' to do something about the perceived deficiency, which involves changing something in the organisation. It is at this point that we find the kinds of questions formulated by Hage and Finsterbusch (1987), outlined above, indispensable. An analytic framework of this kind can enable the manager to ask relevant questions and avoid rushing into inappropriate, wasteful, ineffective, and sometimes disastrous actions.

For those engaged in the development of managers, the management of change presents a challenge which we will deal with in more detail in Chapter 13. This concerns the question: which managerial skills – if any – can be learned in the classroom? As we have indicated in this chapter, change is an extremely complex process. To initiate, anticipate, monitor, understand, cope with and manage the processes of change demands various abilities, which are difficult to analyse and describe, let alone teach. It is probable that those involved in the training and development of African managers will have to look beyond the book and the classroom if they are to make any contribution to organisational change and development. They will need to get close to the working environments of managers, to understand what managers do in their employing organisations, what problems they experience in relation to the changing environment, and how they currently cope. We have earlier in the chapter briefly introduced some of the concepts of the management of change developed by Revans in his experiences with Action Learning. We believe that these ideas assist in understanding the nature of change and offer workable strategies for helping managers to learn how to learn from their experience. For management educators they present a challenge because they call into question the assumption, commonly encountered in Africa, on which most management development practices are based – that management skills can be learned in the classroom. As we shall see in Chapter 13, Action Learning offers management educators concrete strategies for helping working managers to learn, to cope with change.

Whether they experiment with Action Learning or with alternative strategies, the challenge for Africa's management educators is to recognise that the classroom-based methods which predominate at present are, by themselves, ineffective in preparing individuals for the real, tough job of management. There is a pressing need for strategies and practices which are effective in preparing managers for the challenges of innovation and change, *and* which are sensitive to African contexts.

Chapter 11:   Role Conflict and Stress

The main character of Chinua Achebe's novel *No Longer at Ease* is a young Nigerian intellectual named Obi Okonkwo who has just returned from a four-year sojourn in England where he earned a degree in classics. The novel is concerned largely with analysing Obi's attempts to reconcile a number of strongly conflicting demands and expectations arising from within himself and from a number of different groups within Nigerian society. The Igbo people of his village who had financed his studies in England had one set of hopes and expectations. These were designed to ensure that Obi repaid their investment in kind by enhancing the reputation of the village, observing local customs of marriage and social interaction, and attending generally to his people's interests. Then there were those people with whom Obi came into contact as part of his work in the public service who sought to harness his influence through 'donations', a practice which he knew to be commonplace, though usually discreet. These pressures conflicted with the values Obi had acquired during the course of his university education in England. There, he had become convinced that corruption was an evil which hindered the development of his country and should be eliminated, and that egalitarianism and individualism were virtues.

After some initial success, Obi found it increasingly difficult to behave according to his ideals. His inability to reconcile the demands of his conscience with those of his fellow Nigerians caused him great torment. Eventually, as a result of financial mismanagement and the considerable amount of psychological strain he was under, Obi succumbed to the temptation of a 'bribe', was apprehended and brought to trial.

This brief example contains elements of what we shall refer to below as 'role conflict', and 'stress'. Obi's case, while fictional, is nevertheless representative of the experiences of many people in Africa. Magid (1976) has described them aptly as 'men in the middle': people caught between two worlds. This chapter attempts to provide a framework for analysing and understanding their behaviour, particularly as it is manifested by managers in Africa's formal organisations.

11.1   Role Conflict and Role Ambiguity

A number of seminal studies conducted by Kahn, Wolfe, Quinn, Snoek, and Rosenthal (1964) in the USA were responsible for drawing the attention of organisational researchers to the problems of *role conflict* and *role ambiguity*. Role theory has subsequently become popular among researchers as a framework for assessing the stresses associated with working in modern organisations in industrialised settings (e.g., Jackson & Schuler 1985; Greenhaus & Beutell 1985; Miles & Perreault 1976; Moch, Bartunek & Brass

1979), and to a certain extent in developing countries as well (e.g., Blunt, Richards & Wilson 1989; Price 1975). As so often happens, a special language developed to describe the major concepts involved. These concepts are briefly defined below.

11.1.1 Role

This is defined as that set of activities associated with any given position in an organisation. These will include *potential behaviours* of any individual in that position, not only those of the current incumbent. Mullins (1989) makes the important point that behaviour is influenced both by the individual's personality and role (p. 387).

11.1.2 Role Set

A role set is made up primarily of a web of linked positions or 'offices'. The role set for any particular position therefore comprises those positions to which it is directly linked. Included in such a role set might be colleagues, bosses, subordinates and others within the organisation with whom the incumbent interacts. In addition, a role set encompasses people from outside the organisation such as clients, friends and relatives.

11.1.3 Role Expectations

All the members of an individual's role set depend upon one or more aspects of her behaviour in some way. As a consequence of this dependency, members of a particular role set develop attitudes about what the individual in question (the *focal person*) should or should not do as part of her role: these attitudes are known as *role expectations*. Such expectations are concerned with both the content (what she should do) and form (how she should do it) of the role. Role expectations also deal with beliefs and values, as well as actions.

11.1.4 Role Pressures

Attempts by members of the role set to influence the focal person so as to bring about conformity with their expectations are referred to as role pressures. Such pressures, which may emanate from formal and informal sources, are frequently contradictory. For example, pressures from superiors may be directed at the maintenance of high standards of work performance, while pressures from subordinates may be designed to ensure more leisure or more autonomy or a better quality of working life. The magnitudes of role pressures vary tremendously according to the perceived consequences of non-conformity.

11.1.5 Role Conflict

As indicated above, the various members of a particular role set may have quite different role expectations of the focal person. As a result, role pressures will be brought to bear which are aimed at producing different behaviours. These conflicting expectations form the foundations of role conflict. House and Rizzo (1972) have broken down the concept of role conflict into four distinct types:

Person-role conflict: the degree to which role expectations clash with the values or orientations of the focal person.

Intersender conflict: the degree to which role expectations from one member of the role set oppose those from one or more of the other members of the role set.

Intrasender conflict: the degree to which two or more role expectations from a single member of the role set are mutually incompatible.

Overload: the degree to which the various role expectations perceived by the focal person exceed the amount of time and resources available for meeting them. This may be regarded as a form of intersender conflict in which members of the role set hold quite legitimate expectations that the focal person should perform a wide variety of tasks, all of which may be mutually compatible in theory but not in practice. In this situation, overload takes the form of a conflict of priorities.

Mullins (1989: 388) has noted two additional types of role conflict:

Underload: may occur when the role holder feels that the demands of the role fall short of his abilities, either in their size or variety. This is common, for instance, for new appointees to the organisation, and in cases where managers do not delegate sufficiently. This latter point is of significance for African management because empirical studies point consistently to a reluctance by African executives to delegate and to share information with subordinates (e.g., Blunt & Jones 1986; Jenkins 1982; Jones 1988a; Montgomery 1986b).

Incompatibility: may arise where two role expectations are simultaneously contradictory, making it difficult or impossible for the role holder to comply with both. Mullins (1989) notes the common example of the supervisor as the 'man in the middle' faced with conflicting demands from management and workers. This notion is analogous to that of intersender conflict, mentioned above.

11.1.6   Role Ambiguity

Role ambiguity is defined in terms of the availability of clear and timely information regarding the expectations associated with a particular role, methods for fulfilling known role expectations, and the consequences of role performance. This means, according to Van Sell, Brief and Schuler (1981), that role ambiguity could take one or more of the following forms: "(a) information is unclear regarding which potential role expectation – A, B or C – should be performed; (b) it is understood that expectation A should be met, but information is unclear regarding what behaviour will in fact yield A; (c) the consequences of behaviour A are unclear" (p. 44).

Inadequate job descriptions are a common source of role ambiguity. All too often job incumbents are unclear about the precise scope and nature of their responsibilities, or what it is they are supposed to do and how they should do it. There may also be ambiguity with regard to *whose* expectations should be met. The focal person may, initially, be unable to distinguish between important members of his role set and those whose expectations can safely be ignored. As Mullins (1989) notes, this is likely to be the case in large, diverse groups and in situations of change when issues of work methods, appraisal, standards, and responsibilities may cause concern and uncertainty. Ambiguity can also be a function of time: that is to say, it is often difficult to foresee clearly the long term consequences of behaviour. It is also a feature of the adhocracy configuration of organisational structure (Mintzberg 1989), as we saw in Chapter 7.

Perhaps the most distressing form of role ambiguity surrounds the short term consequences of behaviour. Some of the most common anxieties here are a function of doubts about the way in which we are being evaluated by members of our role sets. A balanced self-image very often requires clear and consistent feedback from those around us. This feedback is necessary for the accurate anticipation of rewards and punishments, and therefore for effective performance on the job. In some ways, clear information regarding the way others perceive us and our performance may be more important than knowing the precise content of the jobs we are required to perform. This is a key assumption in role theory:

"The behaviour of any organisational performer is the product of motivational forces that derive in large part from the behaviours of members of his role set, because they constantly bring influence to bear upon him which serves to regulate his behaviour in accordance with the role expectations they hold for him" (Kahn et al., 1964: 35).

A role episode model portraying the relationships between the variables described above, and allowing for the effects of other factors which might influence these relationships, is set out in Figure 11.1. The model shows that the interactions between the focal person and members of his role set (the role episode) are influenced by personal factors such as age, education and values; organisational factors such as the tasks to be performed and the physical setting of work; and interpersonal factors such as frequency of interaction and the degree of participation in decision making. There has been a great deal of empirical research conducted in the West on many of the relationships depicted in Figure 11.1, but while 'substantial in quantity', such research has been found to be "irregular in quality and in relevance" (Katz & Kahn 1966: 188; *see* also Jackson & Schuler 1985).

Some of the available Western and African empirical evidence pertaining to these relationships will now be discussed in separate sections.

11.2   Western Studies

With regard to the relationships between the focal person and members of his role set, most investigations have related the focal person's perceptions of role conflict and role ambiguity to his emotional and 'objective' responses. Emotional responses studied have included anxiety, satisfaction, job involvement, and propensity to leave the organisation, while the objective responses studied have included absenteeism, turnover and heart rate (Van Sell *et al.* 1981).

The research findings are not uniform, but role conflict has been fairly consistently associated with job dissatisfaction and job-related tension. Positive correlations have also been found between role conflict and unsatisfactory work group relationships, slower and less accurate group performance, lower commitment to the organisation, and lower performance evaluations. Observed personal effects of role conflict include fatigue, complaints of physical illness, depression, irritation, increased heart rate, feelings of futility, and unhappiness. Similar results have been obtained in relation to role ambiguity, but in neither case does the evidence permit confident general statements to be made regarding the effects of role conflict and role ambiguity on all but a few variables.

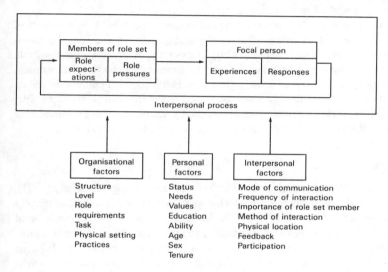

Figure 11.1: The Role Episode Model (Van Sell, Brief & Schuler 1981)

On the basis of their extensive review of the literature, Van Sell *et al.* (1981) concluded:

1. Role conflict and role ambiguity are likely to *cause* lower productivity, higher levels of tension and dissatisfaction, and psychological withdrawal from the work group.
2. The relationship between the focal person and members of her role set is affected (moderated) by differences in the way that the work environment is perceived and adapted to by the focal person. Individual differences with regard to the need for clear, unambiguous information is another possible moderator of the relationships between the focal person and members of her role set.
3. Finally, the evidence indicates that experienced role conflict and role ambiguity are partly a function of a complex interaction between the content of the job being performed, the leadership styles of superiors, and the overall structure of the organis-ation.

11.3   African Studies

Instances of role conflict are commonplace in the literature dealing with problems of administration in Africa. Most early reports referred to the difficulties experienced by chiefs, village headmen and other local officials who had both indigenous responsibilities and responsibilities to the colonial authorities. Magid (1976) has termed this 'exogenous role conflict'. It arises, according to Magid, from the "superimposition on indigenous political structures of European colonial administrations ... Usually such conflict has been observed at the point(s) where administrative positions in two hierarchies, each with its own pattern of social relations, intersect" (1976: 3).

Another type of role conflict which has been frequently identified by researchers in Africa involves role conflict which occurs within indigenous African societies them-selves. Gluckman, Mitchell and Barnes (1949), for example, observed problems of role conflict experienced by village headmen in Central Africa as they attempted to maintain harmonious relationships between kinship groups in their villages. Typically, headmen had great difficulty in separating the roles associated with their own personal involve-ments in kinship networks from their roles as supposedly neutral arbiters of disputes. This type of role conflict has been termed 'endogenous role conflict' by Magid (1976).

11.3.1   Tanzania

A third, and less common, form of role conflict has been described by Abernethy (1971), who has commented that "many (government) officials in the new African states quickly fall victim to an acute case of (it)" (p. 100). Based on fieldwork carried out in rural Tanzania, he claimed that government officials in countries committed to socialist prin-ciples of development suffer from a particularly severe form of role conflict. This happens because, on the one hand, they must act as the agents of the central government "at a time when government is trying to assert, even more strongly than in the colonial era, its right to collect taxes, allocate goods and services and regulate the behaviour of citizens" (Abernethy 1971: 100). On the other hand, such officials are expected, at the same time, to foster the development of decentralised decision making through the creation of participative local government structures, agricultural and industrial cooperatives, and the like. Abernethy argues that in effect what is happening is that government officials in socialist countries are caught between macro-socialist philosophies which accord the public service an important place in the extension of popular rule, and micro-socialist philosophies which seek to establish autonomy, equality, cooperation and self-determina-tion within small communities.

11.3.2   Uganda

Studies of exogenous role conflict on both sides of the African continent have tended to see the problem in terms of a clash between indigenous particularism and bureaucratic universalism. The basic conflict between Western (universalistic) bureaucratic-type organisations and traditional (particularistic) norms and values springs largely from differing views concerning the use or legitimation of authority. As Fallers (1965), in his study of the Busoga of Uganda, made clear, the seeds of this conflict lie in the fact that in the traditional setting authority relations are based on interactions between individuals or groups. In Western bureaucracies, on the other hand, authority is situational, that is, authority is vested in a position or office and not in the person who holds such an office: in Parsons' (1951) terms, universalistic. The point here is that when these values are institutionalised in systems which interact with one another, interpersonal conflicts are likely to arise, and subsequently other symptoms of organisational maladjustment such as job alienation may appear.

Take, for instance, the basic questions of recruitment and selection. These are obvious areas for potential conflict between, on the one hand, the particularistic claims of kinsmen or fellow tribesmen, and on the other, the universalistic principle of selection according to ability. Another example occurs in the daily exercise of authority, where there may be repeated conflict between particularistic loyalties and the bureaucratic norm of disinterested and impartial administration of rules and regulations set down by a small bureaucratic elite. Mazrui's (1980) experience nicely exemplifies this:

"When I was Dean of Social Studies at Makerere University in Uganda, I sometimes used to receive letters from one relative or another making a special plea that his son be admitted to Makerere in spite of the fact that he had not done so well in the School Certificate Examination. Then, to make the case clearer, my correspondent would proceed to remind me of his relationship with me in terms of the extended family ... Any relative who wrote to me in these terms was not necessarily trying to corrupt me. The relative was operating within one moral system of mutual support and fellowship. But the university institution in Uganda was a product of another culture altogether, Western culture, and carried with it a different moral system which presumed the sanctity of merit as a basis of university admission. I, as an African Dean in an African University, was caught up between two moral worlds* " (p. 119) (emphasis added).

Mazrui's poignant final sentence, above, emphasises the dilemma faced by African managers in trying to reconcile the demands of two systems with quite different value positions. In the Western system described by Mazrui there is no possibility of taking into account the attributes of the whole person, as could be the case in the indigenous setting. On the contrary, in indigenous settings impersonality would tend to disrupt the network of particularistic ties and to break down what the community regards as just behaviour; hence the preference is for a leader who knows people as individuals and is known by them in the same way.

Fallers' (1965) study of the Busoga provides numerous illustrations of exogenous role conflict. Chiefs, who were both indigenous and colonial office bearers, were continually subjected to conflicting role expectations. For instance, kinsman A might ask chief B for special consideration, and at the same time request that a competitor's case be ignored. Magid (1976) illustrates their dilemma:

"Operating in a milieu in which kin, client, and civil service relationships intermeshed, chiefs were apt to experience the following dilemma: while agreeing to the particularistic demands of a kinsman could result in dismissal for nepotism, refusal to agree could be interpreted as a violation of traditional kin obligations. Similarly, while agreement to the particularistic demands of a superior could be interpreted as a violation of civil service norms, refusal to honour the client relationship could be grounds for dismissal on a contrived charge of corruption" (p. 5).

Fleming (1966) made similar observations in East Africa. He noted in addition that after independence problems of role conflict worsened because "local government bodies and technical roles had evolved which complicated the original simple relations between the district commissioner and the chief, and where increasing complexity led to increasing role confusion" (p. 399). Chiefs were required to carry out many new duties, which were not always clearly defined, and to attend to the directives of new technical officers. For example, a chief might be expected to maintain roads in accordance with public works department regulations, follow the advice of agricultural officers on methods of planting and harvesting, and police the marriage by-laws of the local council. All of these duties were likely to bring him into varying degrees of conflict with the customary procedures of his own people.

11.3.3   Northern Nigeria

The roots of role conflict among local officials in Northern Nigeria have been investigated by Magid (1967, 1976). The district councillors studied by Magid experienced the same type of role conflict as their counterparts in East Africa. The Nigerian officials had a dual role which was conducive to a wide range of conflicts. As statutory agents of the 'Native Authority', they had the power, amongst other things, to appoint tax collectors, to levy taxes on villages and individuals, to sanction the expenditure of council funds, to maintain law and order, and to supervise the use of communal labour. At the same time, however, they were expected to "faithfully represent ... the people of the various districts" (Magid 1967: 324).

11.3.4   Ghana

The difficulties faced by modern government officials in Africa have been well illustrated by Price (1975). His study of role orientations among Ghanaian civil servants clearly depicts the role expectations and pressures directed at them from members of their role sets outside of the civil service. The data upon which the study was based were collected in three attitude surveys: a civil servant survey, a client survey and a comparison client survey. This approach allowed Price to assess the degree to which the civil servants' social environment was supportive of the behaviour formally required of them by virtue of their positions in a government department. The civil servant respondents were therefore required to provide information on the composition of their role sets, their perceptions of likely role expectations held by members of their role sets, and the sanctions which were likely to be applied in the event of their not complying with role expectations. From their clients, information was obtained on how they thought the focal person (civil servant) might react to certain role expectations, and, again, what the consequences might be for the focal person if role expectations were violated by him. In all, 434 Ghanaian civil servants were interviewed, and 385 'clients' – students at the University of Ghana – completed a lengthy questionnaire. An additional group – the 'comparison/client group' – of 81 Ghanaians, picked at random from urban areas in Southern Ghana, served to provide the view of the ordinary man in the street, and a 'reality check' on the client sample. This study probably represents the most comprehensive analysis of organisational role conflict yet conducted in sub-Saharan Africa, and will therefore be discussed in some detail.

To ascertain the civil servants' perceptions of role expectations and pressures, and the consequences of non-compliance, a type of projective technique was used. This involved an imaginary – yet likely – situation involving conflict. In one such scenario, respondents were asked to "suppose a civil servant arrives at his office one morning and finds several people waiting to see him about routine business. One of these is a relative of his". The civil servant respondents would then be asked, "would it be proper to keep this relative waiting because others have come before him?" (Price 1975: 63). The intention was to determine which set of role expectations – civil service or family – the respondent would be likely to comply with. If the respondent said that the relative should be kept waiting, this was interpreted as his giving precedence to the universalistic, civil service role expectations. If, on the other hand, he felt that the relative should be attended to first, he was seen as favouring particularistic modes of behaviour, and complying with that set of role expectations. The respondent was then asked what he thought "the average civil servant in Ghana would actually do in this situation. Would he receive his relative before the others?" Here the intention was to discover what was considered to be normal behaviour under such circumstances. Finally, the respondent was asked about the relative's expectations in the imaginary situation: "Would he be likely to expect to be seen before the others, or would he expect to be seen only after those who came before him had taken care of their business?" (Price 1975: 64). The results of this part of Price's study are set out in Table 11.1. The data indicate that there is very little relationship between what the civil servants thought to be proper and what they considered likely to happen. Indeed, as can be seen from Table 11.1, the vast majority of civil servants felt that the actual behaviour in such a situation would be the opposite of what was considered correct for a civil servant. These findings are very similar to those of Berger (1957) in Egypt.

Two other imaginary scenarios employed by Price confirmed the findings obtained from the first hypothetical role conflict situation. The second situation, which involved a potentially far more serious role conflict than the first situation, is set out below.

"A civil servant is officially informed that he is to be transferred from Accra to a new post in Tamale. The civil servant is from Accra, he speaks the local language, has all his friends and relatives there, and he is looking after his aged parents who are too old to

move to the North with him. For all these reasons he does not want to be transferred to Tamale. He therefore goes to the head of his department, who happens to be his cousin, and asks to be kept in Accra" (Price 1975: 66).

Table 11.1:   Responses of Ghanaian Civil Servants to an Imaginary Role Conflict Situation (N = 434)
              (Price 1975)

	R believes legitimate role behaviour to be:	R's estimate of normal behaviour in situation	R's perception of the relative's role expectation
Universalistic (i.e. comply with civil service role expectations)	75.3%	19.4%	5.1%
Particularistic (i.e. comply with role expectations of kin)	23.7%	80.0%	92.6%
No answer	0.9%	1.6%	2.3%
Total	99.9%	101.0%	100.0%

Again, the civil servants were asked to say whether "in this situation" the head of department's relatives would "be likely to expect him to arrange to have his cousin stay in the Accra post". The overwhelming response was that the relatives would expect their demands to be met: 85 per cent of the civil servants indicated that in such a situation the head of department would be expected to ensure that his cousin was not transferred. Nevertheless, the majority of respondents also indicated that relatives did not have the right to expect the head of department to behave in this way. Despite the widespread agreement among the civil servant sample regarding the illegitimacy of relatives' role expectations, however, only a minority thought the head of department would actually refuse to help his cousin.

Rank and tenure in the organisation had some effect on attitudes; those with long tenure and those with high rank being less likely to feel that civil servants should give in to the demands of relatives. Even so, there was still a majority of high-ranking and long-service civil servants who expected the demands of relatives to be satisfied. Price (1975) concluded: "the preponderant opinion in all categories is that in normal practice a civil servant yields to particularistic familial role expectations" (p. 68).

The next step was to enquire about the effects of refusal: "What are the head of department's relatives likely to think of him if he refused to help his cousin stay in the

Accra post?" (Price 1975: 69). The main feature of the civil servants' responses to this question was that relatives were seen as having no conception of the conflicting role pressures that were being brought to bear on them. In other words, civil servants felt that relatives would fail to understand that they (the civil servants) had organisational obligations which made it difficult for them to satisfy the wishes of their families. Instead, relatives were likely to perceive refusal to help as an indication of some general failing of character, such as selfishness or anti-family bias. Of the 327 civil servants who responded to this question, 43 per cent thought that a civil servant who refused to help his relatives would be regarded as a 'wicked', 'bad', 'cruel' or 'hard-hearted' man. More than half of the civil servants interviewed indicated that the head of department's refusal to help his cousin would be interpreted as anti-family bias by his relatives: that "he did not care for his relatives' well-being", that he had 'abandoned' them, or that he had ill-feeling toward his family and was trying to 'insult' it. Typical (verbatim) responses included: "They would think that he is not helpful to the family and that he is cruel ... that he does not want the aged dependents of his cousin to live comfortably." "They would say that because he has got somewhere he no longer wants to help his people." "He lacks the typical Ghanaian family feeling" (Price 1975: 71–72).

Given the central role of the extended family, it is clear that the sanctions of kin carry considerable weight and that heavy pressures to conform can therefore be exerted on their members in positions of power. Pressures to conform are increased by the perception that the civil servant has of how his relatives will *behave* towards him. About 20 per cent of civil servant respondents in Price's study felt that the head of department would be ostracised for refusing to help his cousin: "The head of department would not feel easy to move among the relatives because of the strained relations that have been created .... He would be isolated. Events like births, marriages, deaths, and so forth are of great family significance, and after this event I doubt if the head of the department will be entertained at any of these functions" (Price 1975: 72–73).

The predictions made by the Ghanaian civil servants about the reactions of relatives to the head of department's lack of cooperation were confirmed by the responses of the client group. More than 80 per cent of those questioned thought that a member of their family in the 'cousin's' situation would have asked the head of department to nullify his transfer. His refusal to do so evoked the type of response anticipated by the civil servants. For example,

"My family would feel it had been let down by somebody whose duty it was to help it ...
The relative would be looked upon as somebody who ignored a most essential duty to his
kinsmen ... He would be regarded as a bad man and members of his family might refuse
to have anything to do with him again" (Price 1975: 9).

Some members of the client group felt that their relatives would react negatively because they would see the head of department's behaviour as constituting a violation of traditional norms and values. For instance, a member of the coastal Fanti ethnic group remarked,

"Yes, relations between the head and my family will be greatly affected. In Akan custom the service of any member of the family should be placed at the disposal of other members of the family. His refusal is a flagrant violation of what obtains in our traditional custom" (Price 1975: 79).

Civil servants are likely to be subjected not only to role pressures from kinsmen and their organisations, but may also frequently be approached by strangers who wish to establish particularistic relationships with them either directly or indirectly in order to get things done. Price assessed the public's views on what they thought was the most effective manner of getting things done at government offices by asking University of Ghana students to respond to a questionnaire which included the following item:

"We are interested in the most effective ways of getting things done at government offices in Ghana. Let us say you had some routine business with a government bureau or agency. Below are listed five alternative ways of getting your business done. Which of these would be the most effective, i.e. would get the business completed successfully in the shortest time?

1. You see a friend who knows the official with whom you must deal.
2. You go straight to the government office and state your business.
3. You visit the official in charge at his house prior to going to his office, and offer to 'do something'.
4. You find someone to 'fix things' with the responsible official.
5. You go to the office and 'dash' the official with whom you must deal" (Price 1975: 113).

A majority of the student sample felt that the most effective method of getting things done when dealing with a government office was to establish some form of particularistic connection with an official (alternatives 1, 3, 4 and 5 above). When the business to be conducted was described as *urgent* rather than routine, the proportion of students favouring the particularistic approach rose to almost 70 per cent of the sample.

Of the particularistic methods mentioned in the questionnaire item, the giving of material benefits – so-called 'dash' – is widespread in West Africa, in other parts of the continent, and elsewhere in the world, although it may go under different names, and its form and prevalence varies. Dash is often an integral part of the most routine transactions in Ghana, and unlike the 'tip' in Western societies, it precedes rather than follows the performance of the service in question. The term dash, however, should *not* be seen as analogous to the English word 'bribe'. According to Price (1975), dash performs two social functions which are not normally associated with the giving and taking of bribes. First, it is a socially acceptable method of establishing a personal relationship between a client and a civil servant (or anyone else in authority) who are strangers to one another. Second, dash acts as a symbol of the unequal status of the two individuals. In effect, by giving dash the client is, at the same time, seeking to establish a personal tie with the official and acknowledging his superior status. This giving and taking of material rewards and the functions it serves has roots in many African traditional social systems.

LeVine (1970), for example, has observed that personal relationships among African people are characterised "primarily in terms of the type of material transaction involved: who gives what to whom and under what condition ... Africans emphasise ... obligations to give material goods – food, gifts, financial help, property, and babies" (p. 288). Indeed, almost all social events of importance in African societies involve the sharing of food and drink, thus testifying "to the personal links between community members – both living and dead – and (symbolising) the unity of the group" (Price 1975: 119). This emphasis on the exchange of food and drink in traditional, and other, societies provides an important clue to the meaning of the modern institution of dash. A commonly used euphemism for dash, on both sides of the African continent, is the term 'drink'. In Kenya, for instance, it is often said that 'I gave him some tea', meaning that some form of informal payment for services (about to be) rendered had been made. In Ghana, when government officials accept such payments they are said to have received their 'chopping money' – this is a pidgin English expression which means, amongst other things, 'to eat'.

In both the modern and the traditional contexts, social exchanges of this sort impart a degree of predictability to interpersonal relationships. When organisations operate, as most do, according to universalistic principles, the employee is placed in a difficult dilemma. Interestingly, most of the clients surveyed by Price expected that civil servants facing such role conflict would resolve it by submitting to particularistic demands involving dash. To confirm this finding, Price (1975) presented the following more specific situation to the university students.

"Now, suppose you were attempting to carry out some routine business at a government office. You have visited the office three separate times, but each time the civil servant in charge says your forms are not ready and that you should 'go and come'. What would you conclude is the trouble?" (Price 1975: 124).

Subjects were asked to say which one of five alternative explanations was the reason for the delay. It is clear from Table 11.2 that the vast majority of students felt that delays in the Ghanaian civil service were due to the fact that officials need to be encouraged to perform through the payment of dash. Almost 64 per cent of the sample thought that the 'civil servant in charge' was looking for dash. Data from the comparison/client sample corroborated these findings.

To conclude, the data gathered by Price allow the following major inferences to be drawn:

1. That Ghanaian civil servants perceive strong role pressures emanating from members of their role sets who are outside of the organisation: relatives, friends, fellow tribesmen, and so on.
2. That Ghanaian civil servants feel that when faced with particularistic role pressures from relatives, civil servants will give in to them and comply with their demands.
3. That clients perceive the likely behaviour of civil servants faced with particularistic role pressures in the same way.

4. That the giving and taking of material rewards, or dash, is a commonly-used method of establishing particularistic ties with officials, and in the eyes of clients is necessary to ensure that things get done in government offices.

Table 11.2: Perceptions of Reasons for Delays at Government Offices Among Ghanaian University Students (N = 372) (Price 1975)

Alternative Reasons for relay		Percentage of Respondents
1	The staff is overworked	3.8
2	The staff is lazy	12.4
3	The official is looking for dash	63.7
4	The staff is incompetent	11.3
5	The official is trying to show his importance	0.8
	Total	100.00

In terms of the definition provided at the beginning of this chapter, the civil servants studied by Price are likely to experience considerable intersender role conflict: that is, conflicting expectations from different members of their role sets. On the one hand, they must deal with particularistic demands from kinsmen, friends and fellow tribesmen, and on the other, they are expected to conform to the universalistic role requirements of the organisations they work for. The intensity of experienced role conflict in such situations, however, is a function of the strength of the individual's commitment to one or the other set of expectations. We would expect to find, therefore, that where commitment to the organisation is low, the intensity of experienced role conflict is also low. Price's findings on this question revealed that:

"Neither the intensity nor the content of the commitment to the civil service revealed by the survey respondents suggests that the extent and character of organisational role orientations is likely to lead Ghanaian civil servants to resist externally-generated role pressures. The attachment of most civil servants in the survey sample to their careers appears to be relatively weak, which suggests that their organisational commitment is not likely to override loyalty to such competing external reference groups as extended families, home villages, and the like" (1975: 202–3).

Price's study addresses issues which have serious effects on the functioning of public organisations in many parts of Africa.

Recently, similar results have been obtained in the oil rich Southeast Asian State of Brunei where the extent and nature of particularism was observed to be broadly similar to that observed in Ghana by Price (1975). The authors noted:

"... one of the most distinctive features of modernity is the dichotomisation of public and private spheres of social intercourse. It would appear that in Brunei this dichotomy has not yet been internalised: rationality and impersonality may still sometimes be seen as alien impositions rather than necessary and perhaps even beneficial criteria for the administration of society. Particularism is not perceived negatively by Bruneians: rather, the opposite is the case. A particularistic official is a good person not a corrupt one. Particularism is not seen by Bruneians as the equivalent of corruption; rather, particularism would appear to have moral precedence" (Blunt et al. 1989: 427–428).

11.3.5 Malawi

This picture of the African manager's sensitivity to the demands of his extended family is reinforced by data from an investigation by Jones (1986b) of managerial thinking in Malawi. Jones quotes managers reflecting on this issue in semi-structured interviews. A welfare administrator felt obligated to meet such demands as far as possible, even where they were unreasonable, adding "I would carry a bad name if I refused". A training officer observed that "luck stems from your relationships". A personnel manager described his obligations in looking after a sister and her sons, in addition to his own twelve children; he had himself been brought up by an uncle, and he accepted his reciprocal obligations "as a duty to be fulfilled ... if I did not, I would be regarded as inhuman". A personnel officer observed, "If people of my blood were to think I am a bad man because I don't help, then I would expect to have bad luck. That is how we feel" (Jones 1986b: 274). And a shipping manager commented, "This is Africa. We have to help each other. I would not like to think of what would happen if I didn't" (Jones, 1986b: 272).

It is interesting to note here that Jones's findings reinforce those of Price's Ghanaian study in respect of the perceived consequences of refusing to help relatives: like the Ghanaian civil servants, the Malawian managers in Jones's interview survey did not seem to suffer from role conflict when faced with the conflicting demands of their formal organisations and those of kinsmen. Jones (1986b) notes that during the interviews all the managers, with one exception, not only stressed that these obligations are natural, but expressed pride in this aspect of Malawian culture:

"– I had expectations of people in jobs myself. I try to help now. I feel obliged. (Senior Civil Servant)
 – I am looking after a widowed grandmother and divorced mother. This is natural that I should do so. (Sales Manager)
 – My mother's sister and her kids are my responsibility, of course, since she has no husband to support her. It is not sponging. They have no choice. (Planning Manager)
 – It is an inherited obligation. (Senior Civil Servant)

  *– I was put through school by my brother. Until recently, I had thirteen living with me
  including my wife and two children. It is mutual insurance. (Personnel Manager)*
  – It is no problem because it is our tradition. (Senior Personnel Officer)
  *– You expect to help people when you get a job. This is a tradition which you cannot
  escape ... My father has three wives. He educated me but the five younger sons by the
  two wives were put through schooling by me. (Senior Civil Servant)*
  *– Family relationships are our strength and security. Contributing to them is a moral
  responsibility. (Civil Servant)" (pp. 272–273).*

Jones notes that the Malawian interviewees invariably felt it necessary to explain the
extended family system as a preface to their answers. They frequently used phrases like
'you Europeans' and 'in our African society', indicating that this was a distinctive feature
of African life which Westerners did not experience and perhaps found difficult to
understand. These explanations, Jones reflects, "were usually given with a degree of
gentle amusement and pride" (1986b: 272).

   Perhaps what is illustrated here is the danger of misunderstanding cultural and organisational realities by the tendency to interpret what we observe through our own culturally
constructed spectacles. As Jones (1986b) suggests,

*"Western commentaries on this (Malawian) social reality often assume or imply that for
the individual in paid employment the expectations of his extended family and kinship
group present a problematic burden. The wage or salary he receives reflects an assumption that he will live in the urban area, supporting his nuclear family, for which an
appropriately sized house is often provided. If he faces demands on his income from a far
more extensive group to whom he feels some sort of obligation then he must be in a very
uncomfortable position. In addition, he may be expected to help members of this wider
group to obtain employment, particularly if he is in a managerial position. This line of
reasoning perhaps reflects how a Westerner might feel in such a situation. It did not
emerge as an accurate account of how Malawian managers experienced this aspect of
their lives. Although a minority explained that they experienced problems in reconciling
competing demands, this was viewed as a technical difficulty rather than a cause for
discomfort or embarrassment. With only one exception, all the interviewees stated unequivocally that they viewed the expectations of their extended family and kinsmen as one
side of a normal relationship involving accepted and unexceptional obligations ... Not
only were these traditional obligations viewed as normal; they were spoken of with pride
and affection, as a fundamental strength of Malawian society and a distinctive feature of
African life" (pp. 282–283; 294).*

11.3.6 Nigeria

It seems that the urban poor of Nigeria also believe that particularistic methods are the
most effective when it comes to obtaining personal material advancement and to getting
things done. Gutkind (1975) implies that their tolerance of the ever-widening gap between
themselves and the rich is due in no small measure to the fact that:

"The poor have placed their faith in slow evolutionary change – at least for the time being – which they hope to achieve by a series of manipulative personal and, at times, collective manoeuvres using networks of kin, friends, occupations, neighbourhood contacts, past political friendships ... and what might be called ethnic brotherhood. The Ibadan poor have great faith that they can eventually find a true 'helper' who is both willing and able to create for them opportunities productive of upward mobility" (p. 7).

If Gutkind is right, dismantling current methods, involving the particularistic distribution of services, jobs and resources, may have the effect of closing off an avenue of progress, which, while far from satisfactory, is at least clearly understood by the poor, and for the moment accepted by them.

These problems pose an urgent and difficult challenge to those concerned with organisational behaviour in Africa: the necessity to achieve the twin aims of organisational effectiveness and a desirable quality of working life increases the complexity of the challenge. Innovative solutions are required which make allowance for dominant social values and methods of interaction and, at the same time, ensure a just, equitable and effective distribution of government services and other organisational outputs. This problem-solving process will need to be informed by additional, and continuing, research into the functioning of organisations in African countries. Price's (1975) study provides a solid foundation and model upon which to build in so far as the crucial issue of (exogenous) role conflict is concerned.

Instances of endogenous organisational role conflict (that which is the result of conflicting role expectations arising from within the organisation) have not been researched as widely in Africa as they have in the West. It is unlikely, however, that problems associated with endogenous organisational role conflict are less serious in Africa, but simply that in relation to other forms of (exogenous) role conflict, such as those studied by Price, their effects on organisational functioning are less severe. In addition, however, role conflict situations which could be characterised as purely endogenous in the West are likely in Africa to be affected by exogenous considerations.

Take, for example, the position of supervisor, which is widely regarded in the West as being a job which is subject to high levels of endogenous role conflict (Miles & Perreault 1976). It is said that role conflict arises in supervisory positions because the supervisor is faced with expectations from senior management that he ensure high levels of performance on the one hand, and, on the other, expectations from the work groups that he supervises that he will represent their interests at higher levels in the organisation. This conflict of loyalties can be the cause of considerable stress among supervisors in organisations, and has been the subject of extensive study in the West.

One way of describing the site of these conflicts, in a general sense, is to regard them as taking place at 'intraorganisational boundaries' (Kahn et al., 1964; Miles & Perreault 1976); boundaries here are interpreted as the limits of units within organisations. A supervisor operates at the boundary of his work group in that his work activities consist in mediating between it (the work group) and other parts of the organisation – this type of work is referred to in the literature as 'boundary spanning' activity. Conflict and stress arise frequently at intraorganisational boundaries because one or more of the following factors are in operation.

1. The boundary spanning role (supervisor, for example) lacks formal power or control over role senders in other systems or work units (e.g., other supervisors or work groups upon which his own group depends for inputs).
2. To compensate for the lack of formal power or control, people at organisational boundaries attempt to create *informal* links involving friendship, trust and respect. These bonds are difficult to maintain, and the need to do so imposes considerable strain on people occupying boundary spanning roles.
3. The maintenance of good relations with other units and individuals within the organis- ation is hindered by the fact that perceived failures of a supervisor's work group are often seen by outsiders as a failure of the supervisor himself.
4. Similarly, the deficiencies of people or units outside the supervisor's work group are often perceived by members of the work group as deficiencies in the supervisor himself.

In many African organisations the situation depicted above is complicated further by the fact that supervisors and others in boundary spanning roles are assessed not only in terms of organisational criteria, but also according to their social status outside the enterprise. We might find, for example, that a very young, though highly educated, supervisor would have difficulty obtaining the respect and cooperation of older members of his work group because authority relations in the organisation invert the accepted traditional pattern associated with age. The same supervisor may also have to face resistance and resentment from older, yet less qualified, superiors who see him as a potential threat to their own positions. Ethnic considerations can work in the same way. That is to say, ethnic hostilities which exist outside the organisation are sometimes carried over into the work situation and, according to the circumstances, will facilitate or impede the activities of the occupants of boundary spanning positions (Blunt 1978; Lamouse-Smith 1969).

As was indicated at the beginning of this chapter, Western research has shown that role conflict is an important source of stress, usually manifested in various forms of psycho- logical and physical disturbance (Mullins 1989). There is little research evidence pertain- ing to the incidence and nature of organisational stress in Africa, but given the prevalence of role conflict, and other causal factors which we shall discuss below, it is not unreason- able to assume that it exists. It is therefore important to be able to recognise the symptoms, and to have some understanding of possible causes apart from those discussed so far.

11.4   Stress

Our short description of Obi Okonkwo's predicament at the beginning of this chapter showed how he was subjected to a variety of role expectations which caused him considerable psychological discomfort. He reacted to the role conflict by becoming extremely anxious and irritable. He went off his food, and generally behaved less rationally than usual. These reactions are symptoms of psychological stress. The purpose of this section is to discuss those factors, known as *stressors*, which contribute to the development of stress in the individual, and to outline the different types of stress reactions. We shall also consider variables which have been found to mediate the relationship between stressors and stress reactions. Finally, some methods of coping with stress are briefly discussed. Following Cooper and Marshall (1978), the major relationships involved are described in Figure 11.2.

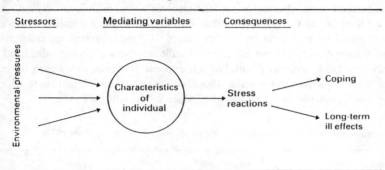

Figure 11.2: A Model of Individual Stress (Cooper & Marshall 1978)

Stressors

It is now widely accepted that the development of stress reactions or symptoms is a function of factors peculiar to the individual (internal needs and values, and personality) and factors operating in the external environment. The nature of the interaction between these variables "will determine the prevalence, causes, and consequences of stress reactions" (Kets de Vries 1979: 5). The stressor variables involved are very similar to those included in the role episode model (Figure 11.1) discussed earlier, and are set out in Table 11.3. Some of the research evidence concerning a sample of the stressors mentioned in Table 11.3 is described below, and the meanings of the terms are clarified.

Physical Work Environment

A great deal of research has been done on the links between the physical conditions of work and physical and psychological health. A review of blue collar stressors by Poulton (1978) draws attention to the following variables: poor visibility from too little light, glare and flicker; noise, and the effects of different intensities in terms of blurred vision, shaky hands and feet, muscle tension and motion sickness; heat, cold and wind; harmful atmospheric pollution; increased and reduced atmospheric pressure; and perceived danger.

Work Overload and Underload

Work overload and underload are often caused by an irregular flow of work. This means that short periods of intensive work are interspersed with periods of relative inactivity.

Public transport systems are subject to predictable peaks and troughs of this kind: the peaks occurring in the morning when everyone is travelling to work and in the evening when they are going home. Similarly, telephone operators have their peak period around the middle of the morning, partly as a result of the fact that managers have been through their morning's mail and are making calls connected with it. Work overload can be differentiated in terms of whether it involves *qualitative* or *quantitative* overload. The overload referred to above is clearly quantitative overload, that is, when there is *too much to do* in the available time. Qualitative overload involves work which is too *difficult*. A review of the literature by Cooper and Marshall (1978) indicated that quantitative work overload was associated with coronary heart disease (CHD), escapist drinking, absenteeism, low motivation to work and low self-esteem. Qualitative overload, on the other hand, is often only found to be associated with low self-esteem. However, as we shall see in more detail later, "objective work overload should not be viewed in isolation but relative to the individual's capacities and personality" (Cooper & Marshall 1978: 14).

Table 11.3: Organisational Factors Contributing to Stress (*Adapted from* Kets de Vries 1979)

Organisational Design Variables	Interpersonal Variables	Career Variables
Physical work environment (noise, heat or cold, long working hours, dangerous job conditions, shift work, repetitive work)	Leadership style	Occupational level
	Lack of group cohesion	Entry
Incentive system	Lack of participation	Mid-career
Role pressures (role conflict and role ambiguity)	Responsibility for people	Retirement
		Demotion
Work overload and underload (qualitative and quantitative)		Stagnation Obsolescence

Work underload occurs in the same jobs as work overload, in the troughs when there is little or nothing to do. Boredom and inefficiency frequently result. According to Poulton (1978), "the jobs can be described as 'waiting for nothing to happen'" (p. 74). Unlike work overload, however, work underload seems to be associated with dysfunctional outcomes only among certain groups. Cooper and Marshall (1978) refer to empirical evidence which suggests that work underload leads to high levels of job dissatisfaction among those who value high levels of complexity in their work, such as scientists and administrators, but not among policemen and assembly-line workers.

In the African context it is perhaps relevant to refer to developments mentioned in Chapter 1 relating to the economic and public service structural reforms currently underway in a number of the continent's countries. A common strand running through these reforms is the perceived necessity to cut the size of the civil service, frequently by drastic – and often arbitrary – amounts. Many reports (e.g., ZPSRC 1989) draw attention to degrees of overstaffing in African public administrations, and there is little argument against the need for some streamlining. It is noticeable, however, that the main argument for such surgery is to cut wage bills and associated costs; a human resource management perspective – rather than an economic one – would tend instead to emphasise the costs of overstaffing in terms of low morale, which is common among individuals who have no worthwhile work to perform despite having a title, an office and a salary cheque (work underload).

Responsibility for People
A distinction is normally made here between responsibility for people and responsibility for things (e.g., items of equipment, money, etc.). Responsibility for people has been found to be more likely to lead to CHD than responsibility for things. It is supposed that this is because increased responsibility for people usually entails spending more time interacting with others, attending meetings and meeting deadlines.

Career Variables
One of the most consistent findings concerning the relationship between career variables and stress indicates that a higher incidence of certain stress reactions occurs among lower-level occupations: "In terms of almost all the major and many of the minor causes of death among persons in the working population age groups, the blue collar and unskilled are at greater risk than the white collar and professional groups" (Cooper 1980: 49). There are many reasons for this. Lower socioeconomic groups generally have poorer diets, are more likely to experience unhealthy and unsafe working conditions, are less likely to have their stress reactions diagnosed, and have less control over their work environments. White collar workers are more likely to "reflect the pressures of work in mental illness" (Cooper 1980: 50).

Three stages in a person's career appear to be particularly stressful: the beginning, the middle and the end. At the beginning, individuals frequently experience a reality shock. This was Obi Okonkwo's experience when he started work in the Nigerian civil service: it was simply not as he had thought it would be, and conflict and stress resulted. Dissatisfaction and boredom are common features of the early part of a person's career as well. This is because new recruits are often not provided with challenge in their jobs or the opportunities to use their abilities to the full. The case incident entitled 'Joe's First Job' (p. 256) illustrates this point.

Case Incident : Joe's First Job[1]

William Kyode had failed his second year at university and, as a result, had wound up in Joe's year. In due course, he graduated,to his great relief and surprise, with a third class degree. Joe, on the other hand, had passed with distinctions in all but two subjects. Three months or so after graduation they had met casually in a bar they both frequented. Their conversation soon turned to questions of employment and finance. It transpired that only two weeks after leaving university, William had found an excellent job as a trainee marketing manager with a major tobacco firm. He was driving a new Japanese car, had a company house, which was unusual for non-government employees and was, he said, enjoying life immensely. Naturally, Joe was eager to discover the secret of William's success and plied him with questions. They had been fairly close friends at university, having played on the same soccer team, and Joe had on more than one occasion helped William with assignments, particularly in the more numerate subjects. They were also of the same ethnic group and from the same rural area. Joe could therefore be quite frank, and besides, in view of everything he had done to help William through his degree, he felt he was owed a few favours.

'Look, William, here I am with a good degree, no failures, all the right subjects, and still no job; and there you are on the way to marketing director. Where have I gone wrong?'

'Personality, my boy,' retorted William, beaming. 'Marketing is one field where bullshit matters more than brains every time .... Seriously though, you need an introduction to the right person. Without that you won't get anywhere no matter how bright or worthy you are. But you know all that anyway.'

'Yes, of course I do,' said Joe. 'I had just hoped to begin my career on the right foot. I'd convinced myself that the only way of avoiding that sort of thing myself when I'm in the driving seat is to start out the hard way. It's more and more beginning to seem as if I was wrong.'

'Of course you were wrong,' retorted William.

'The trouble with you Joe has always been that you were too idealistic. It must have been that religious upbringing you had.You've just got to change your tactics if you want work. We're not playing campus politics now you know. This is life with a capital 'C' for corruption.' William laughed loudly at his own joke, and then continued:

'What about your uncle ...? He has a thriving little manufacturing business, doesn't he? He must know a couple of people in the right places surely. What was he in again, shoe polish or something wasn't it?'

'No, he manufactures shoes,' Joe replied quietly, and then more loudly: 'But I think you're right, William. What is the use of my sitting around being ethical and

---

1   Adapted from Blunt and Popoola (1985).

proper if the rest of the world is leaving me to eat its dust while they use other channels? I'll see my uncle early next week. We always got on well, and I think he will help.'

Three weeks later it had all been fixed. Joe was a trainee manager in a chain of shoe shops. His uncle had been supplying the owner of this chain for nine years, and a small present together with the hint of a threat that supplies might dwindle during peak selling periods unless it was accepted was enough to do the trick. As a matter of courtesy, however, Joe had to 'donate' ten per cent of his monthly salary for a period of six months to his uncle who would give it to 'a charity of his choosing or some other worthy cause'. Joe naturally did not enquire too deeply into the ultimate destination of the money.

But Joe did not last long in the shoe business. More than anything, having to fit shoes to all those dirty feet during his training period had done it. It was beneath his dignity. And besides, the atmosphere of the small retail outlet was too frantic. The shop manager was always breathing down your neck, making sure that you made sure that others were doing what they were meant to be doing.

The shop manager was responsible for seeing that what he claimed to be completely unrealistic sales targets were met. Head office had decided on an 'appropriate' target without consulting him. They also decided unilaterally what lines of shoes he should stock, many of them unsuited to the clientele in his area. His dissatisfaction made him touchy and irritable. The morale among the sales personnel was low and requests for transfers, and absenteeism, were high. In any case, a shop manager's salary, which Joe would have been earning after a year or two, was not up to his expectations. After three months in the job he began to cast around for another.

As it turned out, one of the sales girls in the shoe shop named Isabelle – a Yoruba like himself, who also happened to be young, single, vivacious, and highly attractive, and in whom Joe developed a more than passing interest – was extremely friendly with a senior official in the Customs Department. He was an elderly, jovial man, also a Yoruba, whose family home was very close to Joe's own. He came to the store once or twice a week to take Isabelle out to extended lunches. Joe noticed that occasionally Isabelle returned from these 'lunches' looking slightly ruffled, and sometimes even breathless. His observations led him to believe that Isabelle might have considerable influence over Mr. Okunowo, the Customs official. Joe began seriously to consider the merits of the Civil Service, and at the same time to cultivate, with absolute decorum, the friendship of Isabelle.

Mid-career stress is associated with an individual's realisation of the departure of youth, and his assessment of his accomplishments during the course of his career and his prospects for the future. For many workers this is a sobering process, and they are left with feelings of disappointment and frustration. This is particularly true, of course, for those who regard work as a central life interest. It is this group who also suffer most when the

time to retire comes. Given their commitment to work, and their close personal identification with their jobs, retirement can be traumatic. In many cases, retirement "evokes an
image of uselessness and disrupts the rhythm of life. It is also a time when the (worker)
reviews his past career. For some ... this is an experience of despair – when the feeling
prevails that one's one-and-only life has been a failure and a waste" (Kets de Vries
1979: 10). Reactions of this sort may not be as common in Africa as in the West because,
as we have noted in an earlier chapter, relatively fewer workers appear to regard work as a
central life interest. This seems to apply not only to lower-level workers but also to large
numbers of managers and other relatively senior personnel: recall Price's (1975) findings
regarding the low levels of job commitment to be found among Ghanaian civil servants.

Career variables which are more likely to result in stress reactions among African
workers are therefore those which affect instrumental rewards: financial and other forms
of material incentives. Demotion or dismissal would be likely to cause stress for this
reason, but also because it might be perceived as a humiliating (public) blow to self-
esteem, generally a matter of considerable importance to African workers. Anticipation of
demotion or losing one's job can be stressful for the same reasons.

Lack of Autonomy
Mullins (1989) discusses research findings which indicate a correlation between a perceived lack of autonomy by individual managers and stress at work. Lack of autonomy
may be the result of lack of delegation by more senior executives or of the structure of the
organisation itself. We noted earlier in this chapter the evidence concerning the apparent
reluctance of African managers to delegate authority to subordinates, and we have
referred in earlier chapters to the common model of African formal organisations,
particularly in the public sector, of the change-resistant, hierarchical bureaucracy. Thus it
is apparent that these conditions for stress resulting from a perceived lack of autonomy
occur in African organisations. Jones' (1988a) investigation of managerial thinking in
Malawi, for example, found that a major source of dissatisfaction among managers was a
perceived lack of autonomy. Ironically, the same managers indicated a reluctance to
delegate authority and share information with their own subordinates!

Mass Production
Mullins (1989) notes that research findings have indicated a link between the demands of
mass production and work stress, caused primarily by a combination of high workload
and low discretion. This is significant for African organisations, because many of the
continent's nations are industrialising, necessitating the use of mass production methods.
We could reasonably anticipate that such methods, and the imperatives which they
impose on African managers and workers, might have even more serious consequences
than those noted in Western countries where there is a well established industrial tradition.

In addition to these stressors, and referring more specifically to the African context, an
interesting study by Jenkins (1982) of problems experienced by Malawian managers
identified several factors in the managerial job which caused stress and discomfort,
including:

1. *Interpersonal Problems.* These concerned relationships with more senior managers, with subordinates and with clients. As Jenkins notes, this is not an unexpected finding, but in the Malawian situation the problems are apparently exacerbated by the following associated factors.
2. *Problems of Personal Security.* The managers in the Jenkins investigation included under this heading difficulties with decision making and planning, again an unexceptional finding, but they also found it difficult to cope with "what would be regarded in an industrial society as the normal, everyday pressures of management, such as meeting targets and deadlines" (Jenkins 1982: 25). The requirements of efficient performance, Jenkins suggests, may "provide a source of pressure not experienced by people to whom such requirements are familiar (e.g., Western managers)" (1982: 26) (parenthesis added). A perceived need for more training was another factor in the feeling of personal insecurity and lack of confidence, which in turn leads to reluctance to work outside well specified guidelines: "a high level of specification is desirable, and discretion can be a source of discomfort" (Jenkins 1982: 27). Again, Jenkins points out that this finding would not be expected among managers in the industrialised nations of the West, neither would it find support in Western theories of managerial motivation.

Jenkins' (1982) findings concerning the stress caused among Malawian managers by feelings of personal insecurity are supported by an investigation of managerial thinking in the same country by Jones (1988a). In a questionnaire survey Jones asked managers what they considered to be 'the best thing' and 'the worst thing' about being a manager. As might be anticipated considering the prime characteristic of the management job, the best things about being a manager reflected the power, authority, status and privileges of the managerial job. What was unexpected – from the Western view of the responsibilities which are the axiomatic concomitants of managerial power – was the overwhelming choice, as the worst thing about being a manager, of accepting responsibility for the consequences of decisions and for the mistakes of subordinates.

An investigation of perceived stressors among 1,065 executives drawn from ten countries on five continents illustrates the universality of the points made thus far. Cooper and Arbose (1984) asked managers from Brazil, Great Britain, Egypt, Germany, Japan, Nigeria, Singapore, South Africa, Sweden, and the United States about their perceptions of the major causes or sources of job stress (that is, stressors). Table 11.4 sets out the fifteen stressors most frequently mentioned by the managers and how this varied according to country.

As can be seen from Table 11.4, time pressures and deadlines were the most frequently mentioned stressors, closely followed by role or work overload, long working hours, meetings, and so on. Nigerian managers found long working hours and the demands of work on family relationships to be particularly stressful. Nevertheless, the data presented in Table 11.4 need to be interpreted carefully. For example, it would not be safe to conclude from the Table that Nigerian managers travel more than others, only that they find travelling to be more stressful, perhaps due to the generally severe problems of city traffic (e.g., Lagos) and road transportation generally in Nigeria.

Similarly, the last column in Table 11.4 should not be taken to imply that Brazilian executives experience less stress than others (because four stressors were mentioned less frequently by them). Indeed, one of the most interesting aspects of the study (not reported in Table 11.4) was that managers in developing countries like Brazil, Egypt, and Nigeria showed more *symptoms* of stress than did managers in industrialised countries. The researchers speculated that the environments in which developing country executives must work – such as those we mention in Chapter 1 – are changing rapidly and unpredictably and that managers in these environments are subjected to more severe constraints.

11.5   Stress Reactions

Schuler (1980) has identified three major classes of symptoms of stress in organisations (*see* Table 11.5: physiological, psychological and behavioural reactions). Over a period of time an individual may exhibit symptoms falling within one or more of these classifications – to that extent, the classes of symptoms are interrelated, although they will be presented separately below.

11.5.1   Physiological Reactions

Most research on the physiological correlates of stressors has concentrated on the cardiovascular system. In his review of 'hazardous occupations and the heart', Carruthers (1980) asserts that man's physiological make-up has failed to keep pace with the rapid change experienced in the last century: "the idea has emerged that man's stone-age biochemistry and physiology has in several important respects failed to adapt to his present space-age situation" (p. 11). The most dramatic examples of this, he claims, involve modern methods of transport. He cites the following evidence.

Air Crew

Much of the debate as to whether aviation, or any other occupation, is associated with heart disease depends on how the statistics are interpreted. These are usually expressed in terms of the standardised mortality ratio (SMR). This is a simple representation of the number of deaths observed in a particular occupational group compared with the number of deaths expected in that group expressed as a percentage:

$$\frac{\text{Deaths observed}}{\text{Deaths expected}} \times 100$$

A score of below 100 is therefore better than average and a score of more than 100 worse than average. However, Carruthers rightly points out that the simple SMR of an occupation is not only a product of the special factors associated with that occupation, but also a

Table 11.4: A Ten-Country Comparison of Work Stressors (*Adapted from* Hellriegel, Slocum & Woodman 1986: 524)

Source of Stress	Percentage of Respondents Mentioning Source	Most often Mentioned by Managers in	Least Often Mentioned by Managers in
1. Time pressures and deadlines	55.3	Germany (65.4%)	Japan (41.8%)
2. Work overload	51.6	Egypt (76.7%)	Brazil (38.1%)
3. Inadequately trained subordinates	36.4	Egypt (65.0%)	Britain (13.1%)
4. Long working hours	29.0	Nigeria (40.5%)	Brazil (19.6%)
5. Attending meetings	23.6	South Africa (28.5%)	United States (16.3%)
6. Demands of work on my private and social life	22.1	Sweden (31.7%)	Singapore (12.9%)
7. Demands of work on my relationship with my family	21.4	Nigeria (29.7%)	Brazil (8.2%)
8. Keeping up with new technology	21.4	Japan (32.8%)	Egypt (10.0%)
9. My beliefs conflicting with those of the organisation	20.6	United States (30.2%)	Egypt (13.3%)
10. Taking my work home	19.7	Egypt (30.0%)	Japan (13.4%)
11. Lack of power and influence	19.5	United States (46.5%)	Sweden (11.0%)
12. Interpersonal relations	19.4	Japan (29.8%)	Singapore (12.9%)
13. The amount of travel required by my work	18.4	Nigeria (29.7%)	Brazil (9.3%)
14. Doing a job below the level of my competence	17.7	Brazil (23.7%)	Sweden (10.3%)
15. Incompetent boss	15.6	United States (30.2%)	Britain (9.1%)

Table 11.5: Individual Symptoms of Stress (Schuler 1980)

1   Physiological

      Short term: Heart rate, GSR, respiration, headache
      Long term: Ulcer, blood pressure, heart attack
      Nonspecific: Adrenaline, noradrenaline, thymus deduction,
                      lymph deduction, gastric aid production, ACTH production

2   Psychological Responses (affective and cognitive)

Flight or withdrawal	Inability to organise self
Apathy, resignation,	Inner confusion about duties or roles
boredom	Dissatisfaction
Regression	High intolerance for ambiguity,
Fixation	do not deal well with new or strange situations
Projection	Tendency to begin vacillating in decision making
Fantasy	Tendency to become distraught with trifles
Expression of boredom	Inattentiveness: loss of power to concentrate
with much of everything	Irritability
Forgetfulness	Procrastination
Tendency to misjudge people	Feelings of persecution
Uncertainty about whom to trust	Gut-level feelings of unexplainable dissatisfaction

3   Behavioural

    A   Individual consequences
        Loss of appetite
        Sudden, noticeable loss or gain of weight
        Sudden change of appearance: decline/improvement in dress
        Sudden change of complexion (sallow, reddened, acne)
        Sudden change of hair style and length
        Difficult breathing
        Sudden change of smoking habits
        Sudden change in use of alcohol

    B   Organisational consequences
        Low performance-quality/quantity
        Low job involvement
        Loss of responsibility
        Lack of concern for organisation
        Lack of concern for colleagues
        Loss of creativity
        Absenteeism
        Volutary turnover
        Accident proneness

function of broader social and environmental factors which go with it. These have to be controlled for. One way of accomplishing this is to compare the SMRs of the job occupants with the SMRs of their wives: as the wives share the same non-occupational influences as their husbands, it is reasonable to assume that differences in their SMRs are due to their occupations. When this is expressed as a quotient, it soon becomes clear that aircraft pilots, navigators and flight engineers are doing jobs which involve high risk of coronary heart disease. Some comparative data on occupational groups at high risk are set out in Table 11.6.

Table 11.6: Occupations at Risk of CHD: Groups with Highest Men/Wives SMR Quotients (Carruthers 1980)

	SMR men	SMR wives	SMR quotient
Aircraft pilots, navigators and fight engineers	70	25	2.80
Sales managers	97	47	2.06
Professional workers	106	54	1.96
Judges, barristers, solicitors	93	50	1.86
Electrical engineers	59	33	1.79
Radio and radar mechanics	120	68	1.77
Draughtsmen	101	57	1.77
Authors, journalists	92	53	1.74
Printing workers	101	59	1.71
Textile machine operators	158	93	1.70

Everyday Traffic Drivers

Studies conducted on people driving in daily London traffic indicate that it causes the build-up of relatively high levels of noradrenaline (noradrenaline is the hormone most likely to cause the accelerated aging of the cardiovascular system underlying coronary heart disease). These results, together with those of previous studies, confirm the suggestion that driving brings out the 'demon' in man's nature. They also support "the idea that aggression, anger, and frustration are the emotions which may contribute significantly to coronary heart disease" (Carruthers 1980: 18).

Attempts to explain why people take up hazardous occupations recognise that situations which cause noradrenaline secretion are usually pleasurable. As passengers in an aircraft or drivers of a motor vehicle, we have all at some time experienced a thrill or excitement associated with the activity in question. We shall see shortly that some people (showing what is known as Type A behaviour) are, in a sense, 'thrill seekers', and the incidence of CHD in this group is especially high. Stressful occupations, which are frequently exciting and challenging too, are therefore attractive to this group.

This is another relatively unexplored area of research in Africa. Comparative research on physiological reactions to stressful work in Africa is sorely needed. The same can be said of psychological reactions.

11.5.2   Psychological Reactions

A general feeling of anxiety is usually an early and important indicator that the individual is unable to cope with the stressors he encounters at work. The individual may also find it difficult to concentrate or to think clearly, and will therefore tend to work towards short-term goals. Irritability, anger, aggression, an inability to relax and psychological withdrawal may also feature prominently in psychological stress reactions. In their more serious forms, stress reactions can be almost totally debilitating, as the following extreme example, of an English professor of psychology suffering from a severe psychological trauma, clearly illustrates:

"At times I did fight to gain some measure of control. I would drag myself into my office for two or three hours at a time thinking I was being very courageous. When I went to work, I could do none: instead I bored my colleagues with my troubles and telephoned home every half-hour. I was supposed to be examining a doctoral thesis, and for a fortnight I struggled with it morning and afternoon sitting in my garden. I tried to make notes on the contents, but I never succeeded in understanding a paragraph: my notes, penned with a shaking hand, turned out to be gibberish ... I tried from time to time to resume my normal activities. There was one book on psychology that I pathetically carried around with me and which several times a day I would attempt to read. In the ensuing months I must have opened it several hundred times, but I never succeeded in getting past the first page.

There were three activities that gave me some slight respite. Two were pursuits that in my normal state I would have condemned as a waste of time: they were driving a car and doing The Times crossword. Perhaps I could concentrate on these tasks because neither requires one to carry forward anything in memory from one moment to the next. I could not read because I could never remember the sense of what I had just read; to solve a crossword, however, one does not need to remember the answer to one clue in order to tackle the next, and I could find just sufficient gaps in my obsessive thought-processes to enable me laboriously to complete a puzzle clue by clue" (Sutherland 1977: 5–6).

The onset of the psychological reactions described in this example were largely caused by the professor's discovery of his wife's infidelity with one of his closest friends. And although the professor's job itself was hectic and stressful, and his 'normal' behaviour could be described as quite frantic – for example, he 'bathed rarely and hastily', shaved in the car on the way to work, and according to a former secretary, would dictate letters (presumably into a dictaphone) while seated on the lavatory – the major cause of his stress reaction emanated from outside the work place. This raises the important point that stress reactions *observed at work* may not be caused entirely by work-related factors.

This was true of Obi Okonkwo in Achebe's novel. The stress he experienced could not be neatly compartmentalised into work and non-work related. The point is particularly noteworthy in Africa, where the non-work sphere of social relations intrudes frequently and forcefully into the work place. As we saw earlier, Cooper and Arbose (1984) report this finding in relation to the stressors perceived by Nigerian managers.

11.5.3 Behavioural Reactions

Stressors have been associated with the following individual behaviours: smoking, drinking, losses of appetite and changes of appearance. Organisational consequences include low performance, low job involvement and higher absenteeism and turnover. The case of the English professor cited earlier shows how behavioural, psychological and organisational reactions tend to occur together. As indicated in Figure 11.2, the degree to which individuals experience stress reactions is dependent upon a number of mediating variables, including needs and values, abilities and experience, and personality.

11.6   Mediating Variables

One of the most thoroughly researched aspects of organisational stress concerns the part played by personality. The last three decades have seen a dramatic rise in the number of studies of the relationship between personality and certain types of stress reaction.

11.6.1   Personality

The coronary prone Type A behaviour pattern has received considerable attention from researchers. This line of enquiry began with a study by Friedman, Rosenman and Carroll (1958), who found that the incidence of CHD seemed to be associated with what is now widely known as the Type A behaviour pattern. The precise pattern of behaviour taken as indicative of Type A is as follows:

1. An intense, sustained drive to achieve self-selected but usually poorly defined goals;
2. A profound inclination and eagerness to compete;
3. A persistent desire for recognition and advancement;
4. A continuous involvement in multiple and diverse functions constantly subject to deadlines;

5. A habitual propensity to accelerate the rate of execution of many physical and mental functions;

6. Extraordinary mental and physical alertness.

The most important features of the above profile are sustained drive and competitiveness and a chronic sense of time urgency. When assessed through interviewing, a person showing a fully developed Type A behaviour pattern exhibits rapid body movements, tense facial and body musculature, and/or teeth clenching, excessive unconscious gesturing, explosive conversational intonations, and a tendency to finish the interviewer's questions for him, together with a general air of impatience. On the other hand, individuals who are relaxed, speak slowly, make few tense gestures, move slowly and calmly, display no muscular tension or impatience, deny even moderate levels of drive or ambition, avoid deadlines, dislike competition , and feel no sense of urgency, are likely to be classified as having a Type B behaviour pattern. It is worth noting here that the structured interview of Type A is now regarded as the best measure of the behaviour pattern, and the best predictor of CHD (*see* Friedman & Booth-Kewley 1988).

Some of the most notable research carried out on the Type A behaviour pattern (Rosenman, Friedman, Strauss, Wurm, Kositcheck, Harn & Werthessen 1964) – conducted in the USA and based on a national sample of over 3400 men – showed that Type A men between the ages of 39 and 49, and 50 and 59 had, respectively, 6.5 and 1.9 times the incidence of CHD found among Type B men. The importance of this study is that it was prospective rather than retrospective – that is, none of the 3400 men had CHD when the investigation began: at the same time, all the men were rated, by psychiatrists after intensive interviews, as either Type A or Type B. Subsequent diagnoses, at periods of 2.5 and 4 years after the study began, were carried out by heart specialists who had no knowledge of the subjects' behavioural patterns.

Recent analyses of empirical research conducted since the original study have confirmed that Type A behaviour is clearly associated with CHD (Booth-Kewley & Friedman 1987; Byrne & Reinhart 1989; Friedman & Booth-Kewley 1988), although the increased risk of CHD if one is Type A may not be as great as first thought. Byrne and Reinhart (1989) are emphatic about the relationship: "prospective evidence establishing the link between Type A behaviour pattern and CHD now places its status as a risk factor beyond dispute" (p. 123).

Chesney and Rosenman (1980) have summarised the organisational implications of the Type A behaviour pattern. The results of laboratory studies indicate that Type A people at work:

1. Experience time pressures because they allow themselves too little time in which to accomplish their work.
2. Prefer to work quickly, and exhibit impatience and depressed job performance if required to work slowly.
3. Ignore, suppress or deny physical or psychological symptoms when working under pressure, and may report such symptoms only on completion of the work.
4. Are physiologically aroused and work harder when a task is seen as challenging.

5. Are generally hard driving and competitive and express hostility and/or irritation in response to challenge or threat.

6. Need to control their immediate environments. Lack of control may result in a hostile, competitive Type A response (Ganster 1986). Lee, Ashford and Bobko (1990) have found that perceived control interacts with Type A behaviour to facilitate high job performance and satisfaction, that is, "the performance of people high on Type A behaviour is enhanced in situations in which they have a high degree of perceived control" (p. 877).

7. Are likely to be found in greater numbers at higher occupational levels. Byrne and Reinhart (1989), on the basis of research among Australian public servants, conclude that the Type A behaviour pattern "might well facilitate (career) advancement ... (and) that, where the occupational environment allows unhindered expression of the Type A behaviour pattern, the Type A individual enjoys job satisfaction, experiences no work-related distress and shows no elevation in risk factors for CHD. Where the nature of the job frustrates expression of the Type A behaviour pattern, thus inhibiting progress towards occupational achievement, the reverse may well be true" (p. 133).

Recent research has suggested that the anger-hostility dimension of the Type A personality is the aspect most predictive of CHD (e.g., Booth-Kewley & Friedman 1987) and that the overall Type A behaviour pattern is positively associated with academic performance (e.g., Ivancevich & Matteson 1988).

With regard to the mediating role of the Type A behaviour pattern, Chesney and Rosenman (1980) have found that taken together the research evidence indicates "that psychological distress and situational arousal will result when Type A workers are presented with work situations that are challenging, pressured or controlling" (p. 206). Lee *et al.* (1990) on the basis of their findings in the USA suggest that Type A managers are likely to be better motivated in circumstances where they feel they have greater control, and that organisations might achieve this by reducing role conflict and role ambiguity, by increasing opportunities for participation in decision making, and by providing high degrees of control over work scheduling and work methods.

11.6.2   Other Personal Mediating Variables

A number of researchers are persuaded by the idea that personal variables such as age and ability moderate the relationship between stressors and stress reactions (e.g. Kahn *et al.* 1964; House 1974). But there are few corroborative studies reported in the literature. Beehr and Newman (1978) assert that there is insufficient evidence available at present upon which to base firm conclusions. This is an obvious area for future research. Moderating variables such as age and status, which are of particular significance in African interpersonal relations, merit special attention. The final section of this chapter explores what the individual can do in order to cope with stress reactions.

11.7   Personal Methods of Coping

The number of publications dealing with individual methods of coping with stress reactions has increased tremendously (e.g., Burke & Weir 1980; Cooper & Marshall 1978; Ellis 1978; Levi 1981; Mullins 1989; Nelson & Sutton 1990; Newman & Beehr 1979). This increase reflects both a growing concern among practitioners about the prevalence of stress-related reactions in organisations, and a growing awareness among people in general of the serious health implications of stress. More people are aware of the potentially damaging consequences of stressors at work, and more people want to know how to cope with their effects (Bailey 1991). The methods set out below are those which have been found to be effective in the West. Some of the more practical, work-specific, suggestions will no doubt apply as much in Africa as they do elsewhere. The more general coping strategies mentioned, however, may or may not be appropriate in African settings. They are listed here as possibilities only; and perhaps as a starting point for research into these questions. Some general strategies for dealing with stress reactions are dealt with first, followed by some practical, work-specific strategies.

11.7.1   General Strategies

These can be employed to cope with stress reactions of any kind (not just work-related), and can be aimed at changing the individual's psychological or physiological condition or his behaviour (Newman & Beehr 1979). Some examples include:

Meditation
The purpose of meditation is to restrict physical and mental activity with the aim of producing a state of tranquillity or a general calming of the mind and body. This state is usually achieved through prolonged concentration or reflection upon a word, object or subject. There are many variations of meditation, and some of these are clearly spelt out by McLean (1979) and by Bailey (1988).

Psychological Withdrawal
This is often achieved by attaching less importance to the stressors in question so as to minimise their effects.

Physical Fitness and Diet
Little controlled research has been carried out on the effects of regular exercise and nutrition on stress reactions, but accumulating evidence and informed opinion agree that they serve to ameliorate the harmful effects of stressors (Burke & Weir 1980; Hellriegel et al. 1986).

Social Support
Research indicates that individuals who receive a great deal of social support from others in their work environments and elsewhere are less likely to experience severe stress reactions (Burke & Weir 1980). Generally speaking, social support appears to act as a buffer between stressors and stress reactions, although a study by Blau (1981) suggests

that this is not always the case. Extended family relationships and ethnic ties in Africa provide powerful and continuing sources of such support, as illustrated by Jones's (1988a) study of managerial thinking in Malawi.

11.7.2   Work-specific Strategies

A sound practical guide for dealing with stress reactions in the work environment, which applies particularly to managers, has been developed by Moore and Pratt (1981):

Block Interruptions
This involves restricting contact with others in the organisation by screening out all but the most essential telephone calls and visitors.

Make Use of Alternative Hours of Work
Where the organisation allows work to be done at various times during the day, time spent in the office when others are not present should be maximised. That is to say, where possible work should be scheduled for times when other members of the organisation are not there to provide distractions.

Restrict Meetings
Some meetings are difficult to avoid because they are essential to work performance, but others are wasteful, and according to Moore and Pratt (1981) are subject to the "laws of diminishing returns: they go on for longer than necessary" (p. 10). Time spent in meetings can be reduced by judicious assessment of a meeting's worth; opting out of some, and attending others for only half the time.

"Informal meetings which take place are more difficult to control. One way of exercising control over informal contacts is to ensure that they take place in other people's offices. This enables you to say, 'Must go now ...' when you feel that discussions have reached the diminishing-returns stage. If you are in your own office, you are trapped" (Moore & Pratt 1981: 10).

Restrict Travel
This is an obvious and effective way of saving time.

Delegate
Allow subordinates more autonomy to decide on matters directly affecting them and their work. It may have the dual effect of reducing pressure and stress reactions at upper levels in the organisation and improving quality of working life at lower levels. We have noted the problems associated with delegation among African managers.

Self-Diagnosis
This entails watching out for behavioural and psychological signs which indicate that more severe forms of stress reactions are likely to follow. Being able to recognise symptoms of the Type A behaviour pattern, for example, may help to avert associated stress reactions. This will involve developing a self-consciousness about personal man-

nerisms and behaviour such as fist-clenching or finger-tapping while talking, impatience, irritation and continual lane-changing while driving, and surreptitious glances at the clock while engaged in conversation. This is not to say that the Type A behaviour pattern is inherently bad, but some individuals are more likely to suffer adverse reactions to it than others, and it is for those for whom the Type A behaviour pattern is a potential hazard that these comments are intended.

In addition to these personal strategies for coping, Mullins (1989) and Bailey (1988) suggest several measures which management might try in order to remove or reduce role stress, including:

— clearer job descriptions and guidelines concerning work;
— better matching of individuals to required roles;
— medical monitoring for potential stress-related problems;
— more appropriate job design;
— better management of inter-group conflict;
— changes in management styles and systems; and
— being more *assertive*, rather than passive or aggressive, that is, communicating honestly, directly, fairly, and firmly (*see* Table 11.7).

Table 11.7: Non-Verbal Behaviours Associated with Being Aggressive, Passive and Assertive (Bailey 1988)

	Aggressive	Passive	Assertive
Facial expression	Teeth clenched, frown, eyes staring, curled lip	Head hung down, eyes look up to others, lips quiver	Mouth relaxed, firm, head level, eyes steady
Tone of voice	Loud, sharp, threatening	Quiet, strained, child-like	Low pitched, steady, modulated
Timing	Interrupts, "bulldozes"	Hesitates, quiet, waffles, long gaps	Puts own view concisely
Eye contact	Hard gaze, glaring	Avoids looking into others' eyes	Direct gaze but not staring
Posture	Stoic stance hands on hips, feet/legs stiff	Round-shouldered, slumped head down	Upright balanced, facing squarely, suitable distance
Gesture	Poking/pointing, stabbing finger, banging fist, jaw-grinding, "hand-cruncher", "back-slapper"	Fidgety, hands/arms/ legs, fiddling movements, e.g, crossing/uncrossing legs	Open flow of co-ordinated movements relaxed, "composed gesticulation"

Dealing with stress reactions in organisations may not be as much of a priority in Africa at present as it is in the West. The dearth of data on the incidence, causes and nature of stress reactions in African organisations effectively prevents an assessment of the African condition in these respects. It is reasonable to suppose, however, that stress reactions occur among African workers, and that their incidence and severity may increase in the future. Indeed, the findings of Cooper and Arbose (1984), referred to earlier, suggest that the incidence of stress among managers in developing countries may be higher already than it is among similar groups in industrialised nations.

11.8   Conclusion

There can be little doubt that the social contexts in which many African workers find themselves are conducive to levels of role conflict in excess of those experienced by their counterparts in the West. The extent to which such role conflict emerges as a problem for individuals and organisations depends largely on the ways in which individuals choose to resolve it. The data reviewed in this chapter indicate that, in most instances, Ghanaian (and perhaps other African) civil servants resolve the dilemmas which result from role conflict by giving way to demands from outside their organisations: in other words, where conflicting expectations arise, they elect to satisfy the particularistic role expectations of kin and friends rather than the universalistic role expectations of the organisations they work for. Price (1975) explains the 'inefficiencies' of government organisations in West Africa in terms of this choice and the low levels of organisational commitment which it reflects. The relationship between methods of role conflict resolution and organisational effectiveness is not thereby established. It is clear, however, at the very least, that Price's conclusion provides an hypothesis to be tested.

The consequences of role conflict for the individual also depend partly on the method of conflict resolution adopted. The method favoured by the respondents in Price's study makes it unlikely that role conflict will be a major stressor in African organisations. If, as we have seen, many African workers appear not to regard work as a central life interest, there are correspondingly fewer organisational role expectations which carry great weight, and therefore their conflict with other role expectations is relatively easily dealt with. This allows us to hypothesise that, at present at any rate, role conflict is not a major cause of stress reactions in African organisations. But this state of affairs may change, if, as we predicted in Chapter 9, more Africans come to regard work as a central life interest in the future.

We have also seen in this chapter, however, that stress reactions may be caused by a number of other factors such as the physical work environment, work overload and underload, responsibility for people, and so on. There is no reason to suppose that some of these factors do not have effects in African organisations similar to those in Western ones. Recognising potential stressors and the symptoms of stress reactions is therefore no less important in Africa than it is anywhere else. It follows from this that personal strategies for coping with stress reactions in organisations also need to be considered (some organisational strategies have already been dealt with in Chapters 6, 7, 8, and 9).

11.9   Implications for Managers and Management Development

The nature of managerial work is the subject of much discussion, research and argument. To a greater extent than is the case with the majority of occupations, the job of the manager defies universal description and definition; it is for this reason, primarily, that there can be no agreement on the status of management as a profession. Managers function in an enormous variety of organisational settings; their work is affected by organisational and national cultural factors; they use authority to get things done, so inevitably their work is affected by political issues; they use scarce resources including people to achieve organisational goals, and thus the workplace is a social arena as well as a political one; they have to accept responsibility for failure, which becomes more problematic as they try to manage a changing environment. For these and other reasons the work of managers is complex, difficult and stressful, as our quotation from Revans (1980) in the previous chapter so strikingly illustrates.

It is not difficult to see, therefore, why managerial work should attract so much attention from researchers of stress at work. Bailey (1991), for example, reveals that in 1984/85 there was "a staggering loss to (British) industry and business of 111 million working days caused by stress-related illnesses, three times more than were lost through industrial disputes" (p. 19): little wonder that observers like Bailey urge managers to take the issue of stress at work seriously.

In this chapter we have tried to illustrate the factors in the manager's job which may contribute to stress and we have noted some possible actions which organisations might take in order to reduce the impact of such factors. As is commonplace in the African context, the dearth of empirical research into organisational functioning on the continent makes it impossible to say with any confidence how African managers are affected by stress, what are the stressors, what symptoms they exhibit, or what actions might appropriately be taken. Nevertheless, it is not unreasonable to suppose that managerial work in African organisations may be as stressful as, or more stressful than, such work in the Western industrialised settings where so much research has been done (Cooper & Arbose 1984). The implications of this probability we could assume to be similar to those we have explored in this chapter, both for the health and effectiveness of individual executives and for organisational performance.

Role conflict and stress, and their consequences, probably have not found their way to any degree into the concerns of management development practitioners in Africa or into their developmental strategies. It seems reasonable that managers should be made aware of stress and its consequences, and helped to develop ways to anticipate and cope with it. We have examined in this chapter some of the small amount of reliable data concerning African managers' perceptions of problems at work which could be expected to contribute to stress. Some of these – for example the study of Malawian managers by Jenkins – appear to reveal perceived difficulties in their managerial work which would not be expected in the Western industrialised world, and therefore look distinctly African. African management development strategies and emphases could usefully address these particular issues by helping managers to anticipate them and reduce their stressful impacts.

Our focus on the work of Revans prompts us to consider the promise of Action Learning for the development of African managers. As his words suggest, a central element of Action Learning strategies is the notion of 'comrades in adversity' – managers learning with and from each other to overcome the problems which face them as an inevitable part of their work. We will examine this possibility in more detail in Chapter 13.

11.10 Examples and Questions[1]

Example 1

Mwangi – 42. Married, one child, son aged 11. Sales Manager.

Significant demands:	Number of salesmen Mwangi has to see each day.
Stress experienced:	Fatigue/extreme tiredness. Irritable/anxious.
Coping adopted:	Blames salesmen and smokes 65 cigarettes per day.
Outcomes:	Mwangi feels able to 'lay off' his stress to some extent on his salesforce. The smoking helps to calm his irritability. But he continues to feel increasingly tired and abrasive. As the weeks go by he continues to blame the salesforce. They in turn start complaining about his 'managerial style'. Mwangi runs the risk of alienating his salesforce, undermining their morale and sales effort. The source of stress remains. What else could Mwangi do?

Example 2

Alice – 32. Single. Regional manager of a chain of stores.

Significant demands:	Lack of new product knowledge.
Stress experienced:	Anxiety and feelings of helplessness.

---

1   Source: Adapted from Bailey (1988).

Coping adopted:	Starts drinking heavily before visiting store branches and meetings with shop managers to reduce anxiety and give her 'courage'.
Outcomes:	Temporary reduced anxiety. Attempts to catch up with product line knowledge. But still problems of anxiety and lack of confidence to carry out work required. Alice is still drinking too much. Store managers now withhold new product information and have started to stigmatise Alice as 'pombe (beer) Alice'. How can Alice undo her excessive stress and put things right with the branch managers?

Example 3

Kamau – 35. Divorced. Distribution manager.

Significant demands:	Noise at work – particularly the sound of lorries arriving at and leaving the depot.
Stress experienced:	Headaches. General feeling of increased tension and edginess.
Coping adopted:	Shouts at drivers. Appears very off-hand and dismissive of customers. Doesn't listen to drivers' or customers' views any more.
Outcomes:	Some relief for the general tension, but the headaches remain. Continues to shout at drivers and has started to insult customers. Drivers and customers prefer to avoid contact with Kamau. How helpful is this form of coping?

11.11 Case Incident[2]

James R. is a black South African production worker, married, middle-aged, the father of four children. He has worked in his current job for almost three years. Before this, while he was unemployed, he heard from relatives about a company in the Western Cape that was hiring. He travelled there with his family from the eastern part of the country, a distance of about 800 miles.

As he tells it, James was plagued by anxiety during the trip west because he had no permit to settle in the vicinity of Cape Town. On arrival, he and his family stayed with friends in a new black 'township' 30 miles from the city. (Townships are segregated, slapdash communities, usually near white urban centres.) His friends had been ordered to move there from their old home on one month's notice.

2   Source: Beaty and Harari (1987).

The morning after his arrival, James and his friend walked two miles to catch a 3.30 a.m. bus. It was crowded and the two had to stand the whole way, for about an hour. After changing buses downtown, James reached the company at 6.30 a.m. He recounts his visit: "The white recruitment officer asked questions about my background, where I lived, and whether I had the necessary documents to prove I was allowed to live and work in the Western Cape. When I told him I didn't have any documents but that I had moved to the area temporarily while I looked for a job, he told me I had to go and get my documents sorted out before I could be hired. I went to the authorities to get a permit but I was told that there was no housing available for me in Guguletu (one of several townships set aside for blacks who work in the Western Cape) and that I would have to go back to the eastern area where I came from. When I went back to the company and told them what the authorities had said, I was told: 'No documents, no work. Go away.'"

James concludes his story with an exasperated laugh. "This is free enterprise? Free enterprise for who? Not for us. I see how I live, and I see how my friends live." He leans forward. "Do whites really think that we will accept their free enterprise system when we are not free?"

1. What are the major stressors evident in this case incident?
2. Is it any surprise that the productivity of black workers in South Africa is among the lowest in the world?

11.12 Exercise[3]

Are you Under too Much Stress
Check this list

		Yes/No
1.	Have you been drinking, smoking or eating more than usual?	....
2.	Do you have difficulty sleeping at night?	
3.	Are you more 'touchy' and argumentative than normal?	....
4.	Do you have trouble with your boss?	
5.	Have you or a loved one experienced a serious illness recently?	....
6.	Have you been recently divorced or separated?	
7.	Has there been an increase in marital or family arguments?	....
8.	Have you been experiencing sexual difficulties?	
9.	Has a close relative or friend died?	
10.	Have you married recently or started living with someone?	....
11.	Has there been a pregnancy or birth in your family?	
12.	Do you have financial problems?	

---

3 Source: Bailey (1988).

Yes/No

13. Have you been dismissed from work or become unemployed?   ....
14. Do you feel jumpy, on edge, flying off the handle at little things? ....
15. Do you watch television more than three hours a day?   ....
16. Have you been in trouble recently with the law?   ....
17. Has there been an increase in the number of deadlines
    or hours you are working?   ....
18. Have you recently moved or changed the place where you live?   ....
19. Do you have trouble with your in-laws?   ....
20. Are you exposed to constant noise at home or at work?   ....

If you scored more than 5 Yes's, you need to get more control over the stress in your life.

Part 5: Managing and Developing People

Chapter 12: Motivation and Job Design

"... African organisations may be experiencing serious employee motivation problems. The sources of these problems are varied and not well understood because of lack of empirical research" (Kiggundu 1988: 235).

This quotation from Kiggundu's important survey of management in Africa illustrates the difficulties faced by those – scholars, educators and managers – who seek to understand the functioning of formal organisations there, and to develop strategies to enhance individual and organisational performance. The limited evidence available indicates that African managers, like their counterparts elsewhere, find employee motivation to be a major concern (e.g., Montgomery 1986b). Kiggundu emphasises the seriousness of this issue for managers and other employees by linking it with poor organisational perform-ance, and individual frustration and alienation at work.

Our purpose in this chapter is to introduce a number of theories of human motivation and to consider, critically, some of the assumptions underlying conventional attempts to apply such concepts in the work situation, and the dangers associated with their premature and unquestioning application in modern organisations in Africa. In addition, a widely applied model for designing jobs is presented and discussed.

Broadly speaking, motivation refers to a driving force or state of need deficiency which inclines a person to behave in a particular manner, or to develop a capacity for certain types of behaviour. The urge to act in a certain way may be generated by physiological or psychological needs or states (including unconscious and conscious thought processes) or by external stimuli or by some combination of these. People obviously differ widely in these respects, and accordingly their behaviour also differs. Theories of motivation seek to provide coherent explanations of why people behave in one way as opposed to another, and thus to predict behaviour. The whole issue of explaining and – especially – predicting human behaviour is complicated, however, by the fact that the *reasons* behind a particular action frequently cannot be directly ob-served, and this has limited the testability of theories of motivation and their ability to predict behaviour. It has meant that comparative evaluations between theories have been difficult to make, and in part it accounts for the coexistence of a number of theories of motivation.

A general motivational model which forms the basis of much theorising in the field is set out in Figure 12.1. There are six basic steps in the model. In the first step a state of disequilibrium in the individual arises from some need deficiency. Second, this causes the individual to search for ways to satisfy the need(s), thus restoring the state of equilibrium. In the third step the individual behaves according to the selected strategy to satisfy the need. Fourth, this behaviour is then evaluated in relation to the extent of need satisfaction achieved. Depending on the relative level of need satisfaction attained, fifth, the individual is rewarded or punished. Finally, sixth, the individual takes stock of the performance-reward chain and the degree to which his initial needs have been satisfied.

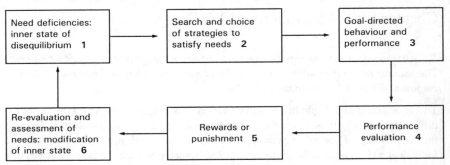

Figure 12.1: A Basic Model of Motivation (Ivancevich, Szilagyi & Wallace 1977)

Theorists interested in motivation in the workplace have taken theories developed to explain human behaviour in general and attempted to apply or adapt them to questions of employee motivation. Let us consider a fairly simple example.

Jani Kayode has recently been appointed assistant marketing manager of a large shoe manufacturing firm in Lagos. She is an ambitious young woman who wants to be promoted to the position of marketing head as soon as possible (need deficiency). Jani feels that one way to improve her chances for promotion is to obtain formal qualifications in marketing management in addition to her degree in business studies (search and selection of strategy to satisfy need). She subsequently attends part-time classes at the University of Lagos in order to attain the marketing qualification (goal-directed behaviour and performance). Eventually, she successfully completes her course of study, her work-related performance improves and is noticed by senior management in the firm (perform-ance evaluation), and she achieves her desired promotion (reward). Now that her initial need has been satisfied, Jani takes on her new role with enthusiasm (re-evaluation of needs), new needs emerge, and so on.

Theories of motivation at work based on the general model described in Figure 12.1 contain a number of, usually unstated, assumptions which need to be addressed before we consider some of the theories themselves.

12.1   The Conventional Approach:
Some Underlying Assumptions and Limitations

An individual's perception of his job and work in general is substantially determined by the stock of cultural values and norms he has acquired from his living environment. Traditionally, theories of motivation at work have placed little emphasis on the perceptual set which the individual brings with him to the work place, preferring instead to analyse in detail those characteristics of the work place itself and the job to be performed which have some bearing on the individual's performance. In crude terms, work motivation theorists have sought answers to questions such as 'how do I motivate employees to increase their productivity?' or 'how can I design the work place so as to get the best out of employees?' that is to say, a clear management bias is evident. Many textbook writers, when dealing with the subject of motivation, begin with justifying statements which indicate quite clearly where their allegiances lie. Some writers are so committed to their alliance with managers that they appear to see them in much the same light as they see themselves. For instance, Dessler (1980), an American organisational theorist, speaks of problems "facing the organisational theorist or manager" (p. 165), as if they have shared interests and a common set of problems, associated with ensuring the *compliance* of employees. The task of organisational theorists and managers in this approach is that of 'out-scheming' the workers. Again Dessler (1980) conveys this attitude well: "Unfortunately, the problem of ensuring compliance is not as simple as it might seem, and there are several reasons for this. First, as we shall see, employees have many ingenious ways of circumventing the sorts of control systems often used to ensure compliance" (p. 165). Dessler continues, "In summary, we will see in the next three chapters that imposing compliance – through rules, formal control systems, and close supervision – is probably a fairly effective technique for ensuring that most routine tasks (as might be found on an assembly line) are accomplished" (1980: 166).

As a result, critics have referred to the activities of many motivation theorists concerned with organisations as 'moo-cow sociology'; the implication being that most of the methods employed are manipulative devices aimed solely at increasing worker docility and productivity.

One such critic is Nord (1974, 1977, 1978). He has argued that partly as a result of the fact that organisational theorists have taken for granted the existing distribution of power within organisations, "which gives certain individuals (managers) the right to determine fundamental organisational goals and procedures" (1977: 1027), and partly as a result of a tendency towards ideological conservatism and the acceptance of the "ideologies of the modern corporation leaders" (1977: 1028), current approaches "are vulnerable to a number of crucial omissions and distortions that render them both incomplete and unrealistic" (1977: 1028). Frost (1980), another critic, has made similar observations: "*We are preoccupied with what managers value and with their definitions of organisational problems.* The failure of researchers and practitioners to recognise the interrelationship of values and observation frequently blinds them to the essentially conservative nature of much of the prescription and implementation in the field" (p. 502). How does this preoccupation with what are essentially management problems affect conventional approaches to motivation at work? Nord (1977) has identified a number of omissions and limitations and it is worth describing some of these in detail.

12.1.1   A Biased and Limited Range of Variables is Studied

The interests of management are directed primarily at matters which include reducing worker absenteeism and turnover, improving productivity and job involvement, facilitating the introduction of change, and so on. These interests have largely determined the activities of the vast majority of organisational researchers. This has meant that other variables such as "self-actualisation, organisational democracy, feelings of self-control and self-worth, equity and justice" (Nord 1977: 1028) have been studied primarily in so far as they serve the managerial interests mentioned earlier. It has also meant that the same biases have found their way to African countries. Bispham (1964), for instance, argued that managerial biases of this kind led to grave distortions about the capabilities and commitment of Nigerian workers, and to serious misinterpretations of labour turnover and absenteeism statistics. Likewise, Odinye and Aduaka (1989) note the importance to Nigerian craftsmen of feelings of self-worth, respect from managers, and understanding.

12.1.2   Job Satisfaction Mostly Studied in Relation to Productivity

Most often, increasing worker satisfaction has been seen as a means of improving productivity. This has meant that the idea of worker satisfaction as a legitimate goal in its own right has not been widely acknowledged. Similar concerns are evident in some African research into such questions (e.g., Munene & Dul 1989).

12.1.3   Extrinsic Sources of Job Satisfaction are Underemphasised

Extrinsic factors which have been relatively ignored by organisational researchers include such basic considerations as pay, job security and safety. These matters merit special attention in Africa because urban unemployment levels are so high, and because the earnings of millions of African workers are so low as to place them perilously close to officially defined poverty levels. Moreover, the existing research evidence indicates that lower-level African workers place much importance on extrinsic factors associated with their work (e.g., Blunt 1982; Gutkind 1968; Kayode 1970). Nellis (1986) indicates that one of the factors explaining the success of the Guma Valley Water Company (GVWC) in Sierra Leone was that its more than 400 employees had their "salaries supplemented by annual bonuses; benefits include free medical and dental care, car allowances and loans for refrigerators. Occasionally the company guarantees housing loans. (He notes) Inducements are quite good in the GVWC" (p. 29). Similar observations have been made of unskilled workers in the USA. Tausky (1969), for example, suggested that "the economic pay off from work may frequently be the main focus of concern rather than rewards stemming from prestige or the intrinsic content of work" (pp. 54–55).

12.1.4   Power and Alienation are Not Widely Studied

In Chapter 9 we discussed the concept of alienation and its relevance for a full understanding of behaviour at work. The worker's feelings of powerlessness are a major feature of alienation. It is the relationship between these two factors which theorists of work motivation have tended to ignore. They have tended to focus instead on job satisfaction – and its relationship to performance – which excludes questions relating to the distribution of power within the organisation (e.g., Clegg 1989; Mintzberg 1983). The point is, as Nord (1977) has suggested, "that the power individuals exercise over the situations that affect them, relative to their expectations of how much influence they should have, may be of greater importance in determining their experiences of alienation (and perhaps their behaviour in general, including productivity) than is the work itself" (p. 1031).

The implications of all this for understanding motivation at work in Africa may be summarised as follows. First, the Western approach has been (and still is) dominated by a managerial ideology which has placed severe limits on the type of knowledge generated. The extent to which the development of the field has been retarded by this bias is difficult to assess, but it is likely that a more even-handed approach – one that took account of the needs and interests of all organisational members – would lead to a fuller understanding of motivation at work. Africans who are interested in motivation at work, at the very least therefore, need to ask themselves whether the management perspective is suited to their own particular environments. The political and economic diversity of the continent suggests that the answers to that question will vary considerably. Second, it is likely that a certain amount of the conflict which takes place in organisations is due directly to the perceived manipulative inclinations of managers and their expert advisers: organisational theorists. In the West, the divide between managers and workers is certainly reinforced by this perception. Were a broader perspective to be applied in Africa, it could well serve the interests of all organisational members, workers and managers alike, and actually result in less conflict, and less sharply defined lines of demarcation between managers and other employees. Third, and finally, making some of the assumptions which underlie Western theories of motivation at work explicit to some degree permits the material covered in this chapter to be presented in a manner which is more value-free than it might otherwise have been.

12.2   Theories of Motivation at Work

It would be neither appropriate nor relevant to attempt to present here anything like a comprehensive review of theories of motivation at work. This chapter deals primarily with those theories which have been the subject of empirical investigation in Africa. As a result a number of theories will be omitted; only *content* theories are discussed. Content theories seek to identify the major variables which exert an influence on behaviour. These theories are to be contrasted with those which attempt to explain the mechanics of the *process* of influencing behaviour. Content theories direct their attention, for example, at classifying the basic needs which people try to satisfy. What rewards do people find most attractive? What incentives are the most effective? Or what aspects of the job to be performed or the work environment lead to desired work-related performance or outcomes? In short, these theories provide a fairly comprehensive appraisal of factors which influence individual behaviour, but they are not, in general, capable of predicting such behaviour accurately (Campbell & Pritchard 1976). They are best regarded, therefore, as frameworks which deepen our understanding of motivation at work without really enabling us to make law-like generalisations about it.

These theories have their historical roots in the clinical-qualitative domain of psychology, while the process theories have their beginnings in the experimental-quantitative domain. The historical underpinnings of these classes of theories hint at how the theories themselves might be interpreted and applied. The clinical basis of the content theories implies that they were developed and intended to be used and interpreted in this light. What does this mean in practice? Simply put, it means that each situation or piece of behaviour which we might want to explain should be treated as if it were a more or less unique case. Our understanding of such behaviour might, therefore, be informed by one theory rather than another not because we are committed to a particular theory but because that theory explains the behaviour in question better than other available alternatives. In the same way, on another occasion we might wish to make use of a number of theories in attempting to understand some aspect of organisational behaviour.

12.2.1   Maslow's Need Hierarchy

This is one of the most popular theories of motivation in the organisational theory and behaviour literature. Maslow developed his theory some forty years ago. It has provided the basis for much research and writing by organisational theorists, and a readily interpretable framework for practitioners. Maslow (1954), like a number of writers before him, notably Murray (1938), proposed a structured classification system for human needs. Before defining these needs, we should note three fundamental assumptions which form the basis of Maslow's theory.

1. People have needs which influence their behaviour. Only needs which have not been satisfied can act as motivators. When, for example, physiological needs, such as the need for food, are unsatisfied they dominate the individual. Energy is directed at satisfying the unfulfilled need.
2. An individual's needs are arranged in a hierarchy of importance, from the most basic needs, such as those for food and shelter, to more complex psychological needs such as the need for esteem or the need to fulfil creative potential (*see* Table 12.1).
3. Needs at the upper levels of the hierarchy are only activated once needs at the lower levels have attained some minimally acceptable level of satisfaction. In Africa, it is safe to suppose that the vast majority of lower-level workers would, partly because of their obligations to immediate family and kin, be concerned with satisfying more basic

needs. This means that at work they would be most concerned about financial rewards and security of employment.

Physiological Needs

These refer to the recurring needs which people have to eat, drink, sleep, and to reproduce. Such needs are clearly essential to people's very existence. Inattention to physiological needs in some instances can result in death. In the USA, where Maslow developed his theory, it is estimated that something like 85 per cent of the population have their physiological needs relatively well catered for. On the other hand, in Africa the figure would be very much lower, and we would therefore expect this need category to feature prominently in people's motivational make-up. At work, such factors as salary level, working conditions (e.g., heat, noise and shift time), and distance from urban residence would feature prominently in this category. In the larger cities of Africa the latter consideration can be of prime significance to the worker who, because of relatively low levels of pay, cannot afford to buy his own motor transport, or to take public transport if it exists, and must therefore either walk or cycle long distances to and from work.

Table 12.1 : Maslow's Need Hierarchy (Ivancevich, Szilagyi & Wallace 1977)

General Factors Associated With Each Level of Need	Levels in the Need Hierarchy	Organisational Factors Associated with Each Level of Needs
1. Growth 2. Achievement 3. Advancement	Self-actualisation	1. Challenging job 2. Creative opportunities 3. Advancement in the organisation
1. Recognition 2. Status 3. Self-esteem 4. Self-respect	Ego, Status and Esteem	1. Job title 2. Merit pay increases 3. Peer/supervisory recognition 4. Work itself 5. Responsibility 6. Interactions with supervisors and peers
1. Companionship 2. Affection 3. Friendship	Social	1. Quality of supervision 2. Compatible work group 3. Professional friendships
1. Safety 2. Security 3. Competence 4. Stability	Safety and Security	1. General salary increases 2. Job security 3. Fringe benefits 4. Safe working conditions
1. Air 2. Food 3. Shelter 4. Sex	Physiological	1. Base salary 2. Heat and cold 3. Canteen facilities 4. Working conditions

It is important to remember here what is frequently forgotten in these discussions: African countries are in varying degrees poor in natural resources, in money, in skilled manpower, and in experience of managing the complex formal work organisations on which their development so much depends. Kiggundu graphically portrays the reality of much of what constitutes organisational life for many Africans:

"What does the inside of an African organisation look like? It would be characteristically overcrowded and improvising in a number of areas. Jobs would be narrowly defined, and all important decisions would be made by senior management and communicated down through the chain of command. Facilities, equipment, machinery, and buildings would look overutilised and in need of repair and maintenance …. . There would be an atmosphere of management by crisis as events would seem to take everybody by surprise" (1988: 224–225).

Like all generalisations, of course, Kiggundu's pen picture is more true of some African organisations than others: in some the picture would not be so dismal while in others it would be even worse.

Safety or Security Needs
Here the individual is concerned to ensure that he is not deprived of his ability to satisfy physiological needs in the long run. It may be regarded as a need to reduce uncertainties associated with basic physiological need satisfaction. In the work setting, these needs would be reflected in the worker's attitude toward the safety of his work, his job security, and the possibility of pay increases. Ankomah (1985), for example, is of the opinion that:

"Most people in postindependence African countries are not inspired to work, because they lack desire to accomplish something. The African bureaucrat is often motivated by material things he can gain from work. He engages in those activities of work that will result either in immediate financial gains or possessing the potential for such" (p. 395–413).

Security needs would also be reflected in the worker's desire for some continuity in the work process itself especially if, as is often the case, this determines his income (by limiting his productivity). Kapferer's (1972) study of tailors in a Zambian factory provides a good case example:

"The constant changes in the kind of garments being made and the alteration between production methods produces a continual uncertainty among the tailors about the nature of their daily work. Moreover, the factory manager presents to the tailors no clearly defined set of output expectations on which they can base their own behaviour, beyond that of expecting the tailors to work hard and with as few breaks as possible. This leads to 'sweat shop' conditions, with the factory manager continually urging the tailors to maintain a fast rate of work and threatening to dismiss those who slacken pace. Many of the tailors view Patel as an unreasonable task master. In the words of one tailor, 'God made a bad mistake to create such an employer'" (p. 37).

This passage also provides an insight into the importance of social relations at work – in this case the quality and type of supervision – and leads us conveniently to the next level in Maslow's need hierarchy, the social needs.

Social Needs

The social (or belongingness) needs reflect man's social nature, his need for the friendship and the company of others. These needs take effect when the physiological and safety needs have been satisfied to an acceptable degree for the individual. One of the most important social relationships at work, as we saw in the Zambian example, has to do with relationship between managers and workers. This can be a difficult relationship to manage in Africa. One reason for this, as illustrated by Jones's (1988a) investigation of management thinking in Malawi, is the fact that workers typically want to establish close personal contacts with their supervisors, and this cuts across the managerial principle which supervisors are required by the organisation to observe: that all employees should be treated, as far as possible, in the same way (the universal – individual contradiction which we have noted previously). The nature of supervision at work can be the cause of frequent complaint, as noted by Peil in her study of Ghanaian factory workers who disliked the behaviour of their foreman because he supervised too closely: "He comes so often he makes us uneasy while working. He is too enthusiastic" (1972: 95).

Esteem (or Ego) Needs

This category incorporates the needs which people have for self-respect and the respect of others, and needs associated with feelings of self-confidence, status and prestige. At work such factors as job title, the nature of the work itself (e.g., highly skilled, scientific, professional etc.), and the amount of autonomy, power and responsibility associated with the job, would feature prominently in this category. Occupational preferences provide some indication of the degree to which different types of work are seen as satisfying esteem needs. In Nigeria, for example, Morgan (1965) found that the prestige ratings attached to various occupations by a sample of university students were very similar to Western ratings: high ratings were given to occupations such as physician and accountant and the lowest ratings to manual work such as domestic servant. McQueen (1969) has made similar findings among Nigerian secondary school leavers, where over 65 per cent of his sample aspired to professional or white collar occupations while only 5.6 per cent aspired to lower-level jobs such as farmer, trader, and unskilled labourer.

Self-Actualisation

The final and highest class of needs in Maslow's hierarchy is that of self-actualisation. It might also be said to be the weakest since the theory says that all other needs must be relatively well satisfied before this one can begin to take effect as a motivator of behaviour. Self-actualisation refers to the individual's need to realise her full potential. That is, the self-actualising person is someone who strives not just to be good at something but to be as good as she is capable of being. Self-actualisation entails a fundamental change in orientation. Whereas in social needs the individual measures herself in relation to her acceptance by others, and in the esteem need category she seeks, in a sense, to set herself apart in terms of status or prestige, in self-actualisation, she measures herself against her own personal ideal of what constitutes the best of her capabilities. Organisational variables associated with self-actualisation include the challenge of the job, the amount of creativity entailed, the degree of autonomy available, and the opportunity for recognition, achievement and advancement.

Paradoxically, most of the organisational research generated by Maslow's theory, of which there is a great deal (Wahba & Bridwell 1976), has employed quantitative methods of data collection and analysis. It is not at all certain that Maslow would have approved of his theory being used in this way let alone having it tested through the use of sophisticated statistical techniques. Maslow developed his theory from clinical, essentially qualitative, insights, and the flavour of his writing (e.g., Maslow 1954, 1973) is anything but positivist in nature. Indeed, its paradigmatic location could be said to be much closer to anti-organisational theory (see Blunt 1983a). Much of humanistic psychology, for example, which eschews quantitative methods almost entirely, draws strength from Maslow's writing. What, then, is to be made of the vast amount of positivist research conducted on the need hierarchy theory?

To begin with, it has proven difficult to devise a questionnaire which consistently and accurately reflects Maslow's need categories (e.g., Blunt 1977), and there has been debate as to whether the statistical techniques employed to assess the validity of Maslow-type questionnaires have been appropriate (e.g., Blunt & Denton 1979; Mitchell & Moudgill 1976). So, it is safe to draw only tentative inferences from the available evidence.

Most of the empirical evidence pertaining to Maslow's theory has been gathered from American managers (e.g., Porter 1961, 1962; Porter & Lawler 1965). However, there is a small but growing body of literature devoted to the cross-cultural study of managerial attitudes and motivations, and there is some agreement concerning the possible effects of culture on need satisfaction and need importance. The data suggest that culture in its broadest sense – taken, in most cases, to be defined by national boundaries – has a significant impact upon perceived need deficiencies among managerial personnel. Generally speaking, in developing countries, where political and socioeconomic systems may be regarded as less stable and more problematic, managers report much higher levels of need dissatisfaction than managers in relatively developed societies. The pioneering work of Haire et al. (1966) shows this, as do the findings of Badawy (1980) among Middle Eastern executives, Blunt (1973, 1976) among South African and Kenyan managers, Howell, Strauss and Sorensen (1975) among Liberian managers, and Jones (1988a) among Malawian managers. Howell et al. (1975) studied 130 Liberian middle managers drawn from 10 industrial organisations. They found that Liberian managers were much more dissatisfied with security needs than were managers from other countries. The investigators explained this finding in terms of the "political climate of Liberia at the time of this study, creating conditions of uncertainty both in the community and in industrial organisations" (Howell et al. 1975: 226).

With respect to need importance too, the literature reveals some consistency. Previous research has indicated that the importance rankings assigned to the various Maslowian need categories cut across cultures (Blunt 1973; Haire, Ghiselli & Porter 1963; Howell et al. 1975). For example, Haire et al. noted:

"... the most impressive finding in connection with the importance attached to different needs was the relative similarity in the way quite different countries and cultures felt about them ... . The overall similarity among managers in different countries in their evaluations of the importance of needs may indicate that what people want from their jobs is relatively unaffected by the cultural environment in which they operate" (1963: 111).

There are at least two implications which flow from these latter findings. First, they have a bearing upon the original theoretical propositions put forward by Maslow (1954). For example, the results imply a greater degree of need hierarchy fixity between cultures than Maslow had thought likely: "We have spoken so far as if this hierarchy were a fixed order, but actually it is not nearly so rigid as we have implied" (Maslow 1954: 98). Second, and more importantly for the purposes of the present discussion, the findings imply in very general terms that irrespective of culture and local conditions, organisational structures, and administrative and reward systems, should be designed to attribute the same priorities to, and therefore satisfy, a unitary set of managerial needs arranged in the same, predetermined, hierarchical order.

However, a study conducted among a group of (mainly Kikuyu) Kenyan managers (Blunt 1976) indicated that they attached highest importance to security needs. The subjects comprised a highly educated group: 57 had completed high school, 13 had completed a course of technical education (post high school) either in Nairobi or abroad, 40 had either attended or were attending university, and 17 subjects had a university degree. All of the subjects were fluent in English, and follow-up interviews indicated that they had experienced no difficulty in understanding and completing the questionnaire.

A parallel study of 105 managers in Malawi by Jones (1988a) produced similar results: *see* Table 12.2 (see also Blunt & Jones 1986). In addition to the Haire *et al.* instrument, Jones (1988a) asked these managers to record "the best and worst things about being a manager". Table 12.3 (Jones 1986b: 215) displays the results of this question within the framework of Maslow's need hierarchy; the striking aspect of these findings is the overwhelming weight of negative responses at the security level. These data suggest that Kenyan and Malawian managers exhibit a need-category dominance profile which contradicts the assumption of cross-cultural stability among managerial groups with respect to the ordering of need categories. The displacement scores in Table 12.2 provide a convenient index of the degree to which national group scores vary from the predicted pattern, common to most Western countries. It is evident that the assumed similarity between managers from different nations does not stand up to testing in widely dissimilar environments. Managers in the developing world exhibit need importance profiles which depart greatly from the expected range of scores, and differ significantly between themselves. These findings add credence to the conclusion of Badawy (1980) that social and cultural environments need to be studied with care when designing organisational structures and management systems. The consequences of allowing serious mismatches to occur may take any one or more of a number of forms of organisational malaise such as high labour turnover and absenteeism, or damage to company property.

Table 12.2: An International Comparison of 'Need Importance'

Country	N	Self-Actualization	Rank	Autonomy	Rank	Security	Rank	Social	Rank	Esteem	Rank	Displacement Score*
Argentina[a]	198	6.59	1	6.36	3	6.49	2	6.18	4	6.15	5	4
Australia[b]	1,339	6.23	1	5.94	2	5.89	3	5.38	4	5.26	5	0
Chile[c]	159	6.48	1	6.10	3	6.31	2	5.94	5	5.97	4	16
Denmark[a]	149	6.00	1	5.65	2	5.53	3	4.96	4	4.50	5	0
England[a]	239	6.23	1	5.88	2	5.56	3	5.08	4	4.89	5	0
France[a]	154	6.35	1	5.83	2	5.22	3	5.08	4	4.83	5	0
Germany[a]	586	6.19	1	5.96	3	6.04	2	4.66	5	5.28	4	16
India[a]	114	6.37	2	6.16	3	6.42	1	5.66	5	5.82	4	30
Italy[a]	267	6.17	1	5.72	3	5.68	4	5.18	5	5.73	2	35
Kenya	126	6.49	2	6.43	3	6.68	1	6.27	5	6.28	4	30
Liberia[b]	130	6.15	2	6.08	3	6.25	1	5.99	4	5.67	5	12
Malawi	105	6.33	2	6.05	3	6.45	1	5.94	4	5.54	5	12
Middle-East[d]	248	6.57	1	6.35	5	6.40	4	6.55	2	6.47	3	32
South Africa[e]	275	6.28	1	5.92	2	5.86	3	5.08	4	4.93	5	0
United States[a]	464	6.30	1	5.80	2	5.30	4	5.37	3	5.09	5	4

*The 'Displacement Score' is the sum of the differences between predicted and actual 'need' category rankings, multiplied by the number of aberrant categories.

[a]Haire et al. (1963); [b]Clark & McCabe (1970); [c]Howell et al. (1975); [d]Badawy (1980); and [e]Blunt (1973).

Table 12.3: Need Hierarchy: Aspects of Managerial Jobs (Malawi) (Jones 1986b)

Needs	Good (+) and Bad (−) Aspects of Job
Self-Actualisation	Feeling of Achievement (16+) Opportunities for Self-Expression and Fulfillment (12+)
Autonomy	Power and Authority (20+) Making Decisions (11+) Making Unpleasant Decisions (4−) Position to have Broad Understanding (2+)
Esteem	Respect from Others (13+) Privileged Position (4+)
Social	Unpopularity (4−) Disciplining Subordinates (2−)
Security	Financial Rewards (3+) Accepting Blame for Failures of Others (27−) Accepting Responsibility for Decisions (14−) Insecurity and Risk (6−) Public Scrutiny of Actions (2−)

The results reported here indicate the potential for diversity which exists between managerial groups with respect to need category dominance. For example, Table 12.2 shows that Indian, Kenyan, Liberian and Malawian cultures encourage managers to assign highest importance to the security needs. It is possible that in African societies, where particularistic criteria can play a disproportionately great part in employment and promotion decisions, managers are sensitive to possible changes of personnel among decision making groups and subsequent wholesale personnel changes in the organisation.

On the other hand, in societies where job tenure is shielded, and in some instances enshrined, by the formal application of universalistic (Parsons 1951) criteria of assessment and by well-developed protective institutions (e.g., trade unions), security needs are of much less concern. Of course speculations of this kind have yet to be tested, but they incorporate the type of situation-specific notions which are gaining wider recognition among researchers in this field of study. It is perhaps worth noting here that the Middle Eastern executives studied by Badawy (1980) attached very little importance to their security needs, possibly because many of the countries in that region are rich and have relatively small indigenous populations: jobs are not scarce and job insecurity is therefore unlikely to be widely experienced by indigenous managers.

In so far as Maslow's theory is concerned, the data presented here support his general hypothesis regarding the degree of fixity of the hierarchy of needs. However, although Maslow (1954: 98–100) suggested several possible explanations for divergences, he failed to include the possibility of culturally determined variations. Research results suggest that an auxiliary hypothesis pertaining to culturally determined need-category ordering should be added to the original theory.

12.2.2   McClelland's Theory of Need for Achievement

It has been argued that the theory of achievement motivation can be applied with good results to generating entrepreneurial activity and economic growth in developing countries (McClelland 1961). The theory has therefore been tested and applied in a number of developing countries, notably India (McClelland & Winter 1969), but also in Nigeria (LeVine 1966), and Tanzania (Ostheimer 1969). This section provides a brief description of the theory, followed by a discussion of the studies conducted by LeVine (1966) and Ostheimer (1969).

McClelland and his colleagues proposed a theory of motivation which is based upon three major motives: the need for achievement and the fear of failure; the need for power; and the need for affiliation. Most of McClelland's research and writing, however, is based upon the first of these, the need for achievement (nAch). Within this approach, it is said that there are two basic types of people: on the one hand, there are those who strive for success, are challenged by opportunity and are willing to exert considerable effort in order to attain a desired goal. On the other hand, there are those who do not care very much whether or not they are successful. That is to say, some people have an urge to achieve while others do not. The strength of the achievement need is usually assessed through the use of a projective psychological test, the Thematic Apperception Test (TAT). This test requires the subject to interpret pictures by telling a story about what is perceived in the picture – what is going on in the scene, how it came about, and what is a likely outcome. It is assumed that the individual projects himself into the scene, and identifies with one or other of the characters depicted. For instance, one set of pictures might include a work situation (men working on an assembly line), a study situation (a student at work showing her seated at a desk with a book), a boy apparently daydreaming, and a picture featuring interaction between a mother and son. Achievement motivation is inferred from stories which suggest competition with some standard, or anything which implies a "desire to move ahead to the ultimate goal" (Atkinson 1958: 22).

Many years of researching achievement motivation have shown that people who have high needs for achievement display certain common characteristics.

1. They set themselves goals which are moderately difficult to attain and pose a certain amount of challenge to their energy and resourcefulness. If goals are too easily achieved, they feel little sense of accomplishment. A favourite experimental illustration of this characteristic is the ring-toss game. Each subject is simply given three rings, shown a peg in the ground some distance away, and asked to see how many rings he can throw over the peg. Subjects are told that they may stand at any distance they wish from the peg. The experimenter then records where the subject stands in relation to the peg and how many successful tosses ('ringers') he makes. Subjects vary widely

with regard to how far they stand from the peg. Some choose to stand very close, so as to maximise their chances of success, while others stand impossible distances away from it. On the other hand, a few will have calculated, on the basis of previous attempts, what precise distance allows them a reasonable measure of success without making the game too easy. It is this behaviour which is typical of people with high n-Ach.

2. People with high n-Ach are attracted by work situations which allow them to take personal responsibility for goal achievement. They have high confidence in their own abilities to accomplish moderately complex tasks, and feel that their chances of success are greater than most other people's. This inclines them to avoid committees and other work situations where they may be required to work towards goals others have set. Similarly, they are averse to gambling situations where they again have no personal control over outcomes.

3. Concrete feedback on performance is essential for people with high n-Ach, so that they know how well they are doing. Moreover, they are responsive to such feedback. For example, Kagan and Moss (1962) have found that boys with high n-Ach showed considerable skill at 'constructional activities' (where there is more or less immediate feedback and it is directly linked to performance), whereas they were neither particularly good nor bad at academic work or intellectual activities.

   In organisations, feedback on performance varies tremendously. Part of this variation has to do with the nature of the work performed. For example, a Bemba copper miner in Zambia would have much less difficulty in obtaining immediate and direct feedback on his performance than would, say, an African public servant working in a large government department, or a manager in a business enterprise. This is because the miner's work is more concrete and more amenable to fairly objective assessment. As a consequence of this need for feedback, people with high n-Ach, who have jobs which do not provide direct feedback, regard money as a symbol of how successful a person has been at work. Money itself is not the motivator; it is a symbol of accomplishment. Goal achievement is the motivator.

4. Another characteristic of people with high n-Ach is that they are more inquisitive about their environments. They search them more thoroughly; they travel more, and are generally more open to new experiences. This behaviour is interpreted as demonstrating their desire for new opportunities to test their achievement skills. LeVine (1966), for instance, noted how the Igbo of Nigeria were more economically successful and held a disproportionately higher number of senior positions in public and private enterprises than did the Hausa of Northern Nigeria. He argued that the Igbo showed much more initiative and readiness to explore new places and methods than other peoples facing similar problems. Speaking of people in economically depressed areas all over the world, he contends:

   "Such families work on a principle of least effort in which the comfort of remaining in similar surroundings and doing familiar things, even when faced with starvation, outweighs the future economic benefits that might be gained from drastically changing

their way of life. So long as their impoverishment is gradual, they will put up with it, for it affords known and immediate gratifications that would be missing were they to seek new productive activities" (LeVine 1966: 84).

He goes on to suggest that the Igbo might have chosen to respond to these deprivations as the Hausa did by concentrating on traditional trading patterns in the areas they migrated to, thus depressing their upward mobility.

"There were, then, at least three possible courses of action open to the Igbo in response to their acute land shortage: to accept impoverishment at home, to extend traditional trading patterns while remaining as un-Westernised as possible, and to pursue Western-type economic activity with the changes in ways of life that were required for it. Other peoples have adopted the first two alternatives in response to economic adversity; although some Igbo undoubtedly did too, many chose the third course. The difference is not one of rationality, but of energy and effort. In the simplest terms, the successful pursuit of a novel occupation involving a high degree of enterprise or education is not for a lazy man, no matter how hard pressed he is financially" (LeVine 1966: 84).

5. A final characteristic of individuals who have high needs for achievement is that they are more inclined to think spontaneously about how they might achieve a desired objective. They spend considerable time going over possible strategies in their minds, and even dream about achieving certain goals. This point is also well illustrated by LeVine's (1966) findings among Nigerian university students.

One of the tasks LeVine (1966) asked of his subjects was that they write two essays, one on 'How does a boy become a successful man?' and the other on 'What is a successful man?'. He scored the essays for indications of n-Ach and could find no differences between Hausa and Igbo students in terms of the emphasis placed on work, sacrifice and achievement. However, when the scoring method was applied to accounts of dreams written by the same students, Igbo students scored significantly higher on n-Ach. LeVine explained these results by suggesting that in the first exercise the students had responded in a manner they thought was appropriate, whereas their dreams reflected their unconscious or spontaneous mental processes. On this point, McClelland and Winter (1969) add: "What people spontaneously think about is more apt to spill over into relevant actions than their attitudes and opinions as expressed in questionnaires or interviews" (pp. 10–11).

In their efforts to relate need for achievement to economic development in poorer nations, McClelland and Winter (1969) devised a training programme designed to instil the need for achievement. Their findings among Indian entrepreneurs indicated that the effects of motivation training were more noticeable for people in positions of responsibility who had the opportunity to bring about change in their working lives. Where individuals had little power or responsibility, the effects of n-Ach training were so small as to be insignificant.

The relationship between need for achievement and economic development has also been studied in Africa. A study conducted among the Chagga of Tanzania by Ostheimer (1969) examined the degree to which n-Ach explained the relatively high level of economic development among farmers in the Kilimanjaro region. Ostheimer used a number of tests in his attempts to measure n-Ach. Except with a modified version of the Thematic Apperception Test, he was unable to obtain significant differences between samples of Chagga students, Bondei students from an area geographically quite different from the Kilimanjaro district, and a group of Hindu Asians from Kilimanjaro schools. A number of theoretical problems relating to the validity of the tests used, and certain difficulties encountered in administering the tests, were put forward as possible explanations of the negative results.

Ostheimer's results apart, however, it seems that achievement motivation theory provides a useful framework for explaining the behaviour of different groups and individuals within organisations. Moreover, it has provided a sound theoretical framework for training and development activities which result in improved performance and entrepreneurial activity, especially for individuals with jobs which provide them with autonomy and decision making power. But this factor can pose difficulties for people working in large organisations, such as public bureaucracies, because they are less able to be directly involved in all the activities impinging on their jobs, and are less likely to receive concrete short-term feedback.

"A manager, particularly one of, or in, a large complex organisation, cannot perform all the tasks necessary for success by himself or herself. He must manage others so that they will do things for the organisation. Also, feedback on his subordinate's performance may be a lot vaguer and more delayed; than it would be if he were doing everything himself" (McClelland & Burnham 1976: 100–101).

This implies that the theory is not applicable to all organisational settings and groups. Nevertheless, it does provide those of us who are interested in understanding motivation at work with a usable index based on the need for achievement.

12.2.3   Herzberg's Two Factor Theory

A third content theory of motivation which has also been widely researched and applied, and is similar to Maslow's need-hierarchy theory, was proposed by Herzberg, Mausner and Snyderman (1959). Their theory grew in an inductive manner from their study of 200 accountants and engineers in Pittsburgh, USA. Subjects were simply required, in interview, to describe in detail what was happening in their jobs at times when they had been particularly dissatisfied, frustrated or unhappy, and at times when everything seemed to be going well and they felt satisfied, enthusiastic or interested in their work. The interview data were then analysed to see if any clear and consistent patterns emerged. The original investigation, and a number of other studies which have been conducted since that time, produced consistent results. In general, positive reactions to work were associated with jobs which provided opportunity for achievement, recognition of performance, responsibility and scope for individual development, and interesting and challenging work. These factors, which have essentially to do with the *content* of the job, were regarded as having the most power to motivate people. They have much in common with the higher-level need categories in Maslow's theory and also with McClelland's need for achievement theory.

On the other hand, work situations which were regarded as most dissatisfying were characterised by deficiencies in such areas as technical supervision, working conditions and pay, and company policy. These patterns of response provide the basis for Herzberg's theory. It consists of two general propositions.

1. Individual *motivation* at work is a function of the intrinsic characteristics of the job which include:

(a) Achievement
(b) Recognition
(c) Work itself
(d) Responsibility
(e) Advancement
(f) Personal development.

These factors are referred to as *motivators*.

2. Dissatisfaction at work is a function of a set of job conditions called *hygiene* factors. When operating to a sufficient degree, these factors *prevent dissatisfaction*, but they cannot act as motivators. Such factors include:

(a) Salary
(b) Job security
(c) Working conditions
(d) Personal life
(e) Relationship with supervisor(s)
(f) Relationships with fellow workmates and subordinates
(g) Company policies
(h) Fringe benefits.

The theory asserts, then, that no matter how highly a worker is paid or how good his working environment may be, this type of factor alone will not be sufficient to induce high levels of motivation or satisfaction. By the same token, irrespective of how interesting or how challenging a job might be (that is, intrinsically motivating), there will still be dissatisfaction if pay or working conditions are inadequate.

A replication of Herzberg's study has been conducted in Zambia by Machungwa and Schmitt (1983) who asked 341 workers to describe aspects of their work which were good or bad. Their findings, which are set out in Table 12.4, indicated that poor working conditions, poor pay, bad interpersonal relations, and poor supervision were mentioned most frequently as demotivators or hygiene factors. The researchers went on to tabulate

Table 12.4: Demotivating and Motivating Factors of Zambian Workers (Machungwa & Schmitt 1983)

Demotivating Factors, or Bad Aspects, of Working

1. Tribalism, favouritism, racial discrimination.
2. Bad interpersonal relations with supervisors, co-workers, subordinates.
3. Low pay, lack of bonuses or merit raises.
4. Supervisors who do not care to listen to problems of employees.
5. Death/sickness in family.
6. Fringe benefits (lack of transportation, housing).
7. Poorly defined work duties.
8. Domestic quarrels.
9. Too much work.
10. Lack of a chance to learn more about job and/or further training.

Motivating Factors, or Good Aspects, of Working

1. A lot of work.
2. Interesting work.
3. Work that has an urgent deadline.
4. Recognition.
5. Chance to learn more about job and/or further training.
6. Chance for promotion.
7. Achievement (work that allows achievement and proving oneself).
8. Responsibility.
9. Good interpersonal relations with co-workers.
10. Trust and confidence shown by superiors and co-workers.

the frequency of mention of work features that would motivate workers to exert more effort. These results are set out in Figure 12.2. This figure shows that the nature of the work itself and the opportunity for personal growth were important motivators, while relations with others, fairness in organisational practices, and personal problems were mentioned most frequently as having the opposite effect. Interestingly, material rewards and the physical conditions of work were seen as possessing *both* motivating and demotivating potential. Our own interpretation of the latter finding is that it is probable that these factors were seen by workers as the most critical to their frame of mind at work: that is to say, if material rewards were inadequate they were demotivated, but if they were seen as reasonable they acted as motivators. This would contradict Herzberg's theory but would be in accordance with findings made in developing countries elsewhere.

Problems with the Theory
One of the major weaknesses of the theory is that it makes no allowances for the different meanings which individuals attach to work or their orientations. It assumes that all workers will respond in a similar manner to different conditions of work. Other problems which have been identified include the following.

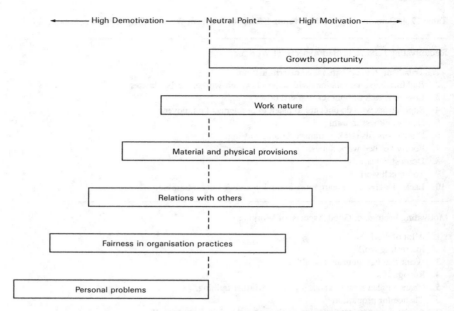

Figure 12.2: Relative Frequency with which Item was Mentioned by Zambian Workers

1. The original results achieved by Herzberg *et al.* (1959), and by other studies which have replicated their findings, may have been partly a function of the data collection methods employed rather than being an accurate reflection of what motivated the individuals concerned. Specifically, it has been suggested that when asked to explain why they feel happy or satisfied people are inclined to explain in terms of their own behaviours (that is, by referring to the sorts of factors listed under motivators). When things are not going so well, however, people tend to lay the blame elsewhere, on extrinsic factors associated with the work environment. Vroom (1966) puts the same point: "People tend to take the credit when things go well, and enhance their own feelings of self-worth, but protect their self-concept when things go poorly by blaming their failure on the environment" (pp. 7–8).

2. The theory has also been criticised on the grounds that a certain job characteristic can cause job dissatisfaction for one person and job satisfaction for another, or vice versa. Lahiri and Srivastva (1966) in a study of 93 Indian middle managers found that both intrinsic and extrinsic job factors caused feelings of satisfaction and dissatisfaction toward the job. They concluded: "the respondents in this study endorsed job factors differently from what the motivator-hygiene theory would have predicted" (Lahiri & Srivastva 1966: 263). Much the same conclusions have been reached by Jibowo (1977) who has studied the effects on job performance of motivators and hygiene factors among a group of 75 agricultural extension workers in Nigeria. Adopting basically the same method as Herzberg *et al.* (1959), Jibowo found some support for

the influence of motivators on job performance. There was also evidence to suggest, however, that hygiene factors, such as poor working conditions, low levels of pay, and poor supervision, depressed productivity, and performance in general, thus contradicting Herzberg's theory. In other words, the hygiene factors – pay, supervision and working conditions – acted as motivators among the Nigerian workers studied by Jibowo.

3. Another criticism is that much of the research on Herzberg's theory has been conducted on workers in interesting jobs, like engineers and accountants. As Jones (1988b: 31) observes, "there are some jobs which have to be performed, cannot be changed, and no normal person would want to do." These "humdrum, boring, repetitive jobs that so many people do in formal organisations" seem to have escaped the attention of these researchers:

"Herzberg's theoretical edifice ... was built on conversations with people in interesting, rewarding jobs. This did not prevent Fred from generalising to the whole of mankind: his book was called Work and the Nature of Man!" (Jones 1988b: 31).

This point is of particular relevance when the theory is applied to African organisations, where there are proportionately far more routine, boring, dehumanising jobs. How much help is to be found in Herzberg's theory for the supervisor who needs to get good work from people in such jobs?

Despite these and other criticisms, Herzberg's theory has been influential. Its most important contribution to our understanding of motivation at work was that it drew attention, in much the same way that Maslow's theory did, to the potential significance of the intrinsic characteristics of work. For many years – and this would be especially true during Africa's colonial days – the 'carrot and stick' approach to motivation predominated. Employee motivation at work was conceived of in terms of rewards and punishments, relating mainly to extrinsic factors such as pay, fringe benefits, working conditions and tight supervisory controls. The work of the so-called father of 'scientific management', the American engineer F. W. Taylor (1947), was primarily responsible for this managerial strategy.

Speaking of employers in Uganda before independence, Elkan (1960) noted that managers looked almost exclusively "to some form of money inducement to obtain larger outputs per man" (p. 121). Elkan's discussion of the behaviour of management in Uganda is illuminating because it shows very clearly the way in which managers have been adamant about the necessity to adopt Western forms of management in Africa, and fairly archaic ones at that. Elkan continues: "success in raising the output of workers is manifestly crucial, and ... it is customarily assumed that this cannot be done unless wage earners become proletarians and respond to Western management techniques" (1960: 125). He points out that managers in Uganda erred in their unquestioning acceptance of Western methods, and that individuals will respond in different ways to monetary incentives according to their ethnic background and whether they are migrants or proletarians. He asserts, for instance, that absence rates among Ganda workers did not decrease in response to bonus payments, but "where there are mainly Banyaruanda, a bonus of this sort is almost invariably a great success" (Elkan 1960: 126). He concluded that European and Asian managers in Uganda, who were convinced of the efficacy of Western management techniques, were too ready to assume homogeneous responses from their workers, and therefore ignored important individual differences. But Elkan made no mention of the possible relevance of intrinsic factors to work motivation, which was an important omission.

To conclude, Herzberg's theory has been well received by managers and management trainers. Part of its appeal rests in the fact that it is easy to comprehend and seems to fit the experiences of many Western managers quite well. It is also attractive because the job design recommendations which flow from it – known as job enrichment – are, again, fairly straightforward and relatively easy to implement in work organisations. In fact, Herzberg (1968) provided a neat recipe-like series of steps to job enrichment which are easy to understand, and unequivocal. They are clear, definite proposals which many managers who are interested in improving their organisation's performance find difficult to resist. For reasons such as these, Herzberg's theory continues to find a degree of approval among managers and researchers alike:

"In sum, what the Herzberg theory does, and does well, is point attention directly to the considerable significance of the work itself as a factor in the ultimate motivation and satisfaction of employees. And because the message of the theory is simple, persuasive and directly relevant to the design and evaluation of actual organisational changes, the theory continues to be widely known and generally used by managers" (Hackman & Oldham 1980: 58).

For similar reasons the theory may be of some value to African managers and practitioners. But in the absence of African data which directly test the theory it would be injudicious to adopt or apply it without a good deal of caution.

The above discussion draws attention to those factors which various theorists have proposed as major determinants of motivation at work. This raises the question of how we assess the presence of such factors in the work setting. It also poses the question: how do we go about designing jobs which are motivating? Job enrichment is one approach, but it has been found to have a number of flaws. A widely accepted approach to job design is that put forward by Hackman and Oldham (1975, 1976, 1980). Although, as we shall see, this model also has limitations, they are perhaps less serious than those associated with job enrichment.

12.3   Job Design

Some people, when they are well matched with the jobs that they are required to do so they can perform effectively, frequently come to enjoy their work because they find it personally rewarding and fulfilling. This condition is referred to by Hackman and Oldham (1976) as *internal motivation*. A state of internal motivation means that the individual identifies closely with her work and obtains high levels of self-reward for performing well: feelings of pride and accomplishment. She simply feels good about a job well done. Poor performance, on the other hand, leads to feelings of unhappiness and perhaps shame, and encourages the individual to try harder so as to avoid these feelings and regain the personal rewards that good performance can bring. The purpose of this section is to consider the ways in which Hackman and Oldham (1976, 1980) propose that jobs should be designed in order to foster such internal motivation, and other desirable outcomes such as general job satisfaction and improved work effectiveness.

The Job Characteristics Model (JCM)

The model proposed by Hackman and Oldham revolves around three psychological states: experienced meaningfulness of the work; experienced responsibility for outcomes of the work; and knowledge of the results of the work performed. These psychological states are strongly influenced by certain features of the job, called core job characteristics. The presence or absence of these psychological states, it is suggested, will determine whether or not desired personal outcomes (e.g., satisfaction or pleasure) and work outcomes (e.g., greater productivity) will result. Hackman and Oldham made some allowance for individual differences by including in their model the notion of *growth need strength* (GNS), and other factors such as knowledge and skill, and context satisfaction (*see* Figure 12.3).

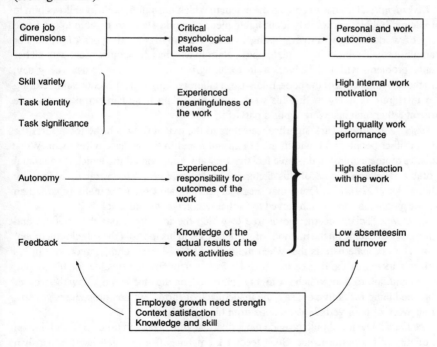

Figure 12.3: The Job Characteristics Model (Hackman & Oldham 1980)

Before defining these terms it is necessary to explain the effects of the moderating variables mentioned immediately above. The moderating variables depicted in Figure 12.3 acknowledge the possibility which Herzberg's theory ignores: that different people will respond differently to the same set of job experiences. As we have suggested, some people are motivated by enriched work while others are not, with some in-between reactions. Many individual characteristics, such as norms and values, can explain these differences, but Hackman and Oldham focus on three variables which they regard as having a major influence: knowledge and skill, satisfaction with the work context, and GNS. What they are saying is that the effectiveness of their job design proposals for particular individuals will depend largely on these three factors. Put another way, for a particular individual, the relationship between the characteristics of her job, and work and personal outcomes such as high productivity and high internal motivation, is *moderated* by GNS, knowledge and skill, and satisfaction with the job context. We now look more closely at the various parts of the model.

Core Job Characteristics

The core job characteristics set out in Figure 12.3 may be defined as follows.

Skill variety: This refers to the number of different skills and abilities a person must have in order to carry out the work required of him.

Task identity: This has to do with the extent to which the individual's job allows him to complete a 'whole' and clearly identifiable piece of work. He must be able to see some piece of work through from beginning to end. This applies to all types of work. For example, a social worker in Accra, Lagos or Nairobi who has the scope to deal with all her clients' problems will find the work more meaningful than someone who deals only, say, with the housing needs of the poor. Likewise, a tailor working in a garment manufacturing firm in Harare is likely to find his work more rewarding if he can complete a whole garment rather than just working on a part of it.

Task significance: Task significance refers to the extent to which the job affects the lives of other people, both within the organisation and in the wider environment. Work becomes more meaningful if people feel that they are doing something which is beneficial to others. The importance of this factor in Africa has been demonstrated recently by Schonmeier (1979), who found that secondary school students in Somalia regarded an ideal occupation as one which served to further national development.

Autonomy: This concerns the degree to which the individual has the freedom and opportunity to decide on the methods of work he uses in his job, and the scheduling of that work. The rationale here is that when the individual has considerable autonomy in his work this increases the degree to which he feels personally responsible for his output, success and failure. Jobs which are highly controlled, on the other hand, allow the worker to lay the blame for failure on, say, the inadequacy of formal written procedures governing his work or poor verbal instructions from his supervisor.

Feedback: The job should provide the individual with clear and timely information on the quality of his performance. Such feedback emanates from the job itself rather than supervisors or co-workers. Thus a doctor who treats a patient and sees the patient recover receives the type of feedback we are talking about. Similarly, a mechanic working on an engine overhaul will derive feedback of this kind from having the engine run smoothly again.

Critical Psychological States
The core job characteristics mentioned above are conducive to the development of the three critical psychological states depicted in Figure 12.3.

Meaningfulness: Work is experienced as more meaningful when the job involves high levels of skill variety, task identity and task significance.

Responsibility: The individual must be able to see clearly that he is personally responsible for the performance of his job. He is more likely to perceive this if he has a job which allows him autonomy to decide on matters which immediately affect his work performance.

Knowledge of results: The job must be able to provide the type of feedback mentioned earlier.

Hackman and Oldham have developed a formula for estimating the potential that a job has for motivating people by combining the core dimensions set out in Figure 12.3 as follows:

$$\text{Motivating Potential Score (MPS)} = \frac{\text{Skill Variety} + \text{Task Identity} + \text{Task Significance}}{3} \times \text{Autonomy} \times \text{Job Feedback}$$

Of course, this formula presupposes that it is possible to assign some numerical value to each of the core job dimensions. Hackman and Oldham (1975) have devised a questionnaire for doing this, the Job Diagnostic Survey (this instrument, along with guidelines and cautions concerning its use, is set out fully in Hackman and Oldham 1980: 275–317). It is clear from the formula that substantial reductions in the MPS of a job occur when the job scores low on either autonomy or feedback. This is because the JCM specifies that both knowledge of results and experienced responsibility should be present if desired personal and work outcomes are to result. Autonomy and feedback are the job characteristics which engender these two psychological states (*see* Figure 12.3).

Moderators
We noted earlier that Hackman and Oldham regard knowledge and skill, GNS and context satisfaction as being the variables which have the greatest influence on how the individual responds to improvements in the core dimensions of his job. These variables are described more fully below.

Knowledge or skill: Where jobs are high in motivating potential they are more demanding of the individual in terms of the skills she must possess, and in terms of her ability to take responsibility and to learn from her mistakes. As a result, people who have sufficient knowledge and skill will enjoy their work. Those with insufficient knowledge and skill, however, are likely to experience frustration and unhappiness. This can lead to their withdrawal from the job, either in a literal sense by resigning or asking for a transfer or job change, or in a psychological sense by telling themselves that really their jobs do not mean that much to them so poor performance does not matter.

Growth-need strength: Hackman and Oldham suggest, in much the same way that Maslow and McClelland do, that some people have strong needs for personal development and accomplishment (similar to n-Ach and self-actualisation), while others do not. People who have these strong 'growth' needs are likely to develop strong internal motivation when their work is interesting and challenging. GNS has a bearing on two relationships in the JCM. First, it affects the link between core job dimensions and critical psychological states: given a job high in MPS, people with high GNS will experience the critical psychological states more strongly than will workmates with low GNS. Second, it affects the relationship between critical psychological states and personal and work outcomes. Again, individuals with low GNS will respond less positively to the psychological states than individuals with high GNS. Hackman and Oldham summarise the effects thus:

"For both of these reasons, individuals with strong needs for growth respond eagerly and positively to the opportunities provided by enriched work. Individuals with low needs for growth, on the other hand, may not recognise the existence of such opportunities, or may not value them, or may even find them threatening and talk about being 'pushed' or stretched too far by their work" (1980: 85).

The number of people who fall into this latter category in Africa may be high, mainly because more basic needs – such as those described in the Maslow hierarchy – have yet to be satisfied. A lower-level Yoruba or Luo or Xhosa worker is unlikely to care very much about self-actualisation if he has difficulty feeding, clothing and housing himself and his family on the money that he earns. This implies that the JCM may have limited applicability to lower-level workers in Africa; perhaps only more senior positions where incumbents are likely to have satisfied their basic needs will respond to enriched work. In the West too, many workers are not interested in enriched jobs. As an American auto worker who had spent several months working in a Saab motor vehicle factory (where jobs are relatively high in MPS) in Sweden put it on his return home: "If I've got to bust my ass to be meaningful, forget it: I'd rather be monotonous" (Goldman, 1976: 31). The point made here – that some workers will not respond to enriched work because of basic need deficiencies – is recognised by Hackman and Oldham in the third moderating variable, context satisfaction.

Satisfaction with the work context: Where an employee feels underpaid, exploited, insecure or unhappy with her work relationships, it is unlikely that she will respond enthusiastically to the prospect of having her job enriched in the manner suggested by the JCM. It is only when these problems have been attended to that motivation through job design becomes a real possibility. Hackman and Oldham predict "that individuals who are relatively satisfied with pay, job security, co-workers and supervisors will respond more positively to enriched and challenging jobs than individuals who are dissatisfied with these aspects of the work context" (1980: 86). This prediction has stood up reasonably well to empirical testing (e.g., Oldham 1976).

Notwithstanding the effects of the moderating variables mentioned above, jobs designed in accordance with the JCM can lead to improvements in general satisfaction with work (apart, that is, from satisfaction with context factors), effectiveness at work in terms of both the quantity and quality of the goods or services produced, and attendance at work (or reduced absenteeism). But what empirical evidence exists to support or refute these claims in Africa? A small number of studies have been directed explicitly at testing the JCM in Africa, and these have been conducted in South Africa. The results are worth reporting particularly because one of these studies is the first true field experimental test of the JCM to have been conducted anywhere (Orpen 1979b).

Empirical Evidence
In the first study to be reviewed here, Orpen (1979a) tested the effects of 'Western' versus 'tribal' orientations among a group of 96 Xhosa machine operators, storemen and book-keepers on the relationship between enriched work (in terms of autonomy, variety, feedback, etc.) and job satisfaction and performance. The findings supported the hypothesis that the relationship between enriched work and job satisfaction was higher for Western-oriented employees than it was for tribal-oriented employees. This relationship was explained in terms of the different norms and values held by the two groups. It was suggested that Western-oriented workers had acquired "a set of values similar to those of middle-class whites ... (consequently) these employees tend to develop an orientation to work which stresses the role of work in one's personality and which regards work as a source of gratification of one's most important needs" (Orpen 1979a: 123). On the other hand, there was no significant difference between the Western and tribal groups with regard to the effects of enriched work on performance.

"The relative lack of responsiveness of behaviour to the four enriching job characteristics or core dimensions of the present study suggests that redesigned jobs can be expected to have a greater positive impact on feelings of satisfaction than on levels of performance" (Orpen 1979a: 123).

At the most general level, then, the results of Orpen's study corroborate some of the points made in Chapter 9. In particular, they indicate that motivation through job design needs to be assessed in the light of the various orientations to work which different people hold. The study also shows that designing jobs according to the JCM may result in improved attitudes towards work, but is not likely to lead to better performance or higher productivity.

A second study conducted by Orpen (1979b) was a field experiment (using a pretest-posttest control group design – *see* Blunt 1983a) which examined the longitudinal effects of job redesign (following the JCM) on a number of personal and work outcomes. The subjects were 72 clerical employees of a large semi-government agency: 36 subjects were assigned to the experimental group (enriched) and 36 were assigned to the control group (unenriched). The results of this investigation indicated "clearly that job enrichment can produce substantial benefits for the employee and the organisation" (Orpen 1979b: 210). More precisely:

1. In the enriched group, job satisfaction, job involvement and work motivation were all significantly higher than they were in the control group.
2. Rates of absenteeism and turnover were also significantly lower in the enriched group.

An advantage of the experimental method employed by Orpen was that it enabled him to draw clear inferences about the direction of causality (correlational studies do not permit unequivocal causal inferences to be drawn). That is to say, it was possible to claim with some degree of certainty that the results achieved, in terms of improved personal and work outcomes, were in fact due to the experimental manipulation (enriched work). In this way, other aspects of the Hackman and Oldham (1976) model were corroborated by this study. To cite one example: it was found that both context satisfaction and GNS had the moderating effects predicted by the JCM. From a practical point of view, Orpen concluded:

"First, that the deliberate redesigning of jobs – to make them more complex and varied – can cause employees to hold more favourable attitudes; second, that the precise extent of this effect depends on particular conditions; and third, that enrichment is likely to have a more direct and stronger impact on jobs attitudes than on productivity" (1979b: 216).

In conclusion, what is it possible to say about the validity of the JCM? Perhaps the most compelling evidence to date, both in terms of its methodological rigour and favourability, is contained in Orpen's (1979b) study. Correlational studies of the JCM have produced more equivocal results, especially with regard to the independence of the core job dimensions; that is, a number of studies have found that the core job dimensions are highly intercorrelated, and in a statistical sense it is therefore difficult to tell them apart. A number of other problems have been identified by Hackman and Oldham (1980), Roberts and Glick (1981), and Blunt (1983b); among them:

1. It has proven difficult, in practice, to determine what constitutes 'job-based' feedback (as opposed to feedback from supervisors and co-workers).
2. It is not clear whether the positive effects of enriched work arise from the *objective* characteristics of work or from employee *perceptions* of those characteristics.
3. The links between psychological states and core job dimensions may not be as straightforward as the model suggests.
4. The moderating effects of growth-need strength have not always been found to be those predicted by the model.
5. Original statements of the theory appear to imply that "all workers, irrespective of their GNS scores, show improved performance, though to varying degrees, as a result of having their jobs enriched" (Blunt 1983b: 196). This takes no account of individual orientations and attachments to work, be they instrumental and calculative or whatever (*see* Chapter 9), which are of great importance in Africa as elsewhere.

The most prudent closing judgment may be that while the model has potential both in terms of further study and as a possible aid in the redesign of jobs, "research based on the job characteristics approach is still exploratory" (Roberts & Glick 1981: 211). Before conclusive statements can be made about its relevance to Africa, therefore, a great deal of careful testing needs to be carried out, preferably through field experiments. Until that point is reached, again the key-word is caution. The need for such caution is argued more fully below.

12.4   Applying Theories of Motivation at Work

It was suggested at the beginning of this chapter that theories of motivation at work have proven remarkably resistant to testing, so much so that some – for example, Maslow's need-hierarchy theory – are regarded as being virtually untestable (Wahba & Bridwell 1976). Of course, this raises serious doubts about the validity of theories of motivation. Do they, in fact, offer complete explanations of human behaviour? Do they enable accurate predictions to be made? These are important questions to raise, not only for scientific reasons, but also because theories of motivation are widely applied to people in practical work settings. It is possible that the current state of knowledge is such as to warrant considerable caution in applying theories of motivation at work. Moreover, the theories of motivation covered in this chapter have their origins in the West. If they are of questionable validity there, then they must be viewed with some circumspection in Africa. In what follows, it is not intended to prejudge the relevance of theories of motivation in Africa but simply to point out some of the dangers of hasty, ill-considered applications.

12.4.1   How Relevant are Theories of Human Motivation to the
Realities of Organisational Life?

Owing to the fact that many managers, including Africans (e.g., Montgomery 1986b), accord prime importance to issues of employee motivation, they continue to find theories of motivation appealing and interesting. Yet in this area, where the interface between theory and practice has received considerable attention, there is little evidence that such theories can be applied by managers in practical ways. Many management trainers, in Africa as elsewhere, have shared the experience of conducting a classroom-based course in which managers have found mentalistic motivation theories fascinating, yet, as Jones (1988b) recalls in a typical account of such an experience, questions asked at the conclusion of the course take the inevitable form 'yes, but what do you actually *do* to motivate workers?'

Academic debate tends to consider theories of motivation in terms of their ability to account for aspects of human behaviour, and is not always of much help to those charged with making complex organisations work. However, some writers have been concerned to look at practical questions. For example, Fitzgerald (1971), in an article provocatively entitled *Why Motivation Theory Doesn't Work*, asserts that theories offer solutions to managerial questions which are not relevant to the reality of the workplace, so "we should discard the dismal vocabulary of motives, motivators, and motivation and think about becoming a society of persons" (p. 65). This call for fundamental changes in the organisation of work and work values is echoed in an equally trenchant contribution by Levinson (1973) called 'Asinine Attitudes Toward Motivation'. Patterns of power distribution in contemporary organisations perpetuate anachronistic structures in which employees are treated as objects and are thus alienated from their work. There is a "great jackass fallacy" (Levinson 1973: 73) about how people should be 'motivated' by managers. It is difficult to see how mentalistic theories conceived to explain human behaviour would be of much help in the organisational revolution which would be needed to change such fundamentally flawed structures (*see* Chapter 10).

Kreitner and Luthans (1987) have put forward an interesting view of the interaction between ideas which may have influenced attempts to control the behaviour of employees in pursuance of organisational goals. Mentalistic motivation theories, (Maslow, McClelland, Herzberg, etc.) which assert that behaviour is caused by internal needs, drives or expectations, have been countered – in terms of applications in the workplace – by attempts to apply B.F. Skinner's radical behaviorist ideas to the workplace. In accordance with behaviorist theories, internal mental states were to be ignored, as non-observable and therefore irrelevant in strategies to control, predict and measure human behaviour. This type of approach is the basis of Luthans' organisational behaviour modification (O.B. Mod.) model, in which behaviour is managed – in behaviorist terminology, 'shaped' – by managing antecedent conditions and contingent consequences of behaviour. Kreitner and Luthans consider that these two approaches are by themselves incomplete and less than effective. They advocate the management of human resources using the insights from social learning theory, which asserts that human behaviour is a function of internal *and* external cues and consequences, *and* cognitive mediation between external stimuli and behavioral responses. Such an approach would have important implications for the management of people and appears worthy of practical attention.

A radical critique of attempts to apply theories of human motivation in the workplace has been advanced by Mant (1979). In his devastating critique of British management, Mant asserts that motivation is *not* something done by one person to another. In the work situation it resides in doing a job which produces a product of quality. Thus the job of the manager is to enforce quality standards and to display commitment to and enthusiasm for the product. The business of making and selling things has been submerged by the preoccupation with 'management', as if it were something separate and distinct. "Against the contemporary background of industrial success in Germany, Japan and other countries, the puzzle, then, is to understand why we downgrade so many jobs that really matter whilst building around the idea of 'management' a plethora of myths, shibboleths and incantations which our most successful competitors seem able to do without" (Mant 1979: 3).

This view is supported by Jones (1988b). He points out that in Britain, for example, like its Freudian predecessors (e.g., the inferiority complex and defence mechanisms), 'motivation' has entered everyday conversation, with unfortunate results.

"An individual's performance, on the football field, in the office, factory, shop or restaurant, is now assumed to depend on some internal process which is provided or stimulated by another person: *motivation has come to mean something one person (the manager) does to another (the subordinate)" (Jones 1988b: 30).*

This distorted account of the motivations which influence human behaviour is, Jones (1988b) asserts, commonly reinforced by management training programmes, but success-ful managers do *not* think in terms of 'motivating' employees. Rather, they set and communicate clear standards for individual performance; make it clear that performance matters and that sub-standard performance is not acceptable; provide relevant opportun-ities for employees to learn the necessary abilities; reward good performance and punish poor performance.

12.4.2   Some Dangers of Premature Application

A review by Pinder (1977) of the validity of theories of motivation at work indicated that practitioners and scholars alike have been guilty of the premature application of theories which cannot yet fully justify the confidence shown in them. What, then, are the dangers of premature application, and how might these be avoided in Africa?

There are at least three groups who stand to lose when premature application takes place and is seen to fail.

1. First, the credibility of the discipline of organisational theory and behaviour itself is threatened, as well as the reputations of those researchers and practitioners who are concerned with the systematic study of organisations.
2. The second group which is clearly at risk are the 'subjects' of premature applications – most often lower-level members of organisations upon whom the practical impli-cations of theory-inspired changes fall with the greatest force. It is they who undergo the readjustments required by new methods of work or supervision, and it is they who suffer the disappointments of failure most acutely. It is little wonder that in many Western countries there is a growing resentment, particularly among lower-level workers, of the intrusions into the work place of behavioral scientists.
3. The third group to lose is composed of the client organisations which 'sponsor' the premature applications in the first place.

12.4.3   What Can be Done?

In Africa, owing to the early stage of development of the discipline, the opportunity exists to avoid some of the mistakes made in the West. The following precautionary measures might be helpful.

1. Researchers interested in testing their theories in a practical setting, or in applying theories as consultants, should be more open from the outset about the fallibilities of their methods. They must be prepared to provide realistic estimates of the chances of success, so that the expectations of the other groups involved (clients and subjects) are not set too high. When client organisations "are offered no miracles, their expectations cannot be easily violated" (Pinder 1977: 390). This brand of honesty will, of course, make it more difficult for researchers and consultants to gain entry to organisations, but the long-term benefits of such an approach for all groups concerned should outweigh the short-term costs.

2. It may be, as Pinder (1977) has suggested, that a code of ethics is needed for all organisational consultants. This would help to ensure that the consumers of organisational knowledge do not have false illusions about the value of what the discipline has to offer, and would serve also to protect the freedom and rights of lower-level members of organisations in particular – the silent army of 'guinea-pigs' whose rights are all too rarely considered. As we have seen, this needs to be done

   "because the absolute levels of predictive and explanatory validity of our best motivation theories are extremely low, (and) some form of professional standard is needed to protect practitioners (and the rest of us) from consultants who 'sell' theories to organisations for the mutual profit of workers and consultants" (Pinder 1977: 390).

3. Perhaps most importantly, students of motivation at work, and of organisational theory and behaviour in general, who are the future managers, trainers and scholars, should learn a critical appreciation of the limitations, strengths and weaknesses of available theories and knowledge. Rather than glossing over or ignoring the limitations of existing knowledge, this should be the starting point so that students can develop the skills which will enable them to assess and apply theories sensibly, thus avoiding the human and organisational costs which arise from an over-simplified view. The continuing relevance of these remarks is reinforced by Adler's (1991) recent comments which openly admit the ethnocentric biases of many content theories of motivation:

   "Unfortunately, American as well as non-American managers have tended to treat American theories as the best or only way to understand motivation. They are neither. American motivation theories, although assumed to be universal, have failed to provide consistently useful explanations outside the United States. Managers must therefore guard against imposing domestic American management theories on their multinational business practices" (p. 160).

Hofstede (1987) has taken this argument further and compared the cultural assumptions implicit in American content theories of motivation with those which obtain in Southeast Asian cultures. It is perhaps worth spelling out his observations in some detail. He outlines the assumptions of American content theories of motivation as follows (Hofstede 1987: 16):

"Work is good for people. It is God's will that people should work.
People's potentialities should be maximally utilised. It is God's will that you and I should
maximally use out potentialities.
There are 'organisational objectives' which exist separately from people.
People in organisations behave as unattached individuals."

He contrasts these assumptions with those which apply in Southeast Asia, namely:

"Work is a necessity but not a goal in itself.
People should find their rightful place, in peace and harmony with their environment.
Absolute objectives exist only with God. In the world, persons in authority positions
represent God, so their objectives should be followed.
People behave as members of a family and/or group. Those who do not are rejected by
society" (Hofstede 1987: 17).

In concluding his analysis, Hofstede (1987) proposes a Theory 'T' based on assumptions
thought by him to be compatible with Southeast Asian cultures:

"(1) In spite of the wisdom in traditions, the experience of change in life is natural, as
natural as work, play or rest.
(2) Commitment to change is a function of the quality of the leaders who lead the
change, the rewards associated with the change, and the negative consequences of
not changing.
(3) The capacity to lead people to a new situation is widely, not narrowly distributed
among leaders in the population.
(4) The learning capacities of the average family are more than sufficient for modern-
isation.
(5) There is an order of inequality in this world in which everyone has his or her
rightful place. High and low are protected by this order which is willed by God.
(6) Children have to learn to fulfil their duties at the place where they belong by birth.
They can improve their place by studying with a good teacher, working with a good
patron, and/or marrying a good partner.
(7) Tradition is a source of wisdom. Therefore, the average human being has an
inherent dislike of change and will rightly avoid it if he or she can" (pp. 17–18).

It seems to us that there is ample opportunity for the application of similar reasoning to
African cultures, which would greatly help to improve the relevance and meaning of
theories of motivation developed in the West.

12.5   Implications for Managers and Management Development

A frequently used shorthand description of management is that managers 'decide what is
to be done, and get it done through others.' Getting others to work for organisational goals
is clearly, then, a crucial function of the manager. We have noted that managers attach a

high priority to this issue and frequently identify it as their major area of concern. The motivation of employees is obviously important. Mintzberg (1989), for example, warns of the consequences for worker motivation of bureaucratic forms of organisation, with their "stifling effect on commitment" (p. 363). Organisational design at the systems and job levels can have important consequences for employee motivation.

A key question in this chapter has concerned the degree to which Western theories of human motivation are of practical use to the manager, particularly the African manager. Our discussion indicates that African managers must adopt a cautious, sceptical approach since there are many unanswered questions in this area. An over-reliance on mentalistic theories, in particular, is likely to produce disappointing results. The impact on employee behaviour of stimuli from the environment, inside and outside the organisation, has to be acknowledged and understood.

In the absence of indigenous theories of human behaviour and sufficient empirical evidence from African formal organisations, the principles of social learning (Kreitner & Luthans 1987), which acknowledge the influence of external stimuli and the role of cognitive mediation on behaviour, appear to offer practical possibilities for managers. They might help in developing an understanding of employee behaviour and in avoiding the futile pursuit of 'techniques' for 'motivating' workers against which Mant (1979) warns.

The continuing fascination of managers with mentalistic theories of human motivation despite the dearth of convincing evidence of their relevance to employee behaviour owes much to the persistence of management educators. Many formal management courses, particularly in African training institutions, continue to include 'motivation' as a standard component. The theories of Maslow and Herzberg in particular are – apparently, at the superficial level – easy to teach, and attractive to learners. Most trained managers, it appears, have heard of these theories and are probably able to quote them, but evidence of their practical application is pretty well non-existent in Africa. It is time for management educators to face this situation and to review the results of their fondness for Maslow and company in the real world of working organisations. Should African managers be taught the necessity of 'motivating' their subordinates, or could their attention more profitably be guided towards real managerial concerns with individual and organisational performance?

Chapter 13:   Management Development

"Who is not satisfied with himself will grow; who is not sure of his own correctness will learn many things." Chinese proverb.

In formal organisations the maintenance and upgrading of managerial capabilities is a continuing need, and frequently a priority area. This is particularly so in situations of rapid change and emerging new demands, as is the case in many African countries. Few would deny the crucial contribution of competent managers to organisational effectiveness and efficiency. As we have noted elsewhere, management is coming to be seen, by donor agencies and others, as the key factor in the pursuit of development in Africa.

It would seem to follow logically that organisations would view money spent on the development of managerial capability in the same light as they would view investments in any other scarce and expensive resource. Strangely, this does not always seem to be the case. Carter (1991) charges that "it is perhaps one of the worst kept secrets of organis-ational life that the measurable improvement in performance, over any given period, resulting from attendance at a management training course is all too often zero" (p. 31). This appears to be an astonishing accusation. Yet Carter is supported by many eminent commentators. Nearly twenty years ago Hague (1974) asserted that "adults abstract little, remember less, and implement nothing" (p. 6) from classroom-based management cours-es. Humble (1973) was equally blunt, claiming that "much of what goes on under the label of 'improving management performance' or 'development' or 'training' is so incredibly wasteful and stupid ..." (p. XV). Yet surely, one is entitled to expect that some improve-ment should have occurred in two decades. If Carter (1991) and other contemporary commentators are to be believed, however, there has not been much improvement.

The impact – or lack of impact – of management development, in the West, is both disappointing and controversial, despite decades of huge investment. Other forms of adult education, training and professional development can demonstrate concrete achievements in contributing to individual and organisational performance, but it is difficult to find any such justification for the investments in management development. In the industrialised Western countries huge sums continue to be pumped into management development activities, especially in formal training institutions. Research continuously explores every conceivable aspect of organisational and managerial life; a succession of trends and approaches engages the interest of practitioners; debates continue about content, process and methodology. Yet the attacks of the critics go largely unanswered. Why should this be so?

13.1   Some Problems with Management Development

We can identify several contributing factors which appear to make management development such a problematic endeavour.

13.1.1   Lack of Commitment by Management

Curiously, it appears that few managers take management development seriously, despite the fact that it is usually extremely expensive. They do not, in fact, seem to *expect* it to make any difference to the performance of individual managers or to organisational effectiveness. To Carter (1991) it is almost as if there is a conspiracy to prevent management development from having any impact; he describes an imaginary scenario in which a 'plant' is operating in the organisation to ensure just this. The 'plant' operates to ensure that: no proper management development records are set up; training programmes are designed without reference to the real learning needs of the organisation's managers; nominations for training are made – and accepted – not on the basis of who needs training, but according to who happens to be available, interested and prepared to pay; managers selected do not discuss the training with their boss or other members of their team before the training; on return to work the manager does not discuss with her boss or colleagues any changes which she might want to make as a result of her new learning; and no effort is made to relate investments in management development to performance on the job (review, validation, evaluation). None of this should be difficult for the 'plant', says Carter, because of lack of interest on the part of line managers. In fact, "this is the way many loyal dedicated professionals (management development practitioners) do it" (Carter 1991: 31) (Our parenthesis).

Carter is by no means alone in this view. Donnelly (1991), for example, discussing the situation in Britain, refers to "the deep-seated indifference to management training which has for so long been a characteristic of senior management" (p. 43). There is, he says, little research on the developmental needs of managers, as individuals or as a group.

Paradoxically though, despite this apparent lack of belief in the potential contribution of management development to organisational performance, managers appear happy to spend money on formal, off-the-job management courses. Donnelly's (1991) view suggests that much of this money is wasted: "a sizable proportion of what goes on under the name of management training, particularly in the short course area, comprises a dubious cocktail of wishful thinking, anecdotal experience, with an admixture of flavour-of-the-month opportunism" (p. 43).

13.1.2   The Nature of Managerial Work

As we have indicated in some detail in Chapter 2, a major difficulty with designing development programmes for managers is that there is no consensus about what managers do. The work of the pioneers of Scientific Management and Classical Management

Principles, some 70 odd years ago, had us believe for decades in the universalistic view: management work is the same whether practised in a university, a soap factory, a ministry or a hospital, consisting of planning, organising, directing, coordinating, and controlling resources. Inconveniently, much more recently empirical research has begun to demonstrate that managerial work is influenced by many important contingent factors – environmental, economic, technological, socio-cultural, political, legal – and that the so-called 'principles' are actually a set of prescriptions which ignore the rich diversity of organisational life.

For management development practitioners this absence of a common set of managerial functions presents serious problems. We know what a bus driver does, what a brain surgeon does, what an aeroplane pilot does, what an accountant does: we can identify and analyse the knowledge and skills required to perform these jobs; and we can design training programmes to enable individuals to learn them to satisfactory standards. (And thus, incidentally, we can classify these jobs as recognised trades or professions. The same cannot be said about the work of managers.) From the pedagogical standpoint, the 'principles' of management presented management educators with a beautifully convenient teaching framework. Generations of managers in the West, and in Africa, have been processed through courses which have slavishly followed Fayol's prescriptions: the first week or first day is used to 'cover' the subject of planning, the second deals with organising, the third, directing (or, as it is currently called, motivating), and so on. The problem with this is that what is being taught – and possibly, learned – is *knowledge* about the subjects called planning, controlling and so on, which alone is insufficient. Managers also need to learn *how* to plan, direct, coordinate; they need *skills* as well as knowledge. The question is: can such skills be learned in the classroom?

13.1.3   The Teaching of Management Skills

Perhaps because of our relative ignorance, until recently, about the work of managers, the content and processes of management development, particularly on formal courses, have tended to neglect the crucial questions: what do managers need to learn, and how do managers learn? As a result, what goes on in management development programmes frequently attracts comments of the kind we have quoted earlier. Management is concerned with the very practical business of producing goods and services, "yet the teaching of management, of all activities, has become rarefied to the point of near disappearance up its own pretensions" (Mant 1983: 226). We shall return later in this chapter to the skills of management and the question of how they are learned.

In African organisations there appears to be a very common additional factor. There is, as Jones (1990b) remarks, "an extraordinarily powerful belief in the ability of training to solve organisational problems", leading to "the expenditure of vast sums on inappropriate and often unnecessary training, and to a belief that training is an act of faith, 'a good thing to do' which need not be rigorously evaluated" (p. 62). Similarly, Moris (1977) observes that "the assumption that managerial effectiveness is primarily a result of adequate training is not only unquestioned; it is unquestionable" (p. 75).

The line of reasoning – or rather, assuming – is represented by Jones (1986a) thus:

Training (equated with classroom-based courses)
leads to
Individual Learning
which leads to
Improved Individual Job Performance
which in turn leads to
Improved Organisational Effectiveness and Efficiency.

At each level the assumption is open to doubt, and the whole sequence can easily break down: "without positive managerial action the training of individuals rarely leads to improved organisational performance" (Jones 1986a: 207).

This assumption, that wherever an instance of sub-standard performance is observed the corrective is training (almost universally equated with off-the-job classroom courses), is frequently reinforced – philosophically and financially – by donor agencies. An example of the assumptions about the power of training to solve organisational problems is reported in the Financial Gazette of Zimbabwe of March 28, 1991. The ministry responsible for the operations of an industrial parastatal were reported as being unhappy with the 'style of management and management qualities' of its general manager. The board and the ministry felt that in order to improve his management style and quality, it was necessary to send him on an intensive management course in the United States. Details of the general manager's weaknesses indicated that he had had 'personality clashes' and 'a physical exchange' with other senior managers of the parastatal (the need for which was doubted by many in the industry). The cost of the general manager's 'short course' was put at ZIM $121,000 (at that time, about US$ 40,000).

Montgomery's (1986b) caution is appropriate: "Training is often oversold as a solution to management problems. Even when it is fully effective, it cannot bring about immediate improvements ..." (p. 25).

13.2   The African Context

"Africa must develop the capacity to turn its ethnic, religious and racial diversity from a source of conflict and misunderstanding to a source of creative strength, mutual interdependence and synergy" (Kiggundu 1991: 41–42).

Perhaps the first thing we should note about management development in Africa is that little is known about activities in the private sector. As Kiggundu (1991) observes: "In general, management development in Africa belongs to the public sector" (p. 35). One of the few relevant studies, by Gershenberg (1987), indicates that in Kenya, for example, "local firms do very little training" (p. 973). Many of the multinational companies which operate in Africa have the resources to run their own internal management development programmes, but objective information about their methods and results is scarce.

In this section, therefore, we focus primarily on management development in the public sector. Since, as we noted earlier, most organisations appear to equate management development with sending managers to formal, classroom-based courses, we examine first the record of the institutions which provide this service, the institutes of public administration, development administration, and management.

13.2.1 Institutional Management Development

The record of the continent's many national institutes of public administration and management is disappointing. Commentators have been pretty well unanimous in their criticisms of the performance of these institutes. The Report to the Regional Training Council of SADCC (NASPA 1985) is representative: "National institutions for training in public management are in trouble" (p. 19). Safavi (1981), describing a study of management education and development programmes in Africa's 57 countries and territories, paints "a gloomy picture" of a number of areas of "conflict between classroom and culture, between Western theory and African reality" (p. 206). Balogun (1986) judges the performance of these institutes to be "well below standard ... they have failed to influence development policy and public sector management practices ... their contribution to the cross-fertilisation of ideas between the public and private sectors is minimal", despite their "unique position" (pp. 233–234). The poor record of these institutes is also recorded by Adamolekun (1989), who calls for them to be reformed since in his view there is no alternative to training to meet the critical shortages of skills at middle and senior management levels.

A UNDP/World Bank (1989) project document confirms that "many institutions continue to have only marginal impact on national development and managerial efforts. Few training institutions enjoy high credibility in the eyes of public and private sector managers because most are far removed from their clients' problems and environment" (p. 3). Kiggundu (1991) notes the dominant role of these institutions and the fact that they "have not had a significant impact on management development in Africa" (p. 36). This appears to be particularly serious because Kiggundu's opinion is that African civil services have 'lost the capacity to manage'.

In the face of such overwhelming criticism, we have to ask why Africa's institutes of public administration and management have performed so badly. A number of commentators (Stifel, Coleman & Black 1977; Hope & Armstrong 1980; Morgan 1984; Seddon 1985a, 1985b; Youker 1986; Balogun 1989; Jones 1989; Schellekens 1989; Kiggundu 1991; Johnston & Dyrssen 1991; SIDA 1991) have suggested reasons. We can briefly summarise these as follows:

- There is little if any systematic attempt to ascertain and analyse the learning needs of clients.
- There is a heavy emphasis on formal, classroom-based courses.
- The 'numbers game' ensures that institutes are judged by the number of courses they run and the number of participants they attract. A 'successful' course is not one which

is shown by rigorous evaluation to have improved job performance, but one which is run as scheduled and manages to attract a reasonable number of managers.
- Courses and course materials are frequently irrelevant to local needs, being imported uncritically from the West.
- There is an over-reliance on didactic, lecture-dominated, teaching methods, which are unsuitable for skill development.
- Trainers are of varying quality, some being academically qualified but lacking teaching skills and experience of managerial work, while others are experienced but incompetent administrators (who may have been 'dumped' on the training institutions in the belief that they can do less damage there than in a ministry).
- There is commonly a lack of contact with the worlds of working managers. This is often caused by the 'numbers game', which leaves very little time for applied research and consultancy work.
- Institutions are often part of the civil service, operating under a parent ministry; they are enmeshed in the bureaucracy with its obsession for control and rigid procedures – the antithesis of a dynamic, responsive enterprise. As Balogun (1989) warns, "an institute unable to reform itself has no leg to stand on when it ventures into the world outside" (p. 235).
- There is usually little effort to involve the bosses and colleagues of participants, before or after the course. Thus there is little chance that newly learned abilities will be applied back at work to enhance individual job performance.
- Thorough review and evaluation, to establish whether courses are actually having any effect on individual and organisational performance, is practically non-existent. 'Evaluation' usually is confined to the reaction level: the end-of-course ritual of asking participants if they enjoyed the course, whether the teachers entertained them, and whether the food was to their taste (the 'happiness measure').
- Training is often viewed as a maintenance function, rather than as an agent for change, resulting in programmes which are designed to reinforce existing bureaucratic systems and practices.
- There is commonly a view that management training is a ritual which one must undergo in order to obtain evidence of study for promotion purposes, rather than a way to enhance managerial performance.

Manamperi (1990) nicely illustrates the kind of management development practices adopted by many African institutes of public administration and management. He sees them as comprising a 'smorgasbord' approach, where the institute offers a 'menu' of formal courses developed and served up to customers without any attempt to find out what training is actually needed to improve organisational performance; the 'bandwagon' approach, in which the institute offers what seems to be currently in fashion, again mostly unrelated to needs and frequently duplicating what is already on offer; the 'excursion' approach, which rests "on the assumption that a correlation exists between the benefits received from training and the distance travelled from the trainees' place of work" (p. 47); the 'welfare' approach, which typifies the view that the purpose of the training is to provide demanded certificates; and the 'justification' approach, in which " 'some sort' of training act is put together" (p. 47) in order to justify the existence of the institute.

What can be done to improve the contribution of these institutes to the enhancement of individual and organisational performance? There is some evidence that some steps are being taken, particularly as political, economic and institutional reform efforts in many African countries gain acceptance and begin to have an impact. Questions can now be asked in many African nations which for several decades have been 'unaskable'. Old ideologies and systems of governance are being questioned. The ability of civil services to activate and manage development is under critical scrutiny. In Zimbabwe, for example, the national Institute of Public Administration and Management (ZIPAM), which has operated since its inception as a branch of the Ministry of the Public Service, is to have its bureaucratic shackles loosened by its conversion to parastatal status. And in Malawi, the country's new Malawi Institute of Management (MIM) has been established from the start in the parastatal form, the intention being that the Institute will shortly operate on a commercial basis as a self-financing enterprise catering for the public and private sectors. It is to be hoped that such institutional change will provide a basis for improvement of many of these institutes.

Many of the other problems listed above could be corrected at little cost by the provision of strong political backing and competent management for the institutes. They have the potential to play an important developmental role if they have the necessary support, autonomy, and professionalism to ensure that their management development activities meet the real needs of their clients as far as possible. Jones (1989) summarises what is required as "a professional, cost-conscious, performance-based approach to the design and implementation of training activities (e.g., accurate identification of real training needs, use of appropriate methodologies, rigorous evaluation of outcomes)" (p. 74). Perhaps the crucial point here is that formal classroom-based management courses have their limitations, particularly in helping individuals to learn the subtle *skills* of management in specific organisational situations. To contribute to this process, institutes will have to get out into the workplace and help managers to learn their skills on the job.

In addition to a number of national initiatives aimed at reviewing and improving the performance of the institutes, several international donor agencies have also shown an interest. The Swedish International Development Authority (SIDA), for example, have developed a set of guidelines which direct their efforts to assist in capacity building with institutes of public administration and management. Their aim is to encourage a coherent action research/consultancy/training profile which will produce practical and relevant training activities and *make a difference* in the performance of public sector organisations (*see* Johnston & Dyrssen 1991). A major initiative was launched in 1988 by the UNDP and the World Bank, aimed at improving the provision of management development in Africa (*see* Palmlund 1991). At present there is little available evidence about the progress and achievements of this programme, now known as UNEDIL (Kiggundu 1991).

In terms of teaching methodology and the building of a learning culture, institutions may have something to learn from the experience of the Agricultural Management Centre, Mananga, Swaziland. The 'Mananga style' has attracted considerable favourable comment (Youker 1986; Marshall 1987). Its essential characteristics have been identified as an emphasis on learners as individuals and as mature adults; a learner-centred (as opposed to teacher-centred or subject-centred) educational approach; emphasis on learning outcomes rather than teaching intentions; encouragement of mutual learning, from fellow participants; and learning from experience. This emphasis in all activities on the learner and learning outcomes has guided Mananga's training strategies and methods, and created its distinctive organisational culture.

13.2.2 Beyond the Classroom

Can Management Skills be Learned in the Classroom?

We have argued earlier in the chapter that formal classroom-based courses have limitations; it is the frequent failure to recognise and understand this reality which is at the root of many of the failures of management education to make an impact on individual and organisational performance. Quite apart from the fact that teaching is itself an inefficient way to facilitate learning – at most, 40% of what is taught is learned, usually the figure is more like 25% (Holt, 1983) – the classroom environment could hardly be more unlike the arena in which managerial skills are exercised, the work organisation. Of course, few would deny that the learning of knowledge about topics relevant to business and management, such as economics, law, marketing, management thought and history, and organisational behaviour is useful in providing an essential understanding of the contexts in which management is practised. It is necessary but by itself insufficient. Learning knowledge is not the same as learning skills. There is a fundamental difference between being able to talk about something – say, decision making – and being able to do it. Donnelly (1991) addresses this issue when he says that it could be argued that knowledge of relevant subjects is required, but it can also be argued that "there is no necessary relationship between competence in such areas and the ability to manage" (p. 44). Noting that current generalisations tend to emphasise the need for competence in areas like decision making, judgment, enterprise, interpersonal skills, he asks 'are these areas teachable?'

Jones (1990a) is concerned with the same issue. He notes that the American Society for Training and Development (1989) identified the essential human abilities required by modern organisations as: learning how to learn (from experience); reading, writing and computing; listening and oral communication; creative thinking and problem solving; personal (self) management; interpersonal skills, negotiation, teamwork; and organisational effectiveness. We can add to this list: monitoring and analysing information about the changing environment; designing and changing to organisational forms capable of rapid response and self-modification at low cost; creative use of conflict; political skills of influencing and persuading; managing organisational relationships, upwards, downwards, and laterally; and training, coaching, and counselling subordinates (Jones 1990a). Of these, obtaining and using effectively information about the environment is essential for African organisations in the 1990s given the changing, complex, and often problematic nature of events in African countries. The ability to change organisations is necessary to achieve the aims of the reform programmes underway in many states, and seems to be especially critical because there is so much evidence that the inherited bureaucracies so characteristic of African public sectors now constitute an immovable obstacle to development in many countries. In the African context of painfully scarce resources, the creative resolution and management of conflict through the exercise of subtle political skills (not to be confused with party politics) is essential. Finally, learning (or, perhaps more accurately, rediscovering) how to learn from our lived experience, and helping others – primarily subordinates – to learn, are indispensable to the management of change.

Can such abilities be learned in the classroom?

"Let us be clear: we are talking here about skills which are difficult (i) to define (consider, for example, 'leadership'); (ii) to describe (what kind of behaviour are we looking for, for instance, when we observe how a manager 'coordinates' the use of resources?); to specify (how would we specify, in any useful sense, the skills required in 'motivating'?); to teach (what teaching methods are available to classroom trainers to teach managers the subtle skills of 'decision making'?)" (Jones 1989: 50).

Stifel *et al.* (1977) refer to the broad range of management skills, from tools, techniques and technologies, which can be taught, to leadership which probably cannot. Similarly, Leonard (1987) notes that Selznick's (1957) classic analysis of the leadership function identifies the ability to define the organisation's mission, to inspire others to work for the mission, to defend the organisation's integrity and values, to manage conflict, to manage relationships with the external environment, to recruit capable, committed people, and to identify and manage problems and opportunities. Leonard (1987) comments that all these except the last "are very hard to effect through training and are not susceptible to the deductive rationality that is the hallmark of Western management science" (p. 903).

The position we are taking here is that, because of the nature of managerial work and organisational life, many aspects of managerial skills are not amenable to educational strategies based solely or mainly on classroom-based courses. If we take just one example, our reasons may become clear. If we want a trainee lawyer to learn how to find and interpret relevant statutes, a competent teacher can arrange for her to practise this activity in the classroom by using real statute books. It would then be easy for the trainee to transfer her learning back to her law office. Consider now how a teacher of management might help a trainee to learn how to make decisions, in the classroom setting. The teacher can lecture on the theories of decision making; he can get the trainee to read and analyse accounts of decisions made by other managers; he might arrange a role play of an imaginary situation in which the trainee is to act out the role of a decision maker; he may ask the trainee and his fellow learners to consider a case study and make decisions about the issues it raises. Yet none of this involves the trainee in making *real decisions and being held responsible for their consequences*. This can be experienced only in the work organisation. Similarly, we can attend a classroom course on the theories of swimming, we can watch a film of top swimmers, we can study the techniques of the various strokes. If our learning stops there, we can then fall in a river and drown. We learn the skill – the behaviour known as swimming – by getting in the water and practising that behaviour and experiencing the consequences when we do it incompetently. This is also the nature of many managerial skills.

What, then, *can* be done to help managers to learn and develop?

How do Managers Learn?

As it has become increasingly accepted that the development of managerial skills presents particular problems for educators, attention has been directed to the nature of managerial work and how managers typically become competent in their jobs. As the lack of impact on managerial skills of teaching management theories became apparent, several contemporary influences on management development have emerged.

The insights of androgogy, the science and technology of adult education – as contrasted to pedagogy, which is based on how children learn – (*see* Jones 1983), has produced a less didactic strand in management teaching. Its influence is apparent, for instance, in the 'Mananga style' mentioned above. Influenced by humanistic psychology, androgogy goes beyond a concern simply with teaching methodology to consider the nature of the relationship between the teacher and the adult learner. The concern is to stress the active nature of adult learning and to challenge traditional notions of dependence on the teacher. This has important implications in cultures, including African ones, where the teacher is regarded as the authoritative 'guru' who bestows wisdom on the passive, dependent learner. Teachers and trainers accustomed to such a relationship often find the idea that their role is to *assist* the learner in attaining his learning goals very threatening. And adult learners frequently find it very difficult to free themselves from dependence on the teacher, to take control of their own learning.

As the unique nature of managerial work has become increasingly recognised, the manager's experience has become, for many educators and theorists, the focus for seeking more relevant and successful management development strategies. It is recognised by many that the distinctive aspect of adult learning lies in the fact that "learning consists much more in the reorganisation of what was already familiar (even if not fully understood in the sense of being operationally applicable) than it consists in acquiring fresh knowledge altogether" (Revans 1980: 277).

A theory of learning which recognises this and attempts to explain how we learn from experience has been very influential on contemporary management development thinking in the West: the Experiential Learning Cycle of Kolb, Rubin and Osland (1991). Learning is a natural process which occurs in our daily encounters with the world. The Kolb model suggests that we learn from our experience when we: 1) reflect upon what happened in a particular experience; 2) try to explain and generalise from the experience; and 3) on the basis of our reflection and generalisation then try out new behaviours, which constitute new experiences for the continuation of the learning cycle. Two points emerge obviously from this explanation of human learning. First, we notice that most of what we call education – which we tend to equate with schooling – starts with studying theories, that is explaining and generalising, and frequently goes no further; which explains why we quickly forget much of what we learned – or more accurately memorised – at school, college and university. Secondly, the old aphorism that we learn from our mistakes is clearly untrue for many people; otherwise we would not repeat our mistakes. We learn from our mistakes, our successes, and our other experiences if we follow the learning cycle, which results in new behaviours. It is easy to see the attraction of Kolb's model for management educators. Managerial work demands the use of many intellectual and social abilities in initiating and managing development and change; it requires the use of authority and political skills in achieving organisational performance. It is essential that managers develop the capacity to learn from their experience. It is, in fact, being asserted that we need to develop our formal organisations as 'learning communities', to recognise that organisations must have the ability to learn from experience if they are to cope with change and survive (Honey 1991; Whipp 1991).

The focus on the manager's experience of the hard reality of organisational life acknowledges the ways in which we learn our jobs and the skills to do them. In Jones's (1986b) investigation of managerial thinking in Malawi, for example, when asked how they learned their managerial abilities, respondents named 'learning by doing the job' as the most important influence, followed by 'discussing real problems with colleagues', 'training by boss', 'observing effective managers', and 'analysing my successes and failures' (p. 212).

However, this recognition of the reality of how management skills are learned presents problems for management educators. How are we to help managers to learn from their experience? Can this be done in the classroom? If not, then where and how? And, from our specific point of view, are their any factors which are particularly important when we are concerned with management development in Africa?

Assisting the Manager's Self-development

If we accept the thrust of contemporary views on adult learning, we see that all individual development is self-development: no one can learn for the individual; the task of the teacher is to assist the learner in that process. For the management educator, the issue is – how? Several possibilities have received attention. Before we discuss some of them we need to remind ourselves that education and training existed for centuries *without schools*. For generations, individuals learned fine skills from master craftsmen, by apprenticeship and long practice. In some traditional communities the education and training of children continues to follow this proven ancient pattern. In the West, the intervention between the master craftsman and the learner of a third party – calling himself a teacher – led to the construction of the giant edifice we now call the education system, based in schools and colleges. If we are to acknowledge the reality of how management abilities are learned, we need to think beyond the almost universal 20th century assumption that in order to learn anything we must sit in a classroom and be taught.

Kiggundu (1991) recognises this when he insists that we must learn from Africa's past. Before the colonial irruption into Africa many rich, complex civilisations had existed for centuries, employing various forms of social and work organisations. According to Kiggundu:

"During this period, management development was done very differently. It tended to be informal and took the form of apprenticeships. Most of it was on-the-job training with

long periods of behavioural observations, tryouts, testing, coaching and feedback from elders and experienced observers. There were no classroom instructions." (1991: 34).

Kiggundu (1991) notes that, in contrast to the situation so common in classroom-based training, there was no problem of transfer of learning to the work situation in the traditional system he describes. He suggests that we might usefully consider a return to that successful system, making appropriate modifications where necessary.

Leonard (1987) similarly laments that "what both host and donor governments ignore is the operationally vital but politically lacklustre category of continuous on-the-job training" (p. 908) in Africa. One donor agency seems to agree with Leonard: SIDA (1991) call for proper attention to be given to on-the-job training. Bas (1989) is convinced that "things cannot go on as they are" (p. 493), and proposes "a more harmonious combination of on-the-job training with the theoretical contributions of the modern sector" (p. 490).

This demand for job-based development to be recognised as essential for managers in Africa acknowledges that much of what the manager needs to learn is not amenable to classroom-based educational strategies. Any teaching technique limited to the classroom, however imaginative, can be nothing more than artificial simulation of the realities of organisational life. The management development practitioner must find ways to assist the manager's development in the only place where such realities are accessible – in the workplace itself, focussing on *real,* as opposed to contrived, issues, events and problems. Mant (1983) states the case succinctly:

"Managers do not in reality learn from experts in the context of 'case studies' ... The problem in 'management development' is therefore to harness, as best we can, the manager's tendency to learn from his own messy experience ... If the manager is seriously attached to his work, the problem is inside him, as well as 'out there' in the form of a detached, intellectualised problem ... Useful management development is, by definition, threatening" (pp. 226–227).

Mant's views reflect his understanding of what is probably the most powerful strategy for the development of managerial abilities, developed by Professor R. W. Revans from his theory of adult development, Action Learning. Revans has been expounding the ideas of Action Learning and helping people around the world, including Africa, to practise it for half a century (*see* Revans 1967, 1991). We examined the profound implications of Revans's work for organisational change and development in Chapter 10. Revans asserts that if C > L (where C represents change and L represents learning), calamity lies ahead; however, if L > C, individuals and organisations can develop the capacity to cope with continuous, accelerating and turbulent change. For Revans, there are two distinct types of learning. Programmed learning (P) is that which is already known and recorded, and taught by 'experts'. P is useful for solving puzzles; to a puzzle there exists a known solution (or several solutions). The task is to use P to locate the solution in recorded knowledge – in books, records or the brains of experts. Since it is knowledge of the past, P may be of little use in dealing with the unknown future, especially at times of rapid change. What is needed to deal with change, the overwhelmingly distinctive feature of the

20th century, is questioning insight (Q). We need both P and Q: $L = P + Q$. Revans recognises that P is essential, but insufficient. Change presents problems, to which there may not exist an answer. For managers, people who try by their decisions and actions to change the future, leadership lies in the ability to learn from lived experience by using Q to solve problems.

Managers learn therefore with and from fellow managers, by reviewing their experience and taking responsibility for acting on problems. For Revans there is, quite literally, no action without learning and no learning without action. In this we see the shortcomings of classroom-based contrived approximations of real life, like case studies, role plays and so on: they involve no real *action* whose real consequences are the real responsibility of the manager. In the Action Learning model, responsibility for action, with all its uncertainties and anxieties, lies at the heart of the management job. Since, in addition, Revans's model, unlike other major learning theories, regards learning as a social process, Revans uses small groups of fellow managers, 'comrades in adversity', to help each other to learn from such uncertainties and anxieties by employing their questioning insight, Q. (Revans advocates small groups, learning sets, because, in his original phrase, 'small is dutiful'.) The role of the management development practitioner in Action Learning is to assist in establishing the learning sets and to be a resource in helping them to function, when such assistance is requested by the managers.

Revans places emphasis, in Q, on learning from uncertainty, failure and anxiety. Strategies for implementing Action Learning, which have been employed by Revans, may involve the manager in dealing with: a) a familiar problem in a familiar situation (the quality circle idea); b) a familiar problem in an unfamiliar situation (a personnel manager looking at a problem in someone else's personnel department); c) an unfamiliar problem in a familiar situation (a personnel manager looking at a production problem in his own organisation); and, most powerful, d) an unfamiliar problem in an unfamiliar situation (a personnel manager looking at a marketing problem in an organisation unlike his own).

Would Action Learning work in Africa? Revans has himself helped with Action Learning initiatives in several African countries, and he is sensitive to some of the cultural issues involved. As long ago as 1967 he was in the Sudan, warning:

"Many of the development problems of Africa can be understood and treated only by those who share the culture of the African, who understand his value system, his sense of fairness, his attitude to authority, and, what is often overlooked by the Western observer, what he wants out of life and what effort he is prepared to make to get it. To attempt to put under the development of the managers of the new Africa the forced draught of Western efficiency without seeing, at least dimly, its consequences for a way of life – or for scores of ways of life – that can be traced back for two thousand years or more, is to invite calamity" (Revans 1967: 174). (Our emphasis)

Jones (1986a) suggests that Action Learning's emphasis on learning in small groups with and from fellow managers appears congruent with the collectivist nature of African cultures. However, Action Learning does assert that failures become sources of learning when they are openly confronted and shared with others; the limited evidence we have suggests that this may be difficult for African managers to accept, unless the learning set develops as a very supportive and confidential environment for its members.

Certainly, Action Learning may appear radical and perhaps impractical for African management educators, especially those in formal training institutes who use overwhelmingly didactic teaching methods – particularly the lecture. However, as we have indicated above, existing strategies and methods are failing to provide African organisations with the skilled managers they so urgently require. The warning which Revans gave in 1967 (above) has been largely ignored, with depressing consequences for African development efforts in the last three decades. New approaches to management development *must* be tried. We have described Action Learning in some detail because it appears to have a powerful potential for developing African managers in ways which are relevant to their situations, and may be rendered culturally consonant with African realities.

We have explored in previous chapters, notably Chapter 9, African socio-cultural factors which appear to influence organisational behaviour. We are woefully short of empirical studies in this area, although it is widely acknowledged that such data are urgently needed if we are to gain a better understanding of how African organisations function and how African managers behave. Such information is vital also if we are to devise more culturally appropriate and effective management strategies. A recent study by Myambo (1991) in Zimbabwe, for example, found that people value achievement, but they value conformity even more highly. In relation to communication, a critical concern for managers, Myambo's investigation showed that formality, especially between those of different age and status, and in meetings, impedes spontaneity: people tend to speak only when asked specific questions and do not elaborate beyond the question; individuals tend to 'withdraw' from sensitive issues by agreeing, by departing, or by remaining silent, which is interpreted as agreement; because public display of anger is not acceptable, individuals convey anger in indirect ways such as 'forgetting' and delaying work; people tend to be very diplomatic, with the result that grievances are not openly confronted. It is not difficult to see how such behaviour, in the work setting, might influence managers in their relations with subordinates, bosses, and colleagues. It is harder to say with any degree of confidence how it might affect organisational performance. Myambo feels that some of the factors she identified might be "incompatible with the demands of a business or organisational setting" (1991: 4).

The task of management development practitioners is to devise strategies and methods which respect and take into account socio-cultural factors of the kind explored in Zimbabwe by Myambo. For this reason, and in view of economic realities, we have focussed on the potential of job-based possibilities such as on-the-job training, coaching by the manager's boss, apprenticeships, and Action Learning. The formal management training institutes can improve their classroom-based activities by practising what they teach, about planning, organising and evaluating; so that they can perform more effectively their role in teaching knowledge of the subjects which will help managers to understand the environment in which their organisations function. But if they want to contribute to the processes by which managers learn their subtle skills, they will have to abandon the safety of the classroom and venture into the real world of organisational life. Jones (1990c) reflects on the "uselessness of teaching theories (mainly conceived in the USA) of leadership, motivation and all the other rigmarole, to practising managers" (p. iii), and reminds us that:

"Managers are crucial people. We must not waste their time by pulling them into classrooms and imposing irrelevant, and usually alien, theories on them" (p. iii).

13.3   Implications for Managers

It is very important that African managers should look critically at the management development strategies they operate (if any). As we have seen, the evidence suggests that current practices are generally both ineffective and very expensive. They should apply to expenditure on management education and training the criteria that competent managers apply to other forms of expenditure. Are the managers who are sent away on courses – in the country or outside – any better at their jobs when they return? Was the investment worth it? What other, better, cheaper ways are possible to develop managerial abilities? Only when African managers apply such normal criteria to management development (indeed, to all forms of training and development) will they be able to force management educators and training institutes to perform.

In particular, we would encourage managers to look closely and imaginatively at the potential of job-based strategies. A simple, but potentially powerful starting point would be to insist that the job descriptions of all managers include as their first duty the coaching of subordinates.

References

Abernethy, D. B. (1971). 'Bureaucracy and Economic Development in Africa'. *African Review*, 1 (1), 91–107.

Abudu, F. (1986). 'Work Attitudes of Africans, with Special Reference to Nigeria'. *ISMO*, 16 (2), 17–36.

Adair, J. (1984). *The Skills of Leadership*. London: Gower.

Adamolekun, L. (1989). *Issues in Development Management in Sub-Saharan Africa*. EDI Policy Seminar Report No. 19. Washington, D.C.: World Bank.

Adamolekun, L. (1991a). 'Public Sector Management Improvement in Sub-Saharan Africa: the World Bank Experience'. *Public Administration and Development*, 11, 223–227.

Adamolekun, L. (1991b). 'Promoting African Decentralisation'. *Public Administration and Development*, 11, 285–291.

Adamolekun, L., Robert, R., & Laleye, M. (1990). *Decentralisation Policies and Socioeconomic Development in Sub-Saharan Africa*. Washington, D.C.: World Bank (EDI).

Adler, N. J. (1991). *International Dimensions of Organisational Behaviour* (2nd ed.). Boston: Kent.

Ahiauzu, A. I. (1986). 'The African Thought System and the Work Behaviour of the African Industrial Man'. *International Studies of Management and Organisation*, 16 (2), 37–58.

Aina, S. (1982). 'Bureaucratic Corruption in Nigeria: The Continuing Search for Causes and Cures'. *International Review of Administrative Sciences*, 48, 70–6.

Aldrich, H. E. (1979). *Organisations and Environments*. Englewood Cliffs, N.J.: Prentice-Hall.

Allen, L. A. (1981). 'Managerial Planning: Back to Basics'. *Management Review*, 70 (4), 15–20.

Aloki, A.O. (1989). 'Rural Development in Sub-Saharan Africa: A Different View of Political and Administrative Decentralisation'. *International Review of Administrative Sciences*, 55, 401–432.

American Society for Training and Development (1989). 'Workplace Basics: The Skills Employers Want'. *Training and Development*, 8.

Analoui, P. (1989). 'Senior Managers and Increased Effectiveness'. *Project Appraisal*, 4(4), 215–218.

Andrews, K. R. (1988). 'The Concept of Corporate Strategy'. In J. B. Quinn, H. Mintzberg, & R. M. James (eds.), *The Strategy Process: Concepts, Contexts, and Cases*. Englewood Cliffs, N. J.: Prentice-Hall.

Ankomah, K. (1985). 'African Culture and Social Structures and Development of Effective Public Administration and Management Systems'. *Indian Journal of Public Administration*, 30, 393–413.

Ansoff, H. I. (1965). *Corporate Strategy*. New York: McGraw-Hill.

Atkinson, J. W. (ed.) (1958). *Motives in Fantasy, Action and Society*. Princeton, N.J.: Van Nostrand.

Austin, J. E. (1990). *Managing in Developing Countries: Strategic Analysis and Operating Techniques*. New York: Free Press.

Ayeni, V. (1987). 'Nigeria's Bureaucratised Ombudsman System: An Insight into the Problem of Bureaucratisation in a Developing Country'. *Public Administration and Development*, 7, 309–324.

Badawy, M. K. (1980). 'Role Orientations of Middle-Eastern Executives: A Cross-cultural Analysis'. *Human Organisation*, 39, 271–5.

Bailey, R. (1988). 'Keeping Key Players Productive: How to Identify and Manage Stress'. *International Journal of Manpower*, 9 (4/5).

Bailey, R. (1991). 'Employee Stress and Counselling at Work'. *Training and Development*, 9, 19–22.

Balogun, M. J. (1986). 'The African Culture and Social Structures: Lessons from Contemporary Public Administration'. In AAPAM, *The Ecology of Public Administration and Management in Africa*. Vikas.

Balogun, M. J. (1989). 'The Role of Management Training Institutes in Developing Capacity for Economic Recovery and Long-term Growth in Africa'. In M. J. Balogun & G. Matahaba (eds.), *Restructuring in African Public Administration*. West Hartford: Kumarian Press.

Barko, W., & Pasmore, W. (eds.) (1986). 'Socio-technical Systems: Innovations in Designing High Performing Systems'. Special issue of *Journal of Applied Behavioural Science*, 22 (3), 195–360.

Barnard, C. (1938). *The Functions of the Executive*. Cambridge, Mass.: Harvard University Press.

Bartolome, F. (1989). 'Nobody Trusts the Boss Completely – Now What?' *Harvard Business Review*, 67, 135–142.

Bas, D. (1989). 'On-the-job Training in Africa'. *International Labour Review*, 128 (4), 485–496.

Bate, P. (1984). 'The Impact of Organisational Culture on Approaches to Problem Solving'. *Organisation Studies*, 5, 43–66.

Bate, P. (1990). 'Using the Culture Concept in an Organisation Development Setting'. *Journal of Applied Behavioural Science*, 26 (1), 83–106.

Beaty, D. T., & Harari, O. (1987). 'South Africa: White Managers, Black Voices'. *Harvard Business Review*, 65 (4), 98–105.

Beckhard, R. (1969). *Organisation Development: Strategies and Models*. Reading, Mass.: Addison-Wesley.

Beehr, T. A., & Newman, J. E. (1978). 'Job Stress, Employee Health, and Organisational Effectiveness: A Facet Analysis, Model, and Literature Review'. *Personnel Psychology*, 31, 665–99.

Bennis, W. (1989). *Why Leaders Can't Lead*. Oxford: Jossey Bass.

Berger, M. (1957). *Bureaucracy and Society in Modern Egypt*. Princeton: Princeton University Press.

Bispham, W. M. L. (1964). 'The Concept and Measurement of Labour Commitment and Its Relevance to Nigerian Development'. *Nigerian Journal of Economic and Social Studies*, 6 (1), 51–9.

Blake, D. H. (1990). 'The Management of Social Policy by Multinational Corporations: A Research Agenda'. In L. E. Preston (ed.), *International and Comparative Corporation and Society Research*. London: JAI Press.

Blake, R. R., & Mouton, J. S. (1985). *The Managerial Grid III*. Houston: Gulf.

Blau, G. (1981). 'An Empirical Investigation of Job Stress, Social Support, Service Length, and Job Strain'. *Organisational Behaviour and Human Performance*, 27, 279–302.

Blauner, R. (1964). *Alienation and Freedom*. Chicago: University of Chicago Press.

Blunt, P. (1973). 'Cultural and Situational Determinants of Job Satisfaction Amongst Management in South Africa: A Research Note'. *Journal of Management Studies*, 10, 133–140.

Blunt, P. (1976). 'Management Motivation in Kenya: Some Initial Impressions'. *Journal of Eastern African Research and Development*, 6 (1), 11–21.

Blunt, P. (1977). ' "Normal" Science and Some of its Dangers for Research into Organisational Theory and Behaviour'. *Australian Psychologist*, 12, 175–85.

Blunt, P. (1978). 'Social and Organisational Structures in East Africa: A Case for Participation'. *Journal of Modern African Studies*, 16, 433–449.

Blunt, P. (1980). 'Bureaucracy and Ethnicity in Kenya: Some Conjectures for the Eighties'. *Journal of Applied Behavioural Science*, 16 (3), 336–353.

Blunt, P. (1982). 'Alienation and Adaptation among Lower-Level Workers in Kenya'. *Civilisations*, 32 (1), 1–29.

Blunt, P. (1983a). *Organisational Theory and Behaviour: An African Perspective*. London: Longman.

Blunt, P. (1983b). 'Motivation Through Job Design and Orientations to Work: A Theoretical Reconstruction and Synthesis'. *Australian Psychologist*, 18 (2), 191–204.

Blunt, P. (1984). 'Conditions For Basic Need Satisfaction in Africa Through Decentralised Forms of Decision Making'. *Journal of Applied Behavioural Science*, 20 (4), 403–421.

Blunt, P. (1988). 'Cultural Consequences for Organisation Change in a Southeast Asian State: Brunei'. *Academy of Management Executive*, 2 (3), 235–240.

Blunt, P. (1990a). 'Strategies for Enhancing Organisational Effectiveness in the Third World'. *Public Administration and Development*, 10, 299–313.

Blunt, P. (1990b). 'Recent Developments in Human Resource Management: the Good, the Bad, and the Ugly'. *International Journal of Human Resource Management*, 1 (1), 45–59.

Blunt, P. (1991). 'Organisational Culture and Development'. *International Journal of Human Resource Management*, 2 (1), 55–71.

Blunt, P., & Denton, S. (1979). 'A Factor Analysis of a Ten-item Questionnaire Designed to Measure Maslow's Need Categories'. *Australian Psychologist*, 14, 41–50.

Blunt, P., & Jones, M. (1986). 'Managerial Motivation in Kenya and Malawi: A Cross Cultural Comparison'. *Journal of Modern African Studies*, 24 (1), 165–175.

Blunt, P., & Jones, M. (eds.) (1991a). 'Management Development in the Third World'. Special issue of *Journal of Management Development*, 10 (6), 1–83.

Blunt, P., & Jones, M. (eds.) (1991b). 'Human Resource Management in Developing Countries'. Special issue of *International Journal of Human Resource Management*, 2 (1), 1–111.

Blunt, P., Jones, M., & Richards, D. (eds.) (in press). *Managing Organisations in Africa: Readings, Cases, and Exercises*. Berlin and New York: de Gruyter.

Blunt, P., & Popoola, O. E. (1985). *Personnel Management in Africa*. London: Longman.

Blunt, P., Richards, D., & Wilson, J. (1989). 'The Hidden-Hand of Public Administration in Newly-Emerging States: A Theoretical and Empirical Analysis'. *Journal of International Development*, 1 (4), 409–443.

Boisot, M., & Guoliang, X. (1988). 'The Nature of Managerial Work – Chinese Style?'. Paper presented at the International Conference on Management in China Today, Leuven, Belgium, 19–21 June.

Booth-Kewley, A. A., & Friedman, H. S. (1987). 'Psychological Predictors of Heart Disease: A Quantitative Review'. *Psychological Bulletin*, 101, 343–362.

Bowers, D. G. (1977). 'Work Humanisation in Practice: What is Business Doing?'. In W. J. Heisler & J. W. Houck (eds.), *A Matter of Dignity: Inquiries into the Humanisation of Work*. Notre Dame: University of Notre Dame Press.

Brown, D. (1989). 'Bureaucracy as an Issue in Third World Management: an African Case Study'. *Public Administration and Development*, 9, 369–380.

Burawoy, M. (1972). 'Another Look at the Mineworker'. *African Social Research*, 14, 239–87.

Burke, R. J., & Weir, T. (1980). 'Coping with the Stress of Managerial Occupations'. In C. L. Cooper & R. Payne (eds.), *Current Concerns in Occupational Stress*. New York: Wiley.

Burns, T., & Stalker, G. M. (1961). *The Management of Innovation*. London: Tavistock.

Byrne, D. G., & Reinhart, M. I. (1989). 'Work Characteristics, Occupational Achievement and the Type A Behaviour Pattern'. *Journal of Occupational Psychology*, 62 (2), 123–134.

Caiden, G. E., & Caiden, N. J. (1977). 'Administrative Corruption'. *Public Administration Review*, 37, 301–9.

Campbell, J. P., & Pritchard, R. D. (1976). 'Motivation Theory in Industrial and Organisational Psychology'. In M. D. Dunnette (ed.), *Handbook of Industrial and Organisational Psychology*. Chicago: Rand McNally.

Carroll, S. J., & Gillen, D. A. (1987). 'Are the Classical Management Functions Useful in Describing Managerial Work?'. *Academy of Management Review*, 12(1), 38–51.

Carruthers, M. (1980). 'Hazardous Occupations and the Heart'. In C. L. Cooper & R. Payne (eds.), *Current Concerns in Occupational Stress*. New York: Wiley.

Carter, A. (1991). 'Management Training', *Training and Development*, 9.

Chandler, A. (1977). *The Visible Hand*. Cambridge, MA: Harvard University Press.

Checkland, P. (1981). *Systems Thinking, Systems Practice*. Chichester: Wiley.

Cherns, A. B. (1972). 'Models for the Use of Research'. *Human Relations*, 25, 25–33.

Cherns, A. B., & Davis, L. E. (1975). 'Assessment of the State of the Art'. In L. E. Davis & A. B. Cherns (eds.), *The Quality of Working Life* (Vol. 1). New York: Macmillan.

Chesney, M. A., & Rosenman, R. H. (1980). 'Type A Behaviour in the Work Setting'. In C. L. Cooper & R. Payne (eds.), *Current Concerns in Occupational Stress*. New York: Wiley.

Child, J. (1972). 'Organisational Structures, Environment and Performance: The Role of Strategic Choice'. *Sociology*, 6, 1–22.

Child, J. (1973). 'Parkinson's Progress: Accounting for the Number of Specialists in Organisations'. *Administrative Science Quarterly*, 18, 328–346.

Child, J. (1978). 'What Determines Organisation Performance? The Universals vs. The It All Depends'. In J. H. Jackson & C. P. Morgan (eds.), *Organisation Theory: A Macro Perspective for Management*. Englewood Cliffs, N.J.: Prentice-Hall.

Child, J. (1984). *Organisation: A Guide to Problems and Practice*. London: Harper & Row.

Child, J., & Wu, X. (1989). *The Communist Party's Role in Enterprise Leadership: At the High Water Mark of China's Economic Reform'*. Occasional Paper. Beijing: China-Europe Management Institute.

Child, J., & Lu, Y. (1990). 'Industrial Decision-making Under China's Reform, 1985–1988'. *Organisation Studies*, 11 (3), 321–351.

Child, J. (1991). 'A Foreign Perspective on the Management of People in China'. *International Journal of Human Resource Management*, 2 (1), 93–107.

China-Europe Management Institute (CEMI) (1990). *The Management of Equity Joint Ventures in China*. Beijing: CEMI.

Choudury, A. M. (1986). 'The Community Concept of Business: a Critique'. *International Studies in Management and Organisation*, 16 (2), 79–95.

Clark, A. W., & McCabe, S. (1970). 'Leadership Beliefs of Australian Managers'. *Journal of Applied Psychology*, 54, 1–6.

Clarke, T. (1989). *Imaginative Flexibility in Production Engineering: The Volvo Uddevalla Plant*. Paper given at Cardiff Business School ERU Conference, Cardiff, September, 1989.

Clegg, I. (1971). *Worker's Self-management in Algeria*. London: Allen Lane.

Clegg, S. R. (1989). *Frameworks of Power*. London: Sage.

Clegg, S. R. (ed.) (1990). *Organisation Theory and Class Analysis*. Berlin: de Gruyter.

Clegg, S., Dunphy, D. C., & Redding, S. G. (eds.) (1986). *The Enterprise and Management in East Asia*. Hong Kong: Centre for Asian Studies, University of Hong Kong.

Cohen, J. M., & Hook, R. M. (1987). 'Decentralised Planning in Kenya'. *Public Administration and Development*, 7, 77–93.

Collier, P. (1988). 'Oil Shocks and Food Security in Nigeria'. *International Labour Review*, 127 (6), 761–781.

Collins, P. (1989a). 'Assessing and Meeting the Management Development Needs of the Public Sector in Africa, Arab States, Asia and Latin America'. Paper presented at Civil Service Improvement Workshop EDI/World Bank, Washington DC, 4–8 December.

Collins, P. D. (1989b). 'Strategic Planning for State Enterprise Performance in Africa: Public versus Private'. *Public Administration and Development*, 9, 65–82.

Collins, P., & Wallis, M. (1990). 'Privatisation, Regulation and Development: Some Questions of Training Strategy'. *Public Administration and Development*, 10, 375–388.

Conger, J. A. (1989). 'Leadership: the Art of Empowering Others'. *Academy of Management Executive*, 3 (1), 17–24.

Conger, J. A. (1991). 'Inspiring Others: The Language of Leadership'. *Academy of Management Executive*, 5 (1), 31–45.

Conyers, D. (1984). 'Decentralisation and Development: A Review of the Literature'. *Public Administration and Development*, 4, 187–197.

Conyers, D. (1986). 'Future Directions in Development Studies: The Case of Decentralisation'. *World Development*, 14 (5), 593–603.

Cooper, C., & Arbose, J. (1984). 'Executive Stress Goes Global'. *International Management Review*, May, 42–48.

Cooper, C. L. (1980). 'Work Stress in White- and Blue-collar Jobs'. *Bulletin of the British Psychological Society*, 33, 49–51.

Cooper, C. L., & Marshall, J. (1978). *Understanding Executive Stress*. London: Macmillan.

Cordery, J. L., Mueller, W. S., & Smith, L. M. (1991). 'Attitudinal and Behavioural Effects of Autonomous Group Working: A Longitudinal Field Study'. *Academy of Management Journal*, 34(2), 264–476.

Cox, T. (1991). 'The Multicultural Organisation'. *Academy of Management Executive*, 5 (2), 34–47.

Crozier, M. (1964). *The Bureaucratic Phenomenon*. Chicago: The University of Chicago Press.

Cummings, T. G., & Srivastva, S. (1977). *Management of Work: A Sociotechnical Systems Approach*. Kent, Ohio: Kent State University Press.

Cummings, T. G. (1986). 'A Concluding Note: Future Directions of Sociotechnical Theory and Research'. *Journal of Applied Behavioural Science*, 22 (3), 355–360.

Dale, E. (1965). *Management: Theory and Practice*. New York: McGraw-Hill.

De Graft-Johnson, J. (1986). 'The African Culture and Social Structures: A Critical Analysis'. In AAPAM, *The Ecology of Public Administration and Management in Africa*. New Delhi: Vikas.

Dessler, G. (1980). *Organisation Theory*. Englewood Cliffs, N.J.: Prentice-Hall.

Donaldson, L. (1985). *In Defence of Organisation Theory*. Cambridge: Cambridge University Press.

Donaldson, T. (1989). *The Ethics of International Business*. New York: Oxford University Press.

Donnelly, E. (1991). 'Management Charter Initiatives: A Critique'. *Training and Development*, 9, 43–46.

Dore, R. (1987). *Taking Japan Seriously*. London: Athlone Press.

Dowling, R. J., & Schuler, R. S. (1991). *International Dimensions of Human Resource Management*. Boston, Mass.: Kent.

Drucker, P. F. (1972). *Technology, Management and Society*. London: Pan.

Drucker, P. F. (1977). *Management*. London: Pan.

Earley, P. C. (1989). 'Social Loafing and Collectivism: A Comparison of the United States and the People's Republic of China'. *Administrative Science Quarterly*, 34, 565–581.

Economist (1990). 'Africa's Cities'. 15 September, 19–22.

Elden, M. (1986). 'Sociotechnical Systems Ideas as Public Policy in Norway: Empowering Participation Through Worker-Managed Change'. *Journal of Applied Behavioural Science*, 22 (3), 239–255.

Elkan, W. (1960). *Migrants and Proletarians*. London: Oxford University Press.

Ellis, A. (1978). 'What People Can Do for Themselves to Cope with Stress'. In C. L. Cooper & R. Payne (eds.), *Stress at Work*. New York: Wiley.

Emery, F. E., & Thorsrud, E. (1964). *Form and Content in Industrial Democracy*. London: Tavistock.

Emery, F. E., & Thorsrud, E. (1975). *Democracy at Work*. Canberra: Australian National University, Centre for Continuing Education.

Emery, F. E., & Trist, E. L. (1965). 'The Causal Texture of Organisational Environments'. *Human Relations*, 18, 21–32.

Emery, F. E., & Trist, E. L. (1981). Sociotechnical Systems. In F. E. Emery (ed.), Systems Thinking, Vol. 1, Harmondsworth: Penguin.

Etzioni, A. (1975). *A Comparative Analysis of Complex Organisations* (2nd ed.). New York: Free Press.

Evans, P., Doz, Y., & Laurent, A. (eds.) (1989). *Human Resource Management in International Firms*. London: Macmillan.

Fallers, L. A. (1965). *Bantu Bureaucracy*. Chicago: University of Chicago Press.

Fayol, H. (1949). *General and Industrial Management*. London: Pitman.

Fiedler, F. (1967). *A Theory of Leadership*. New York: McGraw-Hill.

Fincham, R., & Zulu, G. (1979). 'Labour and Participation in Zambia'. In B. Turok (ed.), *Development in Zambia*. London: Zed Press.

Fitzgerald, T. H. (1971). 'Why Motivation Theory Doesn't Work'. *Harvard Business Review*, 49, 65–72.

Fleming, W. G. (1966). 'Authority, Efficiency, and Role Stress: Problems in the Development of East African Bureaucracies'. *Administrative Science Quarterly*, 11, 386–404.

Friedman, H. S., & Booth-Kewley, S. (1988). 'Validity of the Type A Construct: A Reprise'. *Psychological Bulletin*, 104 (3), 381–384.

Friedman, M., Rosenman, R. H., & Carroll, V. (1958). 'Changes in the Serum Cholesterol and Blood Clotting Time in Men Subjected to Cyclic Variation in Occupational Stress'. *Circulation*, 17, 852–861.

Frost, P. (1980). 'Toward a Radical Framework for Practising Organisation Science'. *Academy of Management Review*, 5, 501–507.

Ganster, D. C. (1986). 'Type A Behaviour and Occupational Stress'. *Journal of Organisational Behaviour Management*, 8, 61–84.

Gershenberg, I. (1987). 'The Training and Spread of Managerial Knowhow: A Comparative Analysis of Multinational and Other Firms in Kenya'. *World Development*, 15 (7), 931–939.

Ghai, Y. (1985). 'The State and the Market in the Management of Public Enterprises in Africa: Ideology and False Comparisons'. *Public Enterprise*, 6 (1), 15–26.

Gleave, S., & Oliver, N. (1990). 'Human Resources Management in Japanese Manufacturing Companies in the U.K.: 5 Case Studies'. *Journal of General Management*, 16 (1), 54–68.

Gluckman, M., Mitchell, J. C., & Barnes, J. A. (1949). 'The Village Headman in British Central Africa'. *Africa*, 19 (2), 89–106.

Goffman, E. (1961). 'The Characteristics of Total Institutions'. In A. Etzioni (ed.), *Complex Organisations: A Sociological Reader*. New York: Holt, Rinehart & Winston.

Goldman, R. D. (1976). *A Work Experiment: Six Americans in a Swedish Plant*. New York: The Ford Foundation.

Goldthorpe, J. H., Lockwood, D., Bechhofer, F., & Platt, J. (1968). *The Affluent Worker: Industrial Attitudes and Behaviour*. London: Cambridge University Press.

Golembiewski, R. T. (1991). 'Third World O.D.: Values, Closeness-of-Fit and Culture-Boundedness'. *International Journal of Human Resource Management*, 2 (1), 39–54.

Gould, D. J. (1980). *Bureaucratic Corruption and Underdevelopment in the Third World: The Case of Zaire*. New York: Pergamon.

Greenley, G. E. (1989). *Strategic Management*. London: Prentice-Hall.

Greenhaus, J. H., & Beutell, N. J. (1985). 'Sources of Conflict Between Work and Family Roles'. *Academy of Management Review*, 10, 76–88.

Gustafsson, L., Blunt, P., Gisle, P., & Sjolander, S. (1991). *The Future of Swedish Support to the Public Administration Sector in Zimbabwe*. Stockholm: SIDA.

Gutkind, P. C. W. (1968). 'African Responses to Urban Wage Employment'. *International Labour Review*, 97, 135–166.

Gutkind, P. C. W. (1975). 'The View from Below: Political Consciousness of the Urban Poor in Ibadan'. *Cahiers d'Etudes Africaines*, 15, 5–35.

Hackman, J. R., & Oldham, G. R. (1975). 'Development of the Job Diagnostic Survey'. *Journal of Applied Psychology*, 60, 159–70.

Hackman, J. R., & Oldham, G. R. (1976). 'Motivation Through the Design of Work: Test of a Theory'. *Organisational Behaviour and Human Performance*, 16, 250–79.

Hackman, J. R., & Oldham, G. R. (1980). *Work Redesign*. Reading, Mass.: Addison-Wesley.

Hage, J., & Finsterbusch, K. (1987). *Organisational Change as a Development Strategy*. London: Lynne Rienner.

Hague, H. (1974). *Executive Self-Development*. London: Macmillan.

Haire, M., Ghiselli, E. E., & Porter, L. W. (1963). 'Cultural Patterns in the Role of the Manager'. *Industrial Relations*, 2, 95–117.

Haire, M., Ghiselli, E. E., & Porter, L. W. (1966). *Managerial Thinking: An International Study*. New York: Wiley.

Hales, C. (1986). 'Management Processes, Management Divisions of Labour and Managerial Work: Towards a Synthesis'. Paper presented at the Labour Process Conference, University of Aston Birmingham, March.

Handy, C. (1989). *The Age of Unreason*. London: Hutchinson.

Harrigan, K. R. (1986). *Managing for Joint Venture Success*. Massachusetts: Lexington Books.

Harrow, J., & Willcocks, L. (1990). 'Public Services Management: Activities, Initiatives and Limits to Learning'. *Journal of Management Studies*, 27 (3), 281–304.

Harvey, E. (1967). 'Technology and the Structure of Organisations'. *American Sociological Review*, 32, 194–208.

Hellriegel, D., Slocum, J. W., & Woodman, R. W. (1989). *Organisational Behaviour*. New York: West Pub. Co.

Hendry, C., & Pettigrew, A. (1990). 'Human Resource Management: An Agenda for the 1990s'. *International Journal of Human Resource Management*, 1 (1), 17–43.

Henley, J. S. (1973). 'Employment Relationships and Economic Development: The Kenyan Experience'. *Journal of Modern African Studies*, 11, 559–589.

Henley, J. S., & Nyaw, M. K. (1986). 'Introducing Market Forces into Managerial Decision-Making in Chinese Industrial Enterprises'. *Journal of Management Studies*, 23 (6), 635–656.

Herzberg, F. (1968). 'One More Time: How Do You Motivate Employees?'. *Harvard Business Review*, 46, 53–62.

Herzberg, F., Mausner, B., & Snyderman, B. (1959). *The Motivation to Work* (2nd ed.). New York: Wiley.

Hickson, D. J., Hinings, C. R., McMillan, J. C., & Schwitter, J. P. (1974). 'The Culture-free Context of Organisational Structure: A Tri-national Comparison'. *Sociology*, 8, 59–80.

Hickson, D. J., McMillan, J. C., Azumi, K., & Horvath, D. (1979). 'Grounds for Comparative Organisation Theory: Quicksand or Hard Core?'. In C. J. Lammers & D. J. Hickson (eds.), *Organisations Alike and Unlike*. London: Routledge and Kegan Paul.

Hofstede, G. (1980). *Culture's Consequences: International Differences in Work-Related Values*. London: Sage.

Hofstede, G. (1984). 'The Cultural Relativity of the Quality of Life Concept'. *Academy of Management Review*, 9 (3), 389–98.

Hofstede, G. (1987). 'The Applicability of McGregor's Theories in Southeast Asia'. *Journal of Management Development*, 6 (3), 9–18.

Hofstede, G., & Bond, M. (1988). 'The Confucius Connection: From Cultural Roots to Economic Growth'. *Organisational Dynamics*, 16 (4), 5–21.

Hofstede, G., Neuijen, B., Ohayr, D. D., & Sanders, G. (1990). 'Measuring Organisational Cultures: A Qualitative and Quantitative Study Across Twenty Cases'. *Administrative Science Quarterly*, 35, 286–316.

Holt, J. (1983). *How Children Learn*. New York: Delacorte.

Honey, P. (1991). 'The Learning Organisation Simplified'. *Training and Development*, 9 (7), 30–33.

Hope, K. R., & Armstrong, A. (1980). 'Toward the Development of Administrative and Managerial Capability in Developing Countries'. *International Review of Administrative Sciences*, XLVI (4), 315–320.

House, J. S. (1974). 'Occupational Stress and Coronary Heart Disease: A Review and Theoretical Integration'. *Journal of Health and Social Behaviour*, 14, 12–27.

House, R. (1971). 'A Path-goal Theory of Leadership'. *Administrative Science Quarterly*, 16, 321–338.

House, R. J., & Rizzo, J. R. (1972). 'Role Conflict and Ambiguity as Critical Variables in a Model of Organisational Behaviour'. *Organisational Behaviour and Human Performance*, 7, 467–505.

House, W. J. (1981). 'Redistribution, Consumer Demand and Employment in Kenyan Furniture-making'. *Journal of Development Studies*, 17, 336–356.

Howell, P., Strauss, J., & Sorensen, P. F. (1975). 'Cultural and Situational Determinants of Job Satisfaction Among Management in Liberia'. *Journal of Management Studies*, 12, 225–227.

Hughes, G. D., & Singler, C. H. (1985). *Strategic Sales Management*. Reading, MA: Addison-Wesley.

Humble, J. W. (1973). *Improving the Performance of the Experienced Manager*. London: Macmillan.

Hutton, G. (1972). *Thinking About Organisations* (2nd ed.). London: Tavistock.

Hyden, G. (1983). *No Shortcuts to Progress: African Development Management in Perspective*. London: Heinemann.

Ivancevich, J. M., & Matteson, M. T. (1988). 'Type A Behaviour and the Healthy Individual'. *British Journal of Medical Psychology*, 61, 37–56.

Ivancevich, J. M., Szilagyi, A. D., & Wallace, M. J. (1977). *Organisational Behaviour and Performance*. Santa Monica, California: Goodyear.

Jackson, D. (1979). 'The Disappearance of Strikes in Tanzania: Incomes Policy and Industrial Democracy'. *Journal of Modern African Studies*, 17, 219–51.

Jackson, S. E., & Schuler, R. S. (1985). 'A Meta-Analysis and Conceptual Critique of Research on Role Ambiguity and Role Conflict in Work Settings'. *Organisational Behaviour and Human Decision Processes*, 36, 16–78.

Jamal, V. (1988). 'Getting the Crisis Right: Missing Perspectives on Africa'. *International Labour Review*, 127(6), 655–678.

Jamal, V., & Weeks, J. (1988). 'The Vanishing Rural Urban Gap in Sub-Saharan Africa'. *International Labour Review*, 127 (3), 271–292.

Jenkins, C. T. (1982). *Management Problems and Management Education in Developing Economies: A Case Study of Malawi*. Working Paper No. 233, University of Aston Management Centre.

Jibowo, A. (1977). 'Effects of Motivators and Hygiene Factors on Job Performance Among Extension Workers in the Former Western State of Nigeria'. *Quarterly Journal of Administration*, 12 (1), 45–54.

Johnston, A., & Dyrssen, H. (1991). 'Cooperation in the Development of Public Sector Management Skills: The SIDA Experience'. *Journal of Management Development*, 10 (6), 52–59.

Jones, M. (1983). *Management Development: A Participative Approach*. Institute for Development Policy and Management, University of Manchester.

Jones, M. (1986a). 'Management Development: An African Focus'. *Management Education and Development*, 17 (3), 202–216.

Jones, M. (1986b). *Managerial Thinking: A Malawian Perspective*. Unpublished Ph.D. thesis, School of Management, University of Manchester.

Jones, M. (1988a). 'Managerial Thinking: An African Perspective'. *Journal of Management Studies*, 25 (5), 481–505.

Jones, M. (1988b). 'Work and the Nature of Fred'. *Management Education and Development*, 19 (1), 30–32.

Jones, M. (1989). 'Issues in Management Education and Training in Developing Countries: Some Evidence from Africa'. *Management Education and Development*, 20 (1), 67–76.

Jones, M. (1990a). 'Critical Skills for African Managers'. *Teaching Public Administration*, 10 (2), 48–53.

Jones, M. (1990b). 'Efficiency and Effectiveness in an African Public Administration Context'. *International Journal of Public Service Management*, 3 (1), 58–64.

Jones, M. (1990c). 'Preface to C. Gamage, *Profile of a Government Agent in the 1990s*. Colombo: Sri Lanka Institute of Development Administration.

Jorgensen, J. J., Hafsi, T., & Kiggundu, M. N. (1986). 'Towards a Market Imperfections Theory of Organisational Structure in Developing Countries'. *Journal of Management Studies*, 23 (4), 417–442.

Jreisat, J. E. (1988). 'Administrative Reform in Developing Countries: A Comparative Perspective'. *Public Administration and Development*, 8, 85–97.

Kagan, J., & Moss, H. A. (1962). *Birth to Maturity*. New York: Wiley.

Kahn, R. L., Wolfe, D. M., Quinn, R. P., Snoek, J. D., & Rosenthal, R. A. (1964). *Organisational Stress: Studies in Role Conflict and Ambiguity*. New York: Wiley.

Kakabadse, A. (1986). *Management Development: an Organisation's Investment in the Future*. Occasional Paper, Cranfield School of Management/Danish Management Centre.

Kanawaty, G., & Thorsrud, E. (1981). 'Field Experiences with New Forms of Work Organisation'. *International Labour Review*, 120, 263–77.

Kanter, R. M. (1991). 'Transcending Business Boundaries: 12,000 World Managers View Change'. *Harvard Business Review*, 69(3), 151–164.

Kapferer, B. (1972). *Strategy and Transaction in an African Factory*. Manchester: Manchester University Press.

Katz, D., & Kahn, R. L. (1966). *The Social Psychology of Organisations*. London: Wiley.

Kaul, M. (1989). 'Strategic Issues in Development Management: Learning from Successful Experiences'. *International Journal of Public Sector Management*, 1 (3), 12–25.

Kayode, M. O. (1970). 'A Re-examination of the Concept and Factors Influencing Productivity with Particular Emphasis on Motivation'. *Nigerian Journal of Economic and Social Studies*, 12, 45–60.

Kelly, J. E. (1978). 'A Reappraisal of Sociotechnical Systems Theory'. *Human Relations*, 31, 1069–99.

Kelly, J. E. (1982). *Scientific Management, Job Redesign and Work Performance*. London: Academic Press.

Ketchum, L. (1984). 'Sociotechnical Design in a Third World Country: The Railway Maintenance Depot at Sennar in the Sudan'. *Human Relations*, 37 (2), 135–154.

Kets de Vries, M. F. R. (1979). 'Organisational Stress: A Call for Management Action'. *Sloan Management Review*, 20, 3–14.

Keys, B. J., & Case, T. L. (1990). 'How to Become an Influential Manager'. *Academy of Management Executive*, 4 (4), 38–51.

Kiggundu, M. (1986). 'Limitations to the Application of Sociotechnical Systems in Developing Countries'. *Journal of Applied Behavioural Science*, 22 (3), 341–353.

Kiggundu, M. N. (1988). 'Africa'. In R. Nath (ed.), *Comparative Management: A Regional View*. Cambridge, Mass.: Ballinger.

Kiggundu, M. N. (1989). *Managing Organisations in Developing Countries*. West Hartford, Conn.: Kumarian Press.

Kiggundu, M. (1991). 'The Challenges of Management Development in Sub-Saharan Africa'. *Journal of Management Development*, 10 (6), 42–57.

Kirkpatrick, S. A., & Locke, E. A. (1991). 'Leadership: Do Traits Matter?'. *Academy of Management Executive*, 5 (2), 48–60.

Knight, K. (ed.) (1977). *Matrix Management*. Aldershot: Gower.

Kolb, D. A., Rubin, I. M., & Osland, J. M. (1991). *Organisational Behaviour: An Experiential Approach* (5th ed.). Englewood Cliffs, N.J.: Prentice Hall.

Kolodny, H., & Stjernberg, T. (1986). 'The Change Process of Innovative Work Designs: New Design and Redesign in Sweden, Canada, and the U.S.'. *Journal of Applied Behavioural Science*, 22 (3), 287–301.

Kotter, J. P. (1982). *The General Manager*. New York: Free Press.

Kotter, J. P. (1988). *The Leadership Factor*. New York: Free Press.

Kotter, J. P. (1990). *A Force for Change: How Leadership Differs from Management*. New York: Free Press.

Krantz, J. (1990). 'Lessons from the Field: An Essay on the Crisis of Leadership in Modern Organisations'. *Journal of Applied Behavioural Science*, 26 (1), 49–64.

Kreitner, R., & Luthans, F. (1987). 'A Social Learning Approach to Behavioural Management: Radical Behaviorists "Mellowing Out" '. In R. M. Steers & L. W. Porter (eds.), *Motivation and Work Behaviour*. New York: McGraw Hill.

Lahiri, D. K., & Srivastva, S. (1966). 'Determinants of Satisfaction in Middle Management Personnel'. *Journal of Applied Psychology*, 51, 254–265.

Lamouse-Smith, W. B. (1969). 'Conflicts in African Industrial Organisations'. *Civilisations*, 19, 498–510.

Lawrence, P. R., & Lorsch, J. W. (1967). *Organisation and Environment*. Boston: Harvard University Press.

Lee, B., & Nellis, J. (1990). *Enterprise Reform and Privatisation in Socialist Economies*. World Bank Discussion Paper No. 104, Washington, D.C.: World Bank.

Lee, C., Ashford, S. J., & Bobko, P. (1990). 'Interactive Effects of 'Type A' Behaviour and Perceived Control on Worker Performance, Job Satisfaction, and Somatic Complaints'. *Academy of Management Journal*, 33 (4), 870–881.

Leonard, D.K. (1987). 'The Political Realities of African Management'. *World Development*, 15, 899–910.

Leonard, D. K. (1988). 'The Secrets of African Managerial Success'. *IDS Bulletin*, 19 (4), 35–41.

Levi, L. (1981). *Preventing Work Stress*. Reading, Mass.: Addison-Wesley.

LeVine, R. A. (1966). *Dreams and Deeds: Achievement Motivation in Nigeria*. Chicago: University of Chicago Press.

LeVine, R. A. (1970). 'Personality and Change'. In J. N. Paden & E. W. Soja (eds.), *The African Experience* (Vol.1). Evanston Ill.: Northwestern University Press.

Levinson, H. (1973). 'Asinine Attitudes Toward Motivation'. *Harvard Business Review*, 51, 73–79.

Likert, R. (1967). *The Human Organisation*. New York: McGraw-Hill.

Lockett, M. (1988). 'Culture and the Problems of Chinese Management'. *Organisation Studies*, 9 (4), 475–96.

Lorsch, J. W., & Lawrence, P. R. (eds.) (1970). *Studies in Organisation Design*. Homewood, Ill.: Irwin and Dorsey.

Luke, D. F. (1984). 'The Political Economy of an African Public Enterprise: A Longitudinal Case Study of the Administrative and Economic Operations of the Sierra Leone Port Organisation'. *Public Administration and Development*, 4, 171–186.

Luthans, F., Rosenkrantz, S. A., & Hennessey, H. W. (1985). 'What Do Successful Managers Really Do? An Observational Study of Managerial Activities'. *Journal of Applied Behavioural Science*, 21(3), 255–270.

Lykken, D. T. (1968). 'Statistical Significance in Psychological Research'. *Psychological Bulletin*, 70 (3), 151–159.

Lyles, M. A. (1990). 'A Research Agenda for Strategic Management in the 1990s'. *Journal of Management Studies*, 27 (4), 363–375.

Macgregor, J. (1990). 'The Crisis in African Agriculture'. *Africa Insight*, 20 (1), 4–16.

Machungwa, P., & Schmitt, N. (1983). 'Work Motivation in a Developing Country'. *Journal of Applied Psychology*, 68, 31–42.

Magid, A. (1967). 'Dimension of Administrative Role and Conflict Resolution Among Local Officials in Northern Nigeria'. *Administrative Science Quarterly*, 12, 321–38.

Magid, A. (1976). *Men in the Middle: Leadership and Role Conflict in Nigerian Society*. Manchester: Manchester University Press.

Makharita, R., & Brunet, J. (1991). 'Institutional Adjustment in Terrafrie: Typical Problems of a Real African Country'. *Public Administration and Development*, 11, 233–237.

Manamperi, S. A. (1990). 'Training Provision and the Trainer's Role in the 1990s'. *Sri Lanka Journal of Development Administration*, 7 (1), 40–64.

Mant, A. (1979). *The Rise and Fall of the British Manager*. London: Pan.

Mant, A. (1981). 'Developing Effective Managers for the Future: Learning from Experience'. In C. Cooper (ed.), *Developing Managers for the 1980s*. London: Macmillan.

Mant, A. (1983). *Leaders we Deserve*. Oxford: Blackmore.

Marsden, D. (1991). 'Indigenous Management'. *International Journal of Human Resource Management*, 2(1), 21–38.

Marshall, D. C. (1987). 'The "Mananga Style": An Analysis of the Education "Culture" of Mananga Agricultural Management Centre'. *Agricultural Administration and Extension*, 27, 171–182.

Martin, R. (1980). *The Management of Participatory Projects: A Consensus Model*. Unpublished paper delivered at a conference organised by the Development Administration Group, Institute of Local Government Studies, University of Birmingham, England, September 1980.

Martinko, M. J., & Gardner, W. L. (1990). 'Structured Observation of Managerial Work: A Replication and Synthesis'. *Journal of Management Studies*, 27(3), 329–357.

Maseko, I. J. (1976). 'Workers' Participation: The Case of the Friendship Textile Mill and TANESCO'. In H. Mapolu (ed.), *Workers and Management*. Dar es Salaam: Tanzania Publishing House.

Maslow, A. H. (1954). *Motivation and Personality*. New York: Harper and Row.

Maslow, A. H. (1973). *The Farther Reaches of Human Nature*. Harmondsworth: Penguin.

Maurice, M. (1979). 'For a Study of "The Societal Effect": Universality and Specificity in Organisation Research'. In J. C. Lammers & D. J. Hickson (eds.), *Organisations Alike and Unlike*. London: Routledge and Kegan Paul.

Mayer, P., & Mayer, I. (1971). *Townsmen or Tribesmen* (2nd ed.). Cape Town: Oxford University Press.

Mazrui, A. A. (1980). *The African Condition*. London: Heinemann Educational.

McClelland, D. C. (1961). *The Achieving Society*. Princeton, N.J.: Van Nostrand.

McClelland, D. C., & Burnham, D. H. (1976). 'Power is the Great Motivator'. *Harvard Business Review*, 54 (2), 100–110.

McClelland, D. C., & Winter, D. G. (1969). *Motivating Economic Development*. New York: Free Press.

McLean, A. A. (1979). *Work Stress*. Reading, Mass.: Addison-Wesley.

Mclennan, R. (1989). *Managing Organisational Change*. Englewood Cliffs, N.J.: Prentice-Hall.

McQueen, A. J. (1969). 'Unemployment and Future Orientations of Nigerian School-leavers'. *Canadian Journal of African Studies*, 3, 441–461.

Mihyo, P. (1975). 'The Struggle for Workers' Control'. *Review of African Political Economy*, 4, 62–84.

Miles, R. H., & Perreault, W. D. (1976). 'Organisational Role Conflict: Its Antecedents and Consequences'. *Organisational Behaviour and Human Performance*, 17, 19–44.

Miller, E. J. (1975). 'Sociotechnical Systems in Weaving, 1953–1970: A Follow-up Study'. *Human Relations*, 28, 349–386.

Miner, J. B. (1980). *Theories of Organisational Behaviour*. Hinsdale, Ill.: Dryden Press.

Mintzberg, H. (1973). *The Nature of Managerial Work*. New York: Harper & Row.

Mintzberg, H. (1979). *The Structuring of Organisations*. Englewood Cliffs, N.J.: Prentice-Hall.

Mintzberg, H. (1983). *Structure in Fives: Designing Effective Organisations*. Englewood Cliffs, N.J.: Prentice-Hall.

Mintzberg, H. (1988). 'The Structuring of Organisations'. In J. B. Quinn, H. Mintzberg, & R. M. James (eds.), *The Strategy Process: Concepts, Contexts, and Cases*. Englewood Cliffs: Prentice-Hall.

Mintzberg, H. (1989). *Mintzberg on Management*. New York: Free Press.

Mitchell, V. F., & Moudgill, P. (1976). 'Measurement of Maslow's Need Hierarchy'. *Organisational Behaviour and Human Performance*, 16, 334–349.

Moch, M. K., Bartunek, J., & Brass, D. J. (1979). 'Structure, Task Characteristics, and Experienced Role Stress in Organisations Employing Complex Technology'. *Organisational Behaviour and Human Performance*, 24, 258–268.

Montgomery, J. D. (1986a). 'Bureaucratic Politics in Southern Africa'. *Public Administration Review*, 46 (5), 407–413.

Montgomery, J. D. (1986b). 'Levels of Managerial Leadership in Southern Africa'. *Journal of Developing Areas*, 21, 15–30.

Montgomery, J. D. (1987). 'Probing Managerial Behaviour: Image and Reality in Southern Africa'. *World Development*, 15 (7), 911–929.

Montgomery, J. D. (1991). Preconditions to Environmental Policy. *International Journal of Human Resource Management*, 2 (1), 7–20.

Moore, B., & Pratt, G. (1981). *Managing in Public*. Melbourne: Cassell.

Morgan, G. (1986). *Images of Organisation*. London: Sage.

Morgan, P. E. (1984). 'Development Management and Management Development in Africa'. *Rural Africana*, 18, 13–15.

Morgan, R. W. (1965). 'Occupation Prestige Ratings by Nigerian Students'. *Nigerian Journal of Economic and Social Studies*, 1, 325–332.

Morgenthau, R. S. (1988). 'Institutionalising Rural Development: Lessons from Evaluation'. In H. Glickman (ed.), *The Crisis and Challenge of African Development*. Westport, Connecticut: Greenwood Press.

Moris, J. (1977). *The Transferability of Western Management Concepts and Programmes: An East African Perspective*. London: International Institute for Educational Planning.

Msekwa, P. (1975). 'Workers' Participation in Management in Tanzania: A Background'. *African Review*, 5, 127–40.

Mullins, L. J. (1989). *Management and Organisational Behaviour* (2nd ed.). London: Pitman.

Munene, J. C., & Dul, R. D. (1989). 'Exploring Normative Commitment with Nigerian Extension Workers'. *Public Administration and Development*, 9, 169–183.

Murray, H. A. (1938). *Exploration in Personality*. Oxford: Oxford University Press.

Murrell, K. L. (1986). *The Managerial Infrastructure of Economic Development: Its Importance and How to Analyse It*. SICA Occasional Paper No. 12, University of Texas.

Myambo, K. (1991). *The Will to Work*. Paper presented at the National Convention of the Institute of Personnel Management of Zimbabwe. August, Harare.

Nash, J., Dandler, J., & Hopkins, N. S. (eds.) (1976). *Popular Participation in Social Change*. The Hague: Mouton.

NASPA (1985). *Improving Management in Southern Africa: Report of the Regional Training Council of SADCC*. Washington, D.C.: NASPA.

Nellis, J. R. (1977). 'Socialist Management in Algeria'. *Journal of Modern African Studies*, 15, 529–54.

Nellis, J. R. (1980). 'Maladministration: Cause or Result of Underdevelopment? The Algerian Example'. *Canadian Journal of African Studies*, 13, 407–22.

Nellis, J. R. (1983). 'Decentralisation in North Africa: Problems of Policy Implementation'. In G. S. Cheema & D. A. Rondinelli (eds.), *Decentralisation and Development: Policy Implementation in Developing Countries*. Beverly Hills: Sage.

Nellis, J. (1986). *Public Enterprises in Sub-Saharan Africa*. Washington, D.C.: World Bank.

Nelson, D. L., & Sutton, C. (1990). 'Chronic Work Stress and Coping: A Longitudinal Study and Suggested New Directions'. *Academy of Management Journal*, 33 (4), 859–869.

Nevis, E. C. (1983). 'Using an American Perspective in Understanding Another Culture: Toward a Hierarchy of Needs for the People's Republic of China'. *Journal of Applied Behavioural Science*, 19 (3), 249–64.

Newman, J. E., & Beehr, T. A. (1979). 'Personal and Organisational Strategies for Handling Job Stress: A Review of Research and Opinion'. *Personnel Psychology*, 32, 1–43.

Nicholson, N., Ostrom, E., Bowles, D., & Long, R. (1985). *Development Management in Africa: the Case of the Egerton College Expansion Project in Kenya*. AID Evaluation Special Study No. 35. Washington, D.C.: World Bank.

Nicholson, N., Rees, A., & Brooks-Rooney, A. (1990). 'Strategy, Innovation and Performance'. *Journal of Management Studies*, 27 (5), 511–534.

Nord, W. R. (1974). 'The Failure of Current Applied Behavioural Science: A Marxian Perspective'. *Journal of Applied Behavioural Science*, 10, 557–577.

Nord, W. R. (1977). 'Job Satisfaction Reconsidered'. *American Psychologist*, 32, 1026–1035.

Nord, W. R. (1978). 'Dreams of Humanisation and the Realities of Power'. *Academy of Management Review*, 3, 674–679.

Nti, J. (1989). 'The Impact of Economic Crisis on the Effectiveness of Public Service Personnel'. In M. J. Balogun & D. Mutahaba (eds.), *Economic Restructuring and African Public Administration*. Hartford, Conn.: Kumarian Press.

Nzelibe, C. O. (1986). 'The Evolution of African Management Thought'. *International Studies of Management and Organisation*, 16 (2), 6–16.

ODA (1989). *Civil Service Reform in Sub-Saharan Africa* (Conference Report). London: ODA.

Odinye, M. O., & Aduaka, E. C. (1989). 'What Motivates Nigerian Craftsmen in a Taskforce Situation: A Case Study of ASCON'. *International Journal of Manpower*, 10 (1), 16–21.

Okediji, O. O. (1965). 'Some Socio-cultural Problems in the Western Nigerian Land Settlement Scheme: A Case Study'. *Nigerian Journal of Economic and Social Studies*, 7, 301–310.

Oldham, G. R. (1976). 'Job Characteristics and Internal Motivation: The Moderating Effect of Interpersonal and Individual Variables'. *Human Relations*, 29, 559–569.

Oliver, N., & Davies, A. (1990). 'Adopting Japanese-style Manufacturing Methods: A Tale of Two (UK) Factories'. *Journal of Management Studies*, 27 (5), 555–570.

Oliver, N., & Wilkinson, B. (1988). *The Japanisation of British Industry*. Oxford: Blackwell.

Orpen, C. (1979a). 'The Reactions of Western and Tribal Black Workers to Job Characteristics'. *International Review of Applied Psychology*, 28, 117–125.

Orpen, C. (1979b). 'The Effects of Job Enrichment on Employee Satisfaction, Motivation, Involvement, and Performance: A Field Experiment'. *Human Relations*, 32, 189–217.

Ostheimer, J. M. (1969). 'Measuring Achievement Motivation Among the Chagga of Tanzania'. *Journal of Social Psychology*, 78, 17–30.

Palmlund, T. (1991). 'UNDP's Management Development Programme'. *Journal of Management Development*, 10 (6), 58–61.

Parkinson, C. N. (1957). *Parkinson's Law*. Boston: Houghton Mifflin.

Parsons, T. (1951). *The Social System*. New York: Free Press.

Pateman, C. (1970). *Participation and Democratic Theory*. Cambridge: Cambridge University Press.

Peil, M. (1972). *The Ghanaian Factory Worker*. Cambridge: Cambridge University Press.

Perrow, C. (1967). 'A Framework for the Comparative Analysis of Organisations'. *American Sociological Review*, 32, 194–208.

Perrow, C. (1970). *Organisational Analysis: A Sociological Review*. London: Tavistock.

Peters, M., & Robinson, V. (1984). 'The Origins and Status of Action Research'. *Journal of Applied Behavioural Science*, 20 (2), 113–124.

Peters, T. J. (1989). *Thriving on Chaos*. London: Pan Books.

Peters, T. J., & Waterman, R. H. (1982). *In Search of Excellence*. New York: Harper & Row.

Phillips, A. O. (1991). 'Institutional Reform in Nigeria'. *Public Administration and Development*, 11, 229–232.

Pinder, C. C. (1977). 'Concerning the Application of Human Motivation Theories in Organisational Settings'. *Academy of Management Review*, 2, 384–397.

Porter, L. W. (1961). 'A Study of Perceived Need Satisfaction in Bottom and Middle Management Jobs'. *Journal of Applied Psychology*, 45, 1–10.

Porter, L. W. (1962). 'Job Attitudes in Management: I Perceived Deficiencies in Need Fulfilment as a Function of Job Level'. *Journal of Applied Psychology*, 46, 375–384.

Porter, L. W., & Lawler, E. E. (1965). 'Properties of Organisation Structure in Relation to Job Attitudes and Job Behaviour'. *Psychological Bulletin*, 64, 23–51.

Poulton, E. C. (1978). 'Blue Collar Stressors'. In C. L. Cooper, & R. Payne (eds.), *Stress at Work*. New York: Wiley.

Presidential Circular No. 1 (1970). Mimeo, Government Printer: Dar es Salaam.

Price, R. M. (1975). *Society and Bureaucracy in Contemporary Ghana*. Berkeley: University of California Press.

Pugh, D. S., & Hinings, C. R. (1976). *Organisational Structure: Extensions and Replications*. Farnborough, Hants.: Saxon House.

Quemby, A. (1975). 'Works Councils and Industrial Relations in Zambia'. In E. Kalula (ed.), *Some Aspects of Zambian Labour Relations*. Lusaka: The University of Zambia.

Rabinowitz, S., & Hall, D. T. (1977). 'Organisational Research on Job Involvement'. *Psychological Bulletin*, 84, 265–88.

Redding, G. R. (1989). *The Spirit of Chinese Capitalism*. Berlin: Walter de Gruyter.

Reilly, W. (1987). 'Management and Training for Development: The Hombe Thesis'. *Public Administration and Development*, 7, 25–42.

Revans, R. W. (1967). 'Development of a Department of Business Administration in the University of Khartoum'. *Journal of Management Studies*, 4, 169–175.

Revans, R. W. (1980). *Action Learning*. London: Blond and Briggs.

Revans, R. W. (1987). *International Perspectives on Action Learning*. Manchester: Institute for Development Policy and Management, University of Manchester.

Revans, R. (1991). 'Action Learning and the Third World'. *International Journal of Human Resource Management*, 1 (2), 73–92.

Rice, A. K. (1953). 'Productivity and Social Organisation in an Indian Weaving Shed'. *Human Relations*, 6, 297–329.

Rice, A. K. (1958). *Productivity and Social Organisation*. London: Tavistock

Richards, D. (1991). 'Flying Against the Wind? Culture and Management Development in Southeast Asia'. *Journal of Management Development*, 10 (6), 19–33.

Robbins, S. R. (1990). *Organisation Theory: Structure, Design and Applications*. Englewood Cliffs, N.J.: Prentice-Hall.

Roberts, K. H., & Glick, W. (1981). 'The Job Characteristics Approach to Task Design: A Critical Review'. *Journal of Applied Psychology*, 66, 193–217.

Rondinelli, D. A. (1986). 'Improving Development Management: Lessons from the Evaluation of USAID projects in Africa.' *International Review of Administrative Sciences*, 52, 421–445.

Rondinelli, D. A., Nellis, J. A., & Cheema, G. S. (1984). *Decentralisation in Developing Countries: A Review of Recent Experience*. Washington, D. C.: World Bank Staff Working Paper No. 581.

Rosenman, R. H., Friedman, M., Strauss, R., Wurm, M., Kositcheck, R., Harn, W., & Werthessen, N. T. (1964). 'A Predictive Study of CHD'. *Journal of the American Medical Association*, 189, 15–22.

Rothwell, S. (1989). 'Strategy and Organisation'. *Journal of General Management*, 13 (4), 103–115.

Rutherford, P. (1981). *Attitudes of Malawian Managers: Some Recent Research*. Unpublished monograph, University of Malawi.

Safavi, F. (1981). 'A Model for Management Education in Africa'. *Academy of Management Review*, 6 (2), 319–331.

Schein, E. H. (1970). *Organisational Psychology*. Englewood Cliffs, N.J.: Prentice-Hall.

Schein, E. (1989). 'Organisational Culture: What It Is and How to Change It'. In P. Evans *et al.* (eds.), *Human Resource Management in International Firms*. London: Macmillan.

Schein, E. H. (1990). 'Innovative Cultures and Adaptive Organisations'. *Sri Lanka Journal of Development Administration*, 7 (2), 9–39.

Schellekens, L. (1989). 'Management Training and Its Contribution to Economic Recovery in Africa'. *Journal of Management Development*, 8 (5), 40–50.

Schonmeier, H. W. (1979). 'Occupational Orientation of Somali Youth: The Perception of Occupational Context'. In L. H. Eckensberger, W. J. Lonner & Y. H. Poortinga (eds.), *Cross-cultural Contributions in Psychology*. Munich: Swetz and Zeitlinger.

Schrank, R. (1978). *Ten Thousand Working Days*. Cambridge, M.A.: MIT Press.

Schuler, R. S. (1980). 'Definition and Conceptualisation of Stress in Organisations'. *Organisational Behaviour and Human Performance*, 25, 184–215.

Schuler, R. S. (1989). 'Strategic Human Resource Management and Industrial Relations'. *Human Relations*, 42 (2), 157–184.

Scott, W. R., Dornbusch, S. M., & Utande, E. D. (1979). 'Organisational Control: A Comparison of Authority Systems in US and Nigerian Organisations'. In C. J. Lammers & D. J. Hickson (eds.), *Organisations Alike and Unlike*. London: Routledge and Kegan Paul.

Seddon, J. W. (1985a). 'Issues in Practice: The Education and Development of Overseas Managers'. *Management Education and Development*, 16 (1), 5–13.

Seddon, J. W. (1985b). 'The Development and Indigenisation of Third World Business: African Values in the Workplace'. In V. Hammond (ed.), *Current Research in Management*. London: Frances Pinter/ATM.

Seeman, M. (1959). 'On the Meaning of Alienation'. *American Sociological Review*, 24, 783–91.

Selznick, P. (1957). *Leadership in Administration*. Evanston: Row & Peterson.

Shostak, A. B. (1980). *Blue-collar Stress*. Reading, Mass.: Addison-Wesley.

SIDA (1990). *Guidelines for SIDA Support to the Development of Public Administration*. Stockholm: SIDA.

SIDA (1991). *Making Government Work*. Stockholm: SIDA.

Singh, J. P. (1990). 'Managerial Culture and Work-related Values in India'. *Organisation Studies*, 11 (1), 75–101.

Sommariva, A. (in press). *Recent Economic Reforms in the Soviet Union, Smaller Eastern European Countries, and China: A Comparative Analysis*. Washington D.C.: Centre for Strategic and International Studies.

Sommer, R. (1987). 'An Experimental Investigation of the Action Research Approach'. *Journal of Applied Behavioural Science*, 23 (2), 185–199.

Steele, F. (1976). 'Is Organisation Development Work Possible in the UK Culture?'. *Journal of European Industrial Training*, 5 (3), 22–28.

Stewart, R. (1967). *Managers and Their Jobs*. Maidenhead: McGraw-Hill.

Stewart, R. (1989). 'Studies of Managerial Jobs and Behaviour: The Way Forward?'. *Journal of Management Studies*, 26 (1), 1–10.

Stifel, L. D., Coleman, J. S., & Black, J. E. (eds.) (1977). *Education and Training for Public Sector Management in Developing Countries*. New York: Rockefeller Foundation.

Sutherland, S. (1977). *Breakdown*. London: Paladin.

Tabatabai, H. (1988). 'Agricultural Decline and Access to Food in Ghana'. *International Labour Review*, 127 (6), 703–734.

Tannenbaum, R., & Schmidt, W. H. (1973). 'How to Choose a Leadership Pattern'. *Harvard Business Review*, 51.

Tausky, C. (1969). 'Meanings of Work Among Blue Collar Men'. *Pacific Sociological Review*, 12, 49–52.

Taylor, F. W. (1911). *The Principles of Scientific Management*. New York: Harper and Row.

Thompson, J. D. (1967). *Organisations in Action*. New York: McGraw-Hill.

Toffler, A. (1970). *Future Shock*. New York: Random House.

Torrington, D., Weightman, J., & Johns, K. (1989). *Effective Management: People and Organisation*. London: Prentice Hall.

Trist, E. L. (1975). 'Planning the First Steps Toward Quality of Working Life in a Developing Country'. In L. E. Davis & A. B. Cherns (eds.), *The Quality of Working Life* (Vol. 1). New York: Macmillan.

Trist, E. L., & Bamforth, K. W. (1951). 'Some Social and Psychological Consequences of the Longwall Method of Coal-getting'. In D. S. Pugh (ed.), *Organisation Theory*. Harmondsworth: Penguin.

Trist, E. L., Higgin, G. W., Murray, H., & Pollock, A. B. (1963). *Organisational Choice*. London: Tavistock.

Trist, E. L., Susman, G., & Brown, G. W. (1977). 'An Experiment in Autonomous Working in an American Underground Coal Mine'. *Human Relations*, 30, 201–36.

UNDP/World Bank (1989). *Programme for Strengthening Training Institutions in Africa*. Project Document. Geneva: UNDP/World Bank.

Van Sell, M., Brief, A. P., & Schuler, R. S. (1981). 'Role Conflict and Role Ambiguity: Integration of the Literature and Directions for Future Research'. *Human Relations*, 34, 43–71.

Vengroff, R., & Johnston, A. (1987). 'Decentralisation and the Implementation of Rural Development in Senegal: The Role of Rural Councils'. *Public Administration and Development*, 7, 273–288.

Vengroff, R., Belhaj, M., & Ndiaye, M. (1991). 'The Nature of Managerial Work in the Public Sector: An African Perspective'. *Public Administration and Development*, 11, 95–110.

Vroom, V. H. (1966). 'Organisational Choice: A Study of Pre- and Post-Decision Processes'. *Organisational Behaviour and Human Performance*, 1, 212–25.

Vroom, V., & Jago, A. (1988). *The New Leadership: Managing Participation in Organisations*. New Jersey: Prentice-Hall.

Vroom, V., & Yetton, P. (1973). *Leadership and Decision Making*. Pittsburgh: University of Pittsburgh Press.

Wahba, M. A., & Bridwell, L. G. (1976). 'Maslow Reconsidered: A Review of Research on the Need Hierarchy Theory'. *Organisational Behaviour and Human Performance*, 15, 212–40.

Walker, K. F. (1974). 'Workers' Participation in Management: Problems, Practice and Prospects'. *Bulletin of the International Institute for Labour Studies*, 12, 3–35.

Wall, T. D., & Lischeron, J. A. (1977). *Worker Participation*. London: McGraw-Hill.

Wamwala, W. N. (1989). 'Impact of Restructuring the Public Service'. In M. J. Balogun & G. Mutahaba (eds.), *Economic Restructuring and African Public Administration*. West Hartford, Conn.: Kumarian Press.

Warmington, A., Lupton, T., & Gribbin, C. (1977). *Organisational Behaviour and Performance: An Open Systems Approach to Change*. London: Macmillan.

Washington, R. (1988). 'Development and Deviance: A Situational Perspective on African Governmental Corruption'. In H. Glickman (ed.), *The Crisis and Challenge of African Development*. Westport, Connecticut: Greenwood Press.

Werlin, H. (1990). 'Decentralisation and Culture: The Case of Monrovia, Liberia'. *Public Administration and Development*, 10 (3), 251–261.

Werlin, H. (1991). 'Understanding Administrative Bottlenecks'. *Public Administration and Development*, 11, 193–206.

Whipp, R. (1991). 'Human Resource Management, Strategic Change and Competition: The Role of Learning'. *International Journal of Human Resource Management*, 2 (2), 165–192.

White, G. (1991a). 'Urban Government and Market Reforms in China'. *Public Administration and Development*, 11, 149–170.

White, G. (ed.) (1991b). *The Chinese State in the Era of Economic Reform: The Road to Crisis*. London: MacMillan.

White, L. G. (1987). *Creating Opportunities for Change*. London: Lynne Rienner.

Whitley, R. D. (1987). 'Taking Firms Seriously as Economic Actors: Towards a Sociology of Firm Behaviour'. *Organisation Studies*, 8, 125–147.

Whitley, R. D. (1989). 'On the Nature of Managerial Tasks and Skills: Their Distinguishing Characteristics and Organisation'. *Journal of Management Studies*, 26 (3), 209–224.

Whitley, R. D. (1990). 'Eastern Asian Enterprise Structures and the Comparative Analysis of Forms of Business Organisation'. *Organisation Studies*, 11 (1), 47–74.

Willmott, H. C. (1984). 'Images and Ideals of Managerial Work: A Critical Examination of Conceptual and Empirical Accounts'. *Journal of Management Studies*, 21 (3), 349–368.

Woodward, J. (1958). *Management and Technology*. London: Her Majesty's Stationery Office.

Woodward, J. (1965). *Industrial Organisation: Theory and Practice*. London: Oxford University Press.

Woodward, J. (ed.) (1970). *Industrial Organisation: Behaviour and Control*. Oxford: Oxford University Press.

Yoder, R. A., & Eby, S. L. (1990). 'Participation, Job Satisfaction and Decentralisation: The Case of Swaziland'. *Public Administration and Development*, 10, 153–163.

Youker, R. (1986). *Training of African Managers: Some Lessons from Experience*. Paper presented to Conference on International Management Development, University of Lancaster.

Zaleznik, A. (1990). 'The Leadership Gap'. *Academy of Management Executive*, 4 (1), 7–22.

ZPSRC (1989). *Report of the Public Service Review Commission of Zimbabwe*, (2 Vols.). Harare, Zimbabwe.

Zwerman, W. L. (1970). *New Perspectives on Organisation Theory*. Westport, Conn.: Greenwood Publishing.

Index

Walter de Gruyter
Berlin · New York

de Gruyter Studies in Organization
(International Management, Organization and Policy Analysis)

Editor: Stewart R. Clegg

An international and interdisciplinary book series from de Gruyter presenting comprehensive research on aspects of international management, organization studies and comparative public policy.

Vol. 27: **Witold Kieżun**
Management in Socialist Countries
USSR and Central Europe
1991. 15.5 x 23 cm. XIV, 375 pages. Cloth.   ISBN 3-11-010670-1

Vol. 28: **Gerald E. Caiden**
Administrative Reform Comes of Age
1991. 15.5 x 23 cm. XII, 347 pages.
Cloth.   ISBN 3-11-012895-0
Paperback.   ISBN 3-11-012645-1

Vol. 32: **James G. Scoville** (Editor)
Status Influences in Third World Labor Markets
Caste, Gender, and Custom
A Publication of the International Industrial Relations Association
1991. 15.5 x 23 cm. VIII, 329 pages. Cloth.   ISBN 3-11-012647-8

Vol. 33: **György Széll** (Editor)
Labour relations in Transition in Eastern Europe
1991. 15.5 x 23 cm. X, 369 pages. With 9 figures, 18 tables. Cloth.
ISBN 3-11-012648-6

Walter de Gruyter & Co. Berlin · New York
Genthiner Strasse 13, D-1000 Berlin 30 (FRG), Tel.: (30) 2 60 05-0, Fax: 2 60 05-2 51
200 Saw Mill River Road, Hawthorne, N.Y. 10532, Tel.: (914) 7 47-01 10, Fax: 7 47-13 26

Walter de Gruyter
Berlin · New York

de Gruyter Studies in Organization
(International Management, Organization and
Policy Analysis)

Vol. 35: **Bill Ryan**
Making Capital from Culture
The Corporate Form of Capitalist Cultural Production
1992. 15.5 x 23 cm. XII, 209 pages. With 11 figures. Cloth.
ISBN 3-11-012548-X

Vol. 37: **Toyohiro Kono**
Long-Range Planning of Japanese Corporations
1992. 15.5 x 23 cm. XIV, 390 pages. Cloth.   ISBN 3-11-012914-0

Vol. 41: **Sukhan Jackson**
Chinese Enterprise Management
Reforms in Economic Perspective
1992. 15.5 x 23 cm. XVIII, 324 pages. With 46 tables and 4 figures. Cloth.
ISBN 3-11-013480-2

In preparation
Vol. 42: **Jane Marceau** (Editor)
Reworking the World
**Organizations, Technologies and Cultures in Comparative
Perspective**
1992. 15.5 x 23 cm. Approx. 460 pages. Cloth.   ISBN 3-11-013158-7

Walter de Gruyter & Co. Berlin · New York
Genthiner Strasse 13, D-1000 Berlin 30 (FRG), Tel.: (30) 2 60 05-0, Fax: 2 60 05-2 51
200 Saw Mill River Road, Hawthorne, N.Y. 10532, Tel.: (914) 7 47-01 10, Fax: 7 47-13 26

			DUE DATE
			Printed in USA